D0891851

Ageing in a Gendered World:
Women's Issues and Identities

United Nations
International Research and Training Institute
for the Advancement of Women
(INSTRAW)

Santo Domingo, Dominican Republic

1999

Printed in the Dominican Republic
English: 1999-1,000
INSTRAW/Ser.B/53
ISBN 92-1-127054-5
Sales No. E.99.III.C.1

Editorial Panel: Karen Judd, Jeannie Ash de Pou, Julia Tavares-Bucher, Tatjana Sikoska, and Juliet Solomon.
Cover design: UN Dept. Public Information

Contents

Introduction: Ageing as a Women's Issue v

International Initiatives on Ageing 1
    Antony de Bono

Section I: Ageing and Pension Policies in Gendered Society 11

Women and Old-Age Income Security in the United States 13
    Laura Katz Olson

Women in the Development of the Japanese Welfare State 31
    Misa Izuhara

Women's Pensions and the Impact of Privatization in Britain 49
    Jay Ginn and Sara Arber

Life-cycle Income and Motherhood: Simulations for British 75
Women of the 1990s
    Hugh Davies, Heather Joshi and Romana Peronaci

The Effect of Disadvantages in Early Career on Later Career 93
Outcomes: A Canadian Case Study
    Isik Urla Zeytinoglu and Caroline L. Weber

Gender-based Barriers to Career Development in Australia 115
    Russell Rimmer

Section II: Care and Care-giving in Family and Community 131

Caring Women, Cared-for Women: The Discourse of 133
Care-giving in Italy
    Isabella Paoletti

Reaping What You Sow? Older Women, Housing and 153
Family Dynamics in Urban Mexico
    Ann Varley and Maribel Blasco

Family Support Systems and Older Women in Sub-Saharan Africa 179
    Irene Zeilinger

Older Women in Transitions in Estonia: Continuing Care-givers 199
    Silva Tedre and Taimi Tulva

Old Age, Gender and Marginality in Peru: Development for 215
the Elderly
    Fiona Clark

Caring for the Care-givers: Challenges for Italian Social Policy 245
    Giovanni Lamura, Maria Gabriella Melchiorre, Massimo Mengani

Gendered Aspects of Caring for Older Persons in Europe: 273
Policy Data Requirements
    Tatiana Sikoska

Section III: Beyond Care-giving: Identity and Empowerment 289

Identity, Culture and Older Women 291
    Noeleen O'Beirne

Silencing the Voices of Older Women 315
    Rachel Siegel

Gendered Living Environments for the Elderly in Turkey 331
and Sweden
    E. Olcay İmamoglu and Vacit İmamoglu

Navigating in Unknown Waters: Canadian Widows 345
Negotiating Relationships
    Deborah K. van den Hoonaard

Age, Migration, Gender and Empowerment: Older Migrant 367
Women in Europe
    Gail Wilson, Helen Cylwik, Angela Grotheer and Lydia Potts

Notes on Contributors 385

Introduction: Ageing as a Woman's Issue

Ageing as a policy issue has surfaced at various times in national and international arenas over the past four decades, propelled by concerns of population demographics, the quality of life of the elderly poor, and increasingly, the insistence by women that ageing is a women's issue.

Why is ageing a woman's issue? Firstly, the majority of older persons are women. It is estimated that 50 per cent of those over 60 years and 65 per cent of those over 80 years are women. Secondly, ageing is a gendered experience. As Clara Pratt explains, "...throughout life and in all societies, males and females play different roles, receive different rewards and experience different realities. These gendered experiences culminate, but do not originate, in late life."[1] As a result, not only is women's disadvantaged position in society 'felt' during childhood and adulthood of women, but it most often aggravated during old age. In fact, women are amongst the poorest of the elderly.

Julia de Alvarez, who, as Ambassador to the UN from the Dominican Republic, has for two decades urged the international community to confront what she calls the impending "age-quake", has also consistently emphasized the gender dimension of this process. As she points out:

> An overwhelming majority of older women in developing countries now are illiterate, poor, socially dependent, and lacking

---

[1] Pratt, Clara. 1997. "Ageing: A Multigenerational, Gendered Perspective". Bulletin On Ageing No. 2/3. (www.un.org/esa/socdev/agb97232.htm)

personal resources to cope with changing social conditions. Many have suffered throughout their lives from poor health care, malnutrition, illiteracy, and low social status, simply because they were born female.

Not only are women more deprived then men during old age due to the disadvantages experienced throughout their lives, but in many countries they are increasingly burdened with caring for grandchildren without sufficient compensation. There is mounting evidence that, as more mothers of young children enter the workforce, and as one or even both parents migrate to a distant city - or country - to find employment, older women who long ago raised their own children and should be able to look forward to a release from the care-giving burden, are now taking care of their children's children. This trend has been increasing in areas of the developed world as well as countries throughout the developing world, and is often intensified by the ever-increasing toll of AIDS on poor and third world populations. According to HelpAge International, there will be an estimated 9 million AIDS orphans by the year 2000, including those being taken care of by their grandmothers.

On the other hand, as more people survive into old age and families become smaller, there are fewer potential care-givers for the elderly. This is further aggravated by the recent trend toward privatization of elderly care and pension systems to which women have less access given their disadvantaged participation in the formal labour market.

Given the important social role of women in old age and the disadvantages and social risks that they face, it is not surprising that they have been instrumental in putting the issue of ageing on the international agenda and in raising awareness that older people, in particular older women, are productive members of society.

In his contribution to this volume, Antony de Bono, who chaired the International Advisory Committee at the first World Assembly on Ageing in 1982, highlights UN efforts to capture these concerns and bring them to the world stage. He makes clear that at each point along the way, the issues were first articulated by NGOs, local, national and international. And with each decade the constituency these groups represented became more diverse, including family planning agencies, the medical profession, and the financial sector, along with retired persons and family care-givers among them, more and more women.

At the time of the World Assembly on Ageing in 1982, policy objectives were informed by the model of the European welfare state, and the expansion of that model to support a portion of the population in retirement years. Ten years later, thinking had changed. Not only had states retreated from the welfare state model, but advocates for the elderly were beginning to emphasize ways in which older people could continue to live productive lives, engaged with family and community. Women were a vital part of this shift. In 1985, at the close of the United Nations Decade for Women in Nairobi, the final document, "Forward-Looking Strategies", included the statement:

> Ageing, as a stage of development, is a challenge for women. In this period of life, women should be enabled to cope in a creative way with new opportunities. The social consequences arising from the stereotyping of elderly women should be recognized and eliminated.

Subsequent meetings on ageing began to emphasize the integration of older persons into the life of society, regarding them not as a burden on productive members of society but as creative and productive members in their own right. Women, who because they live longer, represent the majority of older people in almost every country, are a particularly neglected resource in their elder years.

Recognizing the need for data and knowledge on women and ageing, as early as 1991, INSTRAW carried out a pioneering study on the changing status and role of elderly women in countries around the world. In addition to providing statistical data on an emerging issue, the study identified gaps in data and the kinds of information needed to address the issue of elderly women in an era of globalization as well as on-going urbanization, including long-term changes in the labour market as well as continuing changes in family and household structures and patterns of care-giving.

Also in 1991, the UN Expert Group Meeting on Integration of Ageing and Elderly Women into Development stated:

> Recognition of the importance of older women's potential, and a departure from the emphasis on their problems and vulnerability, is a major factor for the integration of ageing and elderly women into development.

That year, the UN Economic and Social Council adopted a Statement of Principles for Older Persons, urging governments to develop programmes to support the independence, participation, care, self-fulfilment, security and dignity of older people. And the following year, the UN General Assembly declared 1999 to be the International Year of Older Persons, "in recognition of humanity's demographic coming of age". Its focus would be on the integration of older people as a resource rather than a burden to society, and its goal the formulation of policies designed to enable older people to remain socially engaged and active members of a community--as counsellors and mentors, producers and policymakers, as well as care-givers. Its theme, "Towards a Society for all Ages", was chosen to encourage contributions and foster dialogue across all generations.

Yet still the issue languished, in part due to the perception that ageing was a concern only in the developed world. Then in 1994, at the International Conference on Population and Development in Cairo, advocates for the elderly worked closely with women's groups to insure that references to older people were included in every section of the final document. Their success in part reflected the fact that ageing is a demographic issue; population and family planning agencies had long ago recognized the link. But it also reflected growing awareness of changes occurring in the developing world, as improvements in mortality results in large numbers of people living longer, most of them women and most of them poor. According to UN statistics, there were 208 million women over age 60 in 1985, half of them in the developing world. This number is projected to increase to 604 million by 2025, 70 per cent in developing countries, and 70 per cent living in poverty.

Also becoming apparent was the fact that as the numbers of elderly were increasing dramatically, governments were increasingly unprepared to support them. Throughout the developing world, government pension systems were being privatized, pushing thousands of older people into poverty and greatly increasing the care burden on women. At the World Summit for Social Development in Copenhagen, in 1995, women from Latin America, having experienced the effects of pension privatization then sweeping their region, joined in an effort to get governments to commit themselves to maintaining state pensions. It was clear that what had once been a problem of the developed countries was becoming a global problem - and indeed, a global women's problem.

Women in all regions are now actively engaged in an effort to change the way in which older people, especially older women, are viewed in society. In order that societies everywhere view older people as a vital and valuable resource, it is necessary that people understand that ageing is a process that involves ongoing changes and multiple identities, and that these are shaped by structures and relations of privilege and inequality, including those of gender.

Vital to this effort to change perceptions is ethnographic and statistical information about the realities of older women's lives, information that until recently was not seen as useful and as a result is often non-existent. Thus research concerning women and ageing requires not only an identification of relevant policy and its impact on different segments of the population but also an examination of the myths and assumptions about older women that underpin policy discussions and decisions.

All of these concerns inform the papers that make up this volume. In it, women in countries big and small, North, South, East and West, document a reality that differs only in minor ways: populations are getting older everywhere, and in all cases ageing is a gendered phenomenon. Women live longer, have fewer resources, and are expected to care for elderly relatives as well as young children. In countries where pensions are tied to earnings, women's care-giving roles carry a penalty beyond the postponement of education or career: their tendency to cluster in low-wage and part-time jobs as well as to take time off in order to take care of children or relatives leaving them with lower social security income in their retirement years.

Studies of pension policy in both Japan and the United States look at the shortcomings of pension policies designed for a "male-breadwinner" family model in an era when the number of women who are single, divorced, or widowed, and may be entering the workforce for the first time, increases each year. Yet, the shift towards privatization of pension systems may not offer women a better share of benefits. A study of private pension schemes in Britain reports that low-income people, primarily women, are being persuaded to buy into plans which do not provide an adequate pension and are extremely poor value for money. In Britain, as in most countries, pension policy shifts rest on the belief that gender discrimination is on the way out, and women will soon earn the same as men. Yet research presented here, from countries as diverse as Britain, Australia and Estonia, shows that the reality is much more complex. A study done in Britain, for example, finds that while earnings approach parity for professional women and men, they increasingly diverge for low-skilled workers. A study in Australia focused on skills rather than earnings; it suggests a greater career slide among professionals after a break in the workforce than among lower skilled workers.

Examination of the myths and stereotypes that surround older women shows how gender bias and discrimination intensify in old age everywhere, though the cultural forms may differ. Perhaps the most widespread stereotype is that of women as natural caregivers, a notion that continues to sustain the belief in many countries, especially in resource-poor countries, that the "traditional family" will take care of its elderly. As several papers in this volume point out, the view of women as "natural" family caregivers is one that is continually constructed and constantly reinforced by social expectations and strictures. One study, in Italy, examines the ways in which these expectations permeate even casual conversations: women typically apologize if they are not caring for an additional family member, while men, far from being expected to care for family members, are regarded as peculiar when they do.

While in most societies there is the expectation that widowed women will remarry or be reabsorbed into extended families, there is mounting evidence that in many countries, older women increasingly tend to live alone, to a much greater extent than men. In sub-Saharan Africa, as a paper in this volume points out, about half of all older women are widowed, compared to about a tenth of older men, and in addition, women re-marry far less frequently than men, with the result that while up to 90 per cent of older men are married, only between 24 and 46 per cent of older women are married. The author points out that men can, not only find a new, usually younger, spouse more easily, but have more incentive to do so, since the gender-specific division of labour makes it likely that a man who re-marries will be gaining a nurse and care-taker, which is not the same for a woman. In many countries in the region, moreover, widowed older women are unable or unwilling to move into an extended family household, and so tend increasingly to live alone.

Such trends are by no means unique to Africa, as is shown by papers on both Mexico and Turkey. These findings have enormous implications for policy-makers, not only in terms of health and income support, but also, for example, in terms of housing. Yet the persistence of outdated assumptions means that housing policy typically neglects the housing needs of older women. Moreover, in some cases, the expectations of women as selfless caregivers permeate even the organizations set up to serve elderly women. A study of a few of these organizations in Peru, included in this volume, found that the staff tend to rely on older women to provide the volunteer work for their programmes while ignoring the women's health care and income needs.

What happens to the women who pick up the ever-increasing responsibilities of care giving? A paper on health-care policy in Italy examines the consequences of this increasing burden on women's health and well-being in their own later years, and recommends a set of policy measures to avert this potential new health crisis. Others look at the impact of the cultural silencing of older women's communication, in both family and society; unlike older men, they are rarely treated with dignity and respect, judged more often by physical appearance than for their experience and accomplishments, resulting in depression and loss of confidence and the ability to connect. The loss to society, these studies show, is enormous, pointing to the need for similar research everywhere.

Along with challenging the somewhat contradictory notions of natural caregiver and useless burden, both of which continue to underpin public policy, new identity issues, not previously explored, demand exploration and documentation. Widows, for example, can be expected to increase in virtually every country, yet with some well-known exceptions, such as India, little is known about widowhood as an identity category. One paper in this volume explores the meaning of widowhood for women in Canada, who experience it as an entirely new world, one for which they were not prepared. Such studies are essential in every country, not only to help craft effective public policy, but also to understand the circumstances under which widows can realize their potential, to themselves and to society.

Finally, the study of older women migrants in Europe looks at the regional and inter-regional implications of the demographic changes occurring worldwide. The study finds that older women who have left countries in Eastern Europe to work in countries in Western Europe choose to live out their lives in the new country, rather than return home as the earlier male migrants had done. These findings have implications not only for demographers and policymakers, but also for those concerned with the ways in which demographic change differentially affects women in the East and the West, the North and the South.

The cumulative knowledge of the experience of ageing in different countries points to the need for more such research. This is especially true now, in an era in which claims on states to take responsibility for its citizens have seemingly lost their power, and new demands must be formulated, new targets identified.

INSTRAW is pleased to issue this volume as its contribution to the 1999 Year of Older Persons, in the hope that the research and ideas, reflections and analysis it presents will contribute to achieve "a society for all ages".

International Initiatives on Ageing
Anthony de Bono

Abstract

While the developed countries of the world have enjoyed mass longevity for decades, the developing countries are only now beginning to reap the benefits of health and other advances that have allowed increasing numbers to reach and enjoy old age. The International Institute on Ageing - United Nations, Malta has played a leading role in training trainers and capacity building in all aspects of ageing in the developing countries. However, the full extent of the implications of mass longevity are still not fully appreciated and urgently need new policies and trained personnel.

"The countries gathered in the World Assembly on Ageing ...

Do solemnly reaffirmtheir belief that the fundamental and inalienable rights enshrined in the Universal Declaration of Human Rights apply fully and undiminished to the ageing; and

Do solemnly recognize that quality of life is no less important than longevity......"
*From the **Preamble,** Vienna International Plan of Action on Ageing, 1982*

The world has been slow to recognise the early stages of the longevity revolution that is now sweeping like a demographic tidal wave through its populations. Indeed even today, after so many international events designed to create awareness of this unprecedented mass increase in ageing, and the most

1

dramatic demographic predictions, a number of countries are either unaware of the phenomenon or do not want to know. The UN International Institute on Ageing - United Nations Malta, established in 1987, currently conducts courses in aspects of ageing for participants from all over the world. The message from the participants from developing countries throughout the world is almost always the same:

'Yes, the number of older persons in our country is indeed growing very rapidly, but there is no policy, no infrastructure, to deal with the situation. There are very few trained personnel and there are so many other problems.'

Although individual longevity has been known since antiquity, it was not until fairly recently, when it became widespread, that it was realized that a fundamental demographic transition was taking place, first in the more advanced developed countries, and now increasingly in the less developed ones. Yet even today, with the exception of a handful of interested experts, most people - including those in the media - are almost totally unaware of the enormity of the change now occurring, and of the fundamental consequences it will inevitably have on the lives of every individual, and on the socio-economic development of nearly every country.

The implications of ageing on a massive scale are often poorly understood even in the developed countries, which have experienced the ageing of their populations for more than a century. It is quite amazing that it has taken so long for the predictable consequences to register. Increasing longevity has combined with a sharp decline in fertility in these countries to produce an ageing population, that is, one with an increasing number of older people - a consequence of what might be viewed as a 'post-agrarian' phenomenon. Suddenly pension schemes, developed on the assumption of a constant ratio of working to retired people, no longer seem sustainable. Health and other services are under increasing strain as the *second* ageing wave, those over 80 years of age, becomes the most rapidly growing part of the population.

While the developed countries have had ample time to evolve social and economic strategies to deal with the ageing of their populations, whether or not these strategies have been successful is very much open to question. Indeed, it is increasingly widely recognized that radical rethinking is required, not only because the state can no longer carry the social and economic burden it once abrogated to itself, but also because the very process of development has eroded the tradition of family care that is now seen as the bedrock of human care. Rethinking is also required because health services in centralized high-tech centres have become unsustainable.

However, it is in the developing countries that mass survival on an unprecedented scale has suddenly become not only significant but urgent. The longevity revolution has been delayed in these countries, since survival on a significant scale is a fairly recent phenomenon. Developing countries did not begin to enjoy the basic health, sanitation and nutritional prerequisites for mass survival until the post-war years. Thus the cohorts born during that period are only now reaching old age in great numbers. However, one must not forget that many of these countries still have not achieved the basic foundation on which to build a healthy society and are condemned by crushing debt, by draught and disease, by violence and starvation to life expectancies that were common two centuries ago. In a few countries, or areas within them, poverty and ignorance, lack of clean water and sanitation, as well as the still-uncontrolled scourge of infectious disease and the emergence of new or resistant strains of disease organisms are so widespread that any chance of mass survival is remote. This fact is an abiding matter of concern and shame to the world community.

Yet in the minds of many the reality of an ageing population is still not appreciated because the *percentage* of the elderly in these countries is still relatively small - though growing rapidly - because the fertility rate remains high. As a result, large population cohorts are beginning to live to old age, causing a sudden, and rapid transition in many countries. These countries are almost totally unprepared, lacking, in many cases, the economic and financial as well as the health infrastructures to cope. To be sure, they have one asset of crucial importance for dealing with the phenomenon of ageing: they still preserve to a greater or lesser extent, the tradition of care in the family or the community. However, this tradition is being destroyed by development and the changes development brings.

This is an overview of the question of ageing from a great height, such as that which U.S. astronaut, septuagenarian John Glenn, might have envisaged as he orbited the Earth. Nearer the ground the picture is infinitely more complex.

There is no doubt that the achievement of longevity is a triumph for the human race. However, that triumph is far from complete. Although the potential for healthy ageing for all remains the goal, it is a goal that has not been reached. We know, or think we know, that healthy ageing - to what is possibly a genetically determined end - can be achieved. At the present time, the rich potential of the added years has by and large not been fully realized, in terms of either personal fulfilment or economic productivity. Quite apart from the geographical unevenness of healthy ageing, largely determined by economic and development factors, the burden of disease, disability and dementia still too often contribute to what the poet Wordsworth described:

"A heavy weight of years has chained and bowed...."

This then is the challenge: to achieve healthy ageing for all. How has the world responded? Although a number of research institutes and several non-governmental organizations (NGOs) have been concerned with the question of ageing for decades, at least in a few countries, the first time the Question of Ageing was formally raised at the United Nations was in 1968 when the representative of Malta asked for it to be put on the General Assembly agenda.

While this was done, very little happened because awareness of the reality and implications of ageing was not widespread, and, as ever, other matters appeared of more immediate concern. Indeed, it was not until U.S. Senator Frank Church and his colleagues, backed by an increasingly well-organized ageing movement, revived the matter in the late 1970s, that the UN, encouraged by a U.S. offer of financial support, agreed to hold a UN World Assembly on Ageing in 1982. The holding of this World Assembly, at the time a rare gathering of all the member nations in the world, to discuss a single theme, demonstrated the dawning awareness that the issue of ageing was a matter of universal concern and importance.

The World Assembly was preceded by a well-organized series of national and regional meetings throughout the world, which succeeded in prompting governments to look at and be concerned with ageing, often for the first time. The meetings also stimulated the production of national and regional reports which served as the building blocks of the foundations on which the World Assembly rested. These documents make extremely interesting reading nearly twenty years later, representing a picture in each country and region of the starting point of the awareness of ageing. National and international NGOs played an important role, not only in stimulating official action but also holding their own meetings and seminars and completing their reports. Research institutes and individual scientists also made an important contribution and many were included in national delegations to the Assembly.

This mass of information on ageing throughout the world was available, together with a Draft of a Plan of Action, to the 23-nation Advisory Committee which met for three two-week sessions in Vienna and New York. The member nations represented both developed and developing countries and were drawn from the five UN regions. I was Chairman of this Committee, which revised the Draft Plan after much debate, producing the Working Document of the World Assembly. The process provided a unique insight into the diverse and often conflicting views on many of the items in the Draft Plan arising from the different ideological, cultural and development background of the delegations.

The World Assembly was held in Vienna, Austria, and attended by over 2,000 official delegates from 125 countries. The Plan of Action contained no less than 62 specific Recommendations based on Principles which covered nine different areas: health and nutrition, housing and environment, family, social welfare, income security and employment, education, data collection, training, and research. The final document was eventually approved and adopted by consensus, with no reservations, the first time this had occurred in the 38 years of the United Nations.

The Vienna International Plan of Action on Ageing provided the foundation on which subsequent international action on ageing has been based. While the role of NGOs was critical, it was also vital that governments take responsibility for implementation. NGOs, however broad their membership and deep their enthusiasm, cannot assume the responsibility that government must continue to bear for the wellbeing of its citizens and for society.

The oft-quoted Preamble to the Plan of Action emphasizes the fundamental importance of the *'quality of life'* of the individual; a concept that has an infinity of meaning, physical and spiritual. Also it underscored the fundamental principle that the rights of a human being are in no way diminished by age.

While the World Assembly on Ageing marked the beginning of global concern for the multifaceted Question of Ageing, stimulating the formation of national and local action groups, it never really captured the interest and attention of the world's media. While there may be many reasons for this, in retrospect I think it is because ageing is not news; indeed it is almost the antithesis of news. In addition to an individual and collective subconscious effort to suppress the notion of personal or peer ageing, ageing is not dramatic, like an earthquake or hurricane, but slow and inexorable, moving at the rate of a day at a time. Thus both individual ageing and that of a whole population is almost imperceptible.

Periodically, the United Nations Ageing Unit convened regional meetings to review the implementation of the Vienna International Plan of Action, stimulating the production of country reports that chronicled progress or changes in individual countries and regions. But much of the impetus was left to the NGOs which expanded their activities steadily both in their own countries and later in the developing countries. A number of them have a considerable international interest and have established and supported satellite NGOs in some developing countries.

Almost ten years after the World Assembly, in 1991, the UN General Assembly adopted the Principles for Older Persons, emphasizing the rights of older persons to everything that can contribute towards their independence and full participation in society, their entitlement to care and self-fulfilment as well as dignity.

In 1997, the last year of this millennium was designated as the UN Year of Older Persons. The UN Programme on Ageing (Department for Economic and Social Affairs-DESA) is coordinating the programme for the UN Year 1999 with the slogan of 'A Society for All Ages' to emphasize the solidarity of interdependence between generations. A Support Group of NGOs and national representatives met in New York in 1997 and 1998, the 1998 meeting coinciding with the launch of the Year of Older Persons by Secretary General Kofi Annan.

One concrete initiative born out of the Vienna International Plan of Action on Ageing was the International Institute on Ageing (INIA) established in 1987. Its main mandate is to assist in implementing the Vienna International Plan particularly as regards education and training of personnel from developing countries in the field of Ageing. To this end regular courses have been held in four main areas: health care, financial aspects of ageing, social gerontology and demography. Courses are held in Malta and increasingly 'on-site' in the developing countries. Hundreds of students from developing countries have been trained, using the services of some of the leading world experts in their field.

However, such is the growing demand that in spite of greatly increasing the number of on-site courses, wider outreach is required in order to build up local capacity in these fields. Working with university and media personnel, INIA is using modern multimedia information technology to establish interactive training links with centres in developing countries, through which the appropriate expertise of the developed world would be made available in a sustained manner to meet the rapidly growing needs of the developing countries in every area of concern for the elderly. The aim is to establish a critical mass of policy makers as well as effective trainers in the main areas affecting the welfare and integration of the elderly.

The Institute collaborates with other bodies and agencies, as well as with universities and NGOs in its activities in the developing countries. This local partnership enables the Institute to act as a catalyst between the local knowledge and resources in the country and the wide range of expertise of the highest level that its International Visiting Faculty provides. Thus, the joint initiative helps to build capacity and establish a base for continued support.

The magnitude of the demographic changes that will take place in the next few decades clearly indicate the necessity for the Question of Ageing to move from being a matter of limited, almost marginal concern, into the mainstream of population policy. In this respect, one must welcome the increased contribution that United Nations Population Fund (UNFPA) has been making since before the International Conference on Population and Development (ICPD) in Cairo in 1994. In the developed countries, falling fertility rates combined with increasing longevity are giving rise to populations that have an ever increasing proportion of old and very old people. In the developing countries it is the *absolute numbers* that will increase very rapidly in the next few decades leading to a doubling, trebling and even quadrupling of the elderly population.

The economic and financial aspects of both the relative and absolute numbers of the elderly in both developed and developing countries clearly have, and will continue to have, a fundamental and permanent impact on every aspect of development. This impact is of great concern to agencies such as the United Nations Development Programme (UNDP) which has actively supported training and research activities in the ageing field. The World Bank and other lending institutions seem less concerned, though clearly the impact of the sudden and rapid explosion in the numbers of ageing people in the developing countries will have a profound impact on their economies, and therefore on their socio-political stability.

The World Health Organization (WHO) has played a leading role not only in creating awareness but also in stimulating research into all aspects of the health of the elderly. It has promoted the concept that in order to achieve healthy ageing the adoption of healthy lifestyle at an early age is essential as many of the disabilities that afflict the elderly are the manifestation of a long accumulation of noxious elements. Areas of particular concern have been diabetes (predicted to increase by 170% in the next few decades), dementias and cardiovascular disease. In a recent speech the Director of WHO spoke of the tremendous challenge posed by the increase of the elderly from 580 million to over 1 billion just two decades from now. She said WHO would develop global strategies, backed by extensive research, to enable countries to put in place policies for healthy ageing.

Although of course there are other dimensions to ageing, health and freedom from disability are fundamental prerequisites. Health promotion and the prevention of disease and accidents could have a dramatic effect in extending not only longevity but also the enjoyment of disability free years of life in the added years. Earlier I noted that longevity was a triumph for the human race. Yet it is very much an incomplete triumph when one considers the burden of disability that often manifests itself, particularly in women over 80 years old. Indications are that this is not an inherent attribute of age. Much effort is needed to achieve the true triumph of human longevity, in which disability and disease are compressed into a very short period before a peaceful end.

From an international viewpoint, the place of gender in the question of ageing is of the greatest importance. Not only do women constitute the majority of the elderly, and even more so, of the very old, but by far the greatest number of elder care-givers are women. In fact, women continue to bear an unequal, and often unrecognized and uncompensated burden of care. In many countries women have few rights and yet do the bulk of physical work. The international community has a fundamental duty to try to rectify these injustices by education and example. Women have played and will continue to play a leading role in the field of ageing. But to meet the ageing challenges of today and in the future, they must have complete equality of opportunity and choice, access to education and policy making and freedom from the additional burden of discrimination or neglect. In this regard it is encouraging that remarkable women are at the helm of both UNFPA and WHO.

What of the Future?

The developed countries will no doubt have to contend with formidable challenges inherent in populations which are steadily becoming older. Radical re-assessment of the very concept of work and occupation will be needed, not only as a result of ageing but also in the light of the very rapid rate of change in technology and developments in the field of robotics. The dwindling ratio of the 'working' population will make existing pension strategies obsolete. Cyberspace and the very rapid evolution of information technology will introduce a whole new dimension and meaning to lifelong education and entertainment. The list is endless - but all too often the elderly are automatically excluded.

The radical re-orientation of health care for the elderly will require a fundamental change of care culture. Can the developed countries possibly reverse the trends of the past two centuries towards hospital-centered care, or have the cumulative effects of development, urbanization, industrialization, not only eroded the tradition of care in the family and community, but actually made it impossible? Some surveys show that even in Europe 80 per cent of informal care comes from family members. If it not too late, and in view of the relentless logic of the unfolding demography, what practical steps can be taken to evolve effective strategies to reverse the erosion of family and community care? What forms of support, education, help and compensation are necessary, affordable or possible?

If the challenge of ageing is formidable in the developed countries with their wealth, productivity, expertise and other attributes; what of that in the developing countries? Here, in relative terms, the problems are far more daunting. Not only will the accumulation of the numbers of the elderly be extremely rapid, but it will be in situations where most countries have little or no previous experience on which to base their policies to meet this challenge; and even fewer resources. Here we are not talking about some time in the future, *but in the next two to three decades*. The urgency of the situation is only made more stark by complacency and lack of awareness that one finds all too frequently. In many instances it is quite understandable as a whole host of pressing problems compete for attention.

The need for training in all aspects of ageing has never been so pressing; yet in almost every developing country the rate and scope of such training, in relation to the enormity of the impending ageing situation and the rapidity of its development, can be described not merely as inadequate but pathetic. If viable strategies are to be evolved, training at all levels must be commenced without delay using every available means of communication and education, from top policymakers to care-givers and the families including the elderly themselves.

The developing countries, to varying degrees, retain traditions of family responsibility and care for the elderly. This is indeed a precious asset. However, it cannot and must not be taken for granted. Very little hard facts are known about the actual situation in specific countries, indeed in different areas. Surveys and research are urgently required to measure demographic change, and to assess the erosion of family and community care. Practical and sustainable strategies must be designed to support the culture of family and community care, which once destroyed can never be restored.

Bold, new international initiatives are needed to mobilize, coordinate and focus the urgent action needed to cope with the challenge of ageing on a global scale. The problem is that though long predictable, the preventable crisis is far too slow in its manifestation to provoke the urgency that other catastrophes evoke. The demographic transition has been described as a tidal wave: this conjures up a picture too dramatic and swift. It is more like a glacier than an avalanche, and just as inexorable.

Far too often, inter-agency rivalry, mistaken concepts of spheres of influence and other impediments to effective coordinated action so sap the will of international bodies that far too little is done, far too late.

SECTION I

AGEING AND PENSION POLICIES IN GENDERED SOCIETY

Women and Old Age Income Security in the United States

Laura Katz Olson

Abstract

This paper looks at changing views about the adequacy of Social Security with regard to older women since the legislation was enacted. It shows that during the 1970s, the U.S. Government was prepared to initiate changes to better meet women's financial needs. However, beginning in the 1980s, attacks on Social Security have forced a retreat from earlier ideas, expectations and possibilities for addressing issues relating to gender. The language and symbols in which the attacks are framed redefine social welfare itself and obscure the ways in which proposed changes fall disproportionately on women, young and old, and especially those who are divorced, widowed, or who never married. In order to improve the economic plight of older women, this paper contends, we must take back the power to define the ideological agenda.

Introduction

Beginning in the 1970s, in many countries, efforts began to analyze the economic situation of women at various stages in their life cycle, and to investigate the differential impact of existing social programmes on males and females. In the United States of America, one target of investigation was the Social Security system: several prominent reports had pointed out that despite lifting the vast majority of older people out of poverty, the programme had serious inadequacies and inequities with regard to women, both young and old. Debate centered on the best means for correcting them.

By the 1980s, however, recurring national budget deficits, the increasing number of older people in the population and the perceived high costs of programmes to protect them, and the growing dominance of a conservative ideology based on market-based solutions have forced attention away from improving social welfare policies and towards reduction in benefits, and even towards the slow dismantling of all social welfare programmes.

Increasingly, attempts to slash aid to the elderly are camouflaged in terms of choice and the free market as well as financial crisis and an end to entitlement, the real aim of which is to challenge and undermine the legitimacy of all government social welfare provisions. Recommendations to 'save' Social Security from supposed bankruptcy include not only reduced benefits, higher Social Security taxes, and increased age of eligibility but also proposals to transform the system into a market-based programme, either wholly or in part. Such changes, like the broader attack on the social welfare state, fall disproportionately on women, especially on those who are divorced, widowed or whomever married.

The Social Security System

Social Security and Medicare represent the major forms of social welfare in the United States, with the former providing $350 billion to 44 million people in 1998 (Gramlich 1998). Despite an early commitment to individual equity, political debate over Social Security during its formative years was driven primarily by a concern to ensure greater protection for all older people (Kingson and Berkowitz 1993). For nearly three decades, Democrats and Republicans alike worked to extend and improve the programme, by adding pensions for workers' wives and widows, extending coverage to nearly all private sector employees, expanding the range and amount of benefits, and protecting retirees against wage increases and inflation.

By 1950, according to one scholar, there was a "movement away from a 'floor' of protection toward 'adequate' protection" (Tynes 1996: 99). As social value concerns increasingly dominated discussion, the public supported greater efforts to meet the economic needs of the elderly. Consequently, legislators regularly passed significant increases in benefit levels - even controlling for inflation - especially during election years. The 1950 amendments alone raised benefits by a whopping 80 per cent; three across-the-board benefit increases from 1969 to 1972 raised real benefits by 23 per cent. Along with another 20 per cent boost, the 1972 amendments automatically indexed pensions to the cost of living. These improvements were made with wide political support, and very little open opposition.

By the 1970s, Social Security was touted as the nation's most effective anti-poverty programme. However, although the programme had reduced the overall poverty rate of older people from 35 per cent in 1959 to 16 per cent by 1973 (Census Bureau, various), it was becoming increasingly obvious that certain groups were not sharing in the programme's economic success. The divorced wife's benefit of 50 per cent, for one, was woefully inadequate to support a person living alone. In fact, over half of all single elderly women, including a large percentage of widows, were economically deprived. Single women without earned income or savings received no protection at all until becoming eligible for Social Security at age 60, impoverishing many divorced or widowed women even prior to attaining old age.

There also was limited but growing recognition that the United States had changed dramatically since the 1930s, and that the Social Security system was based on an outdated set of norms and expectations. In particular, it did not reflect the changing situation of women in society, especially their new work and family arrangements. The legislation that created the programme in 1935 was structured on the assumption of nuclear family households consisting of a male breadwinner and a life-long unpaid female homemaker. Yet during the 1960s and 1970s, an increasing number of women, including those who were married with young children, began to enter the labour force. By the late 1970s, nearly 50 per cent of all women were working: 65 per cent of wives with no children under age 18, and 39 per cent of mothers with children under six had jobs (HEW 1979). Divorce, too, was on the rise; by 1977, about one-third of all new marriages were expected to end in divorce.

As a result, a few congressional leaders, the Congresswomen's Caucus, and government agencies, along with women's groups and age-based organizations, began to take up the problem of gender inequality in the Social Security programme, with some people calling for fundamental reform. Several government studies, including the Justice

Department's Task Force on Sex Discrimination (1977), the Health, Education and Welfare (HEW) Task Force on the Treatment of Women under Social Security (1978), and the Advisory Council on Social Security (1979), concluded that the programme contained serious gender inadequacies and inequities.

The HEW Task Force, in particular, was charged with studying whether the category of dependency itself should, and could, be eliminated under Social Security. Recognizing that both spouses contribute equally to the well-being of the family, one of the Task Force's main recommendations was that homemakers should be covered as such, in their own right, rather than as dependants of wage-earners. Its final report pointed out that most working women were also disadvantaged in the benefit structure as a result of their lower average wages (HEW 1979). In fact, many studies called for some type of earnings-sharing plan for both dual-earner and one-earner couples. Projections indicated that with earnings-sharing arrangements, benefits for men and women would become more equal. One such scheme had already been introduced in Congress in 1976 and 1977, with 60 co-sponsors.

These various inquiries addressed other issues related to equalizing and improving the economic situation of women. Concluding that working women with young children were unfairly penalized, several reports advocated dropout years for childcare when calculating benefits. They also recommended additional protections for divorced women and ageing surviving spouses, including measures to deal with problems faced by near-elderly widows (the so-called widow's gap). The HEW Task force even proposed the establishment of a double-decker benefit structure, with a flat rate first tier for every older person, funded through general revenues (HEW 1979).

The late 1950s saw the formation of numerous groups representing the elderly, notably the American Association of Retired Persons (AARP) and National Council of Senior Citizens (NCSC) (Pratt 1976). "Social Security had successfully cultivated a committed clientele and powerful political allies during the 1950s and 1960s" (Tynes 1996:135). As a result, these organisations were well organized, and throughout the 1970s, their primary focus remained on increasing benefits for all older people.

The Age of Retrenchment

Thus by the late 1970s, it seemed as though the government was prepared to institute some significant changes in Social Security in order to improve the situation of women; it was just a matter of debating the issues and options. However, in 1980, the election of Ronald Reagan as President ushered in an era committed to government retrenchment, decentralization, individualism, and privatization. Social Security immediately became a target; instead of advancing adequacy concerns, the new administration concentrated on cutting the programme and its benefits, including lowering the replacement rates of pre-retirement income, and eliminating the minimum benefit.

However, support for Social Security was strong among the public as well as elderly advocacy groups, and there was vigorous resistance to any attempt to undermine it. Indeed, "the aged enjoyed a political legitimacy that obviated the need for power" (Hudson 1998). Thus it appeared, at first, that not even the president could tamper with Social Security. "Old age insurance seemed relatively inviolable," and Reagan's relatively modest reductions in the programme were rebuffed (Tynes 1996: 2-3). Even in 1981, the National Commission on Social Security's final report, while maintaining that the system did not need to be seriously altered, acknowledged that benefit levels for many women were inadequate, and proposed limited, incremental reforms to address this problem (National Commission 1981).

In Congress, the House Select Committee on Ageing and the Senate Special Committee on Ageing, formed to study the problems of older Americans, continued to issue recommendations and reports championing the programme. While focusing, at times, on issues raised by the administration, these committees continued to examine the unique problems of disadvantaged groups such as women, citing the negative impacts of President Reagan's proposed cuts on them (U.S. House 1981; U.S. Senate 1981).

However, by the mid-1980s, high rates of inflation and increasing unemployment, along with demographic changes such as increased life expectancies and declining fertility rates that had begun to put a financial strain on the system during the late 1970s, provided an opportunity for the president, and other political conservatives, to reframe the terms of the discussion over the reform of Social Security. Arguing that Social Security would soon become bankrupt, Reagan announced "that it would be necessary to slash Social Security in order to save it" (Myles and Quadagno 1994).

In 1982, circumventing the usual Advisory Councils, which he viewed as ideologically resistant to his plans, President Reagan gave control over the programme to a bipartisan group, the National Commission on Social Security Reform, charging them with solving the 'financial crisis'. Their specific mandate, which was to develop a plan that would save at least $40 billion, forced an ineluctably conservative perspective on the deliberations. Consequently, in its final report, which culminated in the 1983 amendments, equity issues between men and women were conspicuously downgraded. And, for the first time, a proposal for privatizing the system was advanced. However, four of the five options offered were far less radical, involving incremental changes within the existing programme (Tynes 1996).

The 1983 amendments, while providing for relatively modest reductions, notably the gradual increase in the age of eligibility for full benefits, reduced payments at early retirement, a six-month delay in cost-of-living increases, and partial taxation of benefits, were indicative of the new age of retrenchment. Many of the costs of these changes would be borne by those in poor health and the economically disadvantaged, especially single older women. The system itself, however, was left largely intact. Some advocacy groups, including labour unions, NSCS, AARP, and the more outspoken Grey Panthers, had been pushing for financing at least part of the programme out of general budget revenues, rather than continuing as a separately financed, earnings-based programme. Conservatives and most business leaders, intent on maintaining the relationship between wages and benefits, successfully fought such proposals. Instead, the 1983 amendments authorized the acceleration of already scheduled payroll tax rates.

President Reagan and his supporters embarked on additional strategies for undermining Social Security. For example, they successfully initiated legislation allowing for Individual Retirement Accounts (IRAs), to which individuals could contribute up to $2,000 annually without paying taxes. The programme was initially devised for people with no access to pensions, but was gradually extended to everyone. The idea was that as people contributed to these private plans, their dependence on and support for Social Security would gradually erode. In the long run, however, only a small percentage of the population could afford to take advantage of these accounts, which cost the public treasury $14 billion annually by 1998.

Moreover, during the late 1980s, the rhetoric of financial crisis and catastrophe intensified, eventually dominating all aspects of discussion over the federal budget and Social Security, and even allowing Reagan and his allies to garner support for reductions in Aid to Families with Dependent Children and other public welfare programmes. Newspapers and magazine articles, along with television reporters and talk-show pundits, joined in the frenzy, thus grabbing the attention of the public. Statistics and numbers were thrown out "as if they alone were sufficient to justify a single, inescapable policy response to a complex social problem" (Marmor, Cook and Scher 1997). The crisis mentality penetrated American society, stirring up intra- and inter-generational competition and conflict, fears of programme bankruptcy, and even concerns that Social Security would destroy the American economy itself.

Instead of income adequacy, the public heard adversarial notions of equity - between past and future generations, retired and working people. 'Facts' were portrayed as indicating that future retired people would not receive their 'money's worth' compared to earlier generations; already, it was argued, newly retired older people had overly low rates of return on their money, while future retirees would accrue even less. The elderly were portrayed as better off, more educated and having more assets than previous generations of elderly. It was also pointed out that though they represented only 12.6 per cent of the population, people aged 65 and over received one-third of the federal budget. Battle cries ranged from the benign (Social Security is overly generous) to the malign (those 'greedy geezers' are seizing more than their share of available resources). And by the 1990s, a new dimension was added: preserving Social Security benefits became linked to cutbacks in programmes serving needy children, thereby causing greater poverty among that group. In other words, older people were robbing the cradle (Minkler 1991; Binstock 1994).

Hysterical predictions of system bankruptcy and collapse became common, especially in the electronic media, with the ageing 'baby boomers' (those born in the years immediately following the Second World War) viewed as a demographic time bomb. Some analysts suggested that younger generations would be paying the costs of their parents, while not receiving any benefits themselves. Social Security and its taxes were blamed for many of the nation's economic woes, ranging from the huge and growing national budget deficit and low national savings rate, to the flight of capital and the country's diminished competitiveness in world markets. In March of 1995, *Time* Magazine headlined: 'The Case for Killing Social Security'.

Thus by the early 1990s the stage was set for even starker proposals, as the Republican Party won a majority in Congress in 1994. President Clinton grimly asserted that government must begin to overhaul the system; Congress, equally grim, agreed. Clinton's 1997 Advisory Council proposed three new approaches to reform, all including some degree of privatization; five of the 13 Council members proposed radical restructuring plans (Gramlich 1998).

Privatizing Social Security was soon advanced as the solution to nearly all of the nation's economic problems. It was argued that investing in the booming stock market, either collectively or as individuals, could provide individual 'money's worth,' save the programme, enhance the national economy, and allow for greater individual freedom as well. The notion of individual liberty took on new dimensions: the right to choose one's type of retirement account (along with one's medical plan). In his 1999 State of the Union Address, the president highlighted the financial crisis in Social Security and proposed market-based measures to 'save' the programme.

Myths and Realities

The crisis mentality increasingly obscured both the goals of the programme and its financial realities. Projections of bankruptcy provided a smokescreen for a larger political goal: to reduce the scope of all social welfare programmes by reducing confidence in Social Security, the nation's most popular federal programme. Far from imminent bankruptcy, the 1983 amendments in fact had produced a large and growing cumulative surplus in the trust funds. According to the 1994 Trustee report, Social Security was adequately financed until about 2030, at which time current tax rates would cover about three-fourths of the total benefits due. Even under the most pessimistic assumptions, the funds would not be depleted until 2014 - and they would not be exhausted at all under the report's most optimistic assumptions. And the Social Security Trust Fund actually is more solvent than most private pension plans. As one former commissioner of the programme argued, Social Security is not facing a crisis but rather a long-term deficit, beginning in about 30 years (*New York Times* 1996).

Importantly, the surplus in the Social Security Trust Fund is currently used by the president and Congress to fund on-going government operations, and mask the actual budget deficit. President Clinton and Congress are squabbling over what to do with the projected $1.4 trillion federal budget surplus over the next ten years, a sum that will accrue mostly from an excess of Social Security revenues over spending. In actuality, without Social Security the deficit would have been $63 billion in 1998. Thus, increasingly burdensome payroll taxes are being used to support general federal programmes and activities.

Moreover, although the elderly enjoy a large share of the federal budget, according to knowledgeable observers, the Social Security programme is considered somewhat modest by European standards. In fact, Social Security takes a relatively small share of the GDP - during 1997, only 4.8 per cent, as compared to 9 per cent in some European countries. And in the United States, it is expected to increase by only 2 per cent of GDP over the next three decades (Bosworth 1997).

The alarm created over getting individual money's worth obscured the fundamental nature of the programme itself. Social Security is not just a savings plan or pension scheme, seeking the highest rate of return. It is an insurance plan, promoting shared risks and shared obligations among the working and retired populations. It provides protections against unforeseen circumstances outside of a person's control: physical or emotional difficulties; unemployment; poor investment decisions; serious illness; death of a partner; or any of the other untold number of life's income and/or asset draining experiences. But it also is about collective responsibility: to help support low income retirees, dependants, and their children. With private investment accounts, every person (and each generation) is entirely responsible for his or her own retirement income. Moreover, there is no doubt that despite the fact that different groups get different money's worth, Social Security provides exceptional money's worth for everyone. The total package - protections against inflation, wage increases and disability, along with life insurance and portability of coverage from job to job could not be provided better or more cheaply in the private market (Chen and Goss 1997).

Moreover, the furor created over inter-generational inequities obscured the fact that Social Security functions to free a large percentage of younger people from the full economic burden of caring for their mothers and fathers. Adult children can direct their attention to other ways to help their parents, such as meeting their emotional or emergency needs (Minkler 1991).

Numerous myths surround the idea of privatization, as well. First, middle-class Americans have been increasingly convinced, despite compelling evidence to the contrary, that they will be able to rely on their own savings in retirement. Yet, the typical baby-boomer household's savings is only at one-third the rate needed to maintain their standard of living. Low-wage workers, who have difficulty providing for their immediate needs, are unable to save anything for their old age. The reality is that Social Security is the principal source of income for the vast majority of retirees today, and those newly retiring. And it is projected to be the most important source of income in the future for younger generations (Reno and Friedland 1997).

To be sure, proponents of privatization have been aided by the booming economic markets of the 1990s. They have been able to convince the population that Social Security is a bad financial deal, and that high returns from stocks could continue indefinitely. As one analyst confidently stated: "assuming historical rates of return, if individuals born in 1970 were allowed to invest in stocks the amount they currently pay in Social Security taxes, those individuals could receive nearly six times the benefits that they are scheduled to receive under Social Security" (Cozic 1996: 58). Americans have become enthralled with the stock market, and until the fall of 1998 largely ignored the fact that stock prices can drop dramatically - and with them their retirement savings.

Moreover, placing all or part of Social Security contributions into individual accounts presents opportunities for widespread fraud and abuse, inappropriately risky investments, and pressure tactics that would seriously affect our most vulnerable populations. Lured by very high rates of return, such problems have already been experienced by sophisticated consumers as well as state and local governments, which have lost millions in public money.

By contrast, several proposals for solving the system's long-range financial problems involve small corrections, including increasing the number of wage-earning years on which to base benefit levels or delaying the age of benefits. While these recommendations, all of which fall far short of privatization, would make the system actuarially sound in 30 years, none of them would address the neglected adequacy and equity issues affecting disadvantaged groups, and most of them would actually worsen their situation. For example, it is proposed that the age of retirement be raised again, beyond age 67, which would be especially hard on low-income groups who rely exclusively on Social Security at retirement. Another proposal would alter the benefit formula by basing pensions on the highest 38 years of earnings instead of the current 35. Such a change would translate into more zero years for women who leave the labour force for care-giving obligations. And any across-the-board cuts, such as delaying, skipping, or permanently reducing cost-of-living increases would be hardest on low-income retirees.

On the financing side of the equation, one suggestion is for a 1.9 per cent increase in the payroll tax on employees and employers in 2029, with a gradual rise thereafter, a change that could correct the entire shortfall (Ball 1996). Another (less regressive) proposal would raise the income level at which contributions are currently capped, meaning those with higher salaries would pay more of their share. However, both proposals focus only on wages, as does the Social Security system itself. Yet wages constitute only a portion of individual income and wealth; stocks, bonds, real estate, and other income and assets are not tapped. This already imposes an inequitable burden on workers, especially those at the lowest ends of the wage scale, a large number of which are women; under both proposals this inequality would increase.

The Unmet Needs of Women: Adequacy Re-visited

The 1980s and 1990s have been periods of retrenchment, a backing off from earlier ideas, expectations and possibilities for improving the economic situation of older women. By the mid-1990s, those who wanted to reduce or eliminate Social Security had succeeded in convincing the nation that the needs of the elderly have been more than adequately taken care of. And the reality is that the status of the elderly population as a whole has improved and some older people are better off than younger households. However, despite the rhetoric, a significant number of older people continues to live in economically deprived conditions. The poorest among them are, and have always been, women living alone. Moreover, although relative to the population median, U.S. elderly couples fare better than their European and Canadian counterparts, single U.S. women tend to be worse off (Marmor and Smeeding 1994).

Overall, the number of older people in the United States living in poverty has hovered at 12 per cent since 1984. But among single elderly women, the rate of those living in poverty (income less than $8,163 a year) was 23 per cent in 1996, and 50 per cent were living on less than $11,500. The median income for all households in that year was $35,172 and for elderly couples, $29,210, according to the U.S. Bureau of the Census. And, for those aged 85 and over, one third of white women and fully 50 per cent of women of colour are officially classified as poor (Moon 1997); many more are hovering at the poverty line.

The economic disparity among the elderly is growing. As Myles and Quadagno (1994) put it: "Quite simply, the phenomenon of the 'declining middle' - the polarization of wages, salaries, and pension entitlements - observed among the non-elderly since the 1970s is now making its way through the age pyramid." Poverty will likely be even more concentrated on single older women in the future, with many experiencing serious hardship. One knowledgeable observer submits that "By 2020 poverty among the elderly will be almost exclusively a problem among elderly women" (Calasanti 1993).

Age-based organizations remain potent actors in attempts to preserve Social Security benefits. There are about 40 such groups in Washington alone, together with an enormous lobbying network of public and private non-profit agencies serving the old. However, instead of critically evaluating the programme and calling for improved benefits and remedies for gender inequalities, these groups and their supporters have been forced to defend the system in its current form. And to do so, they too promote older people as a monolithic force, downplaying any social and economic differences among them. Voices representing women, especially those living marginally close to poverty, have been muffled not only by the ascendancy of the conservative ideological agenda but increasingly by old age advocacy groups as well.

However, these tactics ultimately could work against the elderly and their associations. According to one analyst, the actual political attitudes and behaviour of older people, similar to younger adults, have always been based on their economic and social characteristics (Binstock 1994). Affluent members of the elderly, along with higher income workers, may become convinced that the attempt to privatize Social Security would not undermine the programme but would, in fact, serve their interests, thereby lowering support for the system overall. If they become more numerous and more vocal, they may give credence to obfuscation strategies that cast conservative "changes as ones of 'individual choice and control' rather than as 'undermining or fragmenting' the programme." Moreover, if more of the aged embrace conservative proposals, the cohesive image of old-age organizations could fall apart (Hudson 1998).

Strategies for Change: A Progressive Feminist Approach

In order to improve the plight of elderly women, those concerned with older people - and the poor overall - must first take back the power to define the ideological agenda. For Social Security, these goals include reversing the redefinition of equity away from getting one's money's worth and back towards adequacy, reinstating the notion of shared responsibilities between generations and among retirees, strengthening the social responsibility of the national government, and elevating the position of women in the welfare state. An additional goal should be to not only maintain but also expand the notion of 'entitlement' (by which everyone who meets the eligibility standards is entitled to benefits, not just those who get there first) so that it includes more rather than fewer individuals.

The conservative approaches to social welfare over the last two decades have represented an assault on women of all ages, reflecting a view of women, especially poor, unmarried women, as a source of various social problems. As several observers have pointed out, mean-spirited and punitive attitudes towards poor, unmarried females currently pervade the American political discourse (Abramowitz 1996; Rose 1995; Sidel 1996). The attack on poor, child-bearing women, labelled welfare reform, (Dunjon and Withorn 1996) resulted in eliminating the entitlement status of the 60-year-old income support programme, according to which everyone who was eligible would receive benefits, and replacing it with a first-come, first-serve arrangement. It appears older women may be next to lose entitlement status, in what is, as one critic contends, an attempt to stigmatize and residualize the needy under the guise of Social Security reform (Hudson 1998).

The campaign against poor females, and its victim-blaming mentality, places the burden of old-age support squarely on women themselves, ignoring the structural causes of their poverty and the interplay between family and work. We must begin to re-establish the links between the public and private, as well as address the impacts of labour-market policies, and social welfare provision on women's economic status throughout the life cycle. Most importantly, as feminist scholar Ruth Sidel astutely notes, for women "the lives and well-being of the working- and middle-classes are intertwined with the lives and well-being of the poor and near-poor" (1996). For older households, the fact remains that despite their history of work and relative economic comfort, most married older women are still one husband away from poverty.

In addition, a feminist analysis of Social Security should re-invoke critical appraisals of the existing programme, its outmoded assumptions, and the negative consequences for women. The programme's structural design reflects the on-going undervaluing of women's reproductive labour over the course of their lives. Caring for the household and children is legitimate work and these efforts should be acknowledged as such, rather than defining those who carry them out only as married 'dependants'. And, as more and more females are expected to take care of elderly family members, forcing them to leave or take time off from their jobs, this role, too, must be incorporated into the benefit formula. In short, the value of care-taking work in the home must be taken into account, thereby enhancing a woman's benefit in her own right, as well as protecting her joint interest in those benefits accruing to the household. Along with other realities of women's lives, strategies for reform also have to take into account the varied forms of family composition today, including growing numbers of domestic partner arrangements.

In order to restructure the system to better meet the economic needs of our most economically deprived group - single, elderly women, especially those of colour - we can work to reinstate the 1970s proposals now on a back burner, along with new, innovative recommendations based on economic and social developments since that time. Progressive approaches include a renewed interest in earnings sharing, and improvements for two-earner couples. Nearly half of all retired-worker female beneficiaries are dually entitled and their numbers are expected to grow. Yet, such households are clearly at a disadvantage when one spouse outlives the other; the death of a partner plunges many older women into poverty.

A more progressive approach would put less reliance on Social Security payroll taxes, and instead finance more of the programme out of the budget's general revenues. This would allow the government to expand the programme's economic base by taxing all wages, assets, and other forms of compensation. Our entire federal tax system has become notably more regressive, in large part because of the way in which Social Security is financed: a significant and growing percentage of Americans have equal or greater amounts of money taken straight out of their pay cheques for the Social Security Trust Fund than they do for income taxes. At a minimum, political leaders could use general revenues to make up for any future shortfalls in the programme's finances -- when and if they show up 30 years from now.

A feminist analysis also should be grounded in radical political economy, which points to the structural imperatives and failures of the capitalist system itself. Social Security alone cannot and should not solve problems that are caused by the larger society. An example is the proposed elimination of the 'earnings test', proposed by President Clinton in his 1999 State of the Union Address, which would allow Social Security beneficiaries to earn greater amounts of money without having to pay a penalty on their benefits. While the elimination of this earnings test may benefit some elderly people - as was shown when it was liberalized during the 1980s - the policy is motivated by capital's shortage of labour for minimum-wage work. And, among other factors, the existing Social Security programme, and its earnings-related benefits, reflect the gender and class inequalities and discrimination within our labour force and wage system. As one source asserts:

> U.S. historical patterns of wages and employment - and their close link to the pension system which reinforces these differences - have led to a system in which older, widowed, and otherwise single women are particularly prone to be poor or near poor (Marmor and Smeeding 1994).

In the final analysis, the increasing attacks against poor, unmarried women is a form of scape-goating, the singling out of those who are particularly vulnerable in order "to shift blame from the affluent and powerful to the poor and powerless" (Gramlich 1998). By fixing responsibility for our economic ills on Social Security, political leaders have been able to divert attention from the more compelling and deep-rooted causes of the nation's economic problems, including federal deficits caused by escalating defence spending and tax cuts for the wealthy during the 1980s; plant closures and massive worker layoffs; the growing gap between the rich and the poor; the deteriorating public infrastructure (schools, roads, bridges, etc.); and the loss of American advantages in the world economy. The large growth in the population of elderly people, who are expected to live longer than previous generations of elderly, and the growing costs to the Social Security system coincided with a serious, unrelated transformation of American economic and political life, beginning in the late 1970s. It is these latter changes which have created a real crisis in the American political economy.

Conclusion

The so-called crisis over Social Security's long-range 'solvency', along with growing federal deficits and the dominance of conservative ideology and rhetoric, has allowed a wide-spread attack on the U.S. Social Security system, restrained spending on all social programmes, and has diverted the American public from demanding attention to some fundamental economic issues, including the restructuring of the economy and growing employment insecurity. It has also created unnecessary, ill-advised rivalries among the generations, antagonisms that have not materialized in other nations experiencing population ageing.

Though old-age insurance remains a popular programme, confidence in its future has waned, with many Americans uncertain and confused as to whether they will receive any benefits at all. Groups concerned with the elderly have been forced to protect benefits, rather than lobby for sorely needed improvements. As a result, women, particularly those who are single, continue to live in seriously deprived economic conditions; the oldest old experience the most hardship while experiencing high medical and long-term care costs. Their situation could worsen considerably, especially if Social Security is 'overhauled', or partially privatized. The conservative agenda seeks to destroy the social welfare system, and replace it with privatized benefits for middle- and upper-income groups, leaving a second-tier state-funded and means-tested system for the elderly poor. Their ultimate objective is to decrease spending for low-income older people and erode political support for their needs.

Americans must begin to reframe the economic and social picture, highlighting the income disparities in society at large. The nation's most meaningful social welfare programmes, Social Security and Medicare, are age-based, unlike the more universal schemes in other industrialized nations. We need to enhance public provisions not only for disadvantaged older people but for younger households facing economic hardships, as well. And such benefits must be under a universal system that does not stigmatize any sectors of society.

References

Abramowitz, M. 1996. *Regulating the Lives of Women: Social Welfare Policy from Colonial Times to the Present.* Boston: South End Press.

Ball, R.1996. Quoted in R. Pear, "Panel in Discord on a Financing Plan for Social Security", *New York Times* (December 8).

Binstock, R.H. 1994. "Transcending Intergenerational Equity", in T.R. Marmor, T.M. Smeeding, and V.L. Greene, *Economic Security and Intergenerational Justice: A Look at North America.* Washington, DC: Urban Institute Press.

Bosworth, B. 1997. "What Economic Role for the Trust Funds?'", in E.R. Kingson and J.H. Schulz. *Social Security in the 21st Century.* New York: Oxford University Press.

Calasanti, T.M. 1993. "Introduction: A Socialist-feminist Approach to Ageing", *Journal of Ageing Studies* 7, pp. 107-10.

Chen Y-P. and S. C. Goss. 1997. "Are Returns on Payroll Taxes Fair?", in E.R. Kingson and J.H. Schulz, eds., *Social Security in the 21st Century.* New York: Oxford University Press.

Cozic, C.P. 1996. *An Ageing Population: Opposing Viewpoints.* San Diego, CA: Greenhaven Press.

Dunjon, D. and A. Withorn, eds. 1996. *For Crying Out Loud: Women's Poverty in the United States.* Boston: South End Press.

Gramlich, E.M. 1998. *Is it Time to Reform Social Security.* Ann Arbor, MI: University of Michigan Press.

Hudson, R.B.1998. "Conflict in Today's Ageing Politics: New Population Encounters Old Ideology", paper presented at the Annual Meeting of the American Political Science Association, Boston, Massachusetts.

Kingson, E.R. and E.D. Berkowitz. 1993. *Social Security and Medicare: A Policy Primer.* Westport, CT: Auburn House.

Marmor, T.R., F.L. Cook, and S. Scher. 1997. "Social Security Politics and the Conflict Between Generations", in E.R. Kingson and J.H. Schulz, eds. *Social Security in the 21st Century.* New York: Oxford University Press.

Marmor, T.R., T.M. Smeeding, and V.L. Greene. 1994. *Economic Security and Intergenerational Justice: A Look at North America.* Washington, D.C.: Urban Institute Press.

Minkler, M. 1991. "'Generational Equity' and the New Victim Blaming", in M. Minkler and C.L. Estes, eds. *Critical Perspectives on Ageing: The Political and Moral Economy of Growing Old.* Amityville, NY: Baywood Publishing Co.

Moon, M. 1997. "Are Social Security Benefits Too High or Too Low?", in E.R. Kingson and J.H. Schulz, eds., *Social Security in the 21st Century*. New York: Oxford University Press.

Myles, J. and J. Quadagno. 1994. "The Politics of Income Security for the Elderly in North America: Founding Cleavages and Unresolved Conflicts", in T.R. Marmor, T.M. Smeeding, and V.L. Greene, eds., *Economic Security and Intergenerational Justice: A Look at North America*. Washington, DC: Urban Institute Press.

National Commission on Social Security. 1981. "Social Security in America's Future", Final Report, Washington, D.C., March.

Pratt, H.J. 1976. *The Gray Lobby*. Chicago: University of Chicago Press.

Reno, V.P. and R. Friedland. 1997. "Strong Support But Low Confidence: What Explains the Contradiction?", in E.R. Kingson and J.H. Schulz, eds., *Social Security in the 21st Century*. New York: Oxford University Press.

Rose, N.E. 1995. *Workfare or Fair Work: Women, Welfare, and Government Work Programmes*. Newark: NJ: Rutgers University Press.

Sidel, R. 1996. *Keeping Women and Children Last: America's War on the Poor*. New York: Penguin Books.

Tynes, S.R. 1996. *Turning Points in Social Security: From 'Cruel Hoax' to 'Sacred Entitlement'*. Stanford, CA: Stanford University Press.

U.S. Bureau of the Census, *Statistical Abstract of the U.S.* Washington, D.C., various editions.

U.S. Department of Health, Education and Welfare (HEW). 1979. *Social Security and the Changing Roles of Men and Women*. Washington, D.C.

U.S. House of Representatives. 1981. "Impact of Administration's Social Security Proposals on the Elderly", Hearing before the Select Committee on Ageing, 97th Congress, first session, Washington, D.C, May 21.

U.S. Senate.1981. "Social Security Oversight: Cost-of-Living Adjustment",Hearing before the Special Committee on Ageing, 97th Congress, first session, Washington, D.C., June 24.

Women in the Development of the Japanese Welfare State

Misa Izuhara

Abstract

In the context of post-war welfare state development in Japan, this paper analyzes issues surrounding the changing role and position of women in the family and society. Sustaining the family as a welfare resource, the welfare state in Japan has taken shape differently than in other industrial societies. The paper investigates the ways in which the post-war social systems and policies have helped to create inequalities and wealth gaps among women in their later years.

Fieldwork consisted of a series of in-depth interviews with older Japanese women, selected from three different welfare sectors (the family, the market and the state) in order to compare them in terms of their socio-economic status, family relations and living arrangement. Results show that the male breadwinner family model has reinforced gender roles within married couples, and the consequent male domination of the labour market has restricted women's access to paid work and weakened their employment status. Social security systems based on 'the family as a unit' have contributed to the relative poverty of older single women. The research concludes that single women (or female-headed households) face many difficulties that prevent them from benefiting fully from social systems and establishing a means for independent living in old age.

Introduction

In Japan, as in most developed nations, societal ageing is an emerging issue. Since the end of the first baby boom in 1949, fertility has decreased very sharply, and now Japan has one of the lowest birth rates in the world - 1.43 in the mid 1990s. This low birth rate, combined with the world's highest life expectancy (83 years for females, 76 years for males in 1995), has recently brought about a sharp increase in the number and proportion of older people in the population. Indeed, the speed of the societal ageing process in Japan has been phenomenal. It has taken only 25 years for ageing rates to double in Japan, from 7 to 14 per cent between 1970 and 1995, compared with 115 years in France and 66 years in the United States (US Bureau of the Census 1984). This tendency is expected to continue until the beginning of the next century, when Japan's rates of societal ageing will become one of the highest in the world. The rapid demographic change will affect the future growth of Japanese economy and the development of the welfare state.

Japan's post-war economic growth has been remarkable.[1] Japan has, within a relatively short period, become one of a handful of non-western nations that is both democratic and industrialized with an established social security system. On the other hand, its welfare programmes have been regarded, by both Western and Japanese observers, as 'lagging behind' its economic achievement, some even suggesting that Japan achieved its post-war economic success partly at the expense of welfare (Lee 1987; Nakagawa 1979; Rudd 1994). Compared with other industrial nations, for example, when measured as a proportion of GDP, public expenditure on welfare in Japan has been relatively low. According to International Labour Organisation (ILO) reports on the Costs of Social Security, most industrial nations were spending two to three times the Japanese rates in the 1960s and 1970s. Although significant improvement has been made since then, current Japanese rates are still very low - approximately equivalent to that of OECD countries in the 1960s (see Table 1).

The relatively low expenditure on welfare as a percentage of GDP does not necessarily indicate, however, that Japan has been a welfare-

---

[1] From 1995 to the first oil crisis in 1973, the Japanese economy enjoyed an average annual growth of 10 per cent. Despite the recession in the early 1970s, the Japanese economy recovered quickly and entered a second period of prosperity in the 1980s Growth accelerated in the second half of the decade, peaking at 5.6 per cent in FY1990 This period, known as the 'bubble economy', burst in the early 1990s.

poor nation. Looked at more broadly, the richness of welfare provision in Japan can be seen in the strengths of other sectors, including traditional family resources, the role of the market, as well as the post-war development of occupational welfare. Nevertheless, changing family traditions, different social values and a restructuring of the employment system as well as rapid demographic change necessitate that existing welfare systems change as well.

Table 1: Social Security Expenditure as a Percentage of GDP (%)

	1970	1980	1983	1990
Japan	5.3	10.8	12.0	14.0
UK	13.7	17.3	20.5	20.5
Sweden	18.6	31.9	33.3	35.2

Sources: ILO, The Cost of Social Security, 1981-1983 (for 1970, 1980, 1983 data); Japan Statistics Yearbook, 1990 (for Japan, 1990); UK National Accounts 1991, HMSO (for UK, 1990); SCB Statistisk Arsbok for Sverige, 1992 (for Sweden, 1990) (Gould 1993).

This paper focuses on the way in which the nature of the Japanese welfare state has both reflected and determined the role and position of women in the family and society. It is often said that institutions such as those of the welfare state shape contemporary forms of social stratification. In Japan, as in most industrial nations, the provision as well as the absence of welfare services may have facilitated the creation of inequalities and new social divisions in the family and society. Taking various welfare services as examples, the paper will investigate the process by which inequalities are created between genders and among families as well as among individuals.

Methodology

Fieldwork was conducted in Kitakyushu City, using a series of in-depth interviews with older Japanese women. Issues of an ageing Japanese society are often issues of older women because higher proportions of the older population are female; due to the greater longevity of females, the age group was likely to be widowed; and women were also likely to be disadvantaged by the prevailing political and economic systems. Therefore, only females who had been married and had children, who had become single through widowhood or divorce, were targeted for interview. A 10-year cohort of women aged 70 to 79 was selected since these women had experienced a common set of post-war legal and socio-economic changes.

Informants were selected from three different welfare sectors (the family, the market and the state) in order to enable a clear distinction to be made in terms of their socio-economic status, family relations and living arrangements. Thus, selection within the family sector focused on women living within the extended family; selection within the market sector focused on women who were relatively well-off, living independently either in their own home or in a special retirement flat; and selection within the state sector focused on those living in state sector housing, such as a public nursing home or on welfare, and thus representative of a lower socio-economic group. Between 9 to 10 women, who met the above criteria, were interviewed from each sector. In quotations, informants are referred to by their initials, ages, and housing sectors.

The Role of the Family in Welfare Service Provision

Based on the traditional system of 'self-help' and 'mutual aid', the contribution of the households to welfare is a significant factor in Japan. In fact, the role of the family as a welfare provider seems to be more explicitly defined in Japan than it is in other industrial nations, and thus the Japanese family contributes more to social welfare, both financially and physically, than do families in other industrial nations. For example, Japanese parents usually fully support their adult children's higher education, and adult children look after their older parents and/or parents-in-law in extended family living arrangements. It was not until the 1970s that Japanese social welfare legislation seemed to acknowledge the end of the family's legal obligation to provide social welfare. Even so, Japanese families still feel morally obliged to provide welfare for their immediate family members.

This continuing family role has resulted in a remarkable imbalance among services and benefits in the development process of the Japanese welfare state. Apart from two major public expenditures (National Health Insurance and Public Pension Schemes), areas of public welfare such as housing and personal social services, are considerably underdeveloped. It seems that the emphasis of the state on traditional family values retards the development of adequate public means of social service delivery. The absence of public welfare provision for children, older people, or people with disabilities has had to be compensated for by relying on traditional family resources.

In contrast, some welfare programmes have been established more universally. It is widely accepted, for example, that the majority of people will send their children to public school under the comprehensive education system, and go to hospitals with the National Health Insurance. Older people usually rely on the state and/or corporations for old age pensions. However, people still look to the informal community and the family for much personal care. Cost and accessibility also play a role. An imbalance in resources, between the health insurance and social service programmes, makes older people depend less on costly or underdeveloped social services and more on accessible alternatives. Older people in general, for instance, tend to use medical care instead of community care services and sometimes ending up being 'socially hospitalized'. However, with changing family values and household structures, including increased numbers of nuclear family households, higher geographic mobility of younger generations, as well as the weakening of the community spirit, particularly in urban areas (Takahashi and Someya 1985), it is increasingly difficult to maintain the traditional practices of family welfare.

Reinforcing Gender Divisions

The post-war development of the Japanese social system, based on 'the patriarchal gender relationship' (Osawa 1993), contributed to the creation of new gender inequalities in the family and society (Langan and Ostner 1991; Yasukochi 1995; Yazawa 1993). The model of the family based on the male breadwinner, which operated most fully among middle-class families in late-nineteenth century industrial societies such as Britain and Ireland (Lewis 1992), was modified only slightly in post-war Japan. Within a 'male-dominated' social system, the social security system in Japan has been developed based on the unit of the family rather than the individual, thus reinforcing gender roles such as the male as breadwinner and the female as unpaid domestic or care worker in order to enhance available resources within the family (Takenaka 1996).

By thus defining the woman's role in the family as one of providing her spouse with basic living security by means of forming a household (Osawa 1993), the Japanese welfare state defined women's welfare entitlement not in terms of their own rights and qualifications, but by virtue of their dependent status within the family as wives and mothers. This mechanism prevented women from becoming economically independent, and also generated an economic 'bond' between couples.

Under 'the family as unit' system, women alone could not gain access to, and status in, paid employment, social security rights and benefits on an equal basis with men. Instead, they tended to make contributions and draw benefits via their husbands. This model particularly disadvantages women who are outside a regular family structure. Since divorce is not considered part of a normatively defined 'proper' life-course in Japanese society, the dissolution of the family unit by divorce or early widowhood often leaves women particularly disadvantaged (Meguro 1987).

Even though more than half of all women in Japan's working population[2] are currently engaged in waged labour, women are often discriminated against and discouraged from equal employment and income opportunities (Yoshida 1993). Since occupational welfare played an important role as a welfare provider during the period of post-war economic growth, substituting for the lack of public welfare provision (Hall 1988), employment discrimination has combined with the allocation of family-based social security benefits to produce high levels of poverty among single women in old age. By excluding women from the regular labour market, Japan has succeeded in maintaining full-employment - unemployment rates remained below 3 per cent until the prolonged recession increased the rate to around 3.5 per cent in 1997, reaching a record 4.3 per cent in June 1998 (*Asahi Evening News*, 31 July 1998). Even after the Equal Employment Opportunity Act in 1986, gender discrimination in salary, promotion, hiring processes and other workplace-related issues remains. Consequently, a married woman who is unemployed is often better off on average than her counterpart who has a career.

Exacerbating this situation are the government's current taxation and pension policies. The discriminatory tax treatment of two-income households discourages wives from taking a full-time job which pays more than ¥1,300,000 (£6,500) annually.[3] Many married women try not to exceed the maximum earning limit and to stay in a dependent status in order to benefit fully from the taxation and welfare system, and maintain maximum income of the two earners (*Asahi Shinbun*, 24 August 1995). According to a 1986 survey by the Ministry of Labour in 1986, among

---

[2] The working population is usually defined as people between 15 and 65 years of age. In 1991, women's labour force participation reached 50.7%, and they were concentrated in the tertiary industry (Sugimoto 1997).

[3] The exchange rate used here is ¥200=£1.

employees in the *paat* [part-time] status[4], 700,000 out of 1,200,000 were women and the majority were assumed to be married. In fact, the rise in female workers since the Equal Opportunity Act has been concentrated on fringe work such as part-time jobs without full occupational benefits (Osawa 1993).

Moreover, in the mid-1980s the pension system was reinforced to protect housewives rather than working women.[5] For instance, widows who have never worked outside the home often receive more money from their widow's pensions than do their counterparts who had a career, meaning married women lose the incentive to take up a full-time job (*Asahi Shinbun*, 26 August 1995). In addition, under the current system, formerly-employed widows are entitled to receive only one pension, either their own or their spouse's (approximately 75% of the occupational component). Reflecting gender-based salary differences, the majority tend to choose their spouse's partial pension and to give up their own despite the contributions paid throughout their working years (Takahashi and Someya 1985; *Asahi Shinbun*, 19 April 1998).

Furthermore, married women can be disadvantaged due to in-built institutional constraints, ranging from the absence of collective social services including childcare and old-age care to the lack of maternity rights. Social and employment structures are insufficiently developed to allow women to become working mothers, so that many women must choose between paid work and having a child. The conventional low participation of males in domestic chores also leaves working wives and mothers with a heavy burden of work and household duties, creating frustration and feelings of guilt about the family (Yasukochi 1995). Women's labour force participation is generally characterised as 'M-shape employment' - the drop from the first peak resulting from marriage and childbirth and the drop from the second peak due to the necessity of taking care of elderly parents (Sugimoto 1997).

---

[4] In Japan, *paat* (part-timer) refers not only to employees with limited working hours, but also those who work full-time hours but are employed for a fixed term at hourly wages without benefits.

[5] There are currently eight public schemes, two of which (the occupational pension scheme and the national pension scheme) cover approximately 90% of the workforce. The national scheme, established in 1961, covers all Japanese residents ages 20 to 59 who are not covered by another public pension scheme. Under the occupational scheme, 17% of a worker's salary is contributed to the scheme, evenly split between employee and employer, while under the national scheme there is a flat contribution (¥13,500 per month in 1998).

37

All these factors have resulted in women postponing marriage and child-bearing in recent years, and has led to a marked decrease in birth rates. The phenomenon known as 'double income, no kids (DINKS)' became popular in Japan in the late 1980s as married couples sought a better living standard. Even after the introduction of paid maternity leave for female employees in the 1990s, birth rates have not increased. This may be related to the low benefit levels - maternity benefit is still as low as 20 per cent of wages - or to social pressure in the workplace, which discourages women from taking maternity leave (instead they may simply leave the firm).

The Persistence of the Male Breadwinner Family Model

This study revealed significant cases of poverty in old age, particularly among women who lived in state sector housing. Many of these women shared common backgrounds and experiences - often reflecting their marital status, family circumstances, or employment history. A dissolution of the family unit through divorce, separation, or early widowhood often placed those women in a disadvantaged position in the male breadwinner family model of Japan. This was largely related to the post-war employment and welfare systems, which developed on the 'family as a unit' basis. Without a male principal worker in the household, it was difficult for single women or female-headed households to establish financial stability within the system.

In Japan, marriage traditionally defined the position and status of women in society. By acquiring a husband, children, and parents-in-law through marriage, women were acknowledged in society, and given certain tasks and obligations to perform in the family - mostly domestic duties and care-giving responsibilities. The gender roles were explicitly defined and carried out, with the result that women were often excluded from, or disadvantaged by, the formal labour market, and their husbands remained unwilling or sometimes incapable of doing 'female' domestic work:

> A.A (72) lived independently in a retirement flat (market sector housing) *'In the past, it used to be said that "men were not allowed to enter the kitchen". Accordingly, my husband was not even able to boil water. So, whenever I had to go out, it was a big hassle for me -- I had to get everything ready for him at home, including leaving hot water in a thermos bottle. He was not an exception, though. That's why, when husbands like him*

without domestic skills are left alone [become a widower], *it is so miserable and pathetic not being able to take care of themselves that they have to move into their adult children's house, residential homes, or nursing homes.'*

Another key reason for women staying at home to carry out domestic duties was the labour market created through post-war industrialization. As Japan changed from an agricultural to an industrial society, the majority of workers, mainly males, were employed in either secondary or tertiary industries, while women continued to accept their domestic role, labouring without direct cash rewards in accord with widely held norms. As a result, the husband's role as sole wage earner was reinforced:

O.K (77) lived with her son-in-law in their own home (family sector housing). She had been a housewife, carrying out all domestic work, child care for her grandson, and old age care for her bed-ridden husband for six years. *'I think that* [such gender roles] *are a lot to do with post-war social and economic change. Maybe the family has become more individualistic. In agricultural society, it was not a problem since all family members had a task, and jobs were distributed equally among them. But, it's a different scenario if your husband is a "salary-man"* [employed].'

Throughout the post-war transformation women continued to have responsibility for caring for the family. Regardless of blood or in-law relations, care in old age was left to women, making it difficult, if not impossible, for married women to take on a full-time paid job. That was one of the reasons why women often remained as secondary wage earners in the households, working part-time or even more casually in order to secure time for such domestic duties. In contrast, male family members, who were supposed to be engaged with full-time paid work, were usually absent from (and frequently not even expected to do) domestic work:

O.M (78) lived with her son's family in their own home (family sector housing). *'Five of us, women, made a schedule to look after my bed-ridden husband. Even when he was in hospital, it was a heavy burden to look after him in the morning, in the afternoon, and over night. All the women in the family, my two daughters and two daughters-in-law, helped out. If I had been on my own, I, myself, would have become ill. My co-resident son's wife was a full-time nursery teacher before. She had a good job which was going very well. So, it was a bit of a shame that she had to quit the job to take care of my husband.'*

O.T (71) lived with her unmarried daughter (46) (family sector housing). After her spouse's early death, her eldest daughter had worked in a bank and supported her family financially. *'If I become bed-ridden, I can't ask my daughter to quit her job and look after me. She is single, and working like a man* [being a breadwinner]. *It's the same thing that you would never ask your son to quit his job in order to give you personal care.'*

Women entering the formal labour market faced additional obstacles when trying to develop their own careers. Unless they had professional jobs, such as teachers, nurses, or civil servants, single women were generally unable to gain economic independence in the family and society. Because such a family model created and reinforced gender roles in households, as well as gender inequalities in employment opportunities and income, 'marriage' used to be the major option for women to survive and secure their financial position in society. This may explain why the nation experienced 'full marriage' rates during the period of post-war economic growth. Such a system inevitably marginalized the position and economic status of women who had never been married or were single as a result of divorce or widowhood.

In recent years, the traditional family model has begun to change, gradually but inevitably. Increasing labour-market participation among women and decreasing compliance with conventional roles in marriage are putting both the employment structure and the welfare system under pressure. With growing numbers of women entering the labour market on a more regular basis, increasing numbers of women are likely to become economically independent both inside and outside of marriage. Despite gender inequalities in the labour market, the options of Japanese women have expanded:

O.K (77) (family sector housing), whose daughter died of cancer at age 42: *'I think that women these days are much more independent. After my daughter died, it was very difficult for her widowed husband (my son-in-law) to find a woman to remarry. We could not find anyone. Suitable and eligible women his age usually had their own income sufficient to support themselves. Even for a young bachelor these days, if he doesn't receive adequate income or isn't attractive enough, no girl wants to marry him, let alone, a middle-aged widower like my son-in-law who earns only a small salary! If women don't need to depend on a man's financial ability, who wants to marry and look after a husband and his parents at home!'*

Women in the Labour Market

Gender roles and inequalities historically expanded from the family into the labour market, where throughout the post-war period women were denied equal access or status. Women's employment opportunities were limited, and they were often disadvantaged at the workplace:

S.Y (74) left her spouse at 20, six months after their marriage. She lived in rental housing (market sector housing). She had worked throughout her adult life to support herself financially. For the last 30 years until her retirement, she had worked as a shop clerk in a big department store. *'Since I wasn't good at flattering my male boss, I had not received much in the way of pay raises. Also, because I was a woman, my salary and retirement allowance were very low. As a single woman, my salary was nothing to compare with my male counterparts "who were supporting a dependent family". In my workplace, there was no concept of fairness in pay awards or equality in income or treatment among employees, especially between genders. When I complained about an unfair pay raise to the personnel department, I was just told that it was my own fault.'*

The research findings suggested that older women currently in poverty, living in state sector housing, were more likely to have worked to make ends meet than more affluent women, who were likely to be supported by their spouses. However, many of those women who had worked for money outside the home were engaged in the informal sector of employment, for example, helping out in their family business. They may also have had an irregular or unstable work status such as *paat*. Marriage breakdown either through divorce or early widowhood, which meant losing the principal male worker of the household, was often the main reason why women were placed in such an unfavourable economic situation. Consequently, these women were forced to enter the labour market without many work skills and experiences in their middle age:

K.H (79) lived in a public nursing home (state sector housing) without any pension or savings. Her spouse had been bed-ridden for 10 years in their 40s while their six children were still growing up. *'Because I had to care for my sick husband, I couldn't take up a formal, full-time job. That's why I worked as "paat" which allowed me more flexibility to look after my husband ... But, instead, in order to make up the time and earn more money, I did lots of overtime in the evening.'*

A.A (74) divorced her spouse a year after their marriage. After her divorce, she had worked as a housemaid for various families, and then as a domestic kitchen and cleaning worker in a private clinic. She moved into a public nursing home (state sector housing) when she was 71. *'For women like me who had only graduated from a former higher-elementary school* [now junior high school, ages 13-15], *work opportunities had been very slim. Places where women alone* [not as a couple doing family business] *could work were very limited - usually bars or night clubs, and a housemaid at best.'*

O.T (71) (family sector housing) had been a widow since the age of 42. *'When my husband passed away, I had to start working. My three children were still of school age. You know, while my husband was alive, I had never worked - I had never done anything outside the house. Since my husband died at 39, we couldn't live on my small widow's pension. Do you think that I could get an office job at 40? No way!* [The only job which middle-aged women could get was] *in the service trade. A waitress in a Japanese restaurant. I used to get dinner ready for my children before going out to work in the evening. I worked there for 13 years until my eldest daughter graduated from high school and started supporting the family.'*

Women and Social Security

The post-war development of the social security system, which allowed married women to access social security and health benefits through their spouse's employment status and welfare contributions, also encouraged women to marry, and further reinforced gender roles and economic relationships among married couples. The system, based on 'the family as a unit', was intended to provide married women with social and financial protection without having to take up full-time employment, thus recognizing their contributions as household care-givers. Yet from another perspective, the system tied these women to their homes and discouraged them from seeking outside employment. At the same time it disadvantaged those who played similar roles without being married.

A good example of this is the national pension scheme, which was reformed in 1986 and strengthened the position of wives without full-time paid work. Under the new system, if a man is employed and has an occupational pension plan, his national pension contributions automatically cover those of his wife, without any extra contributions. This privileged status of wives who do not earn a living outside the home is highlighted by the fact that single males have to make the same amount of contributions as their married counterparts if they earn the same incomes. In contrast, domestic partners, or other relatives, are not afforded the same privileges:

> A.Y (71) had never been married, although she had always been with her older sister. Like a married woman, she had helped her sister's business, working in her beauty salon. Later on, when her sister got divorced and started a cafe in a different city, she also moved with her, continuing to work for her in the cafe. After her sister died, she moved into a public nursing home (state sector housing). Even though she was like a partner to her sister, her financial status was not protected like a housewife. *'I am in limbo at present—my basic national pension* [approximately ¥70,000 (£350) a month] *is too small to live on without any income support. But, since I receive the pension, I'm not poor enough to be fully subsidized by the state. I have little savings and no property. I had always depended on my sister until she died last year. Although I had fulfilled my role helping her business, I wasn't insured as a formal employee. Unlike wives who had supported their husband in the family, I couldn't receive a widow's pension after my sister's death, either.'*

In addition, the system does not privilege married women with careers. Despite having made their own contributions to the pension system throughout their working lives, at retirement, these 'career widows' could not combine their own pensions with their widows benefits, but had to choose one or the other. This study showed that career women were likely to give up their own pension after their spouse's death, reflecting the fact that the life-income of career women is typically less than male workers' partial income. For single career women, the pension to which they had contributed was very likely to be less than that of widows who had never worked outside the home:

U.Y (70) had worked as a nursery teacher until her retirement. Her spouse was a public servant. She lived independently in her own house (market sector housing). *'I had worked as a nursery teacher for 20 years, and then as a chief of a nursery school for another 20 years. As a nursery teacher, I worked for a small school run by a temple. It wasn't an established institution so that my status was informal. Those 13 years working for the particular school made a big empty hole in my contribution years to the occupational pension scheme. That's why I am not eligible to receive my own occupational pension ... You know, my contribution years didn't reach all the required periods. It is now too late to go back and make up the absent years, anyway. When my husband passed away, I chose to receive my widow's pension, which was only half of what we used to receive together, but still much more than my own.'*

N.H (79) had worked for 30 years in the local authority office until she retired at age 60. She lives with her son's family in her own home (family sector housing). *'It must be a rare case that I have been receiving my own occupational pension after my husband's death. Mine was better than 75 per cent of his. I worked as a public servant* [as gender equal as you can get in the Japanese labour market], *while my husband had worked for a small private company.'*

Overall, those who found themselves most disadvantaged in terms of their retirement benefits were informal workers, regardless of gender or marital status. These people had typically lived from day to day without planning for their future financial security. Working as *paat* throughout their lives, they lacked access to the occupational pension scheme. Single women, or women without a principal male worker in the household, were more likely to work in the informal sector and thus most likely to find themselves in this situation. Consequently, this study found greater poverty among single older women who had worked informally and who were left without any pension in their old age:

K.H (79) lived in a public nursing home (state sector housing). *'After my husband got sick and gave up work, I worked very hard instead of him. At that time, there was no occupational pension scheme in my workplace. Since I was working as "paat", I was not insured by the company, anyway. I couldn't even contribute to the basic national pension scheme. If I had paid for pension contributions, our family would not have been able to eat. I had no spare money to contribute towards a pension scheme, let alone set aside money for the future.'*

Y.M (76) rented an old wooden house, subsidised fully by the local authority (state sector housing). *'We had enough money [from selling our house] to be picky about jobs when we first moved to the city. If we didn't like the job, we quit and found another one. We worked as a warden of a company dormitory and in a multi-storey flat, and also worked for places like a public bath. While the money lasted, we were able to do so. Perhaps, that's the reason why we didn't stay in any one job for long. Within two years, we had moved around eight times. Well, by the time my husband got ill, we had exhausted all our money and had no occupational-related insurance. Although it became my responsibility to earn some money for living, such a stressful situation also made me sick. When both of us were hospitalized, we had no choice but to go on welfare.'*

A.A (74) moved into a public nursing home at 71 (state sector housing). She also divorced her spouse one year after their marriage. Leaving her only daughter with her mother, she worked informally as a live-in housemaid for different families. *'I always found something which I did not like about the family, and quit working for them. I repeatedly did so. So, I didn't work for any one of the families for more than three years ... At that time, being on my own, I knew little of the world. So, I had no clue, or never thought about securing my future welfare. Luckily enough, someone told me before it was too late, and I went back and contributed as much as I could to make up for those absent years. Thank God, now, even a little occupational pension, I can receive it! If only I had known about it before, I would have chosen workplaces which offered occupational welfare. If so, my life could have been much easier. I did not have a sense of personal finance.'*

For married women too, it made a noticeable difference to their economic independence in old age whether they had been employed formally or had remained as informal workers. This was true not only among those who had a profession, but those who worked in family businesses. It appears that families that established a small company (employing five or more workers) on a formal basis (with occupational-welfare), rather than remaining self-employed (without occupational-based social security) were able to bring security to the family as well as to other employees. Gender roles were less emphasized in such 'self-employed' families, compared to the 'salaried' ones. In addition, the status of these women was less dependent on their spouse financially, compared with housewives:

N.T (74) lived in her own single-family home with her married son (family sector housing). After her spouse died, her son took over his family plumbing business. *'Indeed, self-employed* [family] *business needs both of our* [husband and wife's] *hands. It won't work if a wife doesn't know the details* [of the business]. *Now, my daughter-in-law is helping my son as I helped my husband for over 30 years. When my husband first started the company, he also employed me as an office clerk with occupational benefits. We used to contribute to the national pension scheme before we started the business. But, at that time, I had no idea how important it was* [to join the occupational schemes] *in order to receive my own pension later on. After my husband died, his pension was cut off, and I'm currently receiving only my own pension. It is enough to live on. There is almost no woman in my age who receives her own pension. Now, I'm very thankful for the situation.'*

O.T (72) and her spouse had run a hotel business for approximately 30 years. She lived in her own house with her married daughter (family sector housing). *'Immediately after we started, my husband turned our family business into a company. In the post-war industrialization period, without occupational welfare benefits, it was very hard to recruit workers. I also switched my pension scheme from the national pension to an occupational one. Due to the wise direction of my husband, his sister, who worked as a kitchen staff in the hotel, also started her own pension scheme. For her, it was quite late to start so that she had to contribute retrospectively in order to make up her absent years of the required periods. Now, she lives in a public nursing home with her own pension. Since we employed many other middle-aged to older women, their pension situations were the same as his sister - some had a national pension scheme, but started very late; others had never contributed even to the basic national scheme! So, we insured all of them with the occupational scheme. Now, all those women receive their own pension. These women currently in hospital and a nursing home are particularly pleased because there are usually no other women who receive pension there. One of them said, "because I receive a pension, even ¥150,000 [£750] a month, I am not treated badly by the care staff in the nursing home."'*

Concluding Comments

Since the structure of the labour market which developed in the post-war period discriminated - and continues to discriminate - on the basis of gender, inequalities based in employment opportunities and conditions have been perpetuated in the status of women in old age. For example, because women's salaries were - and continue to be - so much lower than those of men, the national pension system, which allows married women to receive 75 per cent of their husbands' benefits, merely intensified the inequalities. Thus married women may be relatively well-off in their own home with their spouse's income and occupational benefits; while another group of women, often single, early divorced or widowed, had worked at paid jobs throughout their adult lives, but tended to struggle financially due to a disadvantaged employment status. These contrasts seems to become more pronounced in their old age. Instead of achieving a more equal society regardless of gender, family background, or employment status, the post-war development of the Japanese welfare state has created inequalities among women according to their marital and employment status.

References

Gould, A. 1993. *Capitalist Welfare Systems: A Comparison of Japan, Britain and Sweden.* London: Longman.

Hall, R.1988. "Enterprise Welfare in Japan: Its Development and Role", Discussion Paper, Suntory-Toyota International Centre for Economics and Related Disciplines.

Langan, M. and I. Ostner. 1991. "Gender and Welfare: Towards a Comparative Framework", in G. Room, ed., *Towards a European Welfare State?* Bristol: SAUS.

Lee, H. K. 1987, "The Japanese Welfare State in Transition", in R. Friedmann, N. Gilbert, and M. Sherer, eds., *Modern Welfare States: A Comparative View of Trends and Prospects.* Brighton: Wheatsheaf.

Lewis, J. 1992. "Gender and the Development of Welfare Regimes", *Journal of European Social Policy* 2 (3): 159-73.

Meguro, Y. 1987. *Kojinka suru Kazoku* (Individualizing Family). Tokyo: Keisou Shobou.

Nakagawa, Y. 1979. "Japan, the Welfare Super-Power", *The Journal of Japanese Studies* 5 (1): 5-51.

Osawa, M. 1993. *Kigyo Chuushin Shakai wo Koete: Gendai Nihon wo Gender de Yomu* (Beyond the Firm-Oriented Society: Examine Modern Japan with Gender Studies). Tokyo: Jiji Press.

Rudd, C. 1994. "Japan's Welfare Mix", *The Japan Foundation Newsletter* 22 (3): 14-17.

Sugimoto, Y. 1997. *An Introduction to Japanese Society*. Cambridge: Cambridge University Press.

Takahashi, T. and Y. Someya. 1985. "Japan", in J. Dixon and H.S. Kim, eds., *Social Welfare in Asia*. London: Croom Helm.

Takenaka, E. 1996. *"Danjo Kyousei Shakai no Shakai Hoshou wo Kangaeru Kihon Shiten"* (Basic Viewpoint on Social Security System towards Gender Equal Society), in *Kansai Onna no Roudou Mondai Kenkyu-kai*, ed., *Danjo Kyousei Shakai no Shakai Hoshou Vision*. Tokyo: Domes Shuppan.

U.S. Bureau of the Census. 1984. *Projections of the Population of the United States by Age, Sex, and Race: 1983 to 2080*. Current Population Reports, P-25, 952.

Yasukochi, K. 1995. "Support Problems in the Aging Urban Society", *Review of Social Policy,* March, pp. 43-64.

Yazawa, S., ed. 1993. *Toshi to Josei no Shakaigaku* (Sociology of City and Women: Beyond Collapse of Division of Labour by Gender). Tokyo: Science-sha.

Yoshida, K. 1993. *"Kourei Josei no Seikatsu Jittai"* (Lives of Older Women), in M. Miyamoto, ed., *Kourei-ka to Kazoku no Shakai-gaku* (Sociology of Ageing and the Family). Tokyo: Bunka Shobou Hakubun-sha.

Women's Pensions and the Impact of Privatization in Britain

Jay Ginn and Sara Arber

Abstract

The concentration of poverty among older women is sometimes viewed as a temporary problem, arising from a past era when most women were homemakers. According to this view, gender inequality of income in later life will largely disappear as younger women's greater employment participation is reflected in better pensions. However, gender differences in employment patterns, in earnings and in types and levels of occupations persist.

This paper assesses the prospects for British women's pensions, given the recent policy of expanding the private sector of pension provision while reducing state pensions and trends in women's employment. Data from the British General Household Survey is used to examine trends in working-age women's pension arrangements according to social class and parental status and their employment rates. It concludes that privatization of pensions is likely to widen the gender gap in retirement income and to differentiate increasingly between the minority of women able to pursue full-time continuous employment and the majority of women who cannot.

Introduction

The concentration of poverty among older women in western societies is sometimes viewed as a temporary problem, arising from a past era when most women were full-time homemakers. According to this view, gender inequality of income in later life will largely disappear due to younger women's greater employment participation and to various forms of 'care-giver credits' in state pensions.

British politicians, when they discuss the problem of the gender gap in access to pension income, tend to rely on four different assumptions, or expectations. First, they assume that in later life women generally share a husband's income, ignoring the fact that only two-fifths of women over age 65 are married and that wives may receive much less than an equal share of their husband's income. Second, they repeat the myth that widows' benefits will provide an adequate income, despite of evidence to the contrary (Ginn and Arber 1994). Third, they mention the means-tested safety net, even though receiving financial support in this way leaves older people with a poverty-level income, besides subjecting them to the complexity and stigma of the means test. And fourth, they suggest that the rising employment participation of women and growing gender equality in the labour market will largely reduce the disparity between men's and women's pension income from their own employment. It is this last assumption which we examine here.

Gender convergence in pension income may be more elusive than has been assumed. Gender differences remain in hourly pay, in types and levels of occupations, in hours of work and in continuity of employment (Rubery et al. 1997). In addition, a number of countries are seeking to privatize pension provision, a trend which threatens to undermine any woman-friendly provisions in state pensions. For example, in Britain, the Conservative government set out to persuade individuals to opt out of the state second-tier pension (the State Earnings Related Pension Scheme) through financial incentives, combined with cuts in the value of state pensions and an ideological assault on state welfare. It is likely that other countries will seek to follow Britain's example, encouraged by the World Bank's recommendation to switch to pre-funded private pensions (World Bank 1994). Reforms to curb the cost of public pensions and to encourage increased private-funded pension provisions have been implemented or are planned in most western countries (OECD 1988; 1992; Gillion 1991; Lloyd-Sherlock and Johnson 1996; Street 1996), although the gender impact of such reforms in many, if not most countries, has been largely ignored, at least by policy-makers.

Following a brief review of pension policy in Britain, looking particularly at the position of older women, this paper examines recent changes in pension policy and their consequences for women in the context of trends in women's employment participation. We are primarily concerned with the pension income which women in the future can expect to receive from their own employment, as distinct from widows' benefits or income provided by other family members. Specifically, we examine variation in the pension arrangements made by British men and women of working age, according to parental status, age group and socio-economic position, in order to understand the pension prospects of women in the future and how these are likely to be affected by the changing pensions mix in Britain. Our findings for Britain, where pension retrenchment has been extensive, have some relevance for other countries where similar reforms have been implemented or are under consideration.

Evolving Inequality: State and Private Pension Schemes

Britain first introduced a comprehensive system of social insurance in 1948, following the Beveridge report (Beveridge 1942). Entitlement to the basic National Insurance (NI) pension was eventually based on the number of years of contributions by employees and the self-employed; the full flat rate amount, set at subsistence level, was payable at age 65 (age 60 for women) to those paying contributions for at least 44 years (39 years for women). Married women, who were assumed to be financially dependent on a breadwinning husband, were discouraged from making contributions by the 'half-test', whereby all their NI contributions were void unless covering at least half their married life, and by the fact that they could pay reduced contributions without the pension component. As a result, among older women only a minority receive a full basic pension in their own right, although wives qualify for a basic pension which is 60 per cent of their husband's amount and widows receive the whole of their deceased husband's pension.

The British pension system has undergone many changes since 1948. In 1975, the Social Security Pensions Act under a Labour government specifically addressed the pension needs of women. The 'half-test' and reduced contribution option were removed and the new Home Responsibilities Protection (HRP) allowed years of caring for children or frail adults to count towards eligibility for the basic pension. Thus an increasing proportion of women will in the future qualify for a pension in their own right. Moreover, the amount of the basic pension was indexed to national average earnings.

The 1975 legislation also introduced a second-tier pension, the State Earnings Related Pension Scheme (SERPS), to which all employees (but not the self-employed) with over a minimum weekly earnings must contribute unless contracted out into a private occupational pension. The SERPS was favourable to women, since the pension was based on the average of the best 20 years of relevant earnings. Thus the adverse effect of women's family caring responsibilities on their employment and earnings would have little effect on the amount of this pension. The combination of basic pension and SERPS was redistributive towards the low paid, providing a maximum replacement rate of 50 per cent for a female full-time manual worker, with lower rates for the higher paid (Groves 1991). Widows could expect to receive all of their husband's SERPS pension.

Beginning in the 1980s, however, despite the fact that Britain had, and continues to have, one of the smallest projected rises in the elderly dependency ratio among 20 OECD countries (Roseveare et al. 1996), the Conservative government introduced several major neo-liberal pension reforms, through the 1986 Social Security Act and the 1995 Pensions Act. These had several consequences.

The first is a shift from public to private financing. Prior to 1988, all employees were obliged to contribute either to SERPS or to a 'contracted out' occupational pension scheme; after 1988 the choice of an 'approved' personal pension (APP) fulfilling minimal benefit requirements was added. In contrast to occupational pensions, which are mainly defined benefit schemes incorporating valuable employer contributions, personal pensions are individually-arranged defined contribution schemes, to which employers rarely contribute, apart from the minimum required to replace their contributions towards SERPS.

In addition, changes in state pensions have involved major reductions, all of which have serious consequences for women. First, in 1980 the basic state pension was indexed to prices instead of national earnings. This has eroded its value from 20 per cent of average male earnings in 1980 to 16 per cent by 1990 and to a projected 12 per cent in 2010 (Johnson and Falkingham 1992). Whereas in 1948 the full basic pension for a single person was approximately 10 per cent above the level of means-tested benefits, by 1992 it was about 10 per cent below (Hancock and Weir 1994). Women, with less access to private pensions, are harder hit by the decline in value of the basic pension than men. Those pensioners with income below a certain level - often dubbed poverty level - and whose savings are also small, may be eligible for Income Support (IS), which is the major means-tested public assistance programme in Britain. By 1994, a third of pensioners, predominantly women, required IS or other means-tested benefits such as Housing Benefit (Johnson 1994). Because the basic pension is below the level of IS, a small additional pension brings no financial advantage, merely disqualifying the recipient from IS and associated benefits. As the basic pension falls further below the IS level, increasing numbers of pensioners, mainly women with small amounts of other income, will be caught in the pensions poverty trap.

Second, the value of the State Earnings Related Pension Scheme (SERPS) has been substantially reduced from its 1975 formulation. A series of cuts in SERPS were heralded in the 1986 Social Security Act and will affect those retiring after 1999; the rate of return on contributions will be reduced, falling to 20 per cent by 2027. Most seriously for women, earnings will be averaged over the whole working life instead of the best 20 years so that periods of non-employment or low pay will reduce the pension amount. From the year 2000, widows will receive only half their deceased husband's SERPS pension instead of the whole amount. Although the advantages of SERPS as a portable defined benefit pension scheme remain, the changes have made it less attractive, undermining its role as an additional pension for those unable to join an occupational pension.

Third, the 1995 Pensions Act required that the 1950 state pension age become 65 for both men and women, phasing in the change for women born after 1950. For most occupational pension schemes (private workplace-based schemes), this has resulted in a uniform retirement age of 65, rather than age 60. Although raising the pension age for women may appear to promote gender equality, it will only benefit women in the unlikely event that they maintain full-time employment up to age 65. For women born after 1950, it will further reduce the amount of both basic and SERPS pensions by lengthening the required contribution period (Hutton et al. 1995; Ginn and Arber 1995).

In all of these changes, the ideology of self-reliance and market efficiency played a major role, along with a concern to keep employers' contributions to NI at a low level (relative to other European countries). In addition, the shift from the public sector of pension provision, where NI contributions from workers pay for the NI pensions of pensioners (Pay-As-You-Go pensions), to the private sector, where contributions are held in an invested fund for payment after retirement (pre-funded pensions), has been more radical in Britain than elsewhere in Europe (Pierson 1994). Street (1996) argues that the British pension reforms were not merely cuts, which could later be reversed, but rather involve:

> Purposive policy changes to cut either current or future direct public expenditure for pensions, through ideologically consistent policy changes that permanently restructure pension regimes to increase needs-testing, privatisation or both, and that alter the future political environment of pension policy-making. (Street 1996: 21)

Not surprisingly, the decline in the value of state pensions has limited their role in income redistribution, contributing to increased inequality of pensioner incomes (Johnson et al. 1996), including inequality based on gender (Ginn and Arber 1999). Whereas men and those previously in middle-class occupations generally had occupational pensions to cushion them from the impact of reforms, this was less so for women and for others disadvantaged in the labour market. Cutbacks, including those which will be felt mainly in the future, signalled to the working-age population that state pensions could not be relied upon, creating a climate favourable for marketing the new personal pensions.

The Costs of Privatization

The Social Security Act of 1986 provided financial incentives to encourage employees to switch from SERPS to a personal pension. These, combined with pension industry sales techniques and the government's legislative and ideological attacks on state pensions, persuaded a larger than anticipated number of employees to opt out of

SERPS into a personal pension; many also opted out of an occupational pension scheme. While a half million employees were expected to take up Approved Personal Pensions (APPs), a full 5 million had started an APP by 1993 (DSS 1994: 9). Personal pension coverage among employees had reached 17 per cent by 1994, including 20 per cent of men and 13 per cent of women (Ginn and Arber forthcoming).

Personal pensions provide less generous benefits than do occupational pensions, because of lower employer contributions and the higher cost of administration and sales commissions. The pension amount is unpredictable, depending on the fund's investment performance and on the fees charged, which can absorb 20 or even 30 per cent of the fund. In spite of these disadvantages, many employees with access to an occupational pension were persuaded to opt instead for a personal pension - the notorious mis-selling scandal.

Personal pensions offer women employees a particularly poor deal (Davies and Ward 1992), especially if they ever have children. For those with interrupted employment, additional charges are incurred, so that a higher proportion of the fund is forfeit (Ward 1996: 43-44). The effect of flat rate charges is more serious for women than for men because of women's lower average earnings. A further disadvantage for women is that the same fund buys a smaller annuity than for men, due to the use of sex-based actuarial tables.

The cost of introducing the new personal pensions - due to increased spending for incentives and lost revenue from tax relief - was so great that an Audit Office official remarked, "any more successes like this and we're all ruined" (BBC 1996: 12). Part of the cost was met from the National Insurance Fund, reducing the resources available to improve state pensions; thus the policy effectively robbed the state sector of pensions in order to pay the private sector. A Labour Party politician considered the policy "a major misuse of public funds ... thrusting money into the letter boxes of the private companies" (quoted in ibid.: 11).

Trends in Women's Employment and Earnings

Since much of the gender inequality entailed in private pensions relates to women's employment patterns, we now look at how women's employment is changing in major OECD countries. Can women in the future expect a better pension income than older women today?

Although women's employment rate has increased dramatically since the 1950s, the trend is deceptive in terms of the implications for women's earnings and pension acquisition. Much of the increase has been in part-time employment, as women have sought to combine paid employment with their domestic responsibilities. Part-time employment is likely to contribute little to private pension entitlements (Ginn and Arber 1996; 1998) and may also be less valuable than full-time employment in building state pension entitlements, depending on how state pension schemes in different countries treat part-time employment and low wages.

Figure 1 shows the change in full-time and part-time employment rates of (a) women and (b) men in 11 OECD countries between 1979 and 1995.

Classification of part-time employment by the OECD is based on self-report so that the weekly hours worked by 'part-timers' varies among and within countries. Nevertheless, the data does indicate some trends over time. In all except the Nordic countries and Italy, women's part-time employment showed a significant increase; but full-time employment hardly increased at all in Germany, Italy, Japan, and the UK while in France it declined (see Figure 1a). In Australia, Canada and Sweden, women's full-time employment increased slightly, while in Denmark, New Zealand and the United States of America it increased substantially. In the majority of countries, about 40 per cent of women aged 16-64 were not in paid employment and the rate of female full-time employment remained at about 40 per cent or less, well below men's rate. Men's full-time employment had fallen in most countries from around 80 per cent in 1979 to between 60 and 70 per cent in 1995, while their part-time employment had increased (see Figure 1b).

While these trends suggest some gender convergence of full-time rates of employment, the changes over the 16 years are small relative to the gender gap. In all countries except the United States, convergence owes more to a decline in men's full-time employment than to a rise in full-time employment for women. For example, in Britain, men's full-time employment rate fell by nearly 17 percentage points (from 84 to 67 per cent) while for women it remained stable. Moreover, men's part-time employment occurs mainly in youth or in the latter part of the working life. Women's part-time employment, in contrast, is most common during the reproductive years, the prime years in which occupational status and earnings could otherwise be expected to rise, thereby improving pension entitlements (O'Reilly and Fagan 1998).

56

Figure 1 % employed full and part time, 1979 and 1995, in 11 OECD countries, as proportion of population aged 16-64

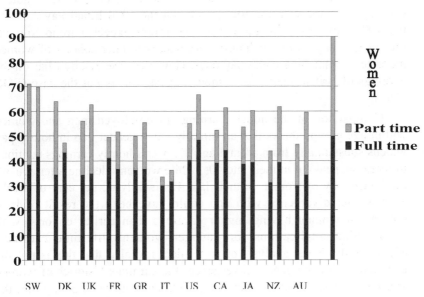

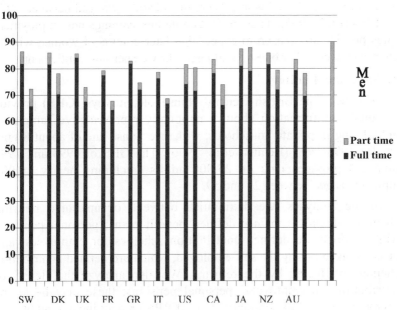

Source: Calculated from OECD (1996) Tables A and E.

A crucial factor in private pension income (and to a lesser extent in state pensions, depending on the benefit formula), is life-time earnings, which depend on years worked, hours worked and the profile of hourly earnings over the working life. Following the 1970 Equal Pay Act and the 1975 Sex Discrimination Act, one might expect a trend towards greater gender equality of hourly earnings, with later cohorts of women more nearly matching men's pay rates. However, research by Elias on the earnings of British men and women suggests this is not the case (EOC 1995).

Comparison of the hourly earnings of employed men and women within age groups shows that an initially small gender gap in hourly pay widens substantially from around age 30. Men's hourly earnings continue to increase, peaking in their late 40s, while women's decline after age 30; the hourly pay of women in their late 40s is only 62 per cent of men's. This gender divergence with age could have been the result of later cohorts of women having higher earnings than earlier cohorts, with encouraging implications for younger women's life-time earnings. Significantly, Elias' analysis of panel data revealed that this is not the explanation for the gender divergence; the earnings histories of women and men closely followed the cross-sectional pattern, showing that the age profile of men's and women's earnings hardly changed between 1976 and 1994 (EOC 1995). Thus, in Britain neither earnings nor employment trends provide any reason to expect that later cohorts of women will be better able than earlier ones to build good private pension entitlements.

Methods and Findings

Data from the British General Household Surveys (GHS) provide high-quality information about a nationally representative sample of adults living in private households, with a response rate of about 80 per cent for 1993-1995 (Bennett et al. 1996). The GHS of 1993 and 1994 combined provides data on 25,000 adults (including nearly 16,000 employees) aged between 20 and 59.

In the analyses, we distinguish between occupational pension schemes, which are mainly defined benefit plans; personal pensions (APPs), which are defined contribution schemes for employees; and pensions taken out by the self-employed, which are defined contribution schemes unaffected by the reforms. We also analyze the 'level' of contributions to employees' personal pensions; these may be at the minimum required to contract out of SERPS or may include additional amounts from the employer or employee.

The effect of parental status on private pension coverage is measured using information on the age of the youngest child and number of dependent children at home (aged under 16 or aged 16-18 but in full-time education). For women, but not for men, information is also available as to whether they had ever borne a child. For employees, socio-economic groups were combined into six categories.

Table 1: Percentage with each type of private pension
      Men and women aged 20-59

	Men	Women	All
Occupational pension	40	25	32
Personal pension (APP)	13	9	11
Self-employed personal pension	9	2	6
No private pension contributions	38	64	51
Col %	100	100	100
N	12,003	12,658	24,661

Source General Household Surveys 1993 and 1994 (authors' analysis).

Private pension coverage: All adults aged 20-59

In 1993-1994, about half the population aged 20-59 (51 per cent) did not contribute to any form of private pension plan (occupational, personal or self-employed pension schemes) (see Table 1). Among women, as many as 64 per cent had no private pension coverage. Thus only a minority of British women, 36 per cent, currently pay into a private pension scheme; this reflects both the proportion of women not in paid employment and those employed part-time, for whom an occupational pension scheme is often not available and for whom contributions to a private pension would generally be hard to afford.

Coverage by occupational and personal pensions has different implications for future pension income, as discussed above. A third of working age adults belonged to an occupational pension and 17 per cent were contributing to a personal pension; this includes 11 per cent contributing to the new personal pensions for employees (APPs) and 6 per cent contributing to personal pensions for the self-employed. Each of the three types of private pension was more common among men than women.

Figure 2: Private pension contributions,
men and women aged 20-59 by age group

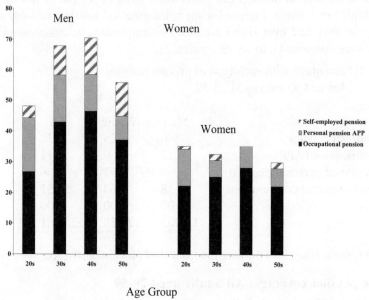

Source: General Household Surveys 1993 and 1994 (authors' analysis).

The age distribution of women with a private pension is important, as it indicates the likelihood of working-age women building good private pension entitlements. Figure 2 shows the proportions of men and women in 10-year age groups with private pension coverage. Whereas men's coverage rises to about 70 per cent from age 30-49, the age coverage profile for women is flatter, reaching 40 per cent only among those in their 40s. With these low rates of private pension coverage among working-age women, the majority of women cannot expect a substantial income in later life from this source.

The gender and age differences in private pension coverage partly reflect differences in men's and women's employment patterns. Men's full-time employment rate rose to over 80 per cent during the prime career-building years from 30 to 49, whereas women's fell from nearly half in their early 20s to about a third from age 30 to 44, rising to 40 per cent in their 40s before falling again to 20 per cent in their late 50s.

The age profile of women's employment and private pension coverage reflects their role in child-bearing and child care, major factors in women's lower full-time employment rate. We therefore analyze the private pension coverage of working-age adults according to their parental status, distinguishing type of pension and level of contribution to personal pensions, in two broad age groups (see Figure 3). Women who had never borne a child were substantially more likely to have pension coverage than other women (see Figure 3a, first bar in each age group). In both age groups of women, a decline in pension coverage with increasing parental responsibility was evident, mainly due to occupational rather than personal pensions; for example, among women aged 40-59, occupational pension coverage was 50 per cent of those who had never had a child, 35 per cent of those with children aged over 10 years old, 30 per cent of those having only one child under 10 years and 25 per cent of those with a child under 10 years and at least one other dependent child at home.

In contrast, men's private pension coverage showed no association with parental status (see Figure 3). Because men had not been asked whether they had ever had a child, we cannot distinguish between those who were not fathers and those whose children were aged over 10 (see first bar in each age group). The low private pension coverage among men aged 20-39 with no child under 10 is likely to reflect that they are younger (and mainly have not yet become fathers), compared with the other two groups of men.

In spite of the much-publicized rise in women's employment in western societies, British women's reproductive role still constrains their employment, with adverse effects on their private pension coverage. This suggests that, on average, working-age women can expect to receive a low private pension income in later life. However, a cleavage is emerging between the experience of women in different socio-economic groups. Typically, child-rearing in Britain means leaving the labour force or reducing hours of work, changes which are associated with a long-term loss of occupational status; only a minority of mothers, predominantly in the higher socio-economic groups, avoid these adverse effects by returning relatively early to full-time employment (Glover and Arber 1995). If policy-makers intend the majority of women to build an adequate private pension through their own employment, policies to ensure the availability of suitable child-care (and parent-care) facilities are essential.

Private pension coverage: Employees

Among employees, the gender gap in private pension coverage was substantial; over 80 per cent of men were covered but only 55 per cent of women, including 72 per cent of full-timers but only 34 per cent of part-timers. Analyzing the change in pension arrangements since the introduction of personal pensions gives some indication of the gender difference in pension income to be expected in the future. Figure 4 compares private pension coverage in 1987 and 1993-1994 in three age groups (20-29, 30-44 and 45-59). Men's occupational pension scheme membership rate had declined slightly between 1987 and 1993-1994 within each age group, while that of women had increased (with the exception of women in their 20s employed full-time). The membership rate of women employed part-time had increased substantially over the seven years, especially among those aged under 45, as a result of European Court judgements concerning equal rights for part-time employees. Nevertheless, the pension prospects of the three quarters of part-time women employees who still lacked private pension coverage by 1994 gives cause for concern. Whereas occupational pension coverage increased with age, personal pension coverage showed the reverse tendency, so that private pension coverage in 1993-1994 peaked between the ages of 30 and 44 for those employed full-time, unlike in 1987. Among women employed part-time, 11 per cent in each age group contributed to a personal pension, with about a fifth contributing to an occupational pension.

Figure 3: Private pension contributions, men and women by parental status and age group

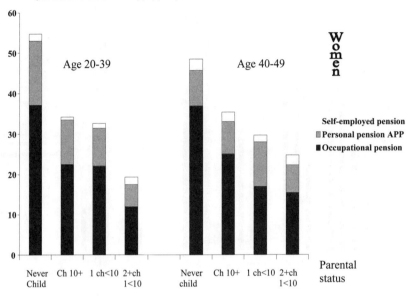

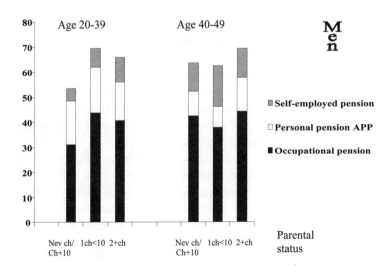

Source General Household Surveys 1993 and 1994 (authors' analysis)

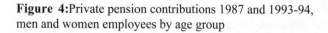

Figure 4: Private pension contributions 1987 and 1993-94, men and women employees by age group

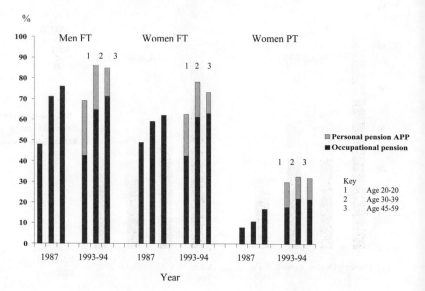

Source: General Household Surveys 1993 and 1994 (authors' analysis).

Differences in coverage by occupational and personal pensions among employees according to socio-economic group, gender and hours of work are shown in Figure 5. The class gradient in pensions coverage was mainly due to occupational pensions, reflecting their differential availability according to occupational group. However, coverage declined more steeply with socio-economic group for women than for men; among women employed part-time the differences in occupational pension membership between the top three groups were particularly marked. In contrast, personal pension coverage was more evenly distributed among socio-economic groups, reflecting their accessibility to all employees. This ostensible class equality may be deceptive because personal pensions are likely to provide a poorer return on contributions for those in the lower socio-economic groups, especially for part-time workers.

Figure 5: Private pension contributions of employees by socioeconomic category & by hours of work for women

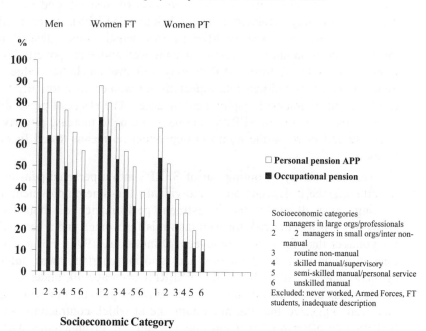

Men   Women FT   Women PT

□ Personal pension APP

■ Occupational pension

Socioeconomic categories
1   managers in large orgs/professionals
2   2 managers in small orgs/inter non-manual
3   routine non-manual
4   skilled manual/supervisory
5   semi-skilled manual/personal service
6   unskilled manual
Excluded: never worked, Armed Forces, FT students, inadequate description

Socioeconomic Category

Source General Household Surveys 1993 and 1994 (authors' analysis)

In this section, we have shown that, although women's private pension coverage has increased in the last decade, it remains substantially lower than men's, in large part due to the constraints placed on women's employment by their reproductive role. Occupational pension membership of those working part-time or in manual occupations is still much lower than for other women. The introduction of the personal pension option for employees, although it has increased access to private pensions, is likely to be of more benefit to those in the higher socio-economic groups and to full-timers. For the low paid, who are predominantly women, the advisability of choosing a personal pension has been questioned and it is this issue that we consider in the next section.

Adequacy of Personal Pensions for Women

The basic National Insurance pension provides an income which, for most women, is substantially below the level of means-tested benefits. The State Earnings Related Pension Scheme (SERPS), as originally formulated, promised a second-tier pension which could substantially improve income in later life, raising income well above the poverty level. Even in its reduced form, SERPS may still provide better value for money than a personal pension, especially for women with low life-time earnings and fragmented employment histories. The effect of persuading individuals to opt out of SERPS may therefore be to increase poverty in later life and increase the numbers dependent on means-tested Income Support.

The advisability of opting out of SERPS into a personal pension is uncertain, since it depends on an individual's life-time employment and earnings as well as on the investment performance of their fund. However, it is a better risk for men than it is for women and a better risk for younger than for older employees (Dilnot et al. 1994). For a young man in a non-manual occupation and ignoring charges, these authors estimate that it is advisable to be in SERPS from age 40, under certain assumptions as to rates of interest and earnings growth. For women, it has been suggested that the maximum age at which contracting out of SERPS into a personal pension upper would be advantageous was as young as 30 (Harrison 1995).

Because of the disproportionate effect of charges on the contributions made by the lower paid, accountants Coopers and Lybrand estimated that those earning less than £10,000 a year in 1993 would not benefit from a personal pension (Durham 1994). In the following analysis of personal pension contributors, we have assumed that those who in 1993-1994 were earning less than £200 per week or were aged over 40 were probably ill-advised to contract out of SERPS into a personal pension.

In Table 2, the proportion of all personal pension contributors who earned less than £200 per week or were over age 40 is shown for men and women. In all, 42 per cent were earning less than £200 per week but two-thirds of women contributing to a personal pension were low paid, compared with a quarter of men. Among women part-timers, 88 per cent were earning too little for a personal pension to be a sensible option.

Over a third of personal pension contributors (36%) were over age 40, with little difference between men and women. If both earnings and age criteria are included, 63 per cent of personal pension contributors (representing 10% of all employees aged 20-59) were likely to have been better off in SERPS. Three-quarters of women contributors were unsuitable for a personal pension on the criteria used, a figure which would be even higher if account were taken of interruptions to employment. Among women part-timers (who comprised 14% of personal pension contributors), 94 per cent were unsuitable due to either the age or earnings criterion.

Table 2: Percentage of personal pension contributors who were low paid or aged over 40, British men and women aged 20-59, by hours of work for women

	All	Men	Women		
			All	FT	PT
Earning <£200pw	42	25	65	52	88
Aged over 40	36	34	38	30	53
Earning <£200/wk or aged over 40	63	54	54	66	94
N	2,278	1,319	959	630	329

Source General Household Surveys 1993 and 1994 (authors' analysis).

Stakeholder Pensions: Are They Any Better?

That personal pensions were sold to many employees whose circumstances made them unsuitable purchasers is increasingly acknowledged, even by the finance industry. Personal pension providers have been castigated by the Consumers Association as providing poor value for money: "We can't think of another major industry where the consumers get such a raw deal or where companies get away with selling such poor products" (quoted in Mackintosh 1998: 11).

The Labour government, although acknowledging the deficiencies of personal pensions and women's particular handicaps in acquiring private pension entitlements, has proposed a more highly regulated form of personal pension - Stakeholder Pensions (SPs). Yet we would argue that it is not possible for any money purchase scheme to provide an adequate pension for those with low life-time earnings - a characteristic that applies to the majority of women. Joshi (1996) calculated that 'Mrs. Typical' in Britain with two children earns £230,000 less (1994 prices) over her lifetime than her childless sister, a loss of 55 per cent.

The precise form that Stakeholder Pensions will take is yet to be determined. In essence, they are personal pensions which fulfil certain quality criteria and which may be operated on a group basis. Although SPs would have advantages over personal pensions in universal access, ease of portability and somewhat lower charges, the main drawbacks remain: losses through charges, which could still be substantial, the close link between benefits and life-time earnings and the risk inherent in any money purchase scheme. Past rates of return on investments are unlikely to be sustained in future (Toporowski 1998; Mabbett 1997). For example, the 1998 fall in share prices and gilt-edged securities has reduced the typical income from a pension fund by 20 per cent for an individual retiring after October of that year, compared with six months earlier (Eaglesham 1998).

It is by no means clear that an SP would provide a better return on contributions than SERPS, even for those with average male earnings (NPC 1998). For women and others with low life-time earnings, the disadvantages of SPs relative to SERPS would be most acute. The pension produced by an SP would be severely reduced for those with gaps in employment and periods of part-time employment during family care-giving.

In Britain, a degree of pension privatization has been accomplished through tax-financed incentives and through substantial long-term cuts in state-provided benefits. Yet British pensions analysts have concluded that state pensions, as currently formulated, are sustainable in the future (Hills 1993; Johnson 1998) and that improvements are affordable (Townsend and Walker 1995). Moreover, public pension spending per person is lower in Britain than in any other OECD country (Hutton et al. 1995), reflecting unusually low contribution rates, especially from employers. It is now widely acknowledged that there is no 'ageing crisis' facing Britain (e.g., Disney 1996) and that demographic change has similar effects in Pay-As-You-Go and funded pensions, in terms of intergenerational equity (Pension Provision Group 1998). It is not surprising, therefore, that some have concluded that British pensions policy has been driven by ideological rather than financial or demographic concerns (see, e.g., Walker 1993). Although other countries face a more rapid ageing of their population than Britain, it is worth questioning to what extent pension privatization is an appropriate response, and what the implications for women are likely to be.

Pension Privatization in other Countries

The gender implications of pension privatization cannot simply be extrapolated from the British case. Countries vary in the extent and quality of part-time employment, in the length of gaps in employment due to child care, in the gender earnings gap and, most importantly, in the existing pension system and popular support for redistributive and collective pension policies. Yet in broad terms a trend to privatization can be expected to diminish the effect of whatever features of state pension schemes protect or compensate women for their care-giving roles.

In spite of an ascendant creed that state pension provision must be replaced by private money purchase schemes, most governments have balked at such wholesale reform - so far. Chile, however, is an exception (Barrientos 1996) and the estimated gender effect of Chile's introduction in 1981 of mandatory private money purchase pensions echoes our assessment of the likely effect of pension retrenchment on British women's pension income in the future.

A comparative analysis of six countries - Australia, Chile, Italy, Poland, Sweden and Britain - (using computer simulation) estimated the differential effect of women's employment histories on their pension income, according to the structure of the pension system (Evans and Falkingham 1997). The performance of each country's mandatory pension system was measured in terms of the amount of expected pension at retirement as a proportion of average gross male earnings, computing the value of 'relative income' for seven hypothetical employment histories. For part-time, low-paid work with child-care gaps, relative income was about 50 per cent in Sweden and Poland, 37 per cent in Italy, 23 per cent in Britain and Australia but only 11 per cent in Chile. The authors conclude that a pension system dominated by private defined contribution pension schemes perpetuates and widens income inequality in retirement, disadvantages women whose employment was restricted by raising children and will lead to pressure for expansion of means-tested assistance. In contrast, minimum pensions, if these are above the level of assistance safety nets, both protect the vulnerable and provide an incentive for additional voluntary provision.

Because of the necessarily long time scale in which pension schemes operate, the effects of pension privatization will not be fully known until well into the next century. Simulations such as the above are therefore most valuable in providing an indication of the likely consequences of privatization. They point to the dangers, especially for women who raise families (the majority of women), of a shift in the balance of pension provision towards the private sector.

Conclusions

Women's need for an adequate pension entitlement of their own is increasingly urgent with the rising rate of divorce, co-habitation and single parenthood: reliance on receiving pension income from a husband or as a widow is an even more risky strategy than in the past. Yet only about a third of working-age women in Britain (36%) currently make contributions to a private pension plan.

For most women, their responsibility to provide care for young children or frail parents conflicts with maintaining the full-time continuous employment required to obtain a good private pension. They may feel that it would be irresponsible and selfish to prioritize their future pension provision over the immediate care needs of their family. Part-time employment facilitates women's juggling of their dual roles; yet, compared with full-time employment, it is much less effective in building private pension entitlements. Only a small minority of highly-qualified, mainly professional, women are able to combine child-bearing with the full-time continuous employment required to obtain a good private pension. Thus a polarization, or class differentiation, among women is emerging, which is likely to result in growing inequality of income among older women in the future. The majority of the next generation of British women will have to rely on state pensions in later life, like the current generation of older women. Yet the value of state pensions is being rapidly eroded.

British pension policy since 1986, which has enabled the finance and insurance industry to make handsome profits, has been portrayed as improving choice and encouraging individuals to take responsibility for their own retirement income. Yet this policy has ignored the inability of low-paid employees, especially women whose employment is constrained by care-giving responsibilities, to save for their retirement through the private pensions sector. It has led many low-paid employees to pay into a personal pension plan which will provide an inadequate pension and which represents extremely poor value for money because of the grossly disproportionate charges levied. The policy has also diverted resources from the National Insurance Fund and incurred substantial losses in tax revenues. The cost of tax relief, which mainly benefits men, is often overlooked, while policy-makers claim that improved state pensions, which would predominantly help women, are unaffordable.

The World Bank's (1994) prescription for extending the use of private-funded pensions and reducing state pensions has been influential in disseminating the view that public pension provision is unsustainable. Yet the World Bank's analysis is gender-blind, ignoring the redistribution effects of pension privatization and in particular the consequences for future cohorts of women when they retire. Although the gender impact of privatization of pensions will vary among countries, the cases of Britain and Chile indicate the difficulties women will face in building good private pension entitlements and highlight the need for state pensions designed to provide an adequate income for those with interrupted and part-time employment.

Looking to the future, state pension provision will become even more important than in the past, due to both social changes and to increasing flexibility of the labour market. Life-long marriage is becoming less common and child-bearing outside marriage more widespread. Attaching women's state pension rights (such as wives' and widows' benefits) to marriage, when it is child-rearing which handicaps them in the labour market and hence in making pension contributions, will become increasingly anachronistic. Men are also working part-time more than in the past, especially towards the end of the working life, and are experiencing more breaks in employment than previously. Women, and to a lesser extent men, are ill-served by a pension system which depends on full-time continuous employment.

The concentration of poverty among older women is likely to be exacerbated unless the trend towards privatizing pensions is reversed. Private pensions cannot fulfil the social function of protecting the pensions of those who raise the next generation.

References

Arber, S. and J. Ginn. 1991. *Gender and Later Life: A Sociological Analysis of Resources and Constraints.* London: Sage Publications.

Barrientos, A. 1996. "Ageing and Personal Pensions in Chile", in P. Lloyd-Sherlock and P. Johnson, eds., *Ageing and Social Policy. Global Comparisons.* London: Suntory-Toyota International Centre for Economics and Related Disciplines.

Beveridge, W. 1942. *Social Insurance and Allied Services*, Cmnd 6404, London: HMSO.

BBC. 1996. "Consequences Programme 4 - Pensions", radio programme transcript, on January 31.

Bennett, N. et al. 1996. *Living in Britain: Results from the 1994 General Household Survey.* London: HMSO.

Davies, B. and S. Ward. 1992. *Women and Personal Pensions.* Manchester: Equal Opportunities Commission.

Department of Social Security (DSS) 1994. *Personal Pension Statistics 1992/3*, rev. ed. London: GSS.

Dilnot, A., R. Disney, P. Johnson and E. Whitehouse. 1994. *Pension Policy in the UK.* An Economic Analysis. London: IFS.

Disney, R. 1996. *Can We Afford to Grow Older?* London: MIT Press.

Durham, P. 1994. "Millions Will Lose Money on Private Pensions", *Independent*, 28 March.

Eaglesham, J. 1998. "Pensionland Gets Colder", *Financial Times Money*, October 10/11.

Equal Opportunities Commission (EOC). 1995. *Women and Men in Britain*. Manchester: EOC.

Evans, M. and J. Falkingham. 1997. "Minimum Pensions and Safety Nets in Old Age: A Comparative Analysis", WSP/131. London: Suntory-Toyota International Centre for Economics and Related Disciplines.

Gillion, C. 1991. "Ageing Populations: Spreading the Costs", *Journal of European Social Policy* 1(2): 107-28.

Ginn, J. and S. Arber. 1991. "Gender, Class and Income Inequalities in Later Life", *British Journal of Sociology* 42(3): 369-96.

_____.1993. "Pension Penalties: The Gendered Division of Occupational Welfare", *Work Employment and Society* 7(1): 47-70.

_____.1994. "Heading for Hardship: How the British Pension System Has Failed Women", in S. Baldwin and J. Falkingham, eds. *Social Security and Social Change: New Challenges to the Beveridge Model*, Hemel Hempstead: Harvester Wheatsheaf, pp. 216-34.

_____. 1995. "Moving the Goalposts: The Impact on British Women of Raising Their State Pension Age to 65", in *Social Policy Review* 7, London: Social Policy Association.

_____.1996. "Patterns of Employment, Pensions and Gender: The Effect of Work History on Older Women's Non-State Pensions", *Work Employment and Society* 10(3): 469-90.

_____. 1998. "How Does Part-Time Work Lead to Low Pension Income?" in J. O'Reilly and C. Fagan, eds., *Part-time Prospects. An International Comparison of Part-time Work in Europe, North America and the Pacific Rim*. London: Routledge.

_____. 1999. "Changing Patterns of Pension Inequality in Later Life", *Ageing and Society* 19(1).

_____. forthcoming. "Personal Pension Take-up in the 1990s in Relation to Position in the Labour Market", *Journal of Social Policy*.

Glover, J. and S. Arber. 1995. "Polarisation in Mothers' Employment", *Gender, Work and Organisation* 2(4): 165-79.

Groves, D. 1987. "Occupational Pension Provision and Women's Poverty in Old Age", in C. Glendinning and J. Millar, eds., *Women and Poverty in Britain*. Brighton: Wheatsheaf.

_____.1991. "Women and Financial Provision for Old Age", in M. Maclean and D. Groves, eds., *Women's Issues in Social Policy*. London: Routledge.

Hancock, R. and P. Weir. 1994. *More Ways Than Means: A Guide To Pensioners' Incomes in the 1980s*. London: Age Concern Institute of Gerontology.

Harrison, D. 1995. "Be Sure You're Secure When You Retire", *Financial Times*, June 10/11.

Hills, J. 1993. *The Future of Welfare. A Guide to the Debate*. York: Joseph Rowntree Foundation.

Hutton, S., Kennedy, S. and Whiteford, P. 1995. *Equalisation of State Pension Ages: The Gender Impact*. Manchester EOC.

Johnson, P. 1994. *The Pensions Dilemma*. London: IPPR.

_____. 1998. "Introduction and Overview", paper presented to Fabian Conference on Stakeholder Pension, London, January 14.

Johnson, P., Disney, R. and Stears, G. 1996. *Pensions: 2000 and Beyond*, Volume 2, Retirement Income Inquiry: London.

Johnson, P. and Falkingham, J. 1992. *Ageing and Economic Welfare*. London: Sage Publications.

Joshi, H. 1996. *The Tale of Mrs. Typical*. London: FPSC.

Lloyd-Sherlock, P. and P. Johnson. 1996. *Ageing and Social Policy. Global Comparisons*. London: Suntory-Toyota International Centre for Economics and Related Disciplines.

Mabbett, D. 1997. *Pension Funding: Economic Imperative or Political Strategy?* Uxbridge: Brunel University.

Mackintosh, J. 1998. "Consumer Group Hits At Personal Pensions 'Rip-Off'", *Financial Times*, July 2, p. 11.

National Pensioners Convention (NPC). 1998. *Pensions Not Poor Relief.* London: NPC.4

O'Reilly, J. and Fagan, C. eds. 1998. *Part-time Prospects. An International Comparison of Part-time work in Europe, North America and the Pacific Rim.* London: Routledge.

OECD. 1992. *Private Pensions and Public Policy* Paris: OECD.

_____.1988. *Reforming Public Pensions*, Social Policy Studies No. 5. Paris: OECD.

_____.1996. *Employment Outlook.* Paris: OECD.

Pension Provision Group. 1998. *We All Need Pensions - The Prospects for Pension Provision.* London: The Stationery Office.

Pierson, P. 1994. *Dismantling the Welfare State? Reagan, Thatcher and the Politics of Retrenchment.* Cambridge: Cambridge University Press.

Roseveare, D., W. Leibfritz, D. Fore and E. Wurzel. 1996. *Ageing Populations, Pension Systems and Government Budgets: Simulations for 20 OECD Countries.* Paris: OECD.

Rubery, J., M. Smith, C. Fagan and D. Grimshaw. 1997. *Women and European Employment*. London: Routledge.

Stone, R. 1989. "The Feminisation of Poverty among the Elderly", *Women's Studies Quarterly* 1 and 2, pp. 20-34.

Street, D. 1996. "The Politics of Pensions in Canada, Great Britain and the United States, 1975-1995", Ph.D. dissertation, Tallahassee, Florida State University.

Toporowski, J. 1998. "Ponzi Finance and Pension Fund Capitalism", paper presented to the Association for Social Economics meeting, Chicago, January 5.

Townsend, P. and A. Walker. 1995. *New Directions for Pensions. How to Revitalise National Insurance.* Nottingham: European Labour Forum.

Walker, A. and T. Maltby. 1996. Ageing Europe. Buckingham: Open University Press.

Walker, A. 1993. "Whither the Social Contract? Intergenerational Solidarity in Income and Employment", in D. Hobman, ed., *Uniting Generations. London: Age Concern England.*

Ward, P. 1996. *The Great British Pensions Robbery.* Preston: Waterfall Books.

World Bank. 1994. *Averting the Old Age Crisis*. New York: Oxford University Press.

Life-Cycle Income and Motherhood: Simulations for British Women of the 1990s

Hugh Davies, Heather Joshi and Romana Peronaci[1]

Abstract

Child-bearing and child-rearing affect women's opportunities in the labour market: both their immediate earning experience and their longer term earning power, which in turn affect their chances of earning a pension. This paper links women's incomes in later life with their history of child-bearing. Individual and family life-time incomes are estimated for hypothetical illustrative British cases.[2] Using new estimates based on data collected during the 1990s, drawn from the British Household Panel Survey, it examines the role of labour market and the state in the foregone income costs of motherhood. The authors explore the following questions: How does the impact of children on gross earnings vary by the woman's education? What is the effect of the tax/benefit system on the earnings costs of motherhood? On conventional assumptions about income pooling, who bears the net costs? How far does motherhood jeopardise financial security in old age? We examine whether these impacts have remained the same in a situation of rising female participation in the labour market.

---

[1] We are grateful to the Leverhulme Trust for supporting this research, under the project "Living Arrangements and Livelihoods over the life cycle" and to the ESRC Data Archive for access to data from the British Household Panel Survey. This paper draws on a revised version of a paper presented at the ESPE Conference, Amsterdam, June 1998.
[2] Earlier work by Heather Joshi provided estimates of the earnings foregone by mothers in Britain, which were then extended in various ways by Joshi and Davies. The behavioural relationships underpinning all of these estimates were, however, based on data collected in 1980.

Introduction

Child-bearing and child-rearing affect women's incomes throughout their lives: women may take time away from paid work in order to look after their children, especially when they are small. Alternatively, or in addition, they may combine child-rearing with part-time employment, often at lower hourly wages than for full-time jobs. Loss of labour-market experience may affect wages later on, so that a woman who has taken time out to have children may never catch up with the wage rate earned by a woman with a continuous employment history. To the extent that pensions are deferred earnings, the income costs of child-rearing will stretch into old age. This paper offers estimates of the size of these effects for Britain's mothers of the 1990s. In particular, we tackle the following questions:

How does the impact of children on gross earnings vary by the woman's education level?

What is the effect of the tax/benefit system on the earnings costs of motherhood?

On conventional assumptions about income pooling, who bears the net costs? How far does motherhood jeopardize financial security in old age?

Our method involves the simulation of life-time incomes for 'typical' women and their partners. Similar calculations based on data collected around 1980 (Joshi 1990, Joshi et al. 1996) provide the basis for comparison with a period of lower female labour-market participation. Following a brief methodological introduction we present some of the simulated life-time participation profiles and life-time gross earnings. We then discuss the earnings foregone due to motherhood as well as the distribution of the net earnings costs of motherhood, taking into account transfers of earnings within the couple and to the state as well as into old age provision. Finally, using these findings we examine the pension consequences of children and the implications for pension and retirement policy.

Method and Assumptions

Our simulation model generates the life-time earnings of illustrative people from estimates of econometric equations and then applies tax, benefit and pension rules to these simulated gross earnings. Briefly, the elements of the model are as follows:

*Participation and earnings.*The simulations are based on participation and earnings functions for 1994 estimated on data from the British Household Panel Survey (Taylor et al. 1996). Wage equations are based on standard human capital specifications, with separate equations fitted for women's earnings in part-time and full-time employment.[3] Educational attainment and (actual) full-time employment experience are the principal explanatory variables; experience in part-time work was not significant in explaining female wages. We also included time out of employment as a variable determining the wage rate: for women this mainly reflects time spent in domestic work (principally child care)[4].

Our estimates imply that a year out of employment produces a decline in the full-time wage of about 1.35 per cent, but only about 0.03 per cent on the part-time wage. The female participation model allows for three outcomes: 'not employed', 'employed part-time' and 'employed full-time'. The specification allows for considerable detail in the way that the number of children and their ages (especially the age of the youngest child) affect participation and the effect of earning power on participation is captured by the predicted wage in full-time work. We did not impose the hypothesis of income-pooling within the family, but allowed a woman's own non-labour income and her partner's net income to affect her participation differently. A woman is assumed to participate when her probability of doing so is greater than 0.5. Hours of paid work depend on sex, occupational grade and whether part-time or full-time[5]. We assume that men in the simulations are continuously employed.

The individuals. Our simulation model allows for three occupational levels, determined by educational attainment. Our central figure ('Mrs Mid') has some formal qualifications gained at secondary school and works in a clerical occupation: think of her as a secretary. We compare her with a graduate (perhaps a teacher), and another woman, who left school with no qualifications and gets only low-skill jobs, such as a shop assistant. We also created a husband for each woman. The husband has

---

[3] Only one wage equation is estimated for men, as very few of them are in part-time employment. A full account of the equations used is available from the authors upon request.

[4] We also included this variable in the male wage equation, but it has a different interpretation for men, primarily reflecting unemployment. The median length of time out of employment for men in the wage regression sample is about four months, whereas for women it is about four years.

[5] Our investigations of hours of work had shown these to be not very sensitive to economic variables within the full- and part-time sector.

some effect on the woman's gross earnings, since in general, a woman is less likely to participate the better paid is her husband (but only to a small extent in these estimates). More importantly, however, the husband's earnings will affect the possibility of income redistribution within the partnership as well as the amount of widow's pension the woman can expect.

In order to focus on the consequences of reproductive work, we assume that the only interruptions to earnings histories are due to child-care responsibilities, so we ignore unemployment for both sexes. Our illustrative people are not statistical averages; rather they are 'typical' individuals in a hypothetical world where male careers are uninterrupted.

There are four types of fertility history in the simulations: married women with no, one, two and four children. A woman marries at age 20, 22 or 24, depending (positively) on her occupational level. If she has two children these are born three years after marriage, and three years after that. If she has four children, the first arrives two years after the marriage, and the others at two-year intervals. In each case the men are assumed to be two years older than all the simulated women[6]. The marriages studied here are life-long partnerships: even today, 60 percent of marriages in Britain are not expected to end in divorce. Men are assumed to live up to age 78, and women up to age 81.

We concentrate on couples in the same skill band as each other, though we also include the case of a man in a high-level occupation married to a woman in a low-level occupation, a combination which is becoming less common as women's skill levels increase in successive cohorts. Emphasis on the equally educationally matched couples is fairly representative of the pattern of partnership in Britain in the 1990s. About half (48.5%) of partnered women have the same educational level as their partners, while in 30 per cent of cases the men are more highly qualified than the women.[7] Among women under age 35, the picture is even more symmetric: about the same percentage of partners are equally qualified, but 25 per cent of these women are more qualified than their

---

[6] Although these marriage and fertility assumptions are rather out-of-date from the perspective of the late 1990s, we use them to facilitate comparisons with our earlier work.
[7] Sample of 2,126 partnered women under 60, not in full-time education, with information available on educational level of both partners. These results refer to a three-fold classification of educational qualifications similar to that employed in the simulation exercise: post school, formal qualifications gained at secondary school, no formal academic qualifications.

husbands. Cases where the woman has higher qualifications than her husband are no longer rare.

Timing. The simulations reported here take place in a time warp. There is no inflation or economic growth: earnings levels are calibrated to January 1998 levels and tax and benefit rates are fixed at their April 1998 levels. Rules for tax, benefit and pension schemes are fixed to be those faced by someone entering the labour force in 1998.

Taxes and benefits. Our model calculates the major components of the (direct) tax, benefit and pension systems as they apply to those who do not suffer from long-term illness or disability. On the tax side, we calculate income tax and National Insurance Contributions (an earnings-related tax). *Child benefit* is non-taxable and is paid to mothers of dependent children (here children under age 16). For a woman with two children it was worth £20.75 per week in April 1998 (the first child attracts a higher rate than others). We also calculate entitlement to two of the main means-tested benefits. *Family Credit* is payable to low-income families with children where at least one partner is in paid work. *Income Support* is the safety-net benefit, payable in certain circumstances to those who do not have significant amounts of paid employment (given the assumptions used here, it is potentially payable only to retired people with very low pensions).

Pensions. We assume a common pension age of 65 for men and women, as will young people today obtain. The *National Insurance Basic Pension* is paid at this age and entitlement depends on a person's contribution history (or their spouse's). There is also a state earnings-related pension scheme (SERPS). It is possible to "contract-out" of this scheme into a private pension scheme (contributions to which are deductible from taxable income). Most of those who are contracted out are in Final Salary pension schemes. We have assigned each person a default pension type. For men the default is a Final Salary Scheme, except that low-skilled men are assumed to be in SERPS. By default, women are assumed to be in SERPS except for the highly-skilled, who are assumed to be in a Final Salary scheme. Those who are contracted out of SERPS pay a lower rate of National Insurance contributions. The benefits paid by SERPS are related to life-time earnings. In the following we count the contributions payable in respect of SERPS as pension contributions rather than as taxes and SERPS benefits as pensions rather than state benefits.

It is arguable that our pension assumptions look backwards rather than forwards. Defined-contribution (money purchase) schemes are beginning to make inroads in private pension provisions at the expense of final salary schemes. The government is reviewing its upper-tier pension arrangements and SERPS is likely to be phased out in favour of 'stakeholder pensions'. Under both SERPS and Final Salary schemes, a survivor's benefit of one-half of the primary beneficiary's annual pension is paid to a surviving spouse (here always a widow).

Life-time Participation Profiles and Earnings

The upper line in each graph of Figure 1 plots the probability of any employment and the lower line shows the fitted probability of being employed full-time. Hence the area between these lines represents the probability of part-time employment.[8] The predictions of the model have been evaluated for four types of women, each of whom may have several family-building scenarios. The four types occupy the four rows of Figure 1: one has no qualifications and neither does her husband (Low-Low); the second couple, Mr and Mrs Mid, have middling levels of education; the third (High-High) are both graduates and the last is an unqualified woman married to a graduate man. The two columns compare scenarios where the woman remains childless and where she has two children. Other fertility scenarios have been computed, and more could be. For present purposes the timing of each woman's fertility is set at the same ages as in our earlier exercise. In practice, the 1990s have seen later child-bearing, particularly among the better educated.

Looking down the column of plots for the childless women, all four have a fairly high level of labour-force attachment over all of their working ages, particularly the middle and the highly educated. Part-time employment is minor for the mid-educated and negligible for the graduate. The two low-skilled women at the top and bottom of the graph have a slightly lower, though still high, propensity to be employed, though this drops off in late middle age, and is somewhat more likely (or less unlikely) to be part-time. The similarity in participation of the low-skilled women with low-skilled and highly-skilled husbands illustrates the relative unimportance of income effects on women's participation. These profiles are, however, sensitive to the wife's earning power.

---

[8] Estimation is based on evidence from 1994 for ages 20 to 59. We extend the simulated lifetimes to age 65, in view of the coming raising of women's pension age from 60 to 65.

This sensitivity to earning power becomes more apparent if we look at the trajectories of employment probabilities when the woman has children. The child-rearing years are associated with a deep trough in the chances of being employed for the two less well-qualified types of women. These display the bi-modal pattern which became common in many countries in the post-war period (OECD 1988). They also involve a relatively high probability of part-time employment, among those employed, once the woman becomes a mother, and even after the children are no longer dependent. The probability of being employed (especially full-time) recovers rather faster for Mrs Mid than for the low-skilled women. At the other end of the skill scale, the graduate woman's probability of employment is hardly perturbed by bearing two children (at the somewhat later ages of 27 and 30), though her chances of working part-time are raised around the time the children are very small.

The low-skilled mother of two (with a low-skilled husband) has 9 years when her probability of employment falls below 50 per cent. This increases to 15 years if she has four children, but it occurs in only four years if she has just one child. For Mrs Mid, the probability of participation drops below 50 per cent for five years if she has two children. If she has four children, there are 12 years when she is more likely to be unemployed than employed. Having two children rather than one increases the number of years when employment is most likely to be part-time from 10 to 20. The graduate mother is always more likely than not to be employed, even if she has four children. Here the difference comes in the number of years when part-time is more likely than full-time: none if she has one child, two if she has two children (as in Figure 1), and seven if she has four children.

It can be seen from Figure 1 that both the unskilled profiles run close to 50 per cent more often than do the others. The latter therefore generate more secure indicators of one representative or 'typical' individual than in cases where almost as many participate as do not, or vice-versa.

Figure 2 shows the earnings trajectories of the four types of woman with zero, one, two and four children. Long breaks in earnings are apparent for most of the low-skilled mothers, and mothers of four in all types have more part-time employment than do those with fewer or no children. The mid-level mother of two (and one) loses earnings relative to her childless counterpart mainly through spells of part-time work; once she returns to full-time work her earnings catch up. The same goes for the graduate mothers, though the period of reduced earnings is shorter. Note that the vertical axes of Figure 2 are on different scales. The mid-level earnings profile is only modestly above and steeper than that of the low-skilled (flattening out at £14,000 p.a. for a continuously full-time employed worker, compared with £11,000 for the least skilled). The graduate earnings profile, by contrast, soars to more than double (£29,000).

Table 1: Forgone Earnings Cost of Motherhood in Britain: Illustrative Couples
(by number of children and skill level)

	New Estimates			Old Estimates		
Number of children	1	2	4	1	2	4
Low-skill couple						
Forgone earnings						
£ '000s, 1998 earnings levels	176	255	402	161	202	234
As % of potential earnings after 1st birth	40	58	89	49	62	70
Composition of loss: percentage due to:				0	0	0
lost years	20	31	30	28	35	40
lost hours	48	37	35	49	41	35
lower pay, due to:						
lost experience	29	31	35	23	23	26
part-time penalty	2	1	0	1	0	0
total, lower pay	*31*	*32*	*35*	*23*	*23*	*26*
Mid-skill couple						
Forgone earnings						
£ '000s, 1998 earnings levels	140	257	460	196	258	318
As % of potential earnings after 1st birth	26	47	82	42	55	67
Composition of loss: percentage due to:						
lost years	16	22	26	28	34	36
lost hours	47	41	36	40	34	31
lower pay, due to:				0	0	0
lost experience	31	31	37	27	27	29
part-time penalty	5	7	1	5	5	4
total, lower pay	*37*	*37*	*38*	*32*	*32*	*33*
High-skill couple						
Forgone earnings						
£ '000s, 1998 earnings levels	0	39	169	72	170	320
As % of potential earnings after 1st birth	0	4	16	8	18	34
Composition of loss: percentage due to:						
lost years	n/a	0	0	51	43	47

	New Estimates			Old Estimates		
Number of children	1	2	4	1	2	4
lost hours	n/a	53	63	0	10	4
lower pay, due to:						
lost experience	n/a	29	32	49	46	49
part-time penalty	n/a	18	5	0	2	0
total, lower pay	*n/a*	*47*	*37*	*49*	*47*	*49*
Mixed skill couple (Man high; Woman low)						
Forgone earnings						
£ '000s, 1998 earnings levels	190	334	401	164	192	220
As % of potential earnings after 1st birth	44	78	92	57	67	74
Composition of loss: percentage due to:				0	0	0
lost years	23	26	32	44	50	53
lost hours	46	40	34	33	26	22
lower pay, due to:						
lost experience	29	33	35	23	24	25
part-time penalty	2	1	0	0	0	0
total, lower pay	*31*	*34*	*35*	*23*	*23*	*25*

Mothers' Foregone Earnings

The areas in the graphs in Figure 2 between the line for the childless woman's earnings and those of the various mothers represent the earnings foregone as a result of responsibility for children, because the women being compared are otherwise identical. The closer the lines, as in the High-High couple, the less the earnings foregone; the bigger the gap, as for the low-skilled woman, the bigger the sum foregone. The (undiscounted) totals represented by these areas are shown in Table 1. Also shown in Table 1 are the results which we have previously obtained, reflecting participation patterns of 1980. In the central case, Mrs Mid foregoes £107,000 or one-fifth of her earnings after the age of child-bearing.

This is remarkably close to our earlier estimate for a similar woman with 1980-style participation, whose foregone earnings for two children amount to over one quarter of a million pounds (£258,000 at 1998 prices). A similar sum is foregone in the present estimates by the woman with two children in a low-skilled couple. This is a higher cash sum than the earlier estimate but, as for the mid-skilled woman, represents a lower fraction of potential earnings after the first birth. The low- and mid-skilled women who have four children are estimated to forego both higher cash sums and higher percentages of their potential earnings in these estimates than in our earlier ones. For the graduates, the estimates of foregone earnings have come down, to nil in the case of the woman with only one child. Her life-time earnings have been unperturbed by the simulation, which does not preclude her having taken paid maternity leave. The graduate mother of two foregoes £39,000, amounting to just 4 per cent of her potential earnings after motherhood, as compared to 18 per cent in the 1980 simulations.

The loss of earnings arises from lost years of work, fewer hours when in employment and lower pay. Lower pay is due both to lost experience and the lower rates of pay associated with part-time work. These components are also shown in Table 1. For the graduates, there is no lost years component, as continuous employment is maintained. The major source of lost income is the reduced hours involved in working part-time rather than full-time. Rates of pay are also reduced, rather more due to loss of full-time experience than to the operation of the part-time penalty. For the mid-skilled mother of two, 22 per cent of the loss is due to lost years, 41 per cent due to fewer hours, 31 per cent due to less experience and 7 per cent due to lower pay in part-time work. Breaks in earnings account for a larger fraction of the total earnings loss among the low-skilled women than the other groups, but the lower hours of part-time work account for the biggest fractions of the lost earnings among all groups.

Distribution of the Earnings Costs

Although the earnings which the mother foregoes would have been earned by her efforts, the cost of not earning them do not fall entirely during the years she is in the labour force, and they do not fall entirely on her. Insofar as earnings-related pensions are reduced by motherhood, the mother may be affected by having less pension in retirement (as well as by having had to make fewer pension contributions from her earnings). She will also be involved in transfer payments each year, to or from the state through taxes and benefits and, if her partner pools his income, within the family. If the net marginal rate of tax minus benefit is around 33 per cent, and all net family income is shared, then every pound not earned by a mother will have an incidence which is roughly split in three equal portions between herself, her partner and the state. This was another threefold division which we found in the 1980 estimates, at leastin the central case (see Table 2). The state's share increased with the number of children (reflecting child benefit), and also with the income level of the family. The higher tax rates paid by better-off families mean that the government loses more from the woman not earning, while child benefit stands in a higher ratio to their lower lost earnings.

The 1990s estimates shown in Table 2 also show this near three-way split for the low-and mid-skilled couples with one or two children. Couples with four children get less help (proportionally) from the state (except for the high-skilled). In the case of graduates in the 1990s

Table 2: Who Pays Revenue Cost of Children?
(by number of children and skill level)
Percentage of Labour Market Income

Number of children	New Estimates			Old Estimates		
	1	2	4	1	2	4
Low-skill couple						
Woman	36	36	37	36	35	32
Man	36	36	38	36	35	34
State	28	28	25	28	30	33
Mid-skill couple						
Woman	34	34	34	34	34	32
Man	34	34	35	34	34	32
State	33	33	31	31	33	36
High-skill couple						
Woman	n/a	10	27	29	31	32
Man	n/a	10	25	28	28	28
State	n/a	79	48	43	40	40
Mixed skill couple (Man high; Woman low)						
Woman	36	37	38	36	36	35
Man	38	38	40	38	38	37
State	26	25	22	25	26	28

Note: labour market income is defined as wages plus earnings-linked pensions minus contributions to those pensions

simulation, the contribution of the state has gone up to 79 per cent for two children and 48 per cent for four. These results reflect the fact that the total lost earnings have become quite small for the higher paid, and so child benefit is a large fraction of earnings foregone. Furthermore, the better paid women pay higher average tax rates on a year's earnings, so that any time they do take out of the labour force is more expensive for the state than is the time of low-skilled women.

The contributions of the man and the woman are nearly identical, but not quite. We assume there is complete pooling of revenue while both are alive, but also that the woman outlives the man and therefore spends some years experiencing a reduced pension without being able to split the deficit with her deceased spouse. If the marginal pound earned by a woman is not put into a family pool (and our participation estimates suggest it is not), the split between man and woman will take different values, which we have not so far explored. If there has been a shift away from intra-family transfers, spreading the net earnings costs of motherhood between men and women, as economist Nancy Folbre (1994) suggests, then women's apparent gains might have to be reconsidered. It is also worth noting that greater continuity of employment involves other costs, notably those of providing maternity leave and child care. We have not attempted to quantify either of these, but some of them may fall on the employer. It is believed that the private costs of purchased child care fall disproportionately on mothers.

The Pension Costs of Child-bearing

Given the current debate about whether there will be enough contributors in the next generation to finance pay-as-you-go schemes in the next century it is instructive to look more closely at the deferred part of these hypothetical earnings streams: that part of the pensions which are related to the woman's own contributions. How far pension is indeed reduced by motherhood depends not only on how far earnings are reduced, but also on how far pension schemes are designed to give credit for time spent on unpaid care-giving duties.

In Britain, the basic state pension provides Home Responsibility Credits for up to 20 years of non-contribution (i.e., years when earnings fall below the 'Lower Earnings Limit' - £64 per week in 1998) and so most of the mothers in our examples do not sustain any loss of pension from this source. The state second tier of earnings-related pensions (SERPS) has an element in its design to reduce the pay penalties of motherhood. This works by excluding years covered by Home Responsibility Credits from the denominator in calculating the average on which SERPS is based. It therefore does not offer any protection for years of low earnings in part-time work, if the amount earned is above the Lower Earnings Limit. This protection is therefore not as great as would have been afforded by the original plan to base SERPS on the Best Twenty Years of earnings only. In our examples, both the mid- and low-skilled woman are assumed to be covered by SERPS, and the graduate woman to be in a final salary type of occupational pension. This is assumed to count years in part-time employment as pensionable, although until a recent European Court judgement, they seldom were (except possibly for some groups such as teachers).

Table 3 shows that Mrs Mid can expect 35 per cent less pension than can her childless counterpart, reflecting the earnings differential (47% of all earnings after age 25 or 18% of life-time earnings). The credits implicit in SERPS do not give much benefit: Mrs Mid earns above the lower earnings limit in 13 of her 20 years of part-time work, and thus gets little help from this source. The low-skilled mother of two is potentially a greater beneficiary of the SERPS credits, but earns so little that they are not worth much to her.

Table 3: Pension Costs of Children
(by number of children and skill level)
As % of childless wife's earnings-linked pension

Number of children	New Estimates			Old Estimates		
	1	2	4	1	2	4
Low-skill couple	30	43	89	48	63	74
Mid-skill couple	14	35	78	30	43	61
High-skill couple	0	0	8	2	13	26
Mixed skill couple (Man high; Woman low)	29	77	88	58	66	73

Note: all these are on assumption that low and mid skilled women are in SERPS, high skilled in Final Salary pension scheme

Paradoxically, the women given a pension scheme with no concessions to motherhood, the graduates, lose even less pension than earnings, if indeed they lose any of either. A graduate mother of four is estimated to forego 8 per cent of her pension and 15 percent of her life-time earnings. The graduate mother of two makes a curious case: she reduces her life-time earnings by 3 per cent but suffers no cut in pension relative to the woman with no (or one) child. This is because we assume (in line with current tax law) that a maximum of 40 years' service is reckonable for a final salary pension.[9] Thus, the two years part-time which she is simulated to take when her children are young do not affect the reckonable years for her pension, and her final salary has itself recovered from the consequences of this discontinuity by age 64.

These estimates show a strong tendency for the least-skilled women to have relatively small pension entitlements if they have children. The possibility that they have access to better pensions held by husbands and extended to them as widow's pensions provides only partial mitigation. Patterns of marriage within similar skill and income levels imply that many of these women will have husbands with quite low pensions. In the event of divorce, these low earners would be most financially vulnerable, in the long-term as well as the short.

Currently, the British government is considering legislation to reform pension arrangements upon divorce. One way to ensure that mothers do not sacrifice pension rights is to make sure they do not sacrifice their own earnings. Those who do earn less in order to take care of their children, however, incur long-term costs, potentially leading to a position of vulnerability or dependency which still needs to be acknowledged.

Conclusions

Highly-qualified women in Britain now appear to be even more attached to full-time employment than they were more than a decade ago. Most women of middle level earning power are now more likely than not to be in the labour force (though on a part-time basis) during most of the years when they have young children. Those of lesser earning power do not appear to have increased their attachment to the labour force during the child-rearing years by much. Our method of simulating the life-time earnings of illustrative individuals suggests that the earnings costs of motherhood have gone down for women of high earning power and have gone down or stayed about the same for women of middle earning power depending on whether they have one or two children. For the least qualified, the earning costs have tended to go up. This adds new evidence to a number of other sources that the experience of employment after child-bearing is becoming polarized. Motherhood is no longer the social leveller it was, since the earnings of two-earner families will tend to grow relative to families with only one breadwinner, who is increasingly likely to be less well-paid himself.

---

[9] The pension cannot exceed two-thirds of the final salary. With the industry standard pension fraction of 1/60, this implies a cap of 40 years in reckonable service.

The conclusions must be qualified by the provisional nature of the results. Our 'first-past-the-post' method of assigning employment status to our illustrative trajectories may be misleading. It ignores cases on the other side of the distribution, which, as Figure 2 shows, may be almost as numerous.

One reason for the growth in participation is probably the spread of maternity leave. Employers have also been introducing various other 'family friendly' practices, particularly for the benefit of more highly-skilled workers (Forth et al. 1997). Another development running parallel to the increase in career continuity is the increased use of child care. Those who can afford these largely private child-care arrangements seem to be making them (though informal child-care arrangements are still very common, particularly for mothers with part-time jobs). The indirect costs of motherhood are being transformed, for more women, into direct expenditure on child care. The model of purchased child care as an intervening factor in the relationship between women's employment and fertility (Ermisch 1989) is becoming increasingly relevant in Britain.

The sources of earnings loss have changed since the 1980 model and become more differentiated by type of woman. In particular, the graduates are now simulated to have no earnings break. The increase in the pay penalty to working part-time has not played a major role in the simulated earnings gaps, as less part-time employment is simulated. On the distribution of the costs of earnings reductions, we find that the threefold division between herself, her husband and the state which we found for the mid-skilled woman of 1980 has remained. As the high-skilled women earn more, and forego less through child-rearing, the fraction lost in taxes (and thus 'borne by the exchequer') increases. There are long-term consequences of motherhood in reduced pension rights, but the effects are also strongly socially differentiated. High earners forego even less pension than earnings (at least on our pensions assumptions), while low earners sacrifice a large portion of their lesser pension rights, and face old age on very different terms than do the higher paid.

The simulations suggest that Britain is becoming one of those countries where the number of children, rather than the age of the youngest child, is the most important predictor of labour-force participation. Although this does not apply across the board, it may have implications for projections of the labour force as well as of fertility.

We have not introduced divorce into these simulations. Even if they were able to increase their labour-market hours after a divorce, the least-skilled women would be in a much weaker position to provide for their children, themselves and their old age than would higher earners. The labour-market advantages of these women, in turn, might be less than those of their former husbands. The model could be elaborated to explore the financial consequences of divorce.

The legacy of motherhood for earning power, earnings and pensions in later life seems less severe in the 1990s than it was in the 1980s, for some groups of women. For those with poor skills, earnings in later life and pensions remain penalised not only by gender but by motherhood.

References

Davies, H. and H.E. Joshi. 1994. "The earnings forgone by Europe's mothers", in O. Ekert ed., *Standards of Living and Families: Observations and Analysis*. Paris: INED John Libbey Eurotext.

_____.1995. "Social and Family Security in the Redress of Unequal Opportunities", in J. Humphries and J. Rubery, eds., *The Economics of Equal Opportunity*, Manchester: Equal Opportunities Commission.

Dex, S., H.E. Joshi and S. Macran .1996. "A Widening Gulf among Britain's Mothers", *Oxford Review of Economic Policy* 12 (1): 65-75.

Ermisch, J.F. 1989. "Purchased Childcare, Optimal Family Size and Mother's Employment. Theory and Econometric Analysis", *Journal of Population Economics* 2, pp. 79-102.

Folbre, N. 1994. *Who Pays for the Kids? Gender and the Structures of Constraint*. London: Routledge.

Forth, J., Lissenburgh S. Callender C. and Millward N. 1997. *Family Friendly Working Arrangements in Britain, 1996*. Department for Education and Empoyment Research Report RR16. Sudbury: Great Britain, Department for Education and Employment.

Joshi, H.E. 1990. "The Opportunity Cost of Child-bearing: An Approach to Estimation using British Data", *Population Studies* 44, pp. 41-60.

Joshi, H.E., H. B. Davies and H. Land. 1996. *The Tale of Mrs Typical*. London: Family Policy Studies Centre.

OECD. 1988. *Employment Outlook, 1988*. Paris: OECD.

Taylor, M.F., ed. with J. Brice, N. Buck and E. Prentice.1996. *British Household Panel Survey User Manual*. Colchester: University of Essex.

Figure 1: Simulated participation probabilities by age, for childless women and mothers of two at various skill levels

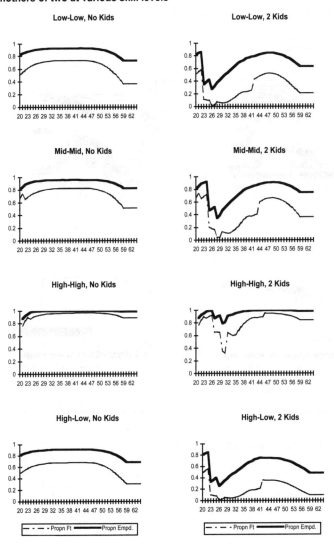

Figure 2: Earnings profiles for childless women and mothers at various skill levels

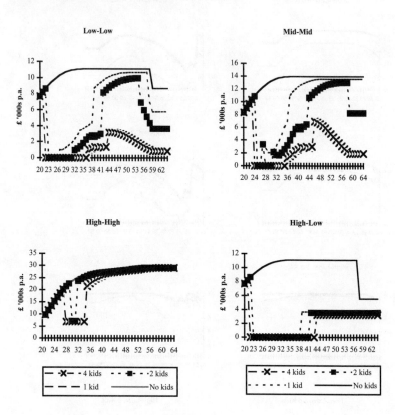

Note: vertical scale differs between panels.

The Effect of Disadvantages in Early Career on Later Career Outcomes: A Canadian Case Study

Isik Urla Zeytinoglu and Caroline L. Weber[1]

Abstract

The economic realities of older women's lives are daunting: more older women than older men live in poverty; older women have more illnesses than men and spend a larger proportion of their lives in poor health. The fact that women live longer than men only makes these facts more appalling. Worldwide, female children are viewed as secondary to male children, and so receive lower investments in human capital, resulting in few employment choices and little opportunity for occupational or professional advancement. The accumulated effects mean that women are often dependent and vulnerable in their old age.

This paper examines the career profiles of men and women by age category in a professional occupation in order to ascertain the effect of the disadvantages faced by women in earlier stages of their careers on employment outcomes in later career stages. Our data set comprises information from 1,055 résumés from industrial relations (IR) and human resource management (HR) professionals from an urban area in Ontario,

[1] This project was completed with financial support from Queen's University-ARC; the Social Science and Humanities Research Council; and the School of Business at Queen's. We would like to thank Katayoun Bagher, F. Cameron Fraser, Liann Joanette, Genevieve Lamorie and Stacey Anderson for expert research assistance and unflagging spirits. Names are listed in no particular order, equal contributions.

Canada, over the period 1962-1991, including not only human capital variables (level of educational attainment, labour-market experience) but also such data as numbers of employers and 'employment gaps'.

We analyze the data for both genders according to age levels. Results show that that although women have the same level of formal education required for the entry to the occupation, they do not demonstrate the same levels of occupational achievement. Women start out and continue their careers at lower occupational levels than men, even in one narrowly defined occupation, in a sample where there are few meaningful differences between men and women with respect to human capital investment.

Introduction

The economic realities of older women's lives are daunting (O'Connor et al. 1999): more older women than older men live in poverty; older women have more illnesses than men and spend a larger proportion of their lives in poor health. The fact that women live longer than men only makes these facts more appalling. Worldwide, female children are viewed as secondary to male children, and women receive inadequate investments in human capital, resulting in low pay, few employment choices and little opportunity for occupational or professional advancement (Date-Bah 1997; Lim 1996; United Nations 1995a; Zeytinoglu 1998). The accumulated effects of these realities are that women are often dependent and vulnerable in their old age.

Though these differences between older women and men are similar in industrialized societies (Collins et al. 1997; Denton and Walters 1996; Zeytinoglu et al. 1999), they have less impact, since health status and standard of living are generally higher in the industrialized economies. The problems that older women face are also downplayed in a context where there is evidence that the 'gender gap' in earnings is narrowing (Almey 1995; Blau and Kahn 1994; ILO 1998; Loury 1997). For managerial and professional occupations, there is evidence of this trend in particular in the United States of America (Gerhart and Milkovich 1989; Jacobs 1992), though the pattern is not consistent in all industrialized countries (for a study from Sweden and the banking industry there, see Acker 1991). Studies show that women in managerial and most professional occupations in North America are well represented in middle- and entry-level positions, but few reach the senior level (Almey 1995; Davidson and Burke 1994;

Denton and Zeytinoglu 1993; Konrad and Cannings 1994; Vinnicombe and Colwill 1995).

As recognized in the International Year of Older Persons-1999, ageing is a continuum where the lifestyle and opportunities in earlier stages of the life cycle affect the well-being in later stages of life. Health Canada funded projects under the *Seniors Independence Program* and *New Horizons: Partners in Aging* programme identified several factors as most important for older persons' health and well-being: income and economic independence, social support networks, education, social environments, physical environments, gender, and inclusive cultural environment (Centre for Health Promotion 1997). Inadequate income and economic dependence on family members and/or government support erodes social status, self-esteem and active involvement of older persons in the society. Low income increases social isolation, lack of information and poor health, and creates education and skill disadvantages. Gender is also a significant factor in poor health in old age, with women - though living longer - living in poorer health than men. Women make up approximately half of the world's population, yet until recently, research on health and its determinants have focused on male populations only, inferring the findings to females. Examination of the determinants of health, including income level, for women in all stages of the life cycle is fairly recent (Zeytinoglu et al. 1997; 1999).

This paper focuses on income and gender factors as they relate to age and the ageing process. It examines the career profiles of men and women in a professional occupation in order to ascertain the effect of the disadvantages faced by women in earlier stages of their careers on employment outcomes in later career stages. By studying differences in career outcomes in only one occupation, we avoid problems that usually arise as a result of the confound between gender composition and occupations (see Solberg and Laughlin 1995). The field of industrial relations/human resources (IR/HR) has been fairly well integrated with respect to gender, as shown in Table 1. We make use of a data set comprised of information extracted from 1,055 résumés from industrial relations (IR) and human resource management (HR) professionals in an urban area in Ontario, Canada over the period 1962-1991. In addition to the usual human capital variables (level of educational attainment, labour-market experience), the résumés are a rich source of more detailed data, such as numbers of employers and unaccounted periods of time, or 'employment gaps'.

As background to our study, we consider the question of why one should focus on work as a determining factor in women's well-being at later stages of their life. We examine the literature on global and national trends in women's employment and its effect on their well-being in older age, as well as that dealing with the gender gap in wage and career outcomes.

Table 1: National and Provincial Gender Composition of IR/HR Occupations

Region and Year	1136 - HR and IR Managers [a]	1174 - HR, IR and Related Officers[b]
Ontario		
1986 - Total	10, 980	14,855
1986 – % Female	39 %	56 %
1991 - Total	16,035	19,675
1991 – % Female	46 %	54 %
Canada		
1986 - Total	31,105	36,850
1986 – % Female	36 %	54 %
1991 - Total	44,010	43,880
1991 – % Female	42 %	57 %

Source Statistics Canada Census Data, based on 1980 Standard Occupational Classification, Cat. No. 93-327, Table 1. The four-digit numbers in the column headings are the Standard Occupational Classification (SOC) codes.

    a. Includes employee relations, industrial relations, and labour relations specialists

    b. Includes analysts, counselors, interviewers, and representatives.

Work as a factor in older women's well-being. Women have been studied as mothers, wives or reproductive agents, but their work as it relates to their quality of life has received attention only recently (Zeytinoglu et al. 1997; 1999). Meaningful employment, economic stability, healthy work environments and supportive social environments are recognized as being critical to the well-being of individuals (Hamilton and Bhatti 1996), and in particular older persons (Denton and Walters 1996).

Work has traditionally been defined as paid work that is largely performed outside the home. This definition rendered much of the traditional work of women invisible and ensured that women's work was neither acknowledged nor recorded by historians and social scientists (Armstrong et al. 1997; Bradbury 1992; Chambers and Montigny 1998,

Messing et al. 1995; Prentice et al. 1996; Teiger 1995). More recently, scholars, notably feminists, have sought to expand the definition of work to include unpaid work, whether performed at home or outside the home volunteering (Zeytinoglu et al. 1997). This is critical, since women will remain an at-risk population until their work, paid and unpaid, is valued and recognized (Collins et.al 1997; Zeytinoglu et al. 1999).

The work of women is not only poorly remunerated, but lacks status and respect within many societies. Women's work is undervalued and underpaid when the knowledge and mental effort involved in the tasks are not considered in the descriptions of their jobs (Teghtsoonian 1997; Teiger 1995). The emotional labour involved in home-care work, neither recognized nor paid, is an example of the invisible work of women (Aronson and Neysmith 1997, Denton et al. 1996; 1999). To overcome this invisibility, researchers argue that women's work must be documented, and its impact on women's lives and well-being, at all stages, must be studied. The diversity among women in terms of age, racial or ethnic background, income level, ability and sexual orientation must be accounted for in all studies (Hajdukowski et al. 1999; Messing 1997; Simkin 1993; Zeytinoglu et al. 1997; 1999).

Global and national trends in women's employment. Globally, women's economic participation rates have climbed from 54 per cent in 1950 to 67 per cent in 1996, and are projected to increase to almost 70 per cent by the year 2010 (ILO 1998). Higher educational attainment and falling fertility rates, particularly in industrialized countries, have played an important role in women's increasing labour-force participation. In the majority of the countries, wage differentials between men and women are gradually narrowing. Still, however, women earn between 50 and 80 per cent of the average male wages (ILO 1998).

In the restructuring of global and national labour markets, the importance of economic sectors is shifting, multinational corporations are becoming important global players, major technological developments are taking place, and the structure of the labour force is changing (ILO 1994). Data on labour-force statistics in Canada show that, particularly since 1982, the incidence of part-time, on-call, shift, contract and temporary work arrangements has grown sharply (Statistics Canada 1998). Self-employment without employees has also increased substantially since the early 1990s (Leckie 1998). The 'typical' full-time, permanent, nine-to-five, Monday-to-Friday job with one employer is now the work arrangement for only a third of the Canadian workforce (Lipsett and Reesor 1998).

These developments are similarly played in industrialized and industrializing economies throughout the world. Globally and nationally, women are the predominant group affected by such changes (Romero 1993; Lim 1996; United Nations 1995a; Zeytinoglu and Crook 1997; Zeytinoglu and Muteshi 1999), with the workforce becoming polarized into those reaping the benefits of the new work environments and those who are left behind. Moreover, women around the world, work in sex-segregated sectors and jobs (Lim 1996). Occupational segregation by sex occurs on both vertical and horizontal lines. As presented in a United Nations report,

> Gender segregation exists from top to bottom of the occupational hierarchy and within individual job categories. Vertical segregation inherently involves many more factors -- skill, responsibility, pay, status and power. Female-dominated jobs often offer less advantaged employment than jobs in which men predominate. Disadvantages include the pay, pensions, sickness benefits, type of work, hours of employment, types of employment contracts and opportunities for promotion (United Nations 1995a: 126).

In occupationally and sectorally segregated labour markets, female workers, worldwide, are more likely than men to work in part-time and temporary jobs (ILO 1998). As the global world of work moves towards labour-market flexibility, the proliferation of atypical or non-standard employment contracts erodes employment security for all workers but particularly for female workers (Lim 1996; Zeytinoglu 1999a). As the United Nations' *Platform for Action of the Fourth World Conference on Women* notes, for female workers the labour-market flexibility and non-standard employment trends have meant "low wages, little or no labour standards protection, poor working conditions, particularly with regard to women's occupational health and safety, low skill levels, and a lack of job security, in both the formal and informal sectors" (United Nations 1995b: Para 158).

Gender wage gap and career outcomes. There is a vast amount of research, begun in the 1970s, documenting and examining the persistent existence of a wage gap between male and female earnings (e.g., Corcoran and Duncan 1979, Malkiel and Malkiel 1973; Mincer and Polachek 1974; Oaxaca 1973). However, most of this work resorts to using proxies or truncated data (Robb 1978) of some sort, either for education or unemployment or work experience, since detailed information about these human capital variables is lacking from most data sets. The problem is so pervasive that some authors (e.g., Nakamura and Nakamura 1985) have suggested methods for modelling information such as employment history.

Focusing on North America, studies show that women in managerial and most professional occupations are well represented in middle- and entry-level positions, but that few reach the senior level (Almey 1995; Davidson and Burke 1994; Denton and Zeytinoglu 1993; Konrad and Cannings 1994; Vinnicombe and Colwill 1995). In the IR/HR profession, as shown in Table 1, there are more women in lower-level positions, although women are reasonably well represented at the managerial levels.

The few studies in Canada using macro-level data (Gunderson 1979; Holmes 1976; Robb 1978; Shapiro and Stelcner 1987) and those based on single-employer data sets (Cannings 1988; Cannings and Montmarquette 1991; Nadeau, Walsh and Wetton 1993) provide further evidence about the gender wage gap. Statistics show that in the mid-1990s the gender wage gap persists, although it seems to be narrowing (Statistics Canada 1998; Almey 1995). The smaller gap is attributed to women's increased investment in human capital (education and training), as well as men's reduced labour-force participation due to job loss in the traditional manufacturing sectors, and the movement of men into the lower paying service sector.

As the literature suggests, many factors can affect wage levels. Investment in education and training (Becker 1964) is well-documented; individuals with more work experience and higher levels of education are expected to earn more. However, even controlling for human capital and other factors such as industry of employment, the gender wage gap persists (Weber and Zeytinoglu forthcoming). It is therefore reasonable, and at this point in our society's history certainly bothersome, to expect that women will earn less than men.

Studying the gender wage gap and arguing about why it exists or when and if it will ever disappear has obfuscated the real impact of the gender wage gap on the lives of women over their lifetimes. By studying wages in cross-section, at one point in time and trying only to understand the reasons for the gap, we have overlooked the longer-term implications of what we know about gender differences in wages. If, as we observe, women earn less than men throughout their careers, for whatever reasons, then they also accrue fewer long-term benefits, leaving them much worse off than men at the end of their labour-market careers. If, as we observe, the structure of society is changing so that more women find themselves as single heads of households *and/or, at the same time*, find themselves confronted with less stability in the employment contracts available to them, which are also arguably inferior, then the existence of a gender wage gap is more than unjust. The longer-term implications of the gender wage gap in this shifting environment are also destabilizing and crippling for society, since the process that generates the wage gap at the same time creates in the long-term a class of people who do not and will not in the future have the resources to care for their families and ultimately, for themselves.

We seek to examine the longer-term implications of the gender wage gap by comparing the differences in wages between men and women in different age groups in one occupational category in an urban area in Ontario, Canada. By controlling for occupation and geographic location, there are fewer variables to explain or to represent alternative arguments.

Methodology and Results

Our data set comprises information extracted from 1,055 résumés of IR/HR professionals in an urban area over the period 1962-1991. The résumés were submitted to a non-profit placement agency, the Technical Service Council, which closed in 1994. In addition to the usual human capital variables (level of educational attainment, labour market experience), they provide such data as numbers of employers, contract and part-time employment, and otherwise unaccounted periods of time, or 'employment gaps'.

The variables and how they were operationalized are presented in Table 2. For most of the variables, information is available for 954 of the original 1,055 résumés.[2] The unfortunate exception is the salary for the last job held, for which there are only 631 observations. All salaries were converted to 1986 Canadian dollars for purposes of comparison.

---

[2] We lose about 100 individuals who submitted résumés as new graduates, with no labour market experience; and calculating full-time experience by job is impossible in instances when only organizational tenure is available on the résumé. Although we could use an organization-based calculation, rather than a job-based one, we are so limited by salary observations that this different calculation is unnecessary.

Table 2: Variables and Descriptions

Variable Name	Description	N
Year	Last year of contact with the TSC	954
High School, College, University, Graduate School (Degrees)	Indicator variables; '1' if degree obtained, '0' otherwise	954
Number of courses	Count of number of courses outside of formal degree programme listed/described on résumé	954
Certificates	Number of professional certificates indicated on résumé	954
Professional Memberships	Number of professional memberships indicated on résumé	954
Gender	'1' if female, based on name or other information referring to gender of applicant	943
Full-time experience (in months)	Sum experience for all jobs that were not contract or part-time	783
Number of employers	Sum number of times résumé indicates applicant changed employers	954
Number of jobs	Sum number of jobs indicated on résumé	961
Contract experience (in months)	Sum experience for all jobs that were contract	950
Number of contract jobs	Sum number of contract jobs indicated on résumé	954
Part-time experience (in months)	Sum experience for all jobs that were part-time	951
Number of part-time jobs	Sum number of part-time jobs indicated on résumé	954
Total employment gap (in months)	Sum of periods of unaccounted time in the career history (sometimes described on the résumé as 'unemployed', other times simply not referred to)	954
Number of gaps	Sum number of employment gaps indicated on résumé	954

Variable Name	Description	N
Industries (Resources, Construction, Manufacturing, Transp/Comm/Util, Wholesale, Retail, Financial, Services, Health, Education & Other, Public Admin.	Indicator variables created for 11 industry categories	954
Occupation Level	Categorical variable ranging from 1 (lowest) to 5 (highest), based on the four-digit Canadian National Occupational Classification codes, where '1' if NOC > 1300 (clerks/clerical and technical levels); '2' if NOC < 1300 and NOC > 1200 (supervisors and officers); '3' if NOC < 1200 and NOC > 1110 (professionals, specialists and consultants); '4' is NOC < 1000 and NOC > 100 (managers); and '5' if NOC < 20 (executives).	945
Last Salary (1986 $)	Last annual salary recorded in application file (sometimes this information is on the résumé, and other times it is recorded on the TSC interviewer's form), multiplied by the CPI in order to get constant 1986 dollars.	631

As Table 3 shows, this is a well-educated population: almost all of the people in the sample report having high school diplomas and 67 per cent hold a university degree. Almost one-third are female. The average of about 12 and one-half years of full-time labour-market experience reflects employment with an average of four different organizations, comprised of five or six different jobs. While there is low reporting of contract and part-time employment experience, on average, each of these individuals reveals one period of unaccounted labour-market time, or an employment 'gap'. Most people report a last job that was in either the manufacturing (32%) or service industry (16%). Average annual gross salary, in 1986 Canadian dollars, is $40,694. Individuals tend to take on average about four courses in addition to their formal degree training.

Table 3: Descriptive Statistics
(Full sample)

Variable Name	Mean or % (std. dev.)	Minimum	Maximum
Year	1986	1962	1991
High School	99 %	0	1
College (2 year education only)	23 %	0	1
University	67 %	0	1
Graduate School	19 %	0	1
Number of Courses	4.37 (4.61)	0	36
Certificates	0.44 (0.85)	0	7
Professional Memberships	0.9 (1.51)	0	25
Gender (1=female)	31 %	0	1
Full-time experience (months)	150.72 (99.80)	1	491
Number of employers	3.96 (2.12)	1	13
Number of jobs	5.61 (2.76)	0	18
Contract experience (months)	2.21 (8.97)	0	98
Number of contract jobs	0.19 (0.57)	0	5
Part-time experience (months)	2.90 (14.95)	0	226
Number of part-time jobs	0.13 (0.50)	0	5
Total employment gap (in months)	14.55 (29.65)	0	288
Number of gaps	0.92 (1.01)	0	5
Industry:			
Resources	3 %	0	1
Construction	1 %	0	1
Manufacturing	32 %	0	1
Transportation/Communication/ Utilities	6 %	0	1
Wholesale	1 %	0	1
Retail	3 %	0	1
Financial	7 %	0	1
Services	16 %	0	1

Variable Name	Mean or % (std. dev.)	Minimum	Maximum
Health	3 %	0	1
Education and other services	6 %	0	1
Public Administration	7 %	0	1
Occupation Level	2.99 (1.25)	1	5
Last Salary (1986 $)	40,694 (16,794)	9,247	24,1361
LN(Last Salary)	10.55 (0.36)	9.13	12.39

Significant differences of means for these variables by gender are presented in Table 4. The difference in the 'Year' variable indicates that the distribution of men and women applying to the placement agency is a little different over time; women apparently applied more recently than men. Males report graduate degrees more often than females, and more professional association memberships, while women report more professional certificates.

Table 4: Difference of Means Tests (T-tests) by Gender Significant Differences Only

Variable Name	Males	Females	T value
Year	1985.5	1986.6	- 3.89***
Graduate School	21 %	15 %	2.38*
Professional Memberships	1.02	0.66	4.14***
Certificates	0.4	0.54	- 2.33*
Full-time experience (in months)	169.98	108.04	9.34***
Number of employers	4.17	3.5	4.71***
Number of part-time jobs	0.1	0.2	- 2.41*
Number of employment gaps	0.87	1.03	- 2.27*
Occupation Level	3.2	2.52	7.96***
Last Salary	$43,518	$33,683	6.85***

* p < .05; ** p < .01; *** p < .001

Women generally are exhibiting less, and perhaps inferior, labour-market experience as compared with the men in this sample, as demonstrated by the differences in full-time and part-time work experience, and in employment 'gaps'[3] Women are in lower occupational levels than men. As expected, women exhibit average annual earnings that are much less than men's: women are earning an average of 77 per cent of what men are earning in this sample.

For the purposes of examining the effects of this gender age gap on older women, we split the sample by gender and then group men and women into age categories of: younger than age 30, age 30-44, and older than age 44, categories favoured by other researchers. For this sample and these age categories, by gender and for the whole sample, cell sizes are reported in Table 5. Admittedly, these categories do not work well for the present data set, since there are few women in the 'older than age 44' category in this sample. Since we are arguing that the work experiences in earlier stages of life will effect the overall well-being of individuals in their elder years, we do not consider the small size of women in 'older than age 44' category as a major deficiency in our analysis, though readers should be cautioned.

Table 5: Cell Sizes for Sample by Age Category, by Gender

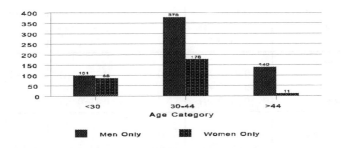

---

[3] Furthermore, women in this sample on average report about two more months of part time experience than men (2.28 for men, versus 4.39 for women) and about four more months of unexplained absence from the labour market (13.37 for men, versus 17.51 for women), although neither of these differences reach acceptable levels of significance (t = -1.85, p = .065 for part time experience, and t=-1.93, p=.054 for employment gaps).

The results of ANOVAs and t-tests are presented in Table 6. Looking within gender and across age categories, and starting with the women (columns 1 and 2), analysis using ANOVA produces predictable results for women's employment experiences: older women have more experience, higher salaries, have changed employers more often, had more employment gaps, have lower levels of formal education (university and graduate degrees) and report higher levels of occupational attainment. The same analysis of men in the sample produces the same general results (columns 3 and 4).

Table 6: Results of ANOVAs and T-Tests by Age Category, Within Gender (ANOVAs) and Between Gender (T-Tests)

Variable	Mean for Women (std.dev.)	F	Mean for Men (std. dev.)	F	T
	(1)	(2)	(3)	(4)	(5)
University degree				4.63^{**}	
< 30	85 %		76 %		-1.5
30 - 44	59 %	10.84^{***}	69 %		2.3^{*}
> 44	45 %		59 %		0.8
Graduate degree					
< 30	21 %	1.91	19 %	2.81	-0.3
30 - 44	12 %		24 %		3.5^{***}
> 44	1 %		14 %		0.5
Professional Memberships					
< 30	0.45 (0.75)	4.10^{*}	0.64 (1.15)	4.19^{*}	1.4
30 - 44	0.77 (1.04)		1.06 (1.81)		2.0^{*}
> 44	0.36 (0.67)		1.28 (1.68)		3.7^{***}
Certificates					
< 30	0.48 (0.95)	0.37	0.33 (0.83)	0.47	-1.2
30 - 44	0.58 (0.93)		0.41 (0.78)		-2.2^{*}
> 44	0.55 (0.69)		0.41 (0.91)		-0.5
Full time experience:					
< 30	33.42 (25.6)	168.68^{**} *	43.12 (36.4)	422.79^{**} *	2.1^{*}
30 - 44	142.39 (57.1)		163.36 (65.4)		3.4^{***}
> 44	253.8 (99.6)		308.88 (74.6)		2.1^{*}
Number of Employers:					
< 30	2.29 (1.25)	31.95^{***}	2.82 (1.77)	32.99^{***}	2.4^{*}
30 - 44	4.06 (1.91)		4.10 (1.98)		0.2

Variable	Mean for Women (std.dev.)	F	Mean for Men (std. dev.)	F	T
	(1)	(2)	(3)	(4)	(5)
> 44	3.45 (1.81)		4.99 (2.35)		2.1[*]
Number of part-time jobs < 30 30 - 44 > 44	0.20 (0.47) 0.21 (0.63) 0.18 (0.60)	0.02	0.16 (0.46) 0.07 (0.39) 0.15 (0.65)	2.09	-0.6 -2.6[*] -0.2
Total Employment Gap: < 30 30 - 44 > 44	6.24 (10.9) 20.78 (31.4) 71.91 (68.3)	27.67[***]	6.97 (9.65) 13.72 (27.68) 18.81 (41.70)	4.70[**]	0.5 -2.6[**] -2.5[*]
Number of Contracts: < 30 30 - 44 > 44	0.28 (0.54) 0.25 (0.71) 0.00 (0.00)	0.95	0.31 (0.73) 0.16 (0.54) 0.11 (0.40)	3.91[*]	0.3 -1.5 3.4[***]
Occupation Level: < 30 30 - 44 > 44	1.95 (1.04) 2.77 (1.20) 2.55 (1.44)	15.17[***]	2.38 (1.10) 3.30 (1.12) 3.46 (1.30)	30.33[***]	2.8[**] 5.0[***] 2.2[*]
Last Salary: < 30 30 - 44 > 44	$25,816 (6,417) $37,035(22,243) $35,616 (3,601)	6.90[***]	$29,948(7,198) $44,390(13,963) $49,053(14,913)	43.59[***]	3.3[***] 3.3[***] 2.0[*]

*** p < .001; ** p < .01; * p < .05

Women in the category greater than 44 years old demonstrate about 7.5 times the full-time experience as women in the youngest category, and men in the oldest age category also demonstrate about 7 times the full-time experience of the men in the youngest age category. Older women have worked for about one and a half times as many employers as younger women, and this ratio is not very different for men. The relative rise in occupational level from youngest to oldest for men is about the same as it is for women. The real differences occur in unaccounted periods of labour-market inactivity, or employment gaps, and in salaries. The total period of gaps reported by older women is 11.5

times that reported for the youngest women, whereas the oldest men report employment gaps that are only about 3 times the amount reported by the youngest men. The oldest women earn about 1.4 times what the youngest women earn, in real terms, while the oldest men earn about 1.6 times what the youngest men earn. That would not be so bad, except that the women earn less than the men do, from top to bottom, so the ratio of 1.4 for the women represents fewer real dollars (just under $10,000 in 1986 Canadian dollars) than those represented by the ratio for the men (1.6 represents a mean difference of about $19,000 in 1986 Canadian dollars).

It is worthwhile to compare the employment patterns for the women to the employment patterns for the men across age groups. (Results of t-tests comparing men and women by age category are presented in column 5 of Table 6. These are provided to show that the level of differences between men and women in each age category are, with few exceptions, statistically significant.) As Table 6 shows, women in each age category, have less full-time experience than their male counterparts, earn lower salaries, and are at lower occupational levels. Moreover, middle-aged and older-women have more employment gaps than their male counterparts. Women in general exhibit lower levels of education than men, but this is only significant for the middle-aged group, and younger people are more educated than older people for both sexes. What is interesting to note, is that even though young women are at least, if not more, educated than young men (no significant differences between men and women in this age category), young women exhibit significantly lower occupational level attainment than men, and thus earn significantly lower salaries.

Discussion and Conclusions

Looking at male and female career profiles we observed that although women have the same level of formal education required for the entry to the occupation, they do not demonstrate the same levels of occupational achievement as men. Women start out and continue their careers at lower occupational levels than men, even when examined in this one narrowly defined occupation, in a sample where there are few meaningful differences between men and women with respect to human capital investment.

The only difference in human capital investment is that after the university degree, more men than women have historically chosen to pursue graduate degrees. Women maintain their professional credentials and perhaps further their education through certificates, which have lower perceived value in the labour market, whereas men continue their careers through professional memberships and the networking opportunities afforded by these. However, the data show that the differences in human capital investment for these professionals is changing. Younger women are no different than their male counterparts in terms of education (university and graduate degrees, certificates) and professional memberships. Still among younger women the same career differences obtain: younger women still start with and earn lower salaries, and are in lower occupational levels than younger men.

The real differences between men and women in this sample are not in pre-market decisions or human capital investment, but in experiences in the labour market. Women, particularly those in their child-bearing and child-rearing years of 30 to 44, leave the paid labour market or take part-time jobs more often than do their male counterparts, presumably to care for family members. This reflects a lack of choices for women - there are few, if any, meaningful family-friendly policies in workplaces, there is no universal child-care programme in Canada, and thus families are left to fend for themselves, with women shouldering the major responsibility for child and family care. Women older than 44 are more inclined to stay outside the labour market or return to the paid workforce on a contract basis. This fact may be related to the belief that the paid labour market in their profession does not provide equal opportunities to make it worthwhile for women to stay on a continuous basis. Thus, the decision to move to the unpaid labour market of homemaking and child-rearing, or to work on a part-time or contract basis at certain periods of their career, even if temporarily, becomes a feasible, and even preferred, option.

Such decisions, however, have longer-term implications for women's economic independence and well-being in their old-age. During their working years, women might be making assumptions and decisions that have impacts on their careers and earnings outcomes. For example, our finding that men are more inclined to be members of professional associations shows that they network well, formally and informally - their names are included in their professional listings, they are informed of professional meetings and other networking activities. Women, on the other hand, are left out of this important networking opportunity, either by choice or due to circumstances beyond their control - such as high membership fees, no time for outside activities, and/or demands of family and work that render such memberships impractical or impossible.

In sum, we see disadvantages faced by women throughout their careers and evidence of discrimination against younger women, in comparison to their male counterparts in the same occupation. The disadvantage and discrimination are not due to any apparent lack of interest or investment on the part of women, but instead are a result of their initial experiences in the labour market and their need to balance paid and unpaid labour throughout their lifetimes. Thus they accrue fewer long-term earnings and benefits, leaving them much worse off than men at the end of their labour-market careers. These results illustrate the longer-term effects of intra-occupation segregation throughout the career cycle.

References

Acker, J. 1991. "Thinking About Wages: The Gendered Wage Gap in Swedish Banks", *Gender and Society* 5(3): 390-407.

Almey. M. 1995. "Labour Force Characteristics", in *Women in Canada*. Ottawa: Ministry of Industry, pp. 64-70.

Armstrong, P., A. Lippman and L. Sky. 1997. "Women's Health, Social Change and Policy Development", paper presented at the Fifth National Health Promotion Research Conference, Dalhousie University, July.

Aronson, J. and S.M. Neysmith. 1997. "You Are Not Just in There to Do the Work: Depersonalizing Policies and the Exploitation of Home Care Workers' Labour", *Gender & Society Journal.*

Becker, G.S. 1964. *Human Capital: A Theoretical and Empirical Analysis, with Special Reference to Education*. New York: Columbia University Press and the National Bureau of Economic Research.

Blau, F.D. and L.M. Kahn. 1994. "Rising Wage Inequality and the U.S. Gender Gap", *The American Economic Review* 84 (May): 23-28.

Bradbury, B., ed. 1992. *Canadian Family History*. Toronto: Copp Clark Pitman.

Cannings, K. 1988. "Managerial Promotion: The Effects of Socialization, Specialization, and Gender", *Industrial and Labor Relations Review* 42(1): 77-88.

Cannings, K. and C. Montmarquette. 1991. "Managerial Momentum: A Simultaneous Model of the Career Progress of Male and Female Managers", *Industrial and Labor Relations Review* 44(2): 212-28.

Centre for Health Promotion. 1997. *Proceedings of Experience in Action: A National Forum for Healthy Aging*, February 9-11, Ottawa.

Chambers, L. and E.A. Montigny, eds. 1998. *Family Matters: Papers in Post-Confederation Canadian Family History.* Toronto: Canadian Scholars' Press.

Collins, B.S., R.B. Hollander, D.M. Koffman, R. Reeve and S. Seidler. 1997. "Women, Work and Health: Issues and Implications for Worksite Health Promotion", *Women and Health* 25(4): 3-38.

Corcoran, M. and G.J. Duncan. 1979. "Work History, Labor Force Attachment and Earnings Differences Between Races and Sexes", *Journal of Human Resources* 14 (Winter): 3-20.

Date-Bah, E. 1997. "Introduction", in E. Date-Bah, ed., *Promoting Gender Equality at Work: Turning Vision into Reality for the Twenty-First Century.* London and New York: Zed Books, pp. 1-23.

Davidson, M.J. and R. J. Burke, eds. 1994. *Women in Management.* London: Paul Chapman Publishing.

Denton, M. and I.U. Zeytinoglu. 1993. "Perceived Participation in Decision-making in a University Setting: The Impact of Gender", *Industrial and Labor Relations Review* 46(2): 320-31.

Denton, M., I.U. Zeytinoglu, K. Barber and P. Pringle. 1996. "Healthy Work Environments in Community Based Health and Social Service Agencies", Stage I Report: Focus Group Findings. *MRCPOWH Technical Report Series* #1, McMaster University, Canada.

Denton, M., I.U. Zeytinoglu, S. Webb and J. Lian. 1999. "Promoting Health in Community Based Health and Social Service Agencies", in M. Denton, M. Hajdukowski-Ahmed, M. O'Connor, I.U. Zeytinoglu, eds., *Women's Voices in Health Promotion.* Toronto: Canadian Scholars' Press.

Denton, M. and V. Walters. 1996. "Age Differences in Canadian Women's Own Perceptions of Their Health", *MRCPOWH Working Paper Series* #6, McMaster University, Canada.

Gerhart, B.A. and G.T. Milkovich. 1989. 'Salaries, Salary Growth, and Promotions of Men and Women in a Large Private Firm', in R.T. Michael and H. Hartmann, eds., *Pay Equity: Empirical Inquiries.* Washington, DC: National Academy Press.

Gunderson, Morley. 1979. "Decomposition of the Male/Female Earnings Differential: Canada 1970", *Canadian Journal of Economics* 12(3): 479-85.

Hajdukowski-Ahmed, M., I.U. Zeytinoglu, L. Chambers and M. Pond. 1999. "Women's Worksite Action Group: A Pilot Participatory Action Research Project", in M. Denton et al., eds., *Women's Voices in Health Promotion.* Toronto: Canadian Scholars' Press.

111

Hamilton, N. and T. Bhatti. 1996. "Population Health Promotion: An Integrated Model of Population Health and Health Promotion", Ottawa, mimeo.

Holmes, R. A. 1976. "Male-Female Earnings Differentials in Canada", *Journal of Human Resources* 11, pp. 109-17.

ILO. 1994. *Note on the Proceedings.* ILO Sectoral Activities Programme, Committee on Salaried Employees and Professional Workers, Tenth Session. Geneva: ILO.

ILO. 1998. *Report of the Director-General: Activities of the ILO, 1996-97.* International Labour Conference, 86th Session. Geneva: ILO. On-line: www.ilo.org.

Jacobs, J.A. 1992. "Women's Entry into Management: Trends in Earnings, Authority, and Values among Salaried Managers", *Administrative Science Quarterly* 37(2): 282-301.

Konrad, A. and K. Cannings, 1994. "Of Mommy Tracks and Glass Ceilings: A Case Study of Men's and Women's Careers in Management", *Relations industrielles/Industrial Relations,* 49(2): 303-35.

Leckie, N. (and Ekos Research Associates Inc.). 1998. *Own-Account Self-Employment In Canada.* Human Resources Development Canada, Evaluation and Data Development, Strategic Policy. Ottawa.

Lim, L.L. 1996. *More and Better Jobs For Women: An Action Guide.* Geneva: ILO.

Lipsett, B. and M. Reesor. 1998. "Flexible Work Arrangements", in P.A. Lapointe, A.E. Smith, and D. Veilleux, eds., *The Changing Nature Of Work, Employment And Workplace Relations, Selected papers from the XXXIVth Annual CIRA Conference* : 29-44. Quebec: ACRI/CIRA.

Loury, L.D. 1997. "The Gender Earnings Gap Among College-Educated Workers", *Industrial and Labor Relations Review* 50(4): 580-93.

Malkiel, B. and J. Malkiel. 1973. "Male-Female Pay Differentials in Professional Employment", *American Economic Review* 63(4): 693-705.

Messing, K. 1997. "Women's Occupational Health: A Critical Review and Discussion of Current Issues", *Women and Health* 25 (4): 39-68.

Messing, K., B. Neis, L. Dumais, eds. 1995. "Introduction", *Issues in Women's Occupational Health: Invisible, La sante des travailleuses.* Charlottetown, PEI: Gynergy.

Mincer, J. and S.W. Polachek. 1974. "Family Investments in Human Capital: Earnings of Women", *Journal of Political Economy* 82(2, part II): S76-S108.

Nadeau, S., W.D. Walsh and C.E. Wetton. 1993. "Gender Wage Discrimination: Methodological Issues and Empirical Results for a Canadian Public Sector Employer", *Applied Economics* 25: 227-41.

Nakamura, A. and M. Nakamura. 1985. "Dynamic Models of the Labor Force Behavior of Married Women Which Can Be Estimated Using Limited Amounts of Past Information", *Journal of Econometrics* 27, pp. 273-98.

Oaxaca, R. 1973. "Male-Female Wage Differentials in Urban Labor Markets", *International Economic Review* 14(3): 693-709.

O'Connor, M., M. Denton, M. Hajdukowski-Ahmed and I.U. Zeytinoglu. 1999 (in press). "Theoretical Framework for Research on Women and Health Promotion", in M Denton et al.,eds., *Women's Voices in Health Promotion*. Toronto: Canadian Scholars' Press.

Prentice, A., P. Bourne, G. Cuthbert-Brandt, B. Light, W. Mitchinson and N. Black. 1996. *Canadian Women: A History*. Toronto: Harcourt, Brace, Jovanovich.

Robb, R.E. 1978. "Earnings Differentials Between Males and Females in Ontario, 1971", *Canadian Journal of Economics* 11(2): 350-59.

Romero, A. 1993. "Multinational Enterprises In the Service Sector: Conceptual and Policy Issues", in P. Bailey, A. Parisotto and G. Renshaw, eds., *Multinationals And Employment: The Global Economy of the 1990s* . Geneva: ILO, pp. 239-66.

Shapiro, D.M. and M. Stelcner. 1987. "The Persistence of the Male-Female Earnings Gap in Canada, 1970-1980: The Impact of Equal Pay Laws and Language Policies", *Canadian Public Policy* 13(4): 462-76.

Simkin, R. 1993. "Unique Health Care Concerns of Lesbians", *The Canadian Journal of Ob/Gyn & Women's Health Care* 5(5): 516-22.

Solberg, Eric and Teresa Laughlin. 1995. "The Gender Pay Gap, Fringe Benefits, and Occupational Crowding", *Industrial and Labor Relations Review* 48(4):692-708.

Statistics Canada. 1998. "1996 Census: Labour Force Activity, Occupation and Industry, Place of Work, Mode of Transportation to Work, Unpaid Work". *The Daily*, March 17.

Teghtsoonian, K. 1997. "Who Pays for Caring for Children? Public Policy and the Devaluation of Women's Work", in S. Boyd, ed., *Challenging the Public/Private Divide: Feminism, Law and Public Policy*. Toronto: University of Toronto Press, pp. 113-43.

Teiger, C. 1995. "Les barrieres cachees a l'integration securitaire des femmes au travail", in K. Messing, B. Neis, L. Dumais, eds., *Issues in Women's Occupational Health: Invisible, La sante des travailleuses*: 202-216. Charlottetown, PEI: Gynergy.

United Nations. 1995a. *The World's Women: 1995 Trends and Statistics*. New York: UN.

United Nations. 1995b. *Report of the Fourth World Conference on Women* (Beijing, 4-15 September), A/CONF.177/20. New York: UN.

Vinnicombe, S., and N.L. Colwill, eds. 1995. *Women in Management.* London: Prentice Hall.

Weber, C. and I.U. Zeytinoglu. forthcoming. "The Effect of Computer Skills and Training on Salaries: A Study of Male and Female Industrial Relations and Human Resource Management Professionals", in R. Chaykowski and L. Powell, eds., *Women and Work.* Kingston, ON: John Deutsch Institute.

Zeytinoglu, I.U. 1998. "Constructed Images as Employment Restrictions: Determinants of Female Labor in Turkey", in Z. Arat, ed., *'The Turkish Woman': Deconstructing Images and Ideologies.* New York: St. Martin's Press, pp. 183-97.

Zeytinoglu, I.U. 1999a (in press). "International Policy-Making: The ILO Standards on Changing Work Relationships". In I.U. Zeytinoglu (ed), *Changing Work Relationships in Industrialised Economies.* Berlin and New York: Walter De Gruyter Publishers.

_____. 1999b (in press). 'Flexible Work Arrangements: An Overview of Developments in Canada', in I.U. Zeytinoglu, ed., *Changing Work Relationships in Industrialised Economies.* Berlin and New York: Walter De Gruyter Publishers.

Zeytinoglu, I.U., M. Denton, M. Hajdukowski-Ahmed, and M. O'Connor.1997. "'The Impact of Work on Women's Health: A Review of Recent Literature and Future Research Directions", *Canadian Journal of Women's Health Care* 8(2): 18-27.

Zeytinoglu, I.U. and M. Crook. 1997. "Women Workers and Working Conditions in Retailing: A Comparative Study of the Situation in a Foreign-controlled Retail Enterprise and a Nationally Owned Retailer in Canada", *ILO Multinational Enterprises Programme,* Working Paper No. 79. Geneva: International Labour Organisation.

Zeytinoglu, I.U., M. Denton, M. Hajdukowski-Ahmed, M. O'Connor and L. Chambers. 1999 (in press). "Women's Work, Women's Voices: From Invisibility to Visibility", in M. Denton et al., eds., *Women's Voices in Health Promotion.* Toronto: Canadian Scholars' Press.

Zeytinoglu, I.U. and J. Muteshi. 1999 (in press). "Changing Work Relationships: Enacting Gender, Race/Ethnicity and Economic Class Variables", in Zeytinoglu, I.U., ed., *Changing Work Relationships in Industrialised Economies.* Berlin and New York: Walter De Gruyter Publishers.

Gender-based Barriers to Career Development in Australia

Russell Rimmer

Abstract

An issue of workplace equity is whether periods of absence from paid work for family reasons are a barrier to women's progress in their working lives. A recent survey of Australian women, reporting their lifetime spells in paid and unpaid work, found that short breaks from paid work are typical. It appears that while some women retain their places on the career ladder, others find that the first break from working involves a career slide. There is some evidence that women can preserve their prospects through taking courses in further education during their spells away from the workforce.

Introduction

Consciousness of the need to address inequity in national labour markets found expression in the United Nations Decade for Women (1976-1985), which focused on recognising women's contributions to society. Australia ratified the UN Convention on the Elimination of All Forms of Discrimination Against Women in 1983. The Sex Discrimination Act followed in 1994.[1]

Some of the markers of progress towards equity in Australia this century are:

- 1902 Non-aboriginal women gained the right to vote.

---

[1] For details of events and legislation see Australian Bureau of Statistics (1995).

- 1912 Minimum wage for women's work set at 54 per cent of men's.
- 1950 Female basic wage set at 75 per cent of the male rate.
- 1967 Aboriginal women and men vote for the first time.
- 1972 Principle of equal pay for work of equal value.
- 1986 Passage of The Affirmative Action (Equal Employment Opportunity for Women) Act.
- 1990 Ratification of the ILO Convention on Workers with Family Responsibilities.
- 1992 Justice Elizabeth Evatt became the first Australian elected to the UN Human Rights Committee.

While these legislative measures brought hope of meaningful change for Australian women and working women in particular, the rate of progress has been disappointing. The Australian labour market remains segregated into women and men's jobs. Women in Australia still do not receive equal pay, equal training or equal promotion opportunities, and they have remained concentrated in the low-paid and low-prestige sectors of the economy. In this respect, Australian experience mirrors the evidence that led the UN to conclude that "labour market conditions for women have developed in a similar way in most countries of the ECE region" (UN 1985: 66).

According to Rimmer (1991) desegregation of occupational employment in Australia would cause a decline in women's average earnings. Further, removing gender bias in the occupational structure could involve a lowering overall in the prestige of women's paid work. She states that "the best hope for improved welfare for women is … through policies to eliminate discriminatory pay practices on other than efficiency grounds, and through policies which ensure equal access to prestigious work within occupations" (*ibid.*: 215-16).

As elsewhere, Australian women are now more likely to return to paid work after family formation begins. This is evident in the rise in the female participation rate from about one-third of women 30 years ago to over one-half now. While more women are working, not all find it possible to sustain their career growth.

Part-time work, segregated jobs, pay differentials, and educational attainment are often separately studied. Rimmer and Rimmer (1997) explored the linkages to earnings of variables such as education, the characteristics of women's jobs, their care-giving roles and their skill levels. They considered that potential experience commences when women leave secondary school or finish the first post-secondary qualification. Thus experience was counted as the proportion of post-school time women actually spent in the workforce.

Generally little knowledge exists about which women are on ascending paths through working life. Equally, evidence is thin about women whose job prospects deteriorate. Responsibility for children is a likely obstacle to career development. But other reasons may be important. For example, returning to part-time work could be a career slide. Alternatively women may think, at least on returning to work, that this provides a way to preserve their attachment to their former position.

Breaks from working may explain some of women's observed inability to achieve equal progress with men in their careers (see Blau and Ferber 1986: 192-96; Dex 1987:76). Lengthy breaks might explain career destruction. Rimmer and Rimmer (1997) found typically short breaks and inferred that little decay in skill would occur. Caring for children stood out in their study as a major barrier for women trying to sustain their career prospects. Few men, compared with women, cited this as a career barrier.

Here we look beneath the aggregated data to examine career progression. Factors such as breaks from working in paid jobs, perceptions of women of their 'best' job, their education, child care, occupational mobility and the sharing of household tasks underlie the discussion. First some summary data give an impression of women's place in the Australian workforce.

Australian Women in the Workforce

In 1998 Australia's population was a little over 18 million. Reflecting the country's immigration policies, a high proportion of the population was born outside the country. The largest group is from Europe followed by the United Kingdom and Ireland and Southeast Asia. Indigenous people remain a tiny minority of the population. Half of the 187,000 aborigines are younger than 20 years old.

The total labour force is 9.4 million, including 4 million women, of whom 2.4 million are married women. Some immigrant women are a little less likely than the Australian-born to participate in paid work. Yet over a quarter of working women were born outside the country. About a quarter of a million women have never worked outside the home.

The workforce participation of Australian women at 64.4 per cent of the population is marginally above that in Japan but well below that in the United States of America. More than two-thirds of the Australian women in the labour force are in their prime years - 25 to 54 years. Part-time jobs are important to women, especially married women who account for 47 per cent of all part-time work.

Educational attainment is interesting. Most employed women do not have post-secondary qualifications, and over 1 million women did not complete the highest level of secondary school. At the other extreme, nearly half a million women have university degrees.

It was noted earlier that women are bunched into traditionally female occupations. In Australia as elsewhere the occupational mix is changing. The fastest growing jobs are in personal service, business, professional and science and medical technicians. Miscellaneous clerical work is declining.

The Survey - Women's Experience

The Australian Bureau of Statistics twice conducted customized cross-section surveys of women of workforce age.[2] Over 3,000 households participated in the survey. In the first year this yielded detailed employment histories for 1907 women aged 20 to 59. The surveyors also gathered a smaller sample of data on 842 men. Weights expanded the survey data to represent the national population.

Women recalled their lives as episodes of paid work and breaks. Absence from paid employment for at least three months constituted a 'break'. Without prompt, most women identified these periods of breaks and employment relative to major life-cycle events such as marriage and childbirth.[3] Data collected included educational attainment, occupation, career prospects, duration of periods in and out of the workforce, flexibility of working conditions, degree of responsibility at work and barriers to career development. Data limitations came from collecting information on three working spells only and on just one main job in each work spell.

Most of the respondents were Australian-born. Almost all had completed their education at the time of the survey. Eighty per cent of the women had finished full-time study before their twentieth birthdays.

---

[2] The author acknowledges the assistance of Theo Neumann of the Australian Bureau of Statistics in customizing these surveys.

[3] Martin and Roberts (1984) relied on an alternative approach of first establishing important events in respondents' lives to gather data on breaks from paid work.

Most of those not working had family care-giving roles. A surprisingly large proportion (11%) of households contained no one in the paid labour force. Not surprisingly, most household responsibility lies with women. Six out of ten Australian women undertake more than half of the household tasks (see Rimmer and Rimmer 1994).

Respondents reported how often their main job involved direction, coordination or supervision of staff. An obvious gender bias emerged. Whereas men 'give orders', women are far more likely to take them. Only a third of women reported flexible working hours to choose starting and finishing times. This implies a tension in accommodating working and home responsibilities. Eighty-four per cent of the women said that their jobs could be done on a part-time basis, while one-third of the men believed that theirs could not. Again, this suggests a barrier to equitable allocation of the home-making and care-giving roles for each of the partners.

Perceptions of career barriers are interesting. The two-thirds of women, who recognized barriers to their progress, easily ranked responsibility for their own children as the key obstacle. Next came discrimination, lack of promotion opportunities, education and marriage. Few men saw their children as a barrier. They first cited the lack of promotion opportunities, followed by educational attainment and discrimination. When asked about the quality and availability of child care, a quarter of the women had found the supply a problem while another quarter appeared to reject using child care.

More than half of the women left school after - or before - the final year of high school, while nearly 60 per cent of men had post-secondary education or training. There are patterns of women partnering with men of similar education. However, there is some tendency for women to partner 'down' rather than 'up' in educational terms. In Australia, two-year diplomas can be taken after the end of high school, usually at colleges of technical and further education. Two-thirds of the women with these diplomas partnered men with only high school or trade certificates. Trade (vocational) certificates are received after several years of on-the-job training and instruction at colleges. The tendency to partner equally on an educational basis was highest for those with university degrees. The fact that women perceive more blocks to entering occupations than men do may reflect their unequal educational qualifications. Clerical and secretarial work remains important to women. Many reported this work as having sound career prospects.

Breaks in Work Histories

An apparent difference in labour-force behaviour between women and men is in attachment to paid work. Conventional text-book analyses 'explain' unequal labour-market outcomes as consequences of interrupted careers. The expectation that women will have long spells away from paid work may discourage women and their employers from investing in women's training. Only long and frequent breaks could plausibly support arguments that a shortfall in human capital development and de-skilling create inequality.

The survey data allow a focus on breaks. Fifty per cent of the men surveyed never had a break from working compared with 20 per cent of the women. Just over 3 million Australian workers had never been away from work and about 70 per cent of them were men. Further, more than half of the women had two breaks from paid work.

Because child-bearing and child-rearing are major reasons for their absences from the labour force, women who have worked continuously are relatively young. Data show that women's first confinements typically occur by the time they reach their 30s, so that continuous work becomes less likely for women over 30 years old. About half of the women working continuously were in their 20s. These women account for only a quarter of Australia's working women aged 20 to 59 years. Among men, those never having had a break were mainly in their 30s or 40s.

Women in their 20s and 50s were slightly under-represented among continuous workers compared with corresponding male workers. For these women the text-book case about gender incidence of breaks from work is substantiated, but what of the duration of breaks? The survey data permit estimates of length of breaks from work as well as spells of work.

Work Histories of Australian women to 1993[i]

Length of spell in:

Length of break	1st period Work[ii]	Break[ii]	2nd period Work[ii]	Break[ii]	3rd period Work[iii]
1 year or less	20.2	51.8	24.0	62.4	40.5
2 or more	78.6	45.8	74.6	32.3	55.7
Don't know	1.2	2.4	1.4	5.3	3.9

i   covers women who ever had a break of at least three months from paid work
ii   percentages in the column are for women reporting a completed spell
iii   length of the third break cannot be measured with the open-ended survey data

Clearly the first break is brief. Of those women with only one break from work, 51.8 per cent had returned to work inside a year. The second period of work was two years or longer for 74.6 per cent of the women completing such a spell. The second break tends also to be fairly brief.

On the basis of these data, across-the-board skill destruction appears unlikely. Indeed it is difficult to see how either the first or second break could be associated with very extensive skill loss. This does not however rule out an initial failure to invest in women's human capital or provide the necessary reason for their subsequent career outcomes. Failure to invest seems based on an incorrect assumption of future lengthy workplace absences.

As with workforce interruptions, it is likely that women and men find that different factors accelerate or retard their career prospects. Respondents to the surveys were asked to report the main barrier, if any to their career development. The Australian Bureau of Statistics coded 21 responses to this question. The key barriers are set out below for women and men who worked continuously and also for those with one break from work. About one-third of women and men reported career barriers, but these barriers differed in some respects.

Career Barriers

Barrier	Continuous		One break	
	Women	Men	Women	Men
Marriage	2.0	3.3	5.1	0.2
Care of own children	8.0	2.7	28.2	2.3
Poor promotion chances	25.9	24.4	10.8	16.3
Education	11.0	15.8	10.4	18.3
Gender discrimination	20.0	2.1	10.0	0.3

Looking first at the continuous workers, poor promotion opportunities and gender discrimination stand out as key barriers for women. For men their lack of promotion prospects and their education are the main barriers cited.

The impact of breaks is evident in the third column, where the care of their own children is reported as the barrier for 28.2 per cent of women. Education and poor promotion prospects again stand out for men. The complete data on barriers show that men perceive a greater diversity of barriers than women do. Being unable to find work, being retrenched and the state of the economy worried a number of the men with one break but troubled fewer of the comparable women. In summary, once a workforce break occurs, it is the care of children that inhibits women, while education and poor promotion prospects matter to men.

The design of the surveys allowed the investigation of career progression for women and men. Many indicated a diverse range of barriers. Accordingly, a considerable degree of dissatisfaction probably existed about working life. Respondents were asked: *Of all the jobs you've had, is your current (main) job the one with the best career prospects?* They were not guided as to what 'best' or 'career prospects' might mean. Below is a summary of the responses to this question.

Current Job is Best?

| | Continuous workers | | At least one break | |
	Women	Men	Women	Men
Yes	71.9	71.4	49.8	52.0
No	28.0	28.6	50.2	48.0

Two things stand out in the table. First, there is almost no difference by gender in the responses. When at least one break from work occurs, then the best job goes for a sizeable number of workers. Workplace frustration was likely to be high because so many workers in Australia were not in their best jobs. To put a perspective on this, recall that about 80 per cent of women had taken breaks and about 50 per cent of men had done so.

Within the survey, respondents named the job they had when first in full-time work and also their current job. The occupation codes are an eight-part classification that provides an approximation to a skill ranking.[4] Making a comparison of an individual's first and current occupation, allows workers to be classified into those whose careers have improved, stayed still or deteriorated since they first worked. Such an exercise is reported below.

---

[4] This is the occupational classification used by the Australian Bureau of Statistics. The category 'Managers and Administrators' is omitted from the table. It is not straightforward enough to interpret the direction of a career shift into or out of that group.

Career Shifts Since First Occupation
Direction of shift
(per cent)

First Occupation	Up		Unchanged		Down	
	Female	Male	Female	Male	Female	Male
Professionals	-	-	63.5	80.0	26.4	5.0
Para-professionals	14.1	17.7	64.2	30.4	16.4	35.2
Tradespersons	3.4	12.9	29.0	39.6	56.0	36.0
Clerks	14.9	24.8	57.2	17.4	21.4	28.9
Sales, personal service	42.7	46.7	35.1	10.0	12.2	29.2
Machine operators	31.7	22.9	23.4	41.9	25.2	30.1
Labourers	47.6	61.9	48.1	29.3	-	-
All Workers	**22.6**	**31.3**	**49.7**	**35.1**	**19.6**	**19.5**

An obvious issue in the interpretation of the table is that because they were at the highest skill category initially, the professionals could not move up. Similarly, labourers could not move down. The last row in the table shows the percentage of the relevant group whose present occupation represented an upward, unchanged or downward career shift. For example, whereas 22.6 per cent of women experienced an upward shift since they began working, 31.3 per cent of men did so. A substantially larger share of women than men stayed still, but the percentages of women and men moving down were the same. The main gender differences are identifiable in the body of the table.

Women who improved their position were mostly in the groups of labourers and sales and personal service workers. The same is true for men. About a quarter of the men who began as clerks subsequently moved up. Men were far less likely to stay still. Most professional men did so, but 10 per cent of the salesmen remained at that level.

Although the overall percentages of women and men moving down are the same, the sources of change are not. For instance only 5 per cent of professional men moved down, whereas this happened for over a quarter of the professional women. Over half of the tradeswomen moved down, compared to just over a third of tradesmen. Women seemed to find it hard to hold their place in the professions and the trades. Men were less likely to move down than were women in the para-professions and personal service work.

There are interesting shifts between particular occupational groups. Below are some tables that indicate what happened to people moving from one occupational group to another. This gives a fairly crude indication of labour-market experience because of the very aggregated classification of the occupations. The first table shows the destination paths of women who moved up from the group of labourers and related workers.

Upward Destinations for Women Labourers
(per cent of women)

Moved to	New occupation	
	Clerks	36.9
	Saleswomen	31.0
	Para-professionals	9.0
Labourers and related ⟶	Plant operators, machinists	8.1
	Trades women	8.1
	Professional	6.1

Recall that nearly half (47.6%) of the women who began their working lives at the lowest skill level managed to move upwards. Clerical and sales work were important sources of their improved jobs. A similar table for men would show that about a third moved up to tradesmen's occupations while another 20 per cent became plant operators or machinists.

For both men and women the 'escape' from being in sales was significant. Below, destination tables show the occupations up to which the sales workers moved.

Upward Destinations for Sales Workers

Moved to	New occupation	
		Per cent of women
	Clerks	63.4
	Para-professional	19.0
Sales workers ⟶	Professional	10.6
	Tradesmen	7.0
		Per cent of men
	Professional	34.6
Sales workers ⟶	Tradesmen	34.3
	Clerks	23.3
	Para-professional	7.8

The women who improved their position from sales workers went largely to clerical and para-professional jobs. For men, the shifts to professional and trades occupations accounted for over two-thirds of the move up from selling. Over all occupations nearly one in five workers moved down to a lower occupation than the one they were in when they first worked full time. Of the eight major classes of occupations this occurred most in the trades group. Some idea of the workers' destinations is set out below.

Downward Destinations for Tradespersons
(per cent)

Moved to	New occupation	Female	Male
	Saleswomen	36.0	12.0
	Clerks	35.7	8.4
Tradespersons ⟶	Plant operators, machinists	17.3	30.7
	Labourers and related	10.9	48.0

The same four major occupational groups are important destinations for the tradespersons - whether women or men. But the women who move down from the trades do not move as far down the skill ladder as do men. It is evident that displaced trades*men* suffer a very substantial decline in the use of the skills. In 1994, 365,000 men in Australia who were formerly tradesmen then worked in lower skilled jobs.

Earlier it was seen that professional work is generally a stable occupational base for men. But of all Australian professional workers who had moved down by 1994, eight in ten were women. Indeed, over 20 per cent of all of the women who had suffered a career slide began their working lives in the professions. Undoubtedly these women had some post-secondary training or qualifications. If their destination jobs did not use these skills, wastage of educational investment seems indicated.

Downward Destinations for Professional Workers
(per cent of women)

Moved to	New occupation	
	Clerks	65.4
	Sales	25.0
	Plant/machinists	6.9
Professional ⟶	Labourers	2.6
	Para-professional	37.0
	Clerks	29.0
	Tradesmen	21.3
	Sales	12.6

Superficially at least, these women move further down the skill ladder than do the men leaving the professions. Clerical and sales work may be providing workplace flexibility for women that the professions do not. Data (not presented here) show that women who leave para-professional jobs go mostly to clerical occupations.

The care of children was said by over a quarter of the women with a break from working to be a barrier to their career prospects. Here we focus on all of the respondents who raised the issue of childcare as a career barrier. First, almost 300,000 women mentioned the care of their own children as barriers. Only 32,000 men gave this response. The small number of men means that very cautious remarks can be offered about their career experience. Nonetheless, it appears that about half of these men began their working lives in the relatively skilled occupations. In their current jobs they mainly worked in the lower skilled occupations. There is evidence of significant de-skilling among this small group of men. Indeed, no men retained jobs in the professions or in para-professional occupations.

The patterns of career shift for the women with the care-of-children barrier were different. Among women, 47.2 per cent were clerks in their first full-time work. At the survey date only 31.4 per cent remained clerks. In addition, more of the women in the care-barrier category became para-professional workers, and, less positively, shifted into labouring and related occupations.

Occupation Changes for Women with the Care Barrier

	First occupation	Current occupation
	(per cent)	
Professional	12.4	15.6
Para Professional	4.9	11.3
Tradespersons	9.8	6.7
Clerks	47.2	31.4
Sales, personal service	15.7	16.8
Machine operators	6.1	1.6
Labourers	3.9	16.5

Career Shifts - Winners and Losers

Survey information was gathered about current work as well as the job in the first employment spell. Thus it is possible to consider the flavour of job satisfaction for some women at opposite ends of the skill ranking. This is conveyed here through examples of teachers and cleaners. Teaching accounts for about 4.5 per cent (170,000) of women's employment in Australia. The first table is about women who were teachers on the survey date. It shows the occupations that these teachers had when they first worked full time.

Occupational Histories of Teachers

Occupation in first work spell	Per cent of teachers
Professional *	71.3
Para-professional	2.4
Tradespersons	1.9
Clerks	14.5
Sales workers	7.0
Labourers	1.9

* Teachers belong to this group.

Teachers appear to sustain their occupational attachment and regard it as their best job. And underlying data show that nearly the entire professional group regarded this as their best work. A similar investigation for nurses showed an even more pronounced attachment to that occupation.

Cleaning is at the bottom of the skill classification. It provides employment for just over 3 per cent (120,000) of Australian women. Quite unlike women in 'good' jobs a minority began their working lives as cleaners.

Occupational Histories of Cleaners

Occupation in first work spell	Per cent of cleaners
Para- professional	2.5
Clerks	21.3
Sales workers	29.9
Plant operators	12.2
Labourers*	30.6

* Cleaners belong to this group

It is possible that the ones who began as cleaners regard it as their 'best' job. On the face of it about two-thirds of the cleaners had become de-skilled when compared with their first jobs. Unreported figures show that previous jobs for cleaners included sales assistants, typists and receptionists and clerks. Cleaning is not generally a young woman's occupation. Some of the cleaners had post-secondary school qualifications and thus it is probable that some of them work well below their skill potential.

The teachers and nurses appeared able to maintain fairly stable career development. But for many other women, the return to paid work after at least one break may be to a secondary labour market such as cleaning. Rimmer and Rimmer (1997: 214) found it intriguing that being further educated after working life commences is a positive force for earnings. Whether this premium comes from education during working or on breaks is not known.

Concluding Remarks - Indications for Extensions

The customized surveys of Australian women show some quite marked differences in economic outcomes. The evidence suggests it is unlikely that the decay of skills occurs as a consequence of interruptions in their paid working lives. This is because the breaks are typically brief and are closely related to family responsibilities.

Whether women retain their career progression seems to depend on the nature of the work. Recall that the outcomes were distinctly different for the teachers and the cleaners. The role of education after working life commences has clear policy relevance in considering how best to protect women from career slides.

This paper has drawn on a small part of the data from the surveys. Earlier work suggested some puzzles connecting household responsibilities and career shifts. From looking at the data on shares of household tasks it seems that continuous workers have a more equitable share than others do. Those on a break pick up the major share of work at home. Once they return to work after the first break they do not shed that disproportionate share. This occurs whether they return to full-time or part-time jobs (Rimmer and Rimmer 1997). Further research could be directed towards unravelling the causality between career deterioration, home responsibilities and the downwards career slide involved in much part-time work.

References

Australian Bureau of Statistics. 1995. *Women in Australia*. Canberra: ABS 4113.0.

Blau, F. and M. Ferber. 1986. *The Economics of Women, Men and Work*. Englewood Cliffs, NJ: Prentice Hall.

Dex, S. *Women's Occupational Mobility: A Lifetime Perspective*. Basingstoke: Macmillan.

Karmel, T. 1993. *Education Levels in the Workforce*. Canberra: Australian National University.

Light, A. and M. Ureta. 1995. "Early-career Work Experience and Gender Wage Differentials", *Journal of Labour Economics* 13(1): 121-54.

Martin, J. and C. Roberts. 1984. *Women and Employment: A Lifetime Perspective*. London: HMSO.

Rimmer, S. 1991. "Occupational Segregation, Earnings Differentials and Status among Australian Workers", *The Economic Record* 67, pp. 205-16.

Rimmer, R.J. and S.M. Rimmer. 1994. *More Brilliant Careers*. Canberra, Australian Government Publishing Service.

_____. 1997. "Employment Breaks, Pay, and Career Development among Australian Women", *Gender Work and Organisation* 4 (4): 202-17.

United Nations. 1985. *The Economic Role of Women in the ECE Region: Developments 1975/85*. New York: UN.

SECTION II

CARE AND CARE-GIVING I
FAMILY AND COMMUNITY

Caring Women, Cared-for Women: The Discourse of Care-giving in Italy

Isabella Paoletti

Abstract

Caring for older disabled relatives appears to be a gender-specific issue (Arber and Ginn 1991; Dalley 1993; Facchini and Scortegagna 1994). In fact, not only are a great number of cared-for elderly women (Dooghe and Appleton 1995), but also the majority of care-givers are women (Arber and Ginn, 1991; Rose and Bruce 1995; Walker 1983). Care-giving can be the source of intense stress, and of physical and psychological problems for care-givers. This paper argues that caring is not just something that women do; it is something strictly related to femininity, that is, to women's social, moral and personal identities.

This study is part of a larger research project (Paoletti 1999; 1998c;1998d), 'The role of women in the family care of disabled elderly', conducted by INRCA, Ancona, Italy. The data consist of audio-recorded interviews on the living conditions of care-givers. Through a detailed discourse analysis within an ethno-methodological framework, instances of identity production in relation to caring practices are highlighted.

Conversationally, males are generally not made responsible for care-giving tasks, except in cases where females are absent or sick, that is, for

---

[1] I would like to thank the Women's Committee of the SPI-CGIL and FNP-CISL in Ferrara for their active participation in this project.

'serious motives'. Care-giving tasks can be seen as gender-specific practices, that is, women's duty, responsibility and ineluctable destiny. Because care-giving can cause serious physical and psychological problems in the care-givers, it is important to provide services that sustain and support their work. However, understanding the way in which care-giving is produced conversationally is essential in order to promote a more shared model of caring.

Introduction: Ageing and Gender

At the beginning of this century, longevity was the privilege of few. Now it is a reality for a large portion of the population in developed countries: "around 150 million of their people, 13% of the total, are aged 65 and over – and more than 35 million are 80 years old or older" (UNDP 1998: 22). At a slower pace, the ageing population is increasing or is expected to increase in developing countries also (ECE and UNFPA 1992:11).

Table 1: Percentage of the World Population Aged 65 and Over

	1950	1970	1990	2025
Pre-initiation Countries	3.5	3.0	2.8	3.9
Late-initiation Countries	3.9	3.9	4.9	9.8
Early-initiation Countries	7.6	9.6	12.1	19.0

The latest UNFPA report states: "as a result of reduced fertility and mortality, there will be a gradual demographic shift in all countries over the next few decades towards an older population. The number of people over 65 will grow by about 9 million this year, 14.5 million in 2010 and 21 million in 2050" (1998: 1). In Italy, in the last 30 years, the actual number of people over 65 years of age has practically doubled; in 1961 there were 4,827,415; in the most recent census, in 1991, the number had risen to 8,700,185 (ISTAT 1997). These changes in the composition of the population pose new and challenging problems, not only at a financial level, but also at a personal and social level. Since the end of the 19th century, average life expectancy has almost doubled; at present, in developed countries, we can hope for a second lifetime compared to the previous century.

Elderliness is often associated with decrepitude, poor health and loss of mental and physical capabilities, and the healthy and active elderly are considered the exceptions; now these images are no longer socially affordable. We need cultural changes that acknowledge the hope and the reality of healthy and socially productive later years for the majority of the population. We must invent a new life for ourselves after 60 years of age and make a space in society for a portion of the population, the elderly, that was not there before. There is a need to rethink all structures of society with this new section of population in mind. If, on the one hand, everything possible should be done in order to include older people as active and important members of society, on the other hand, we have to recognize older people's frailty and their need of care when this occurs.

This study deals with one of the most serious problems posed by the increasing older world population: the need to care for the disabled elderly. It is important to underline, though, that the vast majority of people over age 60 are self-sufficient; even in the eldest cohort, age 80 and over, there are many elderly who are able to cope independently or with minimal help (Dooghe and Appleton 1995; ISTAT 1997; Savage 1996; Walker 1983). Stolnitz, referring to the population over 75 years of age in Europe and North America, states: "over half of the non-institutionalized elderly population in a substantial number of countries report no handicaps, three fourths have such minor limitations that they can continue to live independently" (1994: 6). It is also true, though, that, among disabled people, the vast majority are old.

The issue of ageing is integrally linked to gender, as there is an impressively higher percentage of women aged 65 and over in all European countries, as well as Russia, the United States of America, Canada and Japan (see Table 2). Moreover, the difference between the percentages of elderly men and elderly women increases as age advances (Council of Europe 1997; EUROSTAT 1995; 1996; Dooghe and Appleton 1995), a fact that is largely ignored in the gerontological literature (Ginn and Arber 1991; Harold 1992).

Relating to Stolnitz's (1994) listing of special risk groups among the aged, women are noticeably the most numerous in the various groups described in the UN report, including: the very old (EUROSTAT 1996), the widowed, the elderly who live alone (Dooghe and Appletton 1995; Harold 1992; Mengani and Lamura 1995; Moen et al. 1992), the infirm and disabled elderly (Arber and Ginn 1991; ISTAT 1997) and the elderly with low pensions (Coopmans et al. 1988; Houdart-Blazy 1997). But this fact is not mentioned in the report. For example, in Italy (ISTAT 1997), 48.5 per cent of women age 65 and over are widows, versus 13.4 per cent of men; 12.1 per cent of men age 65 and over live alone versus 36.1 per cent of women. The number of disabled women age 65 and over is double that of men; practically two out of three of those cared-for are women.

Table 2 Percentage of People over 65 in 1994

	M	F
B	6.3	9.4
DK	6.6	9.3
D	5.4	9.9
NOR	6.7	9.4
E	6.2	8.7
F	5.9	8.9
IRL	4.9	6.6
I	6.7	9.6
L	5.3	8.6
NL	5.3	7.9
A	5.4	9.6
P	5.9	8.4
FIN	5.1	8.9
S	7.4	10.1
UK	6.4	9.4
USA (1993)	5.2	7.6
CAN	4.9	6.6
JPN (1995)	5.9	8.5
RUS	5.6	14.5

Source EUROSTAT

Table 3: Gender and Disabilities, people age 65 and over, 1994 (per 1000)

	Females	Males
Population	5,274	3,716
Disabled	1,249	626
Bed Ridden	102	75
Wheel Chair	95	49
Home Confined	297	112
Functional disability	872	461
Mobility Problems	599	267
Hearing & Seeing Impaired	208	136

Disabled women are the most numerous both absolutely and relatively. Why are there proportionally many more disabled women than men? What makes women more liable to become disabled than men? Defining disability is not a straightforward process. As Williams, Lyons and Rowland (1997:95) point out, "one person's limitation may be another's disability", that is, the individual reaction to disease and impairment can vary greatly, resulting in very different degrees of dependence and consequent need of help and services. Qualitative research is needed in order to explore the meanings behind these quantitative data and to investigate the onset of impairment and disability in relation to women's different lifestyles and health history. Which aspects of a woman's life cause her to be more at risk of disability in her old age? What can be done to prevent disability among women? Attempting to answer these questions will result in finding ways to improve the life condition of a significant proportion of the population and also to decrease public expenditure in terms of health and community services.

If we look at the other side of the care-giving relationship, again we find women in greater numbers, providing the bulk of care in terms of number of tasks performed and amount of time devoted to care-giving. Family care-givers are mainly women (Clarke 1995; Facchini and Scortegagna 1994; Jenkins 1997; Matthew and Campbell 1995; Neal et al. 1997; Rose and Bruce 1995; Walker 1983) and more often than is generally thought, they are elderly women (Arber and Ginn 1991). The greater involvement of women in care-giving is difficult to pinpoint. Care-giving, as much as disability, is difficult to define and give shape to in terms of discrete and clear-cut tasks (Graham 1983). Care-giving can take such disparate forms as help in personal care, shopping, transportation, administration of medication, cleaning, emotional support and so on. As Neal et al. (1997:805) point out, "caregiving research that has compared the type and levels of task involvement by gender has been inconsistent with respect to the numbers and kinds of task included in the measures."

Gender bias was highlighted at a more subtle methodological level; that is, women may include tasks such as washing, preparing meals or shopping for the disabled person, for example, in general housework activities in answering a questionnaire, therefore their contribution to care-giving may be underestimated (Clarke 1995; Dalley 1993). In relation to a UK survey directed to care-givers, the OPCS Informal Carers Survey, Arber and Ginn (1991b: 131) state:

The phrasing of the OPCS questions distinguishes 'caring' from 'normal' family care and domestic provisioning work; this may introduce some gender bias because the latter is performed more often by women ... Men may include shopping and cooking for their disabled wife as 'extra family responsibilities', but a woman caring for her disabled husband may not. It may be particularly difficult for a woman to separate time devoted to 'normal' domestic provisioning from the 'extra' care categorised in the survey as 'caring'.

To obtain meaningful and reliable data about gender differences in the contribution to family care-giving for disabled elderly is difficult, but the greater contribution made by women to care-giving with respect to men remains unquestioned. Therefore, support services for elderly people and their care-givers should be planned with mainly women in mind, looking at their specific problems, needs, expectations and priorities.

Community Care-giving

The common opinion that older people are neglected and abandoned and left to the care of public services is not true (Facchini and Scortegagna 1994). The bulk of caring for older disabled people is carried out through informal care provided mainly by the family and informal care-givers (Aronson 1990; Baldassarre 1995; Bulmer 1987; 1992; Caro and Leventhal-Stern 1995; Jenkins 1997); in fact, informal support networks are pushed to their limits (Walker 1995) because of the increasing number of older people, in some cases severely disabled, that have to be supported by a shrinking number of people in the younger cohort.

Contrary to expectations, research has highlighted that many of those cared for would prefer professional help (Clarke 1995). They would feel more in control and they dread impinging on their children's lives, or, very often, they express contradictory feelings about this issue (Aronson 1990). I believe that older disabled people are better cared for in the community, in the environment where they have spent their lives, in which they have ties and interests. Moreover, home care services are highly cost-effective compared to institutionalized care (Caro and Leventhal-Stern 1995). Saying this does not mean endorsing conservative discourses aimed at suppressing any form of help to older disabled people and their care-givers, nor sustaining that family caring should weigh only on women's shoulders. 'Family care', 'community care', and de-institutionalization discourses are presently strongly supported by the new right in various countries, as a means to justify drastic cuts to social services budgets (Walker 1995; Lesemann and Martin 1994). We risk seeing elderly people abandoned in the community, instead of cared for in it. But 'community care' can and should mean the provision of a number of services, such as nursing homes for temporary admissions, day centres, home help, home medical assistance, meals-on-wheels, laundry services, the provision of wheelchairs, hoists, special beds and mattresses, and so on. The fear that providing services could imply the withdrawal of the family support to their older member is baseless (Caro and Leventhal-Stern 1995). Various studies 'provide evidence that informal care may be supplemented, but it is rarely replaced, by formal care' (Williams et al. 1997: 112). Community services could flexibly combine with the existing informal support networks (Caro and Leventhal-Stern 1995; Walker 1995); a more shared model of care-giving should be implemented (EOC 1982), together with adequate legislation fostering the conciliation of working and family life. These changes would provide a better life to older disabled people and would make life bearable to care-givers.

The Effects of Care-giving on Care-givers

Care-giving is a demanding job physically and psychologically (Aronson 1990; Taccani 1994), lasting for decades in some cases. Not only can it imply the fulfilment of tiring tasks such as lifting and handling bed-ridden elderly and coping with mentally impaired elderly or with angry and resentful disabled people, but also it involves a complex array of sentiment and emotions connected to the kin relationship (Dalley 1993; Pohl et al. 1997; Taccani 1994), and feelings of moral obligation and identification issues (Finch and Croves 1983; Joshi 1995). Care-giving often involves contradictory feelings (Pohl et al. 1997); as Aronson (1990:63) points out: "qualitative studies are revealing the complexity of caregivers' experience which may simultaneously include strongly held wishes to support a relative, stress and resentment".

Many care-givers become severely stressed and sick because of their care-giving commitments (Baldassarre 1995; Jenkins 1997; May 1994; Paoletti 1999), and it is the lives of women that are mostly affected by caring for disabled older relatives. They experience proportionally greater stress (Neal et al. 1997) and greater negative consequences on their employment (Joshi 1995) compared to men. The concrete strain produced by the heavy load of daily tasks that care-giving implies is often increased by a construction of the caring relation that excludes any alternative solution. As Taccani (1994:113) effectively points out: "A high level of involvement, understood as taking total responsibility of the older person's well being, perceiving oneself as the only guarantor, a kind of defense against decay and death itself, are almost always accompanied by the onset of somatization and symptoms of anxiety and depression".[2]

The psychological literature and its feminist critique have argued that caring is attributed to women, a basic feature of their identity; the former describing the category as an essential and therefore immutable characteristic of female identity, the latter conceiving the category as a socially constructed attribution of femininity, consequently subject to change and affected by social interventions. Is the relevance of care-giving in relation to feminine identity connected to the greater stress women derive from care-giving? What makes care-giving such an overwhelming burden in some cases, so that care-givers' health and even their lives can be threatened? Why are different solutions not sought? What tangle of emotions, moral obligations, strong identification processes are affecting care-givers? The difficulty of some care-givers in seeking help has already been highlighted (Taccani 1994) and in fact, I myself have been seriously puzzled in talking with some care-givers on the verge of a nervous breakdown who firmly refused to seek or accept help (Paoletti 1999).

How could care-givers be helped? In other instances care-givers were receiving help, but they did not feel relieved by it; in fact, they saw all of their time and all of their thoughts as being occupied, pervaded by care-giving, with no life left for themselves (Paoletti 1998d; 1999). How can some care-givers manage to cope? In order to help care-givers it is important to provide community services that can relieve their heavy load, but also to understand these complex relational and identity issues that, in some cases, make material help useless.

---

[2] Un alto coinvolgimento inteso come "farsi carico" del benessere dell'anziano in modo totalizzante, il percepirsi come l'unico garante, una sorta di baluardo contro il decadimento e la morte stessa, sono quasi semprecollegabili con l'emergere di somatizzazioni e di sintomi di ansia, di depressione (English translation by the author).

From the beginning of my study, I noticed that the way in which care-givers construct their situation appears as relevant as their material condition in relation to their ability to cope, that is, there are instances in the data in which similar material situations (disability of the cared-for, amount of help received, etc.) are constructed in polarized ways and result in very different types of lives for caregivers (Paoletti 1998c; 1999). The aim of the present study is to explore some of the complex moral, relational, and identity issues related to care-giving.

Gender identification is conceived here as produced and reproduced constantly in the course of ordinary activities (Garfinkel 1967). I argue that caring is not an intrinsic property of femininity. 'The will to care' is not just the product of socialisation in childhood, but of something more cogent, pressing and pervasive. Caring is continually attributed to women in ordinary conversation. Conversationally, men are not held accountable for care-giving commitment. If they perform any care-giving task they are appreciated for it, whereas women who provide care to elderly relatives just do what is expected of them. In fact, they can be exempted from it only for serious motives. In the section that follows I will show how care-giving is conversationally constructed as a woman's duty and responsibility, arguing that this is one of the sources of the greater stress experienced by women in care-giving.

The Study

This study is part of an on-going research project conducted by the Social and Economic Research Department of INRCA, Ancona, Italy, with funding from the National Research Council, with a specific focus on the role of women in the family care of disabled elderly. The project comprises a survey study and an action research project. The data are taken from a total of 35 audio-recorded interviews, collected in the first phase of the action research project. The interviews were conducted mainly by women activists in the pensioner Trade Unions in Ferrara, Italy, and were aimed at exploring care-givers' problems and needs, in order to plan support initiatives at the local level. Reference will be made also to other sets of data collected during the pilot phase of the action research (Paoletti 1999) and the pilot of the survey study (Paoletti 1998d).

In this study, interviews are relied upon primarily as relevant interactional instances to document how kinship and gender are made relevant in the talk about caring. The study refers to the ethnomethodological use of interview data to document identity work (Baker 1984; Garfinkel 1967; Paoletti 1997; 1998a; 1998b; Watson and Weinberg 1982) and the display of moral forms (Silverman 1987; 1993). A detailed discourse analysis of transcripts from the interviews will highlight how care-giving is conversationally constructed as a morally relevant issue connected with kin relations and as a gender-specific activity.

The Moral Dimension of Care-giving

In the different sets of data analyzed here, care-giving responsibilities appear to be associated with kin relationship: being a wife, being a daughter or a son are given as good enough reasons for becoming a care-giver (Paoletti 1998d). Care-giving appears as a membership-bound activity to close kin relationship, that is, membership categories such as 'wife', 'daughter', 'son' evoke, make conversationally implicative and a matter of course, a whole series of duties and moral obligations in relation to care-giving. In the following transcript membership category and kinship are evoked in the course of the conversation to account for the motives for performing the care-giving. In this case, kinship duties appear as the only reason left for care-giving.

Marta is 60 years old and she helps her 86-year-old mother by doing all the housework for her. In the following transcript, the interviewer has just asked Marta, if she finds something positive in caring for her mother, she replies negatively and tells a story about her mother's ingratitude.

M   I had her here (   ) between the time in hospital and at home she was here for four months one day she went   in the portuense bar and called a taxi to be taken home that she said she wasn't well in my home
I   sss [(   )
M   [so (I) do it (0.3) I do it because she is my mother
I   [of course
M   [but if I had to do it for another   person (0.4) like her I wouldn't do it

M   l'ho avuta qui (   )tra l'ospedale e casa mia ha fatto 4 mesi un bel giorno è andata nel bar portuense a chiamarsi un taxi e farsi portare a casa sua che ha detto che a casa mia stava ma:: le::
I   sss [(   )
M   [allora (lo\io) faccio (0.3) faccio perché è mia mamma
I   [e certo
M   [ma se lo dovessi fare a un'altra persona (0.4) tipo lei non glielo farei

Action project, Interview 20 (see transcript notes at end).

The tale is constructed by Marta in order to highlight the affronting nature of her mother's behaviour. Reporting her mother's comment about the permanence at her place, *she said she wasn't well in my home*, and in particular detailing about how she terminated it, *one day she went in the portuense bar and called a taxi to be taken home*, Marta portrays her mother as ungrateful and unpleasant. In response, the interviewer utters a hissing sound, showing alignment with Marta. The Collins' dictionary defines a hiss as 'an exclamation of derision or disapproval', generally expressed by an audience to a speaker or performer. In Italy, among other uses, this type of exclamation expresses moral disapprobation in a conversational context; here, it could be translated into an exclamation such as 'how bad of her!'

Marta helps her mother in the housework solely out of duty. The membership category 'mother' is evoked as a sufficient reason for care-giving: *(so (I) do it (0.3) I do it because she is my mother.* This assertion is promptly sustained by the interviewer: *(of course).* Marta is eager to specify that duty is the sole reason for care-giving, given her mother's difficult character: *[but if I had to do it for another person (0.4) like her I wouldn't do it.*

Definite sets of moral duties are attached to kinship membership categories. Their value and strength are highlighted in this transcript. Although Marta finds her mother an ungrateful and bad-tempered human being, she still feels the duty to help her, because of their kin relation. This tale projects a worthy moral identity for Marta. Her care-giving efforts are especially appreciable, because of her mother's bad manners. Projecting a positive moral identity is an important part of ordinary social interaction. Members are constantly involved in projecting moral versions of themselves relevant to the occasion and the setting, in the course ordinary activities.

Care-giving appears primarily as a category-bound activity to kin membership categories, but gender membership categories are also noticeably associated with it. Gender is frequently made relevant by interlocutors in the talk about caring, as will be pointed out in the analysis of the transcripts that follow.

Gender Identification and Care-giving

In all of the data collected in the qualitative pilot project (Paoletti 1999), the interviews of the first phase of the Action Project (Paoletti 1998c) and the pilot phase of survey study (Paoletti 1998d), as well as in relevant literature (Andreini 1994; Bianchin 1994) there are many instances of talk about care-giving in which gender membership is constructed as a relevant issue. 'Being female' or 'being male' appears to imply substantial differences in relation to duties and expectation about care-giving. Close kin relationship constitutes a sufficient reason for becoming a care-giver for both women and men, but not to the same extent and not with the same implications. A woman caring for her close kin just does her duty and if she does not help her relatives, she is liable to moral reproach. If a man performs any kind of care-giving tasks he is appreciated for it and if he does not, he is not held accountable for it. For example, in the next transcript, Nina does not expect her sons to care for her.

Nina assisted her father-in-law till he died a year ago, now she is assisting her 77-year-old mother who has diabetes and who broke two ribs and had pneumonia after a car accident. Towards the end of the interview, the interviewer is inquiring how she envisages her future and her own possible need of assistance.

I: this is a terrible question	I: è una domanda tremenda
N: eh	N: eh
I: if you needed (0.2) help what would you prefer and by who (1.1) let's say	I: se tu avessi bisogno (0.2) di assistenza come la preferiresti e da chi (1.1) metti che
(2.0)	(2.0)
N: not by my sons or by by my daughters-in-law	N: non da i figli e non da da dalle nuore
(2.4)	(2.4)
I: (them [ )	I: (loro [ )
N: [(right) no isn't right that	N: [(già) no non è giusto che
I: of course	I: certo
(2.3)	(2.3)
N: if there are public helpers (1.5)	N: se ci sono le assistenze pubbliche (1.5)
I: can you imagine how many answered I this thing I never thought about it (0.9)	I: sai che tante m'hanno risposto io questa cosa qui non c'avevo mai pensato (0.9)

N: really?
I: yes (1.3) it's a thing
[that
N: [no I think
about it sometimes I have said ( )
because I say (1.2) now when I'm old
what shall I do (0.4) that I have two
males

N: davvero?
I: sì (1.3)   c'è una
cosa   [che
N   [no io ci   penso
invece a volte ho detto ( ) perché dico
(1.2) a::adesso quando sarò::: vecchia
i:o come   faccio (0.4) che c'ho
due maschi

Action Reserch Project, Interview 21 (see transcript notations at end).

The question about Nina's future need of care is constructed by the interviewer as a delicate one through the playful remark, *this is a terrible question*. One's own elderliness and disability is already an unpleasant topic to discuss (Coupland and Coupland 1997). Moreover, demanding care from one's own children is a controversial issue, as is widely documented in the literature (Aronson 1990; Paoletti 1997b; Taccani 1994); many cared for feel bad about impinging upon their children's lives, although their help can make them feel secure. Hesitation is also conveyed by the pauses and inarticulateness in the formulation of the question, *if you needed (0.2) help what would you prefer and by who (1.1) let's say (2.0)*. Notice that, since the interviewer has not finished her sentence, the end of turn pause is attributable to her too; instead, the pause would be regarded as belonging to the next speaker if she had uttered a recognizably complete sentence. Nina's reply, *not by my sons or by my daughters-in-law*, is followed by another pause, *(2.4)*, and an inaudible interviewer's comment: *(them [ )*.

The interviewer seems to hesitate in allying herself with Nina's statement. Nina perceives it as a downgrade assessment (Pomerantz 1984: 68), since she reasserts it: *[(right) no isn't right that* This time, the interviewer acknowledges alignment, *of course*. There is a new pause, *(2.3)*, and then Nina mentions the possibility of being helped by public services, *if there are public helpers*. After a short pause, *(1.5)*, the interviewer changes the subject, *can you imagine how many answered I this thing I never thought about it*. Nina expresses surprise, *really?*, and interrupts the interviewer's next turn, pointing out that the possible future need of care is a cause of worry for her. Her children's gender membership motivates such a preoccupation: *(no I think about it sometimes I have said ( ) because I say (1.2) now when I'm old what shall I do (0.4) that I have two males*. Male children are constructed as unsuitable, undesirable as care-givers; and in any case, they are not supposed to become care-givers. They are exempted from it solely on the basis of their gender membership.

Similar gender typifications are used in the following excerpt from an interview with a male care-giver, whose actions must be justified and explained. Gino is 60 years old and has been caring for his senile 78-year-old mother for the past five years. He had already retired when his mother started to have problems. In this passage the interviewer is inquiring about the help he gets from other relatives in performing care-giving tasks.

I: therefore you cannot rely (0.5) somebody else's (0.3) help or have you any help
G: I have my wife who helps me let's say to ( ) (1.4) to wash her clothes to iron (1.8)
I: I see therefore (0.5) [it is the
G: [these women's jobs
I: you mean you mean you never have (0.3) you mean um woman's job then in a way (0.5) not always because in concrete you are carrying out a woman's role I mean you don't the only thing you don't do you don't iron but for the [rest
G: [yes yes
I: your mother (0.3) eh mm (0.3) I see em (0.3) and (0.2) mm relatives nearby who can help you in your situa[tion who can

G: [I haven't got any=
I: you don't have relatives
G: and I am the only son
I: you are the only son you have nobody (0.6) I see (0.6) therefore the decision (0.4) eh to do this type of caring has fallen on you (0.3) who are a man but it's the same it has fallen on you because you (0.4) then you were the one (0.7) well you were (0.3) let'say

I: tu quindi non puoi contare (0.5) sull'aiuto (0.3) di qualchedun altro oppure hai qualche aiuto
G: ho mia moglie che mi aiuta::: diciamo a ( ) (1.4) a lavare i suoi panni a stirare (1.8)
I: ho capito quindi (0.5) [è la
G: [ste cose   da donna
I: cioè cioè non ha mai::: (0.3) cioè um da donna poi in un ce (0.5) non sempre perchè tu praticamente svolgi anche il ruolo di donna cioè tu non l'unica cosa che non fai non stiri ma per il [resto
G: [sì sì
I: tua mamma (0.3)e::l mm (0.3) ho capito e::m (0.3) e (0.2) mm di parenti qui nelle vicinanze che possano dare:: una mano alla tua situa[zione che possono
G: [no non ne ho
I: =non hai parenti
G: e sono figlio unico
I: sei figlio unico non hai nessuno (0.6) ho capito (0.6) quindi:: la decisione (0.4) e:::h per fare questo tipo di asistenza che è caduto su di te (0.3) che sei uomo però è lo stesso è caduta su di te è caduta perché tu (0.4) allora sei stato quello che (0.7) insomma era (0.3) diciamo

(0.6) the closest to retirement or you	così (0.6) più vicino alla pensione
already had retired=	oppure già in pensione =
G: =( ) to be already	G: = ( ) ad essere già in
retired	pensione
I: ah you had already retired	I: a::h eri già in pensione

Action Research Project, Interview 26 (see transcript notations at end).

Answering the question about the help received in caring for his mother, Gino names two concrete activities carried out by his wife, *I have my wife who helps me let's say to ( ) (1.4) to wash her clothes to iron*. After a short pause, while the interviewer has begun a new turn, he adds a qualification of these activities, *these women's jobs*. Washing and ironing are constructed as category-bound activities to the gender membership category 'female'. The interviewer, through the several restarts, shows the need of taking time and reflecting to utter the reformulation that follows, *you mean you mean you never have (0.3) you mean um*. The hesitation and delay convey also an upcoming disagreement, as Pomerantz (1984:5) points out: "Disagreements are often prefaced." In fact, she repeats the expression and produces two edgings, *woman's job then in a way (0.5) not always*. The category-bound character of the activities is questioned just in relation to the care-giving role performed by Gino that is qualified as specifically female, *because in concrete you are carrying out a woman's role I mean you don't the only thing you don't do you don't iron but for the (rest your mother*. Gino agrees with the statement, *(yes yes*. After various hesitations the interviewer repeats the initial question, *(0.3) eh mm (0.3) I see em (0.3) and (0.2) mm relatives nearby who can help you in your situa(tion who can*. The negative reply is accompanied by an explanation, in which Gino appeals to membership category 'son' to account for his care-giving commitment, *I am the only son*.

In the formulation produced by the interviewer in the following turn she restates Gino's reply and adds a specification, indicating that Gino is caring for his disabled mother because there is nobody else who could do it: *you are the only son you have nobody (0.6) I see*. In fact, she reformulates what has been given as a reason for care-giving, into an account or a justification for what is constructed as a special case: *therefore the decision (0.4) eh to do this type of caring has fallen on you (0.3) who are a man*. Gender identification is evoked; 'being a male' is a sufficient not to become a care-giver, in fact, there has to be a special reason for a man in order to perform care-giving tasks. Gino's position in relation to employment has to be checked too: *you were the one (0.7) well you were (0.3) let's say (0.6) the closest to retirement or you already had retired=*. This interviewer's turn is scattered with short pauses, which conveys a sense of hesitation and increases the sense of out of ordinariness of the turn content. Gino's prompt acknowledgement, *( ) to be already retired*, contributes to constructing the need for a 'sufficient justification' to become a care-giver. Gino not only has the difficult task of caring for his senile mother, but he is also made accountable for it. He has to provide 'good' reasons for being the one in his family who shoulders this commitment.

Understanding among interlocutors in the course of the interviews is granted on the basis that care-giving is a woman's duty. The case of a man care-giver is constructed as a deviation from the norm that needs explanation. Care-giving is conversationally bound to femininity and contributes to defining women's identity and their moral worthiness. The greater stress experienced by women as a consequence of care-giving is attributable also to its relevance in terms of gender identification and moral pregnancy. Some women take total responsibility for care-giving, they own it (Paoletti 1998c). They consider it their load - no alternative care-giving arrangements are conceived or conceivable. Care-giving is their destiny, their sentence, their privilege. Seeking help would mean missing their own moral duty and denying their gender identification as care providers. For a man, not care-giving is acceptable; for a woman it implies not being a morally worthy and a proper woman. Some women get trapped in these constructions.

Conclusion

In this paper I have stressed the importance of considering the gender issue in dealing with the problem posed by the disabled elderly. In fact, women represent the great majority at both ends of the care-giving relationship; their specific needs and priorities have to be taken into account, in order to take effective steps towards providing useful support services.

In particular, I argue that gender identity issues have to be explored in order to understand the greater stress experienced by women care-givers. Additional qualitative studies are necessary to explore these complex issues. Care-giving is not only a time-consuming and physically demanding job, it is also a task in which complex emotional issues are involved. Duties related to kinship, strong relational bonds and gender identification processes are involved in the provision of care to older family members.

This paper describes how care-giving is conversationally constructed as a category-bound activity to close kin relationships, and as a gender specific activity. Care-giving is continually attributed to women in conversation, and mutual understanding is based on the assumption that care-giving is a woman's business. Moving towards a more shared model of care-giving, as promoted by EC recommendations (EOC 1982) means deconstructing and resisting these social constructions, at all levels: personal, social and institutional. It means revising criteria on which support services are produced and allocated, that is, contrasting the tendency to intervene institutionally only in the absence of informal care-giving provisions. As Caro and Leventhal Stern (1995:79) point out: "efforts by policymakers to target scarce home care resource to those with the least informal caregiving resources have surface appeal. However, this targeting is counterproductive if it overburdens or demoralizes the informal care-givers who are the backbone of home care arrangements." It requires legislation to reconcile work and family life in which also men are seen as care providers. It means that women learn to seek help and give space to whoever wants to help.

Transcript notations

. or ,	Stop or pause in the rhythm of the conversation
?	Rising intonation
!	Excited tone
( )	Word(s) spoken, but not audible
(dog)	Word(s) whose hearing is doubtful
((laugh))	Transcriber description
[	Overlapping utterances at this point
=	No gaps in the flow of conversation
(0.4)	Pause timed in seconds
::::::	elongation

References

Arber, S. and J. Ginn, eds. 1991. *Gender and Later Life*. London: Sage Publications.

Andreini, G. 1994. "Il lavoro di cura: cultura e immagine", in P. Taccani, *Dentro la cura*, Milan: Angeli; pp. 191-216.

Aronson, J. 1990. "Women's Perspective on Informal Care of the Elderly: Public Ideology and Personal Experience of Giving and Receiving Care", *Ageing and Society*, pp. 1061-84.

Baker, C. 1984. "The 'Search for Adultness': Membership Work in Adolescent-Adult Talk", *Human Studies* 7, pp. 301-23.

Baldassarre, G. 1995. "Il ruolo della famiglia nell'assistenza all'anziano non auto sufficiente: problemi, risorse", *Il Giornale di Gerontologia* 43, pp. 303-11.

Baruch, G. 1981. "Moral Tales: Parents' Stories of Encounters with the Health Profession", *Sociology of Health and Illness* 3 (3): 275-96.

Bianchin, R. 1994. "Storie: come si diventa caregiver", in P. Taccani, *Dentro la cura*. Milan: Angeli, pp. 87-108.

Bulmer, M. 1987/1992. *Le Basi del Community Care*. Trent: Centro Studi Erickson.

Caro, F.G. and A. Leventhal-Stern. 1995. "Balancing Formal and Informal Care: Meeting Needs in a Resource-Constrained Program", *Home Health Care Services Quarterly* 15 (4): 67-81.

Clarke, L. 1995. "Family Care and Changing Family Structure: Bad News for the Elderly?", in I. Allen and E. Perkins, *The Future of Family Care for Older People*. London: HMSO, pp.19-49.

Coopmans, M., A. Harrop, and M. Herman-Huiskes. 1988. "The Social and Economic Situation of Older Women in Europe". Research Report, Commission of the European Communities, Brussels.

Council of Europe. 1997. *Recent Demographic Development in Europe*, Strasbourg: Council of Europe Publishing.

Coupland, N. and J. Coupland. 1997. "Discourses of the Unsayable: Death Implicative Talk in Geriatric Medical Consultations", in A. Jaworski, *Silence*. New York: Mounton de Gruyter, pp. 117-52.

Dalley, G. 1993. "Caring: A Legitimate Interest of Older Women", in M. Bernard and K. Meade, eds, *Women Come to Age: Perspectives on the Lives of Older Women*. London: Arnold.

Dooghe, G. and N. Appleton, eds. 1995. *Elderly Women*. Brussels: Centrum vor Bevolkings.

ECE and UNFPA. 1992. "Changing Population Age Structures 1990-2015", *Demographic and Economic Consequences*. Geneva: United Nations.

Equal Opportunities Commission (EOC). 1982. *Who Care for the Carers*. Manchester: EOC.

EUROSTAT. 1996. *Statistiche generali dell'Unione Europea*, 33 ed. Luxembourg: Ufficio delle Pubblicazioni Ufficiali della Comunità Europea.

_____.1995. "Les femmes et les hommes dans l'Union Européenne", *Portrait statistique*, Luxembourg: Offices des Publications Officeles des Communites Européennes.

Facchini, C. and R. Scortegagna. 1994. "Italia: Alternative all'istituzionalizzazione e ruolo centrale delle donne", in F. Lesemann and C. Martin, eds. *Assistenza a domicilio, famiglia, anziani*. Milan: Angeli, pp. 33-109.

Finch, J. and D. Croves, eds. 1983. *A Labour of Love: Women, Work and Caring*. London: Routledge & Kegan Paul.

Garfinkel, H. 1967. *Studies in Ethnomethodology*, Englewood Cliffs, NJ: Prentice-Hall.

Graham, H. 1983. "Caring: A Labour of Love", in J. Finch and D. Croves, eds., *A Labour of Love: Women, Work and Caring*. London: Routledge & Kegan Paul, pp. 13-30.

Harold, S. 1992. "Education in Later Life: The Case of Older Women", *Educational Gerontology* 18 (5): 511-27.

Houdart-Blazy, V. 1997. "Age Become Her, Older Women in the European Unions", *The Women of Europe* Dossier n. 45, Brussels.

ISTAT. 1997. Anziani in Italia. Bologne: Il Mulino.

Jenkins, C.L. 1997. "Home, Work, and Caregiving: How Do These Roles Affect Women's Well-Being?", *Journal of Women and Aging* 9 (3): 27-45.

Joshi, H. 1995. 'The Labour Market and Unpaid Caring: Conflict and Compromise', in I. Allen and E. Perkins.1995. *The Future of Family Care for Older People*. London: HMSO, pp. 93- 118.

Lesemann, F. and C. Martin, eds. 1994. *Assistenza a domicilio famiglia e anzian*. *Milan*: Angeli.

Matthews, A.M. and L.D. Campbell. 1995. "Gender roles, employment and informal care", in S. Arber and J.Ginn. *Connecting gender and aging* Buckingham: Open University Press.

May, M.P. 1994. "Il lavoro di cura", in P. Taccani, *Dentro la cura* Milan: Angeli, pp. 25-86.

Mengani, M. and G. Lamura. 1995. 'Elderly Women, Family Structure and Care Patterns in Italy', in G. Dooghe N. Appleton , eds., *Elderly Women in Europe*. Brussels: Centrum vor Bevolkings.

Moen, P., D. Dempster-McClain and R.M. Williams. 1992. "Successful Aging: A Life-course Perspective on Women's Multiple Roles and Health", *American Journal of Sociology* 97 (6): 1612-638.

Neal, M.B., B. Ingersoll-Dayton, and M.E. Starrels. 1997. "Gender and Relationships Differences in Caring Patterns Consequences Among Employed Caregivers", *The Gerontologist* 37 (6): 804-16.

Paoletti, I. forthcoming 1999. "A Half Life: Women Caregivers of Older Disabled Relatives", *Journal of Women and Aging* 11 (1):21.

_____.1998a. "Handling 'Incoherence' According to the Speaker's On-Sight Categorisation", in C. Antaki and S. Widdicombe, eds., *Identities in Talk* . London: Sage Publications.

_____.1998b. *Being An Older Woman: A Study in the Social Production of Identity* , Hillsdale, NJ: Erlbaum Inc.

_____.1998c. "Caring for Older People: A Gendered Practice", paper presented at the ISA conference, Women and Aging, Montreal, 27 July - 3 August 1998.

_____.1998d. "Intergenerational Solidarity: Membership Categorization and Time Appraisal of Carers of Disabled Elderly", paper presented at the conference Crossroads in Cultural Studies, Tampere, Finland, June 28- July 1, 1998.

_____.1997a. "La produzione dell'identità nell'intervista con anziane", in A. Macarino, ed., Analisi della Conversazione e prospettive di ricerca in etnometodologia. Urbino: Edizioni Quattroventi.

_____.1997b. 'A Half Life: Women Caregivers of Older Disabled Relatives', paper presented at: the ESA conference, University of Essex, Colchester, 24-27 August.

Pomerantz, A. 1984. "Agreeing and Disagreeing with Assessments: Some Features of Preferred/dispreferred Turn Shapes", in M.J. Atkinson and J. Heritage, eds., Structures of Social Action. Studies in Conversational Analysis. Cambridge: Cambridge University Press, pp. 57-101.

Pohl, J.M., C. Boyd and B.A. Given. 1997. "Mother-daughter Relationships during the First Year of Caregiving: A Quality Study", Journal of Women and Aging 9 (1/2): 133-49.

Rose, H. and E. Bruce. 1995. "Mutual Care but Differential Esteem: Caring Between Older Couples", in S. Arber and J. Ginn, eds., Connecting Gender and Ageing. Buckingham : Open University Press, pp. 129-143.

Savage, A. 1996. "Qui prendra soin d'eux", Perspectives d'avenir de les familiae aux personnes agées dans lUnion européenne. Dublin: Foudation Europeénne pour l'amélioration des conditions de vie et de travail.

Silverman, D. 1993. Interpreting Qualitative Data. London: Sage Publications.

_____. 1987. Communication and Medical Practices. London: Sage Publications.

Stolnitz, G.J. 1994. "Social Aspects and Country Reviews of Population Aging. Europe and North America". Economic Studies 6, New York: United Nations.

Taccani, P. 1994. "Le relazioni familiari", in P. Taccani, ed., Dentro la cura Milan: Angeli, pp. 109-70

UNDP. 1998. Human Development Report 1998. New York: Oxford University Press.

UNFPA. 1998. The State of the World Population 1998. Press summary. http://www.unfpa.org/SWP/swp98/pressumary2.htm

Walker, A. 1983. "Care for Elderly People: A Conflict Between Women and the State", in J. Finch and D. Croves, eds., A Labour of Love: Women, Work and Caring. London: Routledge & Kegan Paul, pp. 106-128.

Walker, A. 1995. "The Family and the Mixed Economy of Care - Can They Be Integrated?", in I. Allen and E. Perkins, The Future of Family Care for Older People, London: HMSO, pp. 201-20.

Watson, R. and M. Weinberg. 1982. "Interviews and the Interactional Construction of Accounts of Homosexual Identity", Social Analysis 11, pp.56-78.

Williams, J.,B. Lyons and D. Rowland. 1997. "Unmet Long-Term Needs of Elderly People in the Community: A Review of Literature", Home Health Care Services Quarterly 16 (1/2): 93-119.

'Reaping What You Sow'? Older Women, Housing and Family Dynamics in Urban Mexico

Ann Varley and Maribel Blasco

Abstract

This paper asks why it is that older women are more likely than men to live alone in Mexico, and with what consequences. It presents initial findings from our research on 'Gendered housing: identity and independence in urban Mexico', which seeks to broaden our understanding of the significance of gender in relation to housing.[1] To do this we employ a combination of qualitative and survey research methods in four low-income areas of Guadalajara, Mexico's second largest city, and explore questions that have received insufficient attention in work on gender and housing in developing countries. One of these concerns the housing issues affecting older women.

Introduction: Connecting Gender, Ageing and the Family

In their book *Connecting Gender and Ageing*, Sara Arber and Jay Ginn observe:

> There is growing interest in the fact that western societies are ageing and that women predominate in later life, yet the way

---

[1] Research grant R 000 23 6808, Economic and Social Research Council. UK, 1997-2000.

gender and ageing interact has so far been neglected by feminist
researchers. (Arber and Ginn eds., 1995: xii)

They attribute the neglect of ageing to the fact that feminist activists and
researchers are mostly younger women. Research has tended to reflect
the concerns of women from the age groups most likely to be in
employment (Monk and Katz 1993 citing Rosser 1991). As a result,
academic feminists have focused mainly "on gender as it affects people
of working age" (Arber and Ginn 1991: 28). Research also reflects wider
social prejudices and fears in its avoidance of uncomfortable issues such
as ageing or low-status subjects such as elderly women (McMullin
1995). What research has taken place has mostly focused on the care-
giving child rather than the elderly, typically regarded as a problem and a
burden (Jerrome 1996; Marsh and Arber 1992).

Similar arguments surely apply to the neglect of later life in feminist
studies in developing countries. The special place occupied by woman-
headed households in gender and development research and planning
provides a good example. With some notable exceptions, the international
literature on gender and housing, for example, is dominated by discussion
of the problems facing woman-headed households (Varley 1993; but see
Dandekar ed. 1993). This implies that the housing needs of women living
with a male partner are indistinguishable from his needs - leaving many
women, once again, 'invisible'. It is also associated with a tendency to
think of women heading their household as mothers of dependent children,
i.e., relatively young women (Varley 1996, De Vos and Arias 1998). In
Latin American countries, however, female headship rates "increase
steadily by age, reach a maximum between ages 55 to 65 and then
decline" (Arias and Palloni 1996: 14). Misleading stereotypes of female
headship therefore run the danger of marginalizing older women.

There is another disturbing element to this bias towards younger
women. While independence may be seen as a desirable goal for single
mothers still living with their own parents (Buvini et al. 1992), the
dependence of older women on family members is treated as
unproblematic. Some policy-oriented literature explicitly excludes widows
or older women supported by adult sons or daughters from the category
requiring assistance (Varley 1996). It seems that the model of the
benevolent family working impartially for the good of all its members, the
object of sustained feminist critique over the years, resurfaces when
discussion turns towards older women. Yet it cannot be assumed that
widows will be supported by relatives (Owen 1996), or that living with

relatives guarantees older women's well-being. Although the literature on elder abuse is dominated by research on the United Statesof America, Canada and Europe - depicting the 'classic victim' as a woman over age 75 living at home with adult care-givers (Whittaker 1995: 148) - it would be unwise to assume that it is not a problem elsewhere.

We should be doubly wary of the idealization of the caring family, since it serves as a convenient pretext for governments with too many other demands on their budgets to pass the buck to the family. As Esther Contreras de Lehr writes in a multinational study of family support for the elderly commissioned by the World Health Organization:

> policy makers rely on the support of the family and the strength of intergenerational bonds. They expect families to take care of older, frail and dependent persons with a minimum of health and welfare services (1992: 221; see also Tout 1989).

A belief in strong family ties is often regarded as a distinguishing feature of the national soul in Mexico. Vania Salles and Rodolfo Tuirán (1997:62) caution against a series of widely-accepted myths which offer "an idealized vision of [the Mexican family] and distort some of its realities". The first of these is "the myth of the stable and harmonious family" (*ibid.*:66).[2] As Guillermo de la Peña (1984: 211) puts it: "the greater the amount of blood shared, the greater the expectations of mutual benevolence". So entrenched is the notion of the benevolent family that, in spite of her awareness of its political uses, Contreras (1992:218) reports that in Mexico "family members are almost always willing to help other members with problems of any kind". Since family cohesion is a distinctive feature of Mexican culture, the possibility of the family "abandon[ing] its role as care-provider for the elderly" is too remote to be a significant issue (*ibid.*: 221).

One result of this overwhelming belief in the responsible family is the idea that if you are *not* cared for by your children, you must have done something in earlier life to merit this otherwise inexplicable treatment. You 'reap what you sow' according to the personnel of homes for elderly people with whom we talked in Guadalajara. When we asked why elderly people live in these homes, we encountered an implicit and sometimes explicit moral judgement of people whose family did not look after them. Their past behaviour had come back to haunt them, it was

---

[2] All translations from Spanish are by the authors.

suggested. They had somehow deserved to be abandoned in their hour of need: "it's always said that what you sow is what you'll reap".[3]

Older people who have never married are also vulnerable to this type of moralizing, since they may be seen as having failed in the task of developing bonds of affection with others that will sustain them in later life.[4] Such an attitude overlooks questions, for example, of their sexual preferences. Given that women are regarded as having a 'natural' connection with the family, moreover, negative judgement of single people is particularly likely to apply to them.[5] As one social worker in a home for older women said:

> the ones who suffer the most are those who don't have children or anyone to look after them. But it's more a matter of how they were [with other people], because they get paid back in kind [como ellas fueron, reciben].[6]

The older mother, on the other hand, is the archetypal recipient of family charity. As a mother, a woman is supposed to be an object of near-veneration for her daughter and especially her son, and to command great respect in society (Díaz-Guerrero 1982, Leñero Otero 1987). Silvia Llera Lomelí refers to this "special veneration that people have towards the symbol of women as 'mothers'" to help explain her finding, from the census data, that elderly women in Mexico enjoy better physical housing conditions than do their male counterparts. She suggests that "children and, in general, the family are more willing to provide help or financial support to their mother or female relatives than to their father or male relatives" (1996:166). The 'reaping what you sow' ideology therefore

---

[3] Interview with director of a home for abandoned elderly men or women, Guadalajara, May 1998. Interestingly, the same idea was used by both social workers and people living in case-study areas to express the belief that people ought to treat *older* people well, but when examples were provided, they often concerned people's past relationship with their children rather than their own parents or other elderly people.

[4] We are indebted for this observation to Verónica Montes de Oca of the Instituto de Investigaciones Sociales, Universidad Autónoma de México: personal communication, September 1998.

[5] Older women are more likely to be single than older men, with 7.6 per cent of women aged 60 or more single in 1990, compared to 4.9 per cent of men; 9.9 per cent of women in this age group never had children. The highest percentages of single people in the elderly population, over 8 per cent, are found in the Federal District and the state of Jalisco (of which Guadalajara is the capital); and 10.3 per cent of women aged 60 or more in localities of 1 million people or more were childless (INEGI 1993b; 1992).

[6] Interview with social worker in state-supported home for older women, Guadalajara, May 1998.

applies particularly strongly to older Mexican women: "motherhood is the epitome of womanhood - so much so that if a mother's children do not come to her aid in her old age, this is interpreted as a sign that she has been a poor mother, and within the terms of this discourse, to be a poor mother is to be a poor woman" (Melhuus 1996: 244).

And yet there are a large number of older women living alone in Mexico: 231,000, or 8.8 per cent of women aged 60 years or older (Table 1). How are we to explain this observation? What implications does it have for older women's quality of life? Are these women indeed 'reaping what they sowed' or are there other explanations for their situation? How does it compare with that of other women? We first examine the statistics on this subject to try to shed more light on the housing arrangements of older women in urban Mexico.

Table 1: Older People Living Alone in Mexico and the State of Jalisco

	Women	Men	All	I_f
MEXICO 1990				
Percentage of population of 60 years or more	52.9	47.1	100	112.4
Percentage of population 60+ living alone	63.0	37.0	100	170.4
Older persons living alone as % of age/sex cohort	8.8	5.8	7.4	-
CITIES OF 1,000,000+* 1990				
Percentage of population of 60 years or more†	56.7	43.3	100	131.1
Percentage of population 60+ living alone	69.2	30.8	100	224.2
Older persons living alone as % of age/sex cohort†	7.3	4.3	6.0	-
STATE OF JALISCO1990				
Percentage of population of 60 years or more	53.6	46.4	100	115.6
Percentage of population 60+ living alone	65.6	34.4	100	190.9
Older persons living alone as % of age/sex cohort	10.2	6.2	8.3	-
GUADALAJARA‡ 1995				
Percentage of population of 60 years or more	56.1	44.0	100	127.5

Source authors' calculations, data from INEGI 1993a, 1996. The 1990 census recorded 4,988,158 people of 60 years or more, 6.2 per cent of the national population.
Notes: 'living alone' = population living in one-person households.
I_f Number of women per 100 men.
*   Census *localidades* with one million inhabitants or more. Not the same as the total population of metropolitan areas comprising several municipalities, since metropolitan municipalities with less than one million inhabitants are excluded.
†   Calculated on basis of population living in private households rather than institutions (including old people's homes), not total population. Nationally, 98.32% of the population of 60 years or more live in private households.
‡   Calculated from population figures for the metropolitan municipalities of Guadalajara, Tlaquepaque, Tonalá and Zapopan. Data on household structure are not disaggregated by municipality.

Living Alone, Living With Family?

Table 1 compares women and men aged 60 years or more living on their own in Mexico. Nearly two-thirds of older people living alone in 1990 were women. In Mexico as elsewhere there are more older women than men, but those living alone outnumber older men even more. There are 112 women for every 100 men aged 60 years or more, but 170 women for every 100 men of this age living alone. The figures for the largest urban areas reveal as many as 224 older women living alone for every 100 older men doing so.

The preponderance of women in the elderly population is slightly less for the state of Jalisco, but there are 191 elderly women for every 100 elderly men living alone in the state. One in ten older women in Jalisco lives alone.

There are a number of possible explanations for the tendency for women to live alone more frequently than men. As women live longer than men they are more likely to be widowed (Contreras de Lehr 1989; Montes de Oca 1998). In addition, men are more likely to re-marry, and generally marry younger wives (Quilodrán 1991).[7] Consequently, older men are more likely to have a surviving spouse. In 1990, 76 per cent of men aged 65 years or over were married or living with a partner, compared with only 44 per cent of older women. By contrast, 43 per cent of the women were widows, but only 15 per cent of the men were widowers (López Barajas and Izazola Conde 1994).

Unfortunately, census publications do not disaggregate single-person households by age and marital status, but a survey of older people attending clinics of the Mexican Institute of Social Security (IMSS) sheds further light on how marital status affects the likelihood of living alone.[8] Overall, 8.3 per cent of the women surveyed were living alone, compared to only 3.9 per cent of the men (Table 3). If, however, only those people whose marital status means that they are unlikely to have a

---

[7] Seventy-seven per cent of all male heads of household in Mexico are older than their wives; 28 per cent are more than five years older than their wives. INEGI 1998). The greater tendency for men to re-marry is repeated around the globe, such that about 80 per cent of older men are reported as currently married compared with 45 per cent of older women (United Nations 1995: 4).

[8] We are extremely grateful to Sandra Reyes Frausto for giving her permission for us to use this information. The IMSS is the main social security agency in Mexico; its medical services can be used by parents, siblings, spouse and children of formally employed workers affiliated to the IMSS.

current partner are considered, it is elderly *men* who are more likely to be living alone: 17.9 per cent as opposed to only 14.8 per cent of the women.[9] This suggests that the greater tendency for older women to live alone is partly a function of their longer life expectancy and therefore increased chances of finishing their lives without a partner.

Table 2: People Aged 60 or More Living Alone - Mexican Institute of Social Security

	Women	Men	All
ALL OLDER PEOPLE SURVEYED N= 5,493			
As percentage of population surveyed:	59.9	40.1	100
As percentage of those living alone:	76.3	23.7	100
Those living alone as % of all women/men surveyed	8.3	3.9	6.5
SINGLE, SEPARATED, DIVORCED OR WIDOWED N = 2,085			
As percentage of all surveyed in this category:	82.3	17.7	100
As percentage of those living alone:	79.4	20.6	100
Those living alone as % of all women/men surveyed	14.8	17.9	15.4

Source: Questionnaire survey of older people carried out by Dr Sandra Reyes Frausto, Coordinación de Investigación Médica, IMSS: Reyes Frausto et al. (1998).

This leaves unanswered the question of why these women are not living with relatives. Here, too, census data are unable to help us answer the question in sufficient detail, for two reasons. First, the main census publications do not distinguish (by age) between household heads with and without a resident partner, nor give enough information on *how* households are extended. The 60-year-old head of an extended household could be either a married person living with a daughter- or son-in-law and grandchildren, or a single person still living with an 80-year-old mother. Table 2 presents information on *heads of household* aged 65 or over. Women are more likely to live alone than men, and also far more likely to live with other relatives, if they no longer have a partner. But we

---

[9] When the results were disaggregated further by age, men's 'advantage' in not living alone was not reversed until the age of 90-94 years, but there were only a total of five people over 90 living alone.

do not know who those relatives are, and the study cannot deal simultaneously with older people who do *not* head their household.

Table 3: Household Structure of Heads of Household Aged 65 or More, 1990

	Women	Men
Head only	33.7	7.8
Head with partner	0.9	21.7
Head and partner with children	4.9	60.8
Head without partner, but with children	60.5	9.7
All	100	100

Source López Barajas and Izazola Conde 1994, Table 50. Based on 1% sample of 1990 Census.

Second, household headship is defined by the person answering the census questions. We do not know what criteria they have used in identifying someone as household head.[10] In connection with this, there is a flaw in some discussions of older people's living arrangements. People living in extended households are often assumed to have moved into their children's households, particularly if they are also supported financially by them.[11] This is probably a reflection of a widespread tendency to view the role of older people in society as a passive and dependent one (Arber and Ginn 1991, Leñero Otero 1998). It is not, however, a valid assumption, and it ignores the important question of who owns the house (or rents it). There is a considerable social and psychological difference between owning your home and having a son- or daughter-in-law move in with you, and moving in with a married child and his or her family. This difference is lost in statistics which do not relate household structure to the older person in question. To understand people's living arrangements better we need to consider them in relation

---

[10] A recent INEGI publication compares recognized headship with 'economic' headship (the person earning most), and headship on the basis of age (the oldest household member). In 81 per cent of cases the economic head was also the recognized head (INEGI 1998:16). However, in extended households, more likely to be headed by a woman, there is greater discrepancy between these categories.

[11] For a Chilean example, see IECAIM (1991: 113): "the 'extended' family still prevails. That is, older people are mostly taken in [*acogidas*] by their children or relatives, to live with them". For a British one, see Wall (1992: 67-68). Arber and Ginn (1992: 93) provide a more nuanced understanding of the different situations entailed in 'living with relatives'.

to housing tenure (Varley 1994; 1996).

Table 4: Living Arrangements of People aged 60 or More in Four Neighbourhoods, Guadalajara, 1998

	Women		Men		All	
	HHR	NHR	HHR	NHR	HHR	NHR
Living with partner, plus:						
- no-one else	14.3	-	24.6	-	**19.1**	-
- single children only*	18.6	-	34.4	-	**26.0**	-
- with children + partner/child*	11.4	2.9	18.0	4.9	**14.5**	**3.8**
- others	2.9	0	0	0	**1.5**	**0**
No partner - lives:						
- alone	10.0	-	3.3	-	**6.9**	-
- with single children only*	10.0	-	3.3	-	**6.9**	-
- with children + partner/child*	10.0	11.4	3.3	0	**6.9**	**6.1**
- with others	5.7	2.9	8.2	0	**6.9**	**1.5**
All	**100**		**100**		**100**	
N	70		61		131	

Source: Preliminary results, authors' questionnaire survey, Guadalajara, 1998.
Notes: 'Children + partner/child' = at least one daughter or son who themselves has a partner or child. Single 'children' = daughter(s) or son(s) without resident partner or child.
HHR Individual surveyed is the householder (where they have a resident partner, both are identified as householders).
NHR Individual surveyed is not the householder.
• Other relatives/friends in these households are ignored for the purposes of this classification. For example, a person living with an (adult) 'child with partner or child' may also live with single children, or other children in this category.

Table 4 presents results from a survey we undertook in 1998 of housing patterns and the household in four low-income areas of Guadalajara.[12] As with other broadly-based surveys, it yielded individual

---

[12] Two surveys were done in each of four areas. The first was a recent self-help settlement developed illegally on the edge of the city; the second, a similar settlement dating from the 1950s; the third, a government housing project consisting of 4-storey

information on only a small group of older people: 131 people aged 60 years or over. It is interesting, however, because it distinguishes between the living arrangements of those with and those without a partner, and relates them to the question of who is the 'householder': the person (or, for a couple, persons) to whom the house belongs, who originally rented the house, or who were 'loaned' it by others.[13]

As expected, more men than women still had partners - 82 per cent of the men compared with 50 per cent of the women - and more women than men were living alone - 10 per cent and 3 per cent respectively. Considering only those with partners, very similar proportions of women and men were living with only their partner; their partner and children; or their partner, children, daughter/son-in-law and/or grandchildren.[14] But almost one-quarter of women without a partner (11 per cent of all older women surveyed) were living in the home of sons or daughters with their own spouse or child. No older men were found in this category. Instead, three-fifths of them were still living in their own home with their spouse or spouse and children. In all, 17 per cent of the older women we interviewed were living in a relative's house, compared with only 5 per cent of the older men.

Men, therefore, were more likely to have a partner and remain in their own home. As only half the women still had a partner, they were spread more evenly over a wider range of living arrangements, but significant groups lived on their own or had indeed been 'taken in' by adult children. Where men lived with married/single-parent sons or daughters, it was mostly within their own home, but if over one-third of the women did so, it was more often because of children either remaining with a partner-less mother, or taking the mother into *their* home.

In the remainder of this paper, we concentrate on two groups of older

---

apartment blocks; the fourth, an inner-city area with a relatively high proportion of rental housing. The first survey, of 403 households (approximately 100 from each area) yielded information on 1,055 individuals aged 18 years or over; the second addressed the woman householder in 537 households.

[13] A couple are both counted as householders. While some people may have remarried after acquiring the house, their spouse/partner is nonetheless counted as a householder. 'Loaned' refers either to houses being looked after by other people while their owners are away (e.g., in the United States), or to younger households living rent-free on the same plot as one set of parents, but as a separate household (see Varley 1993).

[14] People living *only* with grandchildren are included in the 'other' category, along with single siblings with equal rights to the house - for example, because of a joint inheritance or other relatives.

women: those living with married sons or daughters and those living alone. In our research in Guadalajara, we asked people meeting for a series of discussion groups in different parts of the city where they would like to live when they were older, and what they thought about looking after older people in the home.[15] The results from these groups, from follow-up interviews with participants, the surveys and our interviews with people living or working in *asilos* [homes for the elderly] both support the caring family model and reveal some of its limitations.

Older Women Living with their Children

Why do children continue to live with their elderly parents or take them into their own homes? Our answer to this question includes a number of considerations relating to older people in general, and some specifically to older women. In the interests of simplicity, we will assume that younger people have a choice in deciding whether or not to stay with ageing parents, but this is not necessarily the case. Many authors have argued that as a result of the 1980s economic crisis, more married children remained with their parents because they could not afford independent accommodation (González de la Rocha 1988; Chant 1991; Selby et al. 1990; ECLAC 1991; Gilbert et al. 1993).[16]

Many people did express a feeling of filial duty towards their parents. One man said:

> our parents took care of us when we were little and the boot was on the other foot, and now that they're older we must take care of them. (Lupe, 59, married with four children, is an inner-city tenant who works as a parking attendant)[17]

A woman in the older self-help settlement identified a sense of obligation towards her parents as a specifically female characteristic and, interestingly, a *right* for women:

---

[15] In each area, one group of women, and one of men, recruited via local churches, met for a total of six 90-minute discussions moderated by Maribel Blasco (women) and Martín Ortíz González (men).

[16] Although there are some unresolved methodological questions behind some of these studies (Varley 1994), census data confirm a growth in the complexity of household structure resulting from an increase in the non-nuclear component between 1970 and 1990 (López Barajas and Izazola Conde 1994: 9).

[17] Names have been changed.

We women take care of our parents when they get old, because they're our parents, it's our right and our duty to take care of them. (Anita, 42, married housewife with four children)

The idea of responsibility towards the elderly was often expressed in terms of a 'do-as-you-would-be-done-by' logic:

No, listen, I think that, in the end, looking after an older person [*ancianito*] well ... in a little while it's going to come round to your turn, if it pleases God to let us get to that age, because the way you treated that person, that's the way they're going to treat you. (Luisa, 31, married housewife living in the newer settlement)

This 'moral accounting' is often expressed in terms of an explicitly Catholic morality:

... not to look after [older people] is bad, because whatever you do in this life you pay for tenfold, and if you take care of an *ancianito* you don't know, you're building up your stock of virtue [*son puras indulgencias que te estás ganando*] but you shouldn't expect to be paid back by the person themselves, instead you'll be paid back by other people - you never know what's in store for you - if it's not good news and God is going to punish you, he doesn't need a big stick to do it with - all that you do, He remembers ... We're only on this earth for a short time. (Beatriz, 68, a married grandparent, sells snacks from a stall in the street in the older settlement)

To look after non-relatives, then, is particularly virtuous, underlining the expectation that people will 'naturally' look after their own kith and kin - but also hinting that they do so because they expect to get something in return. Some children stay with their parents in the hope that they will inherit the house when their parents die. There has been a tradition in Mexico of the youngest son or child remaining at home and subsequently inheriting the property (LeVine with Sunderland Correa 1993). Although this is normally described as a rural tradition, women with whom we talked in the inner city agreed that it was usual to leave property to the youngest child, but then qualified this:

Well, not exactly the youngest, but rather people leave their property to the one who's at home with them, even if they're not the youngest.

Yes, it's supposed to be the one who helps their parents most, that's the one who has most right [to the house].

It's a way of thanking their child for having helped them?

Yes, and that's the person who has the most right because they're the one who's been with their parents putting up with everything and helping them, *that's* the one who has the right, even though they're not the youngest.

While in some cases self-interest outweighs other considerations, it is more generally part of a complex pattern of inter-generational reciprocity, and of the mixed bag of motivations affecting people's behaviour to their parents and children (Robertson 1991; Finch 1989).

In this context, people recognize that older women have both special needs and a potential to make themselves useful. Their needs arise partly from women's tendency to suffer worse health than older men. This is a product of their great longevity and a history of poor nutrition and health care, as well as frequent pregnancies in their youth (Contreras de Lehr 1989; Ham-Chande 1996). In response to our survey question about who needs most help in later life, women or men, some women said, for example "women need more care, they get more illnesses - men die quicker" or "women are weaker, they get ill more often".

Older women's special needs also arise from a lifetime of disadvantage in the labour market. In Mexico, welfare provision is scarce, and since women are far less likely than men to have worked in the formal sector, they are rarely recipients of state pensions or other benefits (Bialik 1989; Llera Lomelí 1996).[18] Consequently, women argued that "[older] women suffer more than men - men have got jobs" and "a woman presents more complications while a man can go out and work".

In practice, we found that 11 per cent of older women were still earning money, compared with 36 per cent of older men. Similar figures are reported by other studies in Guadalajara and in the rest of the country (Arias Merino and Orozco Mares 1994; Montes de Oca 1998). As these authors have pointed out, however, older women's contributions to household welfare do not end with income or pensions. They may release

---

[18] See Lloyd-Sherlock (1997) for equivalent findings in Argentina and Tout (1989) for Latin America in general. According to Sennott-Miller (1989), Mexico is among the intermediate range of Latin American countries regarding expenditure on social security.

another family member for work by carrying out domestic and child-care tasks (Lloyd-Sherlock 1997). Women may be acutely conscious of the need to make such a contribution:

> poorer women were having to make themselves as useful as possible to adult children, thereby building up credit for the time when their health failed and they could no longer 'earn their keep' (LeVineand Sunderland Correa 1993: 193).

Thus, 'women fit in better, adapt better', and 'women don't look for problems, they always try to help, to get on well with people'. In short:

> [having an older person around the house] is a good thing, it's nice, because you've got a treasure there, though we don't always want to admit it. You can learn a lot from them, even old forgotten recipes - very good ones, too, for home remedies as well as cooking, and good stories about the past which you'd never find anywhere in books and you've never heard before ... it's good to have an old person around but it's a lot of responsibility, and a lot of expense too, because old people need lots of things. (María, 41, a married housewife with no children, living in the newer settlement)

Finally, the explanation for older people's current situation should not necessarily be sought in their current needs and potential. Sharing living arrangements with a married son or daughter is something which, for some women, is 'inherited' from earlier in their lives. Women-headed households are more likely to be extended than others, regardless of the woman's age, as adult children remain with their mother because of the social perception that a woman 'on her own' is in greater need of support from her family (Varley 1996). Curiously, this may be one way in which earlier disadvantage (if such it is) works to these women's advantage in later life, if living with relatives is indeed an advantage.

Older Women Who Do Not Live with their Children

Although some older people make at least some contribution to household income, and also contribute in other ways, it is often argued that the elderly lose status and respect in the modernization process, with its emphasis on individualism and instrumentalist relationships, and that this leads to their neglect (Tout 1989). As the director of one *asilo* put it:

> We're losing our values and feelings - they're at an all-time low. We're getting very materialistic and losing ourselves in the radio, the TV and having fun, and we don't want to take care of the

elderly any more. It's as though old people have become a nuisance, a waste of time.

She explains that older women may be tolerated only while they can continue to help around the house:

> ... it's always 'look after the children for me' or 'keep an eye on things' or 'make something for me to eat when I get back'. *Then* they're useful. But when they're the ones who need a helping hand, that's when they become too much trouble.

The very reasons why older women are 'useful' also make it easier for people to leave older women to their own devices more readily than they could with older men. Men were often described as 'useless' [*inútiles*] - 'they want you to do everything for them'. Women on the other hand are described as 'more self-sufficient', 'more independent' and 'more of a fighter' [*valiente*], with 'more will-power'.

In Mexico as elsewhere, it is women who have typically cared for elderly relatives (Llera Lomelí 1996; Lloyd-Sherlock 1997). Yet women's role as care-givers can no longer be taken for granted, particularly with increased employment levels.[19] Many women we spoke with felt that their attitudes had changed as a result of greater access to schooling and integration into the labour market (see also LeVine and Sunderland Correa 1993). They no longer unquestioningly submitted to their husband's wishes in the same way as before. This has important implications for younger women's willingness to live with their husbands' mothers. In rural Mexico, as one older woman put it 'you had no choice in the matter - when you got married you went to live with your husband's family'. The anthropological literature records a long history of poor relations between mother- and daughter-in-law, creating lasting bitterness, as the older woman took it on herself to teach her son's wife her place in her new household. This century has seen a growing rebellion against that tradition (Wilson 1991; Varley 1993;1999):

> Women were more submissive in the past -- if they were taken to live with their husband's parents they stayed put and didn't protest. Nowadays they rebel, so when he says 'we're going to live with my mother', they reply, 'no way! Your mother doesn't like me, go and find me a place where we can be on our own' ... I think it's because women work now and we feel we have more

---

[19] In 1995, 39 per cent of women age 12 or more in Jalisco were recorded as economically active (INEGI 1996).

> right to have our say. (Marta, 33, married with three children, works with husband running a *taco* stall in the older settlement)

It is no longer true that although a woman 'may be sharp with her daughters - and even cruel to her daughters-in-law - she is and must be complaisant toward her own mother and her mother-in-law' (Stevens 1973: 95). Consequently, women cannot rely on living with their married sons. This was brought home to us when talking with an older couple who lived on their own in a rented home in the inner city. The wife, in poor health, told us with tears in her eyes that she would love to go live with her son in the south of the city, but her daughter-in-law did not want her there.

Today's older mothers-in-law may, then, be reaping what was sown by earlier generations. Nor is living with one's married daughter necessarily a more likely option, because, according to one social worker interviewed in a state-supported home for older women in Guadalajara, women who are not in employment find it difficult to obtain their husband's consent.[20]

> Men almost never care for them - 'What? How can you expect me to take care of your parents when I've never even cared for my own?' (Anita, see above)

Finally, behaviour in earlier years can indeed come back to haunt people, without defining anyone as irredeemably 'deserving' or 'undeserving' of support:

> I have my mother living with me - she's a bit older now - and my sister, the youngest one, was there once, and my mother says 'the best of my daughters got married and I got left with ....' At times her foot hurts her, or something, and when we're there we rub some ointment in or massage it but that one doesn't - '*hija*, it hurts me here' - but she [sister] turns on her heel and goes .... (Lucia, 31, married housewife with three children living in the older settlement)

---

[20] We found that 46 (47) per cent of women (men) of any age who were living with a married child, were with a daughter, compared with 57 (58) per cent with a son. Some were with both sons and daughters. In an earlier study in three Mexican cities, which also looked at daughters or sons living (more commonly) as a separate household on the same plot, 51 (53) per cent of women (men) living with married children were with daughters, and 70 (71) per cent, with sons (see Varley 1993).

The Older Woman Living Alone: Isolated and Vulnerable?

To this point, we have answered the question of why some women live with their children while others live alone largely from the children's perspective. This overlooks the question of what they themselves may prefer (Arber and Ginn 1992). We should not assume that living alone is invariably seen as undesirable. It obviously has certain practical disadvantages; for example, not having any one around to know if you are suddenly taken ill:

> My mother-in-law says it's not good to live on your own because if you need something in the night, if you need someone to help ... that's why there are people who wake up dead [*amanecen muertos*], because there isn't anyone to get you a glass of water even. (Teresa, 47, married with five children, lives in the older settlement, where she sells sweets and snacks from home)

Even having family nearby, as many people do, is not necessarily going to solve that problem. Arias and Orozco (1994) report that three-quarters of emergency medical cases at a welfare agency for older people in Jalisco were women. Clearly, women in the oldest age groups are more likely to be infirm and in need of medical attention, and most at risk on their own.[21]

In addition, there can clearly be problems of loneliness - 'a killer' - plus an internalization of guilt from the 'reaping what you sow' message: "I haven't been a good enough mother, that's why I'm here on my own". As one woman said "depending on how I've brought them up, that's what's going to make them treat me well" - or not.

That said, people do not necessarily want to live with family. When we asked women householders aged 60 or more where they would like to live as they grew older, over two-thirds of the women expressing a preference said they wanted to carry on living in their own home. Twenty two per cent added 'with their children or husband', while a further 22 per cent said with their children or other relatives, but without specifying that it should be in their own home. Eleven per cent, however, said that it should be in their home, alone.[22]

---

[21] Their alternatives are also, ironically, more limited, as many homes have a policy of not admitting people who are incapacitated [*imposibilitadas*] or ill. Interview with social worker in state-supported home for older women, Guadalajara, May 1998.

[22] Forty-five women aged 60 or over expressed a preference.

When asked why they would want to live alone women (of all ages) often said they would not "want to get on my children's nerves" or did not want to "make a nuisance of myself". A few explicitly mentioned not wanting problems with their daughters-in-law, or causing trouble between their own daughters and her husbands. Some (although fewer older women) said they would rather be in a home, "so my children don't get tired of me, and so as not to be a burden". In general, whether they wanted to live alone or with their family in later life, women expressed great concern about the possibility of being a nuisance to their children.

It is tempting to see in these responses an expression of the traditional feminine ideal of self-denial [*abnegación*], of *marianismo*, the female counterpart to *machismo* (Stevens 1973). They should not, however, always be taken at face value, as they may conceal women's own fears and concerns - particularly about having to look after grandchildren. Some women were happy to express these straight out: "on my own, so no-one can cause me any trouble", or "on my own, so I don't have to be battling, either with my daughters-in-law or with my grandchildren". Others, however, prefaced this with the more usual wish not to be a burden:

> On my own, *solita*, because, on my own, I pray God, for my children, and you really get some peace and quiet, and when they come here to visit they annoy me ... it's as though they were in an amusement park and I don't say anything to them but I'm over here, angry. (Victoria, 55, married housewife with 10 children, from the inner city area)

What this can mean for an older woman was described with great clarity by Margarita, a 55-year-old woman in the younger self-help settlement, who also had ten children:

> I'm surrounded here [by married children], and I don't have problems with my son-in-laws, or with my daughters-in-law, but I do have problems with the grandchildren ... I've hardly finished doing dishes and I want to put them away but they come round and they say '*mamá* Margarita, can I have some water?' then another arrives and she says '*mamá* Margarita can I have some water?' and in a while all the glasses need washing and I have to wash them ... and then I'm knitting and they want things and I say 'go home to your mother a bit' but I take longer to get rid of them than they do to come back ... and they knock again, and it's tiring, because I want to rest a little ...

So the problem isn't always having people living with you, but living nearby, too?

That too. I wish, I say to my husband, I wish we could get shut of all this and they could be a bit further away, not so near. I tell you, we shouldn't say 'I'm going to buy a plot of land for my son straight away so he can live here', no, don't make that mistake, it's a mistake.

For the less forthright, however, the expression of an apparently self-denying wish not to be a burden can provide a convenient smoke-screen for other feelings likely to be less well-received by others, revealing as it does ambivalence towards children and a woman's putting her own needs before her obligations to others.

The Older Woman Living with Her Family: Loved and Cared For?

Older women living with or even near their families can find themselves drawn into an unwelcome continuation of their mothering and housekeeping roles - a reminder that living with relatives does not mean that their well-being is guaranteed (Gutiérrez Robledo 1989). There are also other, more serious, abuses. As one older woman living in a home told us:

I'm happier here than at home, because there they were always saying to me, 'smelly old cow [*diablo de vieja cochina, apestosa*], just look, you've dirtied yourself again'.

Daughters-in-law, if so inclined, get a chance of revenge later on in life, for example:

I saw what happened to my mother-in-law's own mother-in-law .... They brought her here from [city X] with my mother-in-law and she treated her very badly because she was very old when they brought her here, and she could hardly get about by herself, but sometimes she did get up with her walking-stick and walked about and my mother-in-law would get annoyed, and I can really remember it because ... she, my husband's grandmother, suffered a lot because sometimes she would ask my mother-in-law to help her get a bath and she bathed her and I touched the water and I said to her [mother-in-law], 'listen, it's going to hurt her because she's an old woman' but she'd say 'no, she likes it like that' and his grandmother would cry out because the water was freezing and I'd say to her 'let's heat it up for her, let me do it, I'll heat it up a bit' but 'no, that's the way she likes it' and it really made me

> very sad to see it. I wouldn't treat her that way, and my own mother, still less, right? But yes they do suffer, old people with their daughters-in-law - daughters are also a bit hard, cruel, but I think [older people] suffer more with their daughters-in-law. ... (Blanca, 29, married housewife with two children, lives in a government housing project)

In ongoing research on the impact of land-tenure legalization on the residents of 'squatter' settlements, we have also recorded instances of children bullying and cheating their parents in order to claim property for themselves (Varley 1998). Agency officials in Mexico City, for example, were so concerned about this that they devised a system of *testamentos populares* [informal wills], whereby the name of a relative can be entered on a land title as the heir to the property but not its owner. They hope by this means to dissuade older women in particular from putting their children's names down as outright owners in order to save on the taxes and effort involved in transferring ownership after their death. Too often, people doing this have ended up 'out on the street'. One older couple in Mexico City had to fight their sons to get the property legalized in their name, and even though they succeeded in this they were still forced out of the soundly-constructed home they had built over the years and into a shack. The husband had to shield his sleeping wife from the rain coming in through the cracks.[23]

Conclusion

It is tempting to adopt polarized visions of family care for older people: all idealized, or all doom and gloom, 'apocalyptic demography' (Robertson 1997). In Mexico, it has been suggested, the rejection of an automatic 'moral debt' to one's parents means that real engagement with the older generation is in danger of being replaced by a 'strategic affection', thinly-veiled self-interest (Leñero Otero 1998). Abuse is a reality. On the other hand, one of the woman in Guadalajara had this to say about the 'in-law' problem:

> that person already gave of their best, it's only fair they should take it easy now ... We don't want, as daughters-in-law, to be living with her and annoying her with our presence or our way of doing things, because in a while there'll be the grandchildren and then it will be 'we're off to work, listen, *señora*, look after my

---

[23] Interview with regulating agency official, Mexico City, September 1998.

child for me', and she carries on, working and working ... So, I think it's rather cruel to live with the in-laws, because when is that lady going to get a rest? when is she going to go out? or when is she going to be able to say 'here I am, at home in my house'? if she carries on having to be a mother? because first there's the grandchildren and then if God grants her time, in a little while, the great-grandchildren too. (María, see above).

What might at first sight be seen as a lack of caring for the older woman 'left alone' can also reflect thought and consideration of others' needs and entitlements, and a rejection of easy stereotypes about women and the family.

It is important to remember that older women are people with histories, which can indeed affect their likelihood of receiving shelter and support from their relatives. At the same time, it is necessary to do so without falling into the equally tempting trap of equating awareness of individual agency with moral judgement. While some older women, and men, may indeed reap what they sow, others find themselves in difficult situations through no fault of their own. The danger of idealizing the family and adopting moralizing positions towards individuals who do not 'fit' the idealized pattern is that they can easily be dismissed and become invisible. This is particularly worrying as regards older women living alone, because fertility decline means that, regardless of whether or not the Mexican family continues to live up to its idealized image, there will simply be fewer daughters and sons around to live with widowed mothers or offer them a home in the future. Susan De Vos (1990) suggests that it may become less common for elderly people in Latin America to live in extended families. The numbers of women living alone seem likely to increase.

In conclusion, we would draw policy-makers' attention to three groups of older women in urban Mexico who do not fit the stereotypes we have described. First, the older woman who lives on her own and values her independence as much as her counterparts in Europe or the rest of North America have been shown to do. She needs to be supported in that independence as best and as long as she can. Second, the widow who may be supported economically by her children, but who, along with their father, built the house in which her children still live, or to which they have returned. She needs security of tenure, not to be cheated out of what she struggled so hard to build - 'something to leave to the children' - while she still needs a roof over her own head. Third, the older woman who is 'taken in' by her children. Living with family members does not guarantee her well-being, particularly when she becomes too frail to care for grandchildren or help around the house. Finally: they all need more than shelter.

References

Arber, Sara and Jay Ginn.1991. *Gender and Later Life: A Sociological Analysis of Resources and Constraints.* London: Sage Publications.

_____.1992. "'In Sickness and in Health': Care-giving, Gender and the Independence of Elderly People", in C. Marsh and S. Arber, eds., *Families and Households: Divisions and Change.* Basingstoke: Macmillan, pp. 86-105.

_____, eds. 1995. *Connecting Gender and Ageing: A Sociological Approach.* Buckingham: Open University Press.

Arias, Elizabeth and Alberto Palloni. 1996. *Prevalence and Patterns of Female-Headed Households in Latin America*, Working Paper 96-14. Madison: Center for Demography and Ecology, University of Wisconsin-Madison.

Arias Merino, Elva and Imelda Orozco Mares. 1994. "La mujer anciana en Jalisco", in Rosa Rojas and María Rodríguez Batista. eds., *La condición de la mujer en Jalisco.* Guadalajara: Universidad de Guadalajara, pp. 106-9.

Bialik, R. 1989. "Profile of the Mexican Elderly Women: A Comparative Study", in Pan American Health Organization and American Association of Retired Persons, eds., *Midlife and Older Women in Latin American and the Caribbean.* Washington, DC: PAHO/AARP, pp. 242-52.

Buvinic, M., J.P. Valenzuela, Temístocles Molina and E. González. 1992. "The Fortunes of Adolescent Mothers and their Children: The Transmission of Poverty in Santiago, Chile", *Population and Development Review* 18 (2): 269-97.

Chant, S. 1991. *Women and Survival in Mexico Cities: Perspectives on Gender, Labour Markets and Low-Income Households.* Manchester: Manchester University Press.

Contreras de Lehr, E. 1989. "Women and Old Age: Status of the Elderly Woman in Mexico", in Pan American Health Organization and American Association of Retired Persons, eds., *Mid-life and Older Women in Latin American and the Caribbean.* Washington, DC: PAHO/AARP, pp. 389-98.

_____. 1992. "Aging and Family Support in Mexico", in H.L. Kendig, A. Hashimoto and L.C. Coppard, eds., *Family Support for the Elderly: The International Experience.* New York: Oxford University Press, pp. 215-23.

Dandekar, H.C. ed. 1993. *Shelter, Women and Development: First and Third World Perspectives.* Ann Arbor, MI: George Wahr.

De la Peña, G. 1984. "Ideology and Practice in southern Jalisco: peasants, rancheros, and urban entrepreneurs", in Raymond T. Smith. ed., *Kinship Ideology and Practice in Latin America.* Chapel Hill: University of North Carolina Press, pp. 204-34.

De Vos, S. 1990. "Extended Family Living among Older People in Six Latin American Countries", *Journal of Gerontology: Social Sciences* 45 (3): 87-94.

De Vos, S. and E. Arias. 1998. "Female Headship, Marital Status and Material Well-being: Colombia 1985", *International Journal of Comparative Sociology* 39 (2): 177-97.

Díaz-Guerrero, R. 1982. *Psicología del mexicano.* Mexico City: Trillas.

ECLAC (Economic Commission for Latin America and the Caribbean). 1991. *Major Changes and Crisis: The Impact on Women in Latin America and the Caribbean.* Santiago de Chile: United Nations LC/G. 1592-P.

Finch, J. 1989. *Family Obligations and Social Change.* Cambridge: Polity Press.

Gilbert, A.G. with O. Olinto Camacho, R. Coulomb, and A. Necochea. 1993. *In Search of a Home: Rental and Shared Housing in Latin America.* London: UCL Press.

González de la Rocha, M. 1988. "Economic Crisis, Domestic Reorganisation and Women's Work in Guadalajara, Mexico", *Bulletin of Latin American Research* 7 (2): 207-23.

Gutierrez Robledo, L.M. 1989. "The Ageing Situation in Latin America", *Impact of Science on Society* 39 (1): 65-80.

Ham-Chande, R. 1996. "El envejecimiento: una nueva dimensión de la salud en México", *Salud Pública de México* 38, pp. 409-18.

IECAIM (Instituto Ecuatoriano de Investigaciones y Capacitación de la Mujer). 1991. *La mujer de la tercera edad en el Ecuador.* Quito: Centro de Estudios y Datos.

INEGI (Instituto Nacional de Estadística, Geografía e Informática). 1992. *Estados Unidos Mexicanos: Resumen General. XI Censo General de Población y Vivienda, 1990.* Aguascalientes: INEGI.

———. 1993a. *Hogares: Tabulados Tematicos, XI Censo General de Población y Vivienda, 1990.* Aguascalientes: INEGI.

———. 1993b. *La tercera edad en México.* Aguascalientes: INEGI.

———. 1996. *Conteo de Población y Vivienda 1995: Estado de Jalisco .* Aguascalientes, INEGI.

———.1998. *Las familias mexicanas.* Aguascalientes: INEGI.

Jerrome, D. 1996. "Continuity and Change in the Study of Family Relationships", *Ageing and Society* 16 (1): 93-104.

Leñero Otero, L. 1987. "Valores familiares y dramaturgia social", in A. H. Media and L.N. Rodríguez, eds., *Cómo somos los mexicanos*. Mexico City: Centro de Estudios Educativos, pp. 253-99

_____. 1998. "Tercera edad en sus implicaciones familiares y sociales", *El Cotidiano*, 88, pp. 42-56.

LeVine, S. with C.Sunderland Correa. 1993. *Dolor y alegría: Women and Social Chance in Urban Mexico*. Madison: University of Wisconsin Press.

López Barajas, M. and H. Izazola Conde. 1994. *El perfil censal de los hogares y las familias en México*. Aguascalientes: INEGI.

Llera Lomelí, S.R. 1996. "Gender Differentials in the Housing Conditions of the Mexican Elderly, 1970-1990", Ph.D. Dissertation, University of Pennsylvania.

Lloyd-Sherlock, P. 1997. *Old Age and Urban Poverty in the Developing World: The Shanty Towns of Buenos Aires*. Basingstoke: Macmillan.

Marsh, C. and S. Arber, eds. 1992. *Families and Households: Divisions and Change*. Basingstoke: Macmillan.

McMullin, J. 1995. "Theorizing Age and Gender Relations", in S. Arber and J. Ginn, eds., *Connecting Gender and Ageing: A Sociological Approach*. Buckingham: Open University Press, pp. 30-41.

Melhuus, M. 1996. "Power, Value and the Ambiguous Meanings of Gender", in M. Melhuus and K. A. Stolen, eds., *Machos, Mistresses, Madonnas: Contesting the Power of Latin American Gender Imagery*. London: Verso, pp. 230-59.

Monk, J. and C. Katz. 1993. "When in the World Are Women?" in C. Katz and J. Monk, eds., *Full Circles: Geographies of Women over the Life Course*. London: Routledge, pp. 1-26.

Montes de Oca, V. 1988. "Política social y sociodemografía de la vejez", *El Cotidiano* 88, pp. 49-56.

Owen, M. 1996. *A World of Widows*. London: Zed Books.

Quilodrán, J. 1991. *Niveles de fecundidad y patrones de nupcialidad en México*. Mexico City: El Colegio de México.

Reyes Frausto, S., M. del Carmen García Peña, O.M. Hernández and J. Salmeron. 1998. "Population Ageing in the Mexican Institute of Social Security: Economic and Health Policy Implications", preliminary report. Mexico City: IMSS.

Robertson, A. F. 1991. *Beyond the Family: The Social Organization of Human Reproduction*. Cambridge: Polity Press.

Robertson, A. 1997. "Beyond Apocalyptic Demography: Towards a Moral Economy of Interdependence", *Ageing and Society* 17 (4): 425-46.

Salles, V. and R. Tuirán. 1997. "Mitos y creencias sobre la vida familiar", in Leticia Solís Pontón. ed., *La familia en la ciudad de México*. Mexico City:

Asociación Científica de Profesionales para el Estudio Integral de la Niña, Departamento del Distrito Federal and Miguel Angel Porrua.

Selby, H.A, A.D. Murphy and S.A. Lorenzen with I. Cabrera, A. Castañeda and I.R. Love. 1990. *The Mexican Urban Household: Organizing for Self-Defense.* Austin: University of Texas Press.

Sennott-Miller, L. 1989. "The Health and Socioeconomic Situation of Midlife and Older Women in Latin America and the Caribbean", in PAHO and AARP. eds., *Midlife and Older Women in Latin American and the Caribbean.* Washington DC: PAHO/ARP, pp. 1-125.

Stevens, E.P. 1973. "Marianismo: The Other Face of Machismo in Latin America", in A. Pescatello, ed., *Female and Male in Latin America.* Pittsburgh: University of Pittsburgh Press, pp. 89-102.

Tout, K. 1989. *Ageing in Developing Countries.* Oxford and New York: HelpAge International and Oxford University Press.

United Nations. 1995. *The World's Women: Trends and Statistics.* New York: United Nations.

Varley, A. 1993. "Gender and Housing: The Provision of Accommodation for Young Adults in Three Mexican Cities", *Habitat International* 17 (4): 13-30.

_____. 1994. "Housing the Household, Holding the House", in G.A. Jones and P.M. Ward, eds., *Methodology for Land and Housing Market Analysis.* London: UCL Press, pp.120-34.

_____. 1996. "Women Heading Households: Some More Equal than Others?", *World Development* 24 (3): 505-20.

_____. 1998. "Cuestiones de género en la regularización de la tenencia de la tierra", in Edésio Fernandes, ed., *Derecho y Espacio Urbano*, Dikinson de Madrid and Instituto Internacional de Sociología del Derecho, Oñati, Spain.

_____. forthcoming. "Women, the Home, and the Modernization of Patriarchy in Mexican Family Law", in E. Dore, ed., *The Hidden Histories of Gender and the State in Latin America.* Durham, NC: Duke University Press.

Wall, R. 1992. "Relationships Between the Generations in British Families Past and Present", in C. Marsh and S. Arber, eds., *Families and Households: Divisions and Change.* Basingstoke: Macmillan, pp. 63-85.

Whittaker, T. 1995. "Gender and Elder Abuse", in S. Arber and J. Ginn, eds., *Connecting Gender and Ageing: A Sociological Approach.* Buckingham: Open University Press, pp. 144-57.

Wilson, F. 1991. *Sweaters: Gender, Class and Workshop-Based Industry in Mexico.* Basingstoke: Macmillan.

Family Support Systems and Older Women in Sub-Saharan Africa

Irene Zeilinger

Abstract

Because the proportion of those over 60 years old is very low in the sub-Saharan region, the elderly population is largely left out of development programmes and ignored in social service provision. In most countries, if not all, it is assumed that the traditional extended family will provide for the elderly. Yet changing family forms, along with regional conflicts and hardship, have left many old people without a family to care for them, making it uncertain whether or not traditional support systems can in fact meet these expectations. Especially unclear is the ability of older women, who are both entrusted with care-giving responsibilities and the most vulnerable to poverty, to assume these roles. This article examines the role of older women within different family forms as well as the social and economic security of older women. It notes that their dependency on kinship makes older women increasingly vulnerable to poverty, as their access to land and other resources diminishes. At the same time, women continue to work and care for families and communities well into old age, rendering them an important resource to the well-being of their families, communities and the whole society. As result, the paper concludes, a new approach to development planning is needed, one that addresses the needs of older women while acknowledging their contributions to social welfare.

Introduction

> Right now all the old people are working - they're working until they drop dead. So why not support them so they can work with dignity and fulfillment?

Nana Araba Apt, Gabanese gerontologist, 1992

From a demographic as well as a development perspective, sub-Saharan Africa has been in the global limelight as an especially 'problematic' region for several decades. The so-called 'population explosion' is said to be a danger for the whole continent and as a consequence, for the developed regions. The argument is that rapid population growth endangers the demographic and ecological capacities of sub-Saharan Africa - and therefore, is a threat to world peace. Accordingly, development policies often focus on improving family planning programmes to combat this problem. Apart from family planning, which typically focuses on women, the target groups for government development planning are young men; followed by young women. At the bottom of this scale are old men and after them, old women.

The argument that it is not necessary for sub-Saharan African governments to become active on behalf of their older population segments is based on the extremely high proportion of the young in the countries of the region, where overall, the proportion of those over 60 years old is only about 5 per cent (UN 1997). In some southern African states where the process of demographic transition is more advanced, namely, South Africa or Mauritius, this proportion increases by a few percentage points. Relatively, the old are invisible in terms of development politics.

Another reason for the neglect of older persons particularly in sub-Saharan Africa is the assumption that the traditional support systems of the extended family will provide care for the old anyway. In development discussions, the question of what will happen to older persons without a family to care for them often remains left out. Thus, it is essential to find out whether traditional support systems can in fact meet expectations in terms of their ability to care for older people. Investigation must focus on older women, as they are not only the ones typically entrusted with care-giving responsibilities but also the ones who are most vulnerable to poverty, especially in patrilinear societies. To this end, this article will examine different concepts of the family in the region and illustrate them with statistical data on marriage and household composition. It will then examine the role of elderly women within multigenerational households as well as the social and economic security of older women.

The Family in sub-Saharan Africa

Statistical data on such things as living arrangements or status within the family or household tell little about the reality in sub-Saharan Africa. On the one hand, concepts such as marital status are oriented towards conditions in the developed regions and are based on the household, not on the individual. In addition, such statistics are static rather than dynamic, providing information on the status quo, while obscuring the process that leads to this status quo. The marital status of a person does not tell anything about how long this person has been single, married, divorced or widowed.

Users of statistics face even more fundamental problems in the case of sub-Saharan Africa. Statistical concepts of family and household do not take into consideration the variety of cultural and social organizations that exist. Concurring systems of family law, including traditional customary law, colonial law and certain religious influences, all complicate the categorization of living arrangements. Living arrangements that have not been registered officially, particularly non-European family forms such as polygyny or marriage between women puzzle producers and users of statistics as they do not fit into the picture and therefore are invisible.

The view that marriage is a business between two persons of different sex, ends with the death of at least one partner and is the most important component of human life, is based on living conditions in developed regions, but not in - especially rural - sub-Saharan Africa. Here, it is kinship that defines a person's membership in a group and therefore also his or her social roles. Marriage is the bond between two lineages, or descent groups, and it is the woman's role to produce children for her husband's lineage. This is reflected in the custom of the levirate in patrilinear cultures, where a marriage is maintained, even when the husband has died, by one of his male relatives marrying the widow. Often, the dead man is regarded as husband and not the levir. The levirate can differ substantially as regards rights, obligations and living arrangements. In some ethnic groups, such as the Baule of the Côte d'Ivoire or the Bantu Nyika of Tanzania, older widows are thought of as having lost their sexual identity and therefore enjoy the freedom of choice how and with whom they live. They may travel and become traders or, like the Baule, marry a young woman or man (with a young woman) to produce children for her dead husband's kinship group (Owen 1996: 104ff).

In most patrilinear sub-Saharan African cultures marriage is regarded as a union of families, not of individuals. By marriage, a woman loses all her rights in her natal family and can maintain support relationships with her lineage only by making gifts. Her marital duty is to give birth to descendants of her husband's lineage and to work one plot of land for her husband. The rest of her subsistence work is for her own and the children's living. After her husband's death, she theoretically can rely on the subsistence use of communal land and on support from her in-laws and sons. However, due to land scarcity, economic recession or urbanization, a widow may receive little land, traditional inheritance law might be interpreted to her disadvantage, and sons who migrated to cities abroad might not be able to help. For different reasons, she might not be recognized as a widow, because the brideprice has not been paid (fully), competing co-widows appear or her (customary) marriage is not accepted as such. In this insecure situation, she depends on the benevolence of officials and traditional leaders to avoid destitution.

In spite of the limitations of the statistical family concept, data for this region can be interpreted critically. Table 1 shows the elderly population of selected countries by sex and marital status. The low proportion of single persons of both sexes is striking. Marriage seems to be the most successful family form in sub-Saharan Africa. Only in the island countries of Cape Verde, Sao Tome and Principe and the Seychelles are there important proportions of single persons, as for example, 66.8 per cent single women compared to 47.4 per cent single men in Sao Tome and Principe (UN 1993).

Whereas on the continent, the low proportion of single persons is approximately equal for both sexes, considerable gender-specific differences appear in the categories of married and widowed persons. About half of all older women are widowed, compared to one-tenth of all older men. The reason for this disparity lies in the fact that women marry at earlier ages than men, therefore have older spouses, and in combination with women's higher longevity, married women have a high probability of being widowed during their life cycle.

But this cannot explain the extent of gender-specific disparities as regards marital status. A huge proportion of older men are married, up to 90 per cent, compared to 24 to 46 per cent of women. This suggests that men tend to remarry after the death of a spouse, whereas women stay widowed more often. On the one hand, this may be due to the wider acceptance of remarriage for men than for women and the fact that they more easily find a new, usually younger wife. On the other hand, men can expect more advantages from another marriage than women. Due to the gender-specific division of labour, a wife also means a householder and -- if necessary -- a nurse to her husband, which is not the case with a husband. Moreover, women are responsible for the social contacts of a household, and widowers therefore get socially isolated (UN 1994:1).

The Role of Older Women in the Family Household

However the family may be organized, it functions to distribute resources and spread risks between generations. In industrial societies, this function often is transferred to institutions such as child-care facilities or old people's homes. In times of economic recession, these tasks are partially re-transferred to the families which results in a heavier workload for women or even in their being pushed out of the labour market, due to the gender-specific division of labour.

Table 1: Population 60+ by Sex and Marital Status, Selected Countries (in %)

	Single	Married	Widowed
Mali, 1987			
Women	1.4	46.1	46.3
Men	1.7	90.2	5.4
Mozambique			
Women	3.6	32.8	54.0
Men	2.2	83.5	8.9
South Africa, 1985			
Women	6.5	40.8	48.7
Men	6.8	75.8	11.3
Zaire, 1984			
Women	5.8	24.4	53.9
Men	4.3	81.2	9.4

Source: UN 1993 and computation by the author

The support functions of the family, as well as its ability to fulfil them, are dependent on changing social factors. In sub-Saharan Africa, demographic change as well as modernization, urbanization and labour migration have all impacted these tasks. The demographic factor is that -

in the short term - the number of children per family is growing, as is the number of the dependent old, due to improvements in health care and the resulting higher longevity. This puts enormous pressure on the middle-aged groups, which have to care for both the young and the old. In the long run, the number of children per family will decrease in sub-Saharan Africa, whereas the number of the dependent old will continue to rise. Thus, the weight of the pressure on the middle-aged will shift from the young to the old.

There are six main types of families with possible mixed forms (UN 1986):

(a) *the extended family* consists of two or more nuclear families and various dependent kin residing together;

(b) *the limited or modified extended family* comprises one or two nuclear families with one or more members establishing their own households elsewhere, resulting in a greater geographical distance between family units with still close family ties (e.g. visits, financial support);

(c) *the nuclear family* is formed of two partners, married or not, and their children;

(d) *the single-parent family* consists of one adult and one or more children;

(e) *the communal family* comprises several unrelated families residing in the same dwelling for ideological or other reasons;

(f) *the polygynous family* is formed of one husband, two or more wives and their children and other dependants. This occurs when either the man has an elevated standard of living which enables him to support several wives, or when an additional wife means an additional worker with shared tasks and risks.

While the extended family type and its modifications prevails in sub-Saharan Africa, in the urban areas, modernization leads more and more young people, especially those with higher education, to emulate the western ideal of the nuclear family that is associated with well-being and modernity (Dovlo 1992: 151). Of course, this results in conflicts between the generations, because it is not only a question of maintaining values and norms, but also of the responsibility for the social security of the old. However, the extended family still is the most prevalent type of family organization, even in urban areas. In the year 2000, African family size will average 4.7, with a slightly declining trend (UN 1986: 11).

When looking at the age-specific household composition, the example of Burundi illustrates that older persons (want or have to) live independently (see Table 2). In most of Burundi's households, there are no older persons; the largest number of older persons live in one-person households, half of which consist of an old person. Interestingly, in two-person households, it is not old couples who predominate (11%), but younger persons living with an old person (24%). As the number of household members increases, the number of households with older persons declines. Among the 248,597 households with older persons, 17 per cent consist exclusively of older persons. For this considerable part of households, the assumption that older persons are always living in the extended family is not true. However, this statistic does not indicate whether there is any support between households or tell us anything about the living standard of those older persons who live alone or with other older persons.

Table 2: Burundi - Households by Size and Number of Persons 60 +, 1990

	Total	1 pers.	2 pers.	3 pers.	4 pers.	5 pers.	6 pers.	7+ p.
House-holds Absolute	1,145,479	93,520	146,596	181,378	171,007	161,939	142,456	248,583
0 pers. 60 +	896,555	52,090	94,388	139,949	137,138	135,518	122,882	214,590
1 pers. 60 +	190,173	41,430	35,642	27,927	23,338	19,142	14,987	27,707
2 pers. 60 +	57,402		16,566	13,228	10,284	7,068	4,413	5,843
3 + p. 60 +	1,022			274	191	161	117	279
Unknown	327				56	50	57	164
Relative								
0 pers. 60 +	78%	56%	64%	77%	80%	84%	86%	86%
1 pers. 60 +	17%	44%	24%	15%	14%	12%	11%	11%
2 + p. 60 +	5%		11%	7%	6%	4%	3%	2%

Source: UN 1993 and computation by the author

Unfortunately, the data on Burundi are not disaggregated by gender, but there are gender-specific data on older persons living alone for four countries (see Table 3). Apart from Botswana, where the gender-specific difference is minimal, there are generally more older women living alone than there are men. This may be related to men's higher remarriage rate after widowhood. But it also illustrates the fact that women cannot rely on family support in old age, at least not in the same household.

Table 3: Persons 60 + Living Alone by Sex
Selected Countries

Country	Women	Men
Botswana, 1981 (65+)	1,485	1,464
Mali, 1976	20,946	6,908
La Reunion, 1982	3,958	130
Rwanda, 1978	24,491	4,951

Source UN 1993

Taking a closer look on the age-specific distribution of women and men living alone, another gender-specific difference emerges in the case of La Reunion. Whereas in 1982, the number of men living alone declines slowly from 485 to 311 with age, the number of women in the same age groups almost doubles, from 729 to 1,321 (UN 1993). This is further evidence for the fact that women who are more often widowed with age do not remarry as often as men and therefore, also live alone more often than their male counterparts.

Its is reported for Africa that the care and support that are given to the old are not given as a sign of charity but rather is part of the normative and consensual aspect of inter-generational solidarity: the old, by their social age, are assigned certain roles, rights and obligations which complement those of the young (UN 1994:13). For older women, this means that - depending on the culture they live in - they may enjoy high prestige as practitioners and teachers of traditional skills or as midwifes and healers. These roles can empower older women in the family as well as in the community.

> In such societies, when women reach mid-life, and elder status, they become ... less subject to male authority and may engage in a variety of activities not permitted to younger women. Nor do they need to exhibit same degree of deference to males or hold to the same rules of modesty in dress and action. They may ignore some language taboos and begin to speak freely and with authority .... They may also travel from home much more freely than younger women. All this means that older women potentially have more possibility to challenge men in the councils, engage in commerce and trade beyond the boundaries

of their villages, and collaborate in organisation activities. (UN 1993 : 3f)

On the other hand, the empowerment of older women is often connected with the continued submission of girls and young women. This can be seen in the case of female genital mutilation which mostly is performed by traditional birth attendants, that is, older women.

The status or position of old people in any society is influenced by many institutional factors, not only by kinship ties. Other influential factors are the command of the old over knowledge and skills (and the appreciation of these by young), their control over property and thereby over opportunities for the young and the presence of religious and other traditions determining their status (UN 1975: 25). Due to the urbanization and modernization of African societies, these concepts of the status of older persons within the family are undergoing a major change. Statistically, these factors can be measured only indirectly, by looking at headship of household.

In all of the countries for which this information is available, more men over 60 years of age are heading households than women (see Table 4). This is in spite of the generally larger proportion of women in the older age groups and in spite of the fact that a considerable part of the households headed by an old person are single households where women prevail. That means that in multi-person households men are ascribed headship and thus power more frequently than women. This is surely true for the countries where the female rate of headship among the 60 + is lowest, namely Cameroon and Mali, with 19 per cent each. In those countries where households headed by old women reach or even exceed 40 per cent, Botswana, Reunion and Rwanda, there might be more multi-person households headed by old women.

Table 4: Heads of Households 60+ by Sex: Selected Countries

		Absolute		Relative	
Country	Total	Women	Men	Women	Men
Botswana	27,468	11,681	15,787	43%	57%
Cameroon	218,366	40,486	177,880	19%	81%
Congo	59,588	17,810	41,778	30%	70%
Madagascar	274,117	66,336	207,781	24%	76%
Mali	439,423	81,477	357,946	19%	81%
Mauritius	38,144	13,005	25,139	34%	66%
La Reunion	23,513	9,922	13,591	42%	58%
Rwanda	186,439	73,986	112,453	40%	60%
Zambia	202,423	59,874	142,549	30%	70%

Source UN 1997

Table 5 underlines this position: In Burundi, women from 60 to 74 years of age are as often heads of households as they are spouse of the head, namely 44 per cent and 49 per cent, respectively. Women over 75 years of age are twice as often household head than spouse of household head (60% and 29% respectively), which can be attributed to the growing number of widows living alone. This is very different for old men: 96 per cent of men in all old-age groups are heads of household, whereas only 2 per cent are spouse of the head. The same table also shows that the number of women living with their children is ten times higher than the number of men, which again is related to the gender-specific consequences of widowhood. Even in the categories 'other relatives' and 'non-relatives', there are relatively few older women to be found, which indicates that they often have to find a family for support, even if it is not their own.

Table 5: Burundi – Household Members by Age, Sex, Relation to Household Head, 1990

	Total	-15	15 - 24	25 - 59	60 - 74	75 +	n.a.
Women							
Total	2,718,667	1,234,772	479,984	837,346	53,775	110,062	2,728
Head	282,541		13,590	175,857	26,704	65,907	483
Spouse	776,533		138,139	581,929	23,645	32,315	505
Mother	11,048			3,021	1,507	6,468	52
Child	1,471,230	1,132,510	282,932	54,574	328	412	474
Other relative	146,135	90,402	34,538	15,146	1,194	3,920	935
Non-relative	31,180	11,860	10,785	6,819	397	1,040	279
Men							
Total	2,574,126	1,223,468	447,635	757,350	40,322	98,468	6,883
Head	862,938		68,676	658,387	38,883	94,975	2,017
Spouse	18,097		1,620	14,109	663	1,572	133
Father	1,489			548	134	787	20
Child	1,499,766	1,135,146	316,732	47,169	52	87	580
Other relative	32,315	77,950	36,235	14,129	266	653	3,082
Non-relative	59,521	10,372	24,372	23,008	324	394	1,051

Source: UN 1993 and computation by the author

Support and Care for Older Women

Whatever the family type and size, all family arrangements share the same principal goal, namely, the distribution of costs and risks between the generations which results in inter-generational solidarity. Modernization and migration result in the excessive strain of modified extended and nuclear families in sub-Saharan Africa. Nevertheless, the community expects that family members be available to care for the elderly, in the following order (Khasiani 1994: 63f.):

(a) spouses: because women generally marry younger than men, which is even more true for polygyny in East Africa, old men often have very young wives to care for them in their old age;

(b) sons: because they inherit the land and remain geographically close, they are the ones that the old, especially older widows, run to for care;

(c) daughters: theoretically, they are a second-rate choice only, for they often move to their husbands' families at marriage and therefore cannot provide care easily;

(d) siblings: this is more likely for men than for women, because men have access to land of their own; for older women, especially those who are single or divorced, this care is often given only unwillingly because brothers do not want to share their often limited land and shelter. For women, turning to siblings for support is mostly a result of destitution and often begins before reaching old age;

(e) the community: in very few instances, the community will take care of childless women who cannot rely on anyone; mostly this takes the form of symbolic gifts of wood, sugar or tobacco, and only in very extreme cases, neighbours will provide shelter and a piece of land.

The groups at risk of destitution in old age thus are single elderly (never married or divorced), widowed and childless women. For the large majority of older women, support by a spouse is negligible, as husbands usually die earlier and also need care earlier. A study in Sierra Leone showed that husbands are looking for help with their health problems from their wives, but none of the women interviewed expected their husbands to support them (IFA 1985: 22). Among disabled persons, for example, the proportion of women is higher because women live longer and therefore, are more vulnerable to disability in old age than men. On average, women are disabled at later ages, whereas men often are disabled by accidents and war or other conflict situations when they are still young (UN 1993). Due to the gender-specific division of labour, women often have to care for older relatives (e.g., parents-in-law) and then their husbands throughout their life cycle, and when they need help after a life full of hard work, there is no one left to care for them.

Therefore, older women are worrying more about their health. The above-mentioned study in Sierra Leone showed also that nearly half of the women over 65 years old stated that health was their most important problem. The proportion of women who would spend an unexpected gift on health care increased with age (IFA 1985:22). An additional problem is the tendency of formal health-care institutions to target women primarily in their reproductive years and to ignore the needs of older women (HelpAge International 1995: 14).

Another health problem for older women is the spread of the AIDS pandemic, particularly in Eastern Africa. The disease has reached a level where, in some countries, the average life expectancy is decreasing. AIDS is not only a threat to the life of HIV-positive persons, but it also changes the demographic conditions for family organization and for the overall economic situation.

Older women are directly affected by AIDS to a relatively small extent, above all through infection by their husbands, through their role as birth attendants and practitioners of female genital mutilation and through the traditional practice of the levirate. Indirectly, AIDS is influencing their lives much more profoundly. In areas where AIDS is widespread, the number of old widows caring for their sick children and their orphaned grandchildren is growing. Estimates range from 11 per cent to 24 per cent of households containing three generations where AIDS will lead to the extinction of the middle-aged generation (Lee and Palloni 1993: 79). By the year 2000, it is estimated that there will be 9 million AIDS orphans, including those being cared for by their grandmothers (HelpAge International 1995:14). Besides the burden of caring for their children with full-blown AIDS, older women also lose social security by the death of the next generation and have to earn their living for themselves and their grandchildren.

> Damage to the family economy and to the care systems for children and the elderly may begin much earlier than at the time of the death of one or both parents. In fact it may start shortly after the onset of infection in any one of them. If so, the losses incurred by the family will be spread over a longer period of time and their magnitude will be higher than those implied by statistics on orphanhood and widowhood alone. (Lee and Palloni 1993:81)

Therefore, support from their children is essential for old women in case of illness or when they are not able to earn their living for other reasons. A study in rural Kenya revealed that 92 per cent of old women and 88 per cent of old men received help from at least one of their children. The type of help varied considerably, the most vital being -- in order of importance -- non-monetary gifts, money and services, such as fetching wood and water, preparing food and repairing the house (UN 1991:87). Theoretically, it is the sons who are expected to support their mothers (and it is the daughters-in-law who do the work).

The example of the Ankole in southwest Uganda shows the discrepancy between demands and reality. Whereas three-quarters of the female respondents expected old-age support from their sons, they did not expect this from their daughters at all. Nevertheless, when they really need help, their daughters unexpectedly help to a larger extent (UNFPA n.d.). This is different among the Bambara in Mali, where 25 per cent of the young men living in urban areas support their rural families with money and 43 per cent support them with services, whereas only 18 per cent and 25 per cent, respectively, young women help their parents in the same way (Rosenmajr 1993:20). But it has to be underlined that the young women tend to support their families with more money, although they earn less than their male counterparts.

In the Joola society of Senegal and Guinea-Bissau, old age is not endowed with privileges (Attias-Donfut 1994:203ff). Women and men work as long as they are physically capable. Some of the old even prefer to die in the woods rather than depend on their children and one day they will simply disappear. Traditionally, old-age support is organized in such a way that the daughters and daughters-in-law take over the cooking and washing responsibilities of an old woman when her husband is too weak to work with the kajendo, a field tool. Whereas the old man is released from work, the old woman still looks after the animals, produces palm oil, makes baskets and does the necessary sacred rituals. A proverb therefore says that a man gets old, but not a woman (ibid).

The sons' support for their parents has produced another proverb among the Tiriki in Kenya: "Our sons are our legs" (Sangree 1994:227). Therefore, it is a social norm to have at least two sons so as to not be socially 'handicapped' in old age. The lineage of a man will not grant his wife the traditional plot of land with a house, and if necessary the daily food and care, if she has borne less than three children. Childless women have to leave their homes in old age because they are frequently suspected of witchcraft, forcing sterility upon the young. Old women without living children will die or get lost.

The Toucouleurs in Senegal and Mauritania organize old-age differently (Attias-Donfut 1994: 205ff). Here, the principle of seniority enables an old father to appropriate his children's products and redistribute them for living expenses and for the brideprice. The mother is excluded from this system; she is subordinated to any man of any age. Old age therefore, does not give her any advantage, except the possibility of being released from household tasks. Due to her age, she formally has a high status but is marginalized anyway. Only as a midwife, a profession that can only be practiced by women after menopause, can she play an important social role, but with Islamization, this opportunity is steadily diminishing.

Another source of old-age support for women can be the external family economy. In addition to a woman's important role in the internal family economy, through her responsibility for subsistence production, she also works in the external family economy (UN 1994a: 12ff). If women stay close to their families of origin even after marriage, they can expect political, financial and emotional support from their female relatives. If they move away, they lose this support. This is why Igbo women in southeast Nigeria are organizing village support groups for women, especially older women. If there are no female relatives or organized support groups to rely on in times of need, the external family economy is of vital importance to women. To this end, they need a separate income to be able to give presents to their relatives living far away. These gifts oblige the relatives to help them. Beti women in Cameroon receive 34 per cent of their transfer income and 15 per cent of their total income from relatives, not from their spouses. When a woman's income decreases, so too do her chances of maintaining her kinship relations in this way.

Contributions of Older Women

So far, this paper has discussed mainly older women's needs. But especially in sub-Saharan Africa, this group is not waiting idly for family support or government interference. On the contrary, it is for many older women essential to continue to work and contribute to their families' well-being according to their abilities. Not only economic necessity explains women's high economic activity rates in old age. In Burundi, 91 per cent of the women aged 60 to 64 and 74 per cent of those over age 65 are working. Besides a few exceptions in southern Africa and the island countries, activity rates of women aged 60 to 64 range between 30 and 60 per cent and those of women over 65 between 25 and 40 per cent (UN 1997).

It is noteworthy that the activity rate of women 60 to 64 years old exceeds the overall female activity rate in most of the countries. This is due to the fact that older persons are working in traditional sectors which are not as vulnerable to economic recession and unemployment as the modern ones, where more young people seek work. The activity rate of older women will decrease only slowly in Africa (IFA 1985:16).

Apart from their economic activity, older women are still not idle can be seen from the data from Botswana (see Table 6). Whereas the time spent by men in work outside the home is reduced significantly when they reach age 50, the remainder of time is used for other activities. Women continue working at the same rate well into old age and only after age 60 do they have more time for other activities. However, they work longer hours than men at all ages.

The contributions of older women to the well-being of their families do not have to be necessarily economic. In many societies, they are assigned the role of counsellors. For example, among the Bambara in Mali, old mothers enjoy more of their children's trust than fathers, and particularly for their daughters they are important counsellors when there are problems or a partner has to be chosen (Rosenmayr 1993: 26). However, in the course of modernization and urbanization, this role is losing its importance.

Table 6: Botswana - Time Use in Rural Households by Type of Work, Sex and Age (in %)

Type of work	Women			Men		
	40-49	50-59	60+	40-49	50-59	60+
Work outside the home	20	19	16	32	29	26
Household work	32	32	24	9	8	7
Other activities	48	49	60	59	63	67

Work outside the home: crop and animal husbandry, wage labour, trading, hunting, gathering.
Household work: housework, child care, water collection, repair of buildings.
Other activities: school, meetings, illness and health care, leisure.
Source UN 1991: 27f

Attias-Donfut (1994:139ff) reports that Bambara women in the traditional system of age classes age faster than men: they are 'old' at the chronological age of 33, whereas men have to wait until age 60. Although superficially men dominate the political system and women do not have a vote in the village council, old women hold the strings behind the scenes - nothing would work without their consent. The very old women of merit become grandmothers for everyone. They are responsible for the community well-being and receive not only prestige, but also services from the young. "If the field of an old woman is kept especially well, one can assume that she is 'someone' in the village" (*ibid.*: 142).

An example from western Africa is Hajiya Osabe from Nigeria (UN 1991:7). At the age of 80, she still collected herbs, produced medicines and treated women and children. She worked as a midwife, rented room is her compound, traded with henna and was responsible for the organization of burials.

Nana Apeadu, the Queen Mother of Apuri, a town in Eastern Ghana, describes the tasks of old women as follows:

> They help as baby-sitters. The family has someone to represent its interests at meetings of the village councils. The counsellors who advise the Queen Mother of the village are known as the Wise Old Women .... They do counselling - you can just go to an elderly person and pour out your heart about a family problem or a personal problem. People come by early in the morning on the way to work or travel miles to seek their advice, to have someone listen to them. It's said that the older people have 'listening ears'. (UN 1992:1)

In southern Africa in the town of Bakwena (Botswana), more than half of the households are headed by women and there is a rather high number of illegitimate children (Ingstad 1994: 213). This is due to the fact that the majority of men work in the mines of South Africa and have only illegitimate relationships with the women in Bakwena. The single mothers often stay with their children at their widowed mothers' houses. The old women organize the household and look after the children so that the young women have time to work in the fields or in town. The division of labour between women of different generations enables the young to be economically active and provides social security for the old. These and other examples show that in sub-Saharan Africa older women are anything but mere recipients of support and care and contribute to the well-being of their families.

Conclusions

As has been shown, there is a vast variety of family support systems for older women in sub-Saharan Africa. In all cases, older women contribute with work and wisdom to the well-being of their families, communities and the whole society. This means also that a new approach in gender-sensitive development planning is necessary.

First of all, more information will be necessary for the identification of problems and planning of projects targeting older women. This should comprise not only statistics on number, geographical distribution and other demographic indicators on older women but also qualitative research on the roles of older women in different cultures as well as their social and economic status. Older women can influence the acceptance of a project through their role as counsellors. Their support to the family and community also improves the productivity of younger generations. As a result, old women should be targeted in development planning

In terms of policy, measures are needed to improve income security, especially of groups at risk, namely single, divorced, widowed and childless old women. The social security (in the form of independent income), social integration, health status, housing and education of older women have to be put on the developmental agenda to ensure that ageing is possible in security, dignity and self-reliance. In particular it is essential to strengthen the family in its role as a support system, a role which is currently endangered by demographic, economic and social changes. It is to be hoped that the International Year of Older Persons 1999 will encourage such a shift in the focus of developmental politics.

References

Attias-Donfut, C. 1994. "Entre traditions et modernité: les incontournables aînés", in C. Attias-Donfut and L. Rosenmayr, *Vieillir en Afrique*. Paris: Presses Universitaires de France.

Attias-Donfut, C. and L. Rosenmayr, eds. 1994. *Vieillir en Afrique*. Paris: Presses Universitaires de France.

Dovlo, F.E. 1992. "Problems of the Impact of Social Change on the African Family", in N.B. Leidenfrost, ed., *Families in Transition*. Vienna: International Federation for Home Economics.

HelpAge International. 1995. *Older Women in Development*. London: HelpAge International.

International Federation on Ageing (IFA). 1985. *Women and Ageing Around the World*. Washington, DC: IFA Publications Division.

Ingstad, B. 1994. "The Grandmother and Household Viability in Botswana", in A. Aderanti and C. Oppong, eds., *Gender, Work and Population in Sub-Saharan Africa*. London: James Currey/Heinemann.

Journet, O. and A. Julliard. 1994. "Le van des grands-mères", in C. Attias-Donfut and L. Rosenmayr, *Viellir en Afrique*. Paris: Presses Universitaires de France.

Khasiani, S.A. 1994. "The Changing Role of the Family in Meeting the Needs of the Ageing Population in the Developing Countries, with Particular Focus on Eastern Africa", in *Ageing and the Family*. Proceedings of the United Nations International Conference on Ageing Populations in the Context of the Family, Kitakyushu, Japan, 15-19 October. New York: UN.

Lee, Y.J. and A. Palloni. 1992. "Some Aspects of the Social Context of HIV and its Effects on Women, Children and Families", in: *Population Bulletin of the United Nations* 33, pp. 64 - 87.

Owen, M. 1996. *A World of Widows*. London: Zed Books.

Rosenmayr, L. 1993. "Generationenbeziehungen im Entwicklungsprozess Schwarzafrikas", project report, Vienna.

Sangree, W.H. 1994. "Grand-parenté et statut des vieux à Tiriki (Kenya)", in Attias-Donfut, C. and L. Rosenmayr, *Viellir en Afrique*. Paris: Presses Universitaires de France.

United Nations (UN). 1975. *The Aging: Trends and Policies*. New York: UN.

_____. 1985. *The World Aging Situation: Strategies and Policies*. New York: UN.

_____. 1986b. *The Role of the Family in the Development Process*. No. 2. New York: UN

_____. 1991. *The World Ageing Situation 1991*. ST/CSDHA/14. New York : UN.

_____. 1992. *Paths to Productive Ageing*. DPI/1255. New York: UN.

_____. 1992a. *Income Security for an Ageing World*. DPI/1256. UN: New York.

_____. 1993. *Demographic Yearbook. Special Issue: Population Ageing and the Situation of Elderly Persons*. ST/ESA/STAT/SER.R/22. New York: UN.

_____. 1993a. "Older Persons in the Family: Facets of Empowerment". Occasional Papers Series No. 4, V.93-80195. UN: New York.

_____. 1994. "'The Elderly and the Family in Developing Countries". Occasional Papers Series No. 13, V.94-26135. UN: Vienna.

_____. 1994a. "The Intersection of Family, Gender and Economy in the Developing World". Occasional Papers Series No. 9. UN: Vienna.

_____. 1997. "Women"s Indicators and Statistics Database". 3rd Version. CD-ROM, UN: New York.

United Nations Population Fund (UNFPA). n.d. "Investing in Women: The Focus of the '90s". New York.

Older Women in Transition in Estonia: Continuing Care-givers

Silva Tedre and Taimi Tulva

Abstract

This paper examines some critical issues regarding the position of the elderly in Estonia. Ageing is both an individual and a social process which takes place in a situational and temporal context. People grow old within a particular culture, society and political system. Gender is one of the cultural features which determine the ageing process. People carry their life-histories with them and are affected by their past. Because ageing and the position of the elderly were not studied during the Soviet period, there are few studies concerning this issue. Moreover, a gendered approach to ageing is almost completely lacking. The position and problems of the elderly women represent a virtually unexplored area for sciences and official structures. The paper examines some gender-specific aspects of ageing in Estonia.

Introduction

The notion of gender, as used in this paper, is a hierarchically organized relation between men and women. It is produced and reproduced in a complex, multi-originated and multi-dimensional process, inseparable from social structures, institutions and different forms of practice. This system-oriented perspective emphasizes the fact that an asymmetrical gender-bound dichotomy and hierarchy exists on all levels (symbolic, structural and individual) of the gender system (Harding 1986). The structure is not stable, but ongoing. Recent scholars

199

(Acker 1992, Rantalaiho and Heiskanen 1997) have distinguished different levels where gendered processes occur: on the structural level, in interactions, in symbols and ideas.

This paper looks at some gendered structures of social systems and their connections with the position of elderly women in Estonia, exploring the ways in which cultural symbols and ideas construct the image and the status of gendered ageing. It takes a historical perspective on older women's lives, looking at how the ideals of women as well as their responsibilities, rights and opportunities have changed under different economic and political systems.

Unfortunately, available statistical data is sparse and the sources are eclectic, which obliges us to generalize in some instances. Because of the rapid changes in Estonian society statistics and findings tend to be outdated in a few months. The paper draws on two studies, the first of which describes trends in Estonian social policy, the nature of social problems and the areas in which they are concentrated. It examines Estonian history since the period of the first independence and explores the extent to which it has shaped the present situation (Tulva 1995; 1997). The second study is a survey of living conditions of the elderly in Estonia (Tulva 1998; Tulva et al 1999). Theme interviews and group discussions with Estonian women were also carried out in the autumn of 1994.

Anu's Story

Anu was born on 14 July 1930, in Novgorod, which is located in the western part of Russia, close to the border between Estonia and Russia. Her Estonian mother married a Russian man, with whom she moved to Novgorod in 1925. Up to that time Estonia had been an independent state for seven years. In 1937, during the Stalin-led persecutions, her father was taken away from home to an unknown place and accused of spying for Estonia because he was married to an Estonian woman. Anu was seven years old. It took over 50 years until the family learned that the father was not sent to a far-away internment camp as they were told but executed immediately after the pick-up. After his disappearance the mother took up cattle breeding, buying a few cows for the maintenance of the family. Tending the cows was left to seven-year-old Anu, who can still remember how difficult it was to herd them together.

When the Second World War started, the mother tried several times to leave Russia for Estonia where Anu's grandmother and other relatives were living. The border was closed, however, and deportations to Siberia began. Anu and her family - mother, sister and brother - were sent there, too. On the way to Siberia, in a railway station where the crowd was milling around, Anu and the rest of her family were separated and she could not find them. The girl was taken into a children's home in the Urals where she lived over a year until she learned her family's whereabouts. She travelled for many days with no ticket or money, but finally she traced them to a collective farm (*kolkhoz*) for Estonians in Novosibirsk region, deep in Siberia.

Life in Novosibirsk was extremely hard. The mother and children worked hard from morning till night. There was a serious shortage of food even in the kolkhoz. The nearest school was located a long way off, and finally Anu had to give up going to school, although her mother had hoped to avoid this. Since her husband's disappearance the mother longed for Estonia, no matter where they lived, in Novgorod or Siberia.

The mother died in Siberia and the children were sent to Estonia where they lived with their grandmother. During the Second World War Estonia was occupied twice by the Red Army and once by German troops. Already before the war Estonia had lost its independence, becoming a part of the Soviet Union. In Estonia Anu went back to school and qualified as a teacher of Russian. In this profession she worked more than 40 years. At that time, the Russian language gradually strengthened its position in the Estonian Soviet Socialist Republic.

Anu married an Estonian doctor. They had two children, a son and a daughter. She had a full-time occupation, while her mother-in-law did the housekeeping and cared for the children. For Anu education of the children has always been a great concern. In 1982 her son married. At first, the young couple settled in Anu's house sharing a single room, but after the first baby was born they decided to build a house of their own next door. Today the son and his wife have four children.

Anu retired on a pension shortly after Estonia regained its independence. She feels lucky that she managed to retire before the recent changes. She believes that older working people face a lot of problems, related to the new ideology of the free market and a new kind of ageism in society. Pensions in Estonia are low, but according to law a retired person is allowed to make a little extra. Since her retirement Anu has given some lessons in Russian, but there are only few Estonians who want to learn Russian. "I've tried to say to the children that the Russian language is not the one to be blamed for our difficulties during the Soviet regime," Anu says. She also takes care of her father-in-law who is 88 years old and lives under the same roof and occasionally nurses her grandchildren. Her husband is also retired and takes an active part in local politics.

Anu's story is not exceptional in Estonia, as many people share her Siberian experiences. Some people managed to move to the West during the war but those who stayed in Estonia kept the society running. According to the women who took part in group discussions for this study, it was the Estonian women who through these hard times took care of children and old people and formed a significant part of the labour force. They used to send food parcels and letters to their relatives and other Estonian exiles in Siberia. Those young women of war-time are the ageing women of today's Estonia. There are many other elderly people of several ethnic groups in the country. They are mostly Russians, Belarussians, Ukrainians and Ingrians who were sent or who had moved to Estonia. Cultural and social differences on the one hand, the common history of the Soviet regime and communist ideology on the other characterize the lives and circumstances of the older people in today's Estonia.

Women and Ageing in the Changing Social System

The Estonian Republic lies on the southeastern shore of the Baltic Sea and is the smallest of the three Baltic countries. According to the Baltic News Service, there are 1.5 million inhabitants in Estonia, 70 per cent of whom live in the cities. The capital is Tallinn, with about 30 per cent of the population. Since 1990 the population is decreasing because of high emigration of Russians and a decline in the birthrate. Estonians currently make up 65 percent of the population, which is steadily ageing.

In looking at women's position and social policy in Estonia, we can distinguish four different historical periods: the first period of independence (1918-1940), the years of war (1941-1944), the Soviet regime (1945-1991) and the new independence (1991 onwards). Estonia first gained independence in 1918 with the break-up of the Russian empire. This ended in 1940 when Estonia was occupied by the Soviet Union and became one of the Soviet Republics. During the mass deportations in June 1941, over 10,000 people were sent to Siberia, and on 25-26 March 1949, at least 20,700 people were banished. Among these victims were not only representatives of the intelligentsia or the affluent but also ordinary Estonians. Approximately 70,000 people fled abroad during the war, mainly to Germany and Sweden (The Baltic States 1991).

In the late 1980s, with the disintegration of the Soviet Union, women played an active role in the Estonian national movement, which struggled to re-establish the independent state. In 1989, hundreds of thousands of Estonians together with Latvians and Lithuanians protested the 50th anniversary of the Hitler-Stalin Pact (the basis for Soviet occupation) by linking hands and forming a 200-mile human chain that stretched from Tallinn to Vilnius, the capital of Lithuania. In Estonia independence was achieved by the so-called 'singing revolution', without armed conflict, in which women took to the streets and demonstrated alongside men. Political independence was re-established in 1991.

The First and the Second World Wars damaged the Estonian economy and killed a great many people, especially men. Several western studies (Pierson 1989, Satka 1994) have pointed out that during crises and especially in the upheavals of wars women tend to take care of the rest of their families and keep the society running. This seems to have been the case also in Estonia. According to the women we interviewed, women played an important role during each of the different phases of Estonia's history. Both world wars were followed by a lack of men, either because they were killed or had left for the West, or after the Second World War, because they were sent to Siberia or put in prison. In each case, women were employed in all kinds of jobs. During the first independence Estonia was still an agrarian country where most people earned their living in agriculture and women worked hard along with men. In the Soviet period, during Stalin's persecutions women at home supported their men in internment and labour camps, sending them letters and parcels.

Ideologically one image of womanhood is a feminine woman whose place is at home, in the family. Estonian women are said to be strong, sometimes even 'too strong', so that they have taken the responsibility and power away from men in family life. During the Soviet period, the women of the western islands of Estonia are said to have been especially strong because they had to get along without the help of their men in very hard circumstances. In Estonia the ideal takes the form of a mother-woman at the heart of family life who participates in public life mainly for her husband. While women's participation in politics has never been very active in Estonia, in practice, women have always been active in working life.

Yet in the immediate past it was expected that the older people would be helped by their children. The family was also thought to take responsibility for the dependent elderly. On the other hand, the parents were expected to support their adult children, too. In practice, it was often the grandmothers who took care of their grandchildren. This gender-specific system of care providing a great resource for young families with children, remained 'natural' and invisible in social planning and discussions throughout the different periods.

The First World War and the Estonian War of Independence (1918-1920), however, produced special groups who needed help, both invalids and orphans. Special attention was paid to the care of poor single mothers and children in order to improve their living conditions. The women's movement played an important role in the organization of social care and in the 1930s quite a few social care organizations were established for children and adults, among them the Estonian Red Cross, the Women's League and the Estonian Children's Care Foundation. In 1935 the Women's League created the Institute of Social and Home Economy. Women's role in these organizations was crucial. They not only received material aid but worked as volunteers.

After Estonia became annexed to the Soviet Union in 1940, politics, economy and the entire social sphere were subordinated to communist principles. Accordingly, the state social welfare system was centralized, organized primarily on the East European model of socialism that was elaborated in the 1930s. Many of the former social welfare methods were not acceptable in the Soviet system; thus for example social services at local municipality level were abolished. Social welfare depended heavily on grants of state pensions and allowances.

According to Soviet ideology, women's employment was a norm, intended to ensure equality between sexes in Soviet society. At the same time women assumed responsibility for family affairs. Household tasks and care of children or other people needing help were women's duty. While women's participation in working life was encouraged by the state-run day care system, social services for the elderly were not set up until the end of the 1980s, when non-institutional home-help services were developed and nursing homes for older people were built.

If, as some argue (Liljeström 1993: 163-174), one of the fundamental characteristics of the Soviet gender system was its effort to control all aspects of human life, the institution of the family played the major role in sustaining this effort. The family was maintained not only as an economic unit but also as a unit for social security and particularly as a unit for the care of children and old people. Most of the tasks of the private sphere were thought of as natural female tasks that women would automatically take on, despite the fact that they were also expected to take part in full-time working life in the public sphere. The family structures and patterns of socialization remained untouched and unquestioned in Soviet policy and communist ideology.

In Estonia women's employment was the highest in the Soviet Union. During the Soviet period women's wages remained systemically below the wages of men. The main reason for women's lower wages was the gendered division of labour. Therefore the strengthening of the gender dichotomy, the distance between male and female and its institutions is of essential importance for the reproduction of gender-differences of people, including the elderly.

Although civil organizations were banned during the Soviet period, women's activities in their families and social networks made progress. In 1987 the first voluntary organizations for aged, disabled and infirm people came into being, and thereafter the number of nursing homes and care institutions, financed and run by the state, grew. The workers of social institutions and services were mostly women and were often their clients, too.

Because all health care and social services were free of charge in the Soviet period and wages and prices were controlled by the state, the basic needs of retired people were met and the system guaranteed a certain material security for the elderly. According to the Pension Law, retirement age was 55 years for women and 60 years for men. However, people very often kept on working after their retirement. While the different retirement ages for women and men may have benefited women doing hard manual work, it also forced them to give up their full status of worker and enlist in the marginal labour force. Also women's pensions were smaller. Like all allocations and privileges in the Soviet era, pensions were based on the ideological value of people's activities, favouring political and trade union leaders, veterans of the war and work heroes. In these groups women formed a minority.

While the status of retired women seems to have been relatively low during both the first independence and the Soviet periods, elderly women seem to have had some authority within the family. We have no research for Estonia, but according to a study done in post-Soviet Russia (Gerasimova 1996), the image of elderly women in Russian culture is negative. In the age group 50-55, women were worried, for example, about belonging to the female sex, approaching pensionable age and losing their reproductive functions, which earlier guaranteed them a certain set of rights in various state and social institutions and organizations. They worried about the post-socialist social policy of the state, which treats aged people in a discriminatory manner, reflecting gerontophobic stereotypes of the public consciousness.

At the end of the Soviet period nearly 60 per cent of retired Russian working women were supporting their children and grandchildren, a role which reportedly strengthened their self-esteem and material independence (Gerasimova 1996). Nowadays, however, this group of women is often forced to adopt a more humble role in the family. Becoming economically more dependent, grandmothers have to live in the family of their descendants in the position of a servant, regardless of their education and cultural potential or personal history. The women in the countryside, however, help their children in towns with produce from their kitchen gardens.

At the same time, according to this study, many ageing women in Russia evaluate their situation with calm common sense. Their image of old age is idealised. Within these ideals, different symbolic patterns of behaviour are distinguished. Some women ignore the conventions of old age and defend their independence. Others emphasize their place in the social hierarchy. The third group can be characterized as the humble, invisible and subordinated.

Gendered Ageing Today

Ageing and gender differences in age distribution characterize today's Estonian population. Compared to the last years of the Soviet era, life expectancy has dropped for three years in succession. Today, every fifth Estonian is more than 60 years old. Judging by the health and socio-economic situation of the population, life expectancy for people born in 1996-1998 is estimated at about 70 years. At the moment, 43 per cent of the population is of working age, while 27 per cent is on a pension (old-age, disability, survivors' and national pensions). In 1993, the average life expectancy in Estonia was 67.5 years, for women it was 74.3 and for men 61.7 years. Women live approximately 12 years longer than men. In the age group 60-64, approximately 65 per cent of the population are women, in the age group over 80 years women's proportion is nearly 80 per cent.

Anu, the woman in our story above, lives in an ideal situation if we think about the present social policy in Estonia. She has no serious problems with her health. She has her own house and enough room to share with her husband and father-in-law. Her son and his family live in the neighbourhood, ready to help her if needed. At the moment Anu does not need any help. On the contrary, she has many activities and duties. She gives some lessons in Russian language. She is taking care of her father-in-law and sometimes also the grandchildren. Yet she has the feeling that her knowledge is not needed in post-socialist, modern society. From the gender perspective, there also seem to be differences between the norms and expectations concerning her and her husband. Her life is closely connected with family duties, whereas for her husband activity in the public policy arena is very important. She is expected to support opportunities of other people through her family roles and she is willing to do that.

Anu belongs to the family system in which close family connections are appreciated and thought to be 'natural'. As the son says: "We are living here together, four generations around the same yard. To my mind it is the only natural life style." Such family ideology seems to have been common in Russian culture and partly also in Estonian culture. The children's duty to take care of their aged parents is written in the new legislation of Estonia along with liability for maintenance between the grandparents and grandchildren. However, we can point to various trends in real life which will weaken the possibilities of realizing the ideology or of implementing the legislation.

Survey research (Tulva 1997) suggests that 69 percent of the retired people in the western parts of Estonia live alone (n=717). The number of single elderly women is especially increasing. The ideology of individualism and the process of urbanisation are weakening former social networks that were based on physical nearness and common social norms. During the urbanisation process it was the elderly who remained in the country while younger generations moved to the towns. The world wars as well as Stalin's terror destroyed a great many families and spread them all over the world. Moreover, after the new independence many young adults are moving abroad and the elderly stay in Estonia. Besides, the relatives of ethnic minorities might live far away in other parts of the former Soviet Union.

It seems evident that the status of families as well as women's roles and positions both in families and in the labour market are changing rapidly. Changes in the economy have caused increased economic differentiation among individuals and families. The number of single mothers is high as is the number of divorces. The marriage rate has declined since the end of the Soviet era. In 1987, 13,400 marriages were contracted and 6,100 couples divorced in Estonia. In 1996, the number of marriages was 5,510 and that of divorces was 5,499. Younger people prefer cohabitation to marriage and 40 per cent of children are born out-of-wedlock. (Tulva 1997). Also the number of abortions remains high. In 1991, the number of abortions was 152 per 100 births; in 1994, the number was 150 (Tulva 1997). A law was passed in 1994 that tried to reduce the number of abortions by imposing a fee to obtain them. In Soviet times and also afterwards, a shortage of contraceptives, as well as counselling, meant that abortions were used as a means of family planning.

Women do not want to have children because of the difficulties and uncertainty of everyday life. At the beginning of 1995, one in every five families in Estonia was classified as poor. High fees for kindergarten during the post-socialist period have cut family resources for childcare. Younger women are worried about coping and they fear unemployment at the same time as the ideology of housewifery seems to be growing stronger. Gender-segregated labour markets as well as women's lower salaries still exist.

Since 1991, insecurity and the inability to cope with problems in everyday life are increasing. The ageing population in particular is facing economic, social and psychological problems. It may be that the changes involved in the transition are more rapid than society's and individual's ability to adjust. Alternatively, it has been argued that Estonia is intentionally adopting a political-economic system which eliminates any social guarantee for people (Urponen and Vabar 1997). The median pension for the aged is 46 per cent of the median salary. As a result, people over age 71 are two times as likely to be poor as persons of other ages (World Bank 1996).

Estonia is considered to have a high rate of suicide, particularly among elderly women and middle-aged men (see Värnik 1997). More than half of the women who commit suicide are over the age of 54. In general, the suicide rate among men is four times higher than among women. Also the increase of illnesses is revealed by the growing number of disability pensions. The number of people who are able to draw an old-age pension in good health is decreasing every year.

Survey findings (Tulva 1998, Tulva et al 1999) show that old people have many problems with housing conditions. Heat is expensive and the buildings are of poor quality. Also the urban infrastructure is weak, creating difficulties with sanitation and transportation services. Moreover, the study shows that retired people in Estonia are suffering health problems as well as a break-down of social support networks. Over 40 per cent of the interviewees said that they have no children and 10 per cent named the municipal home helper as the closest person. So did most women over 80 years old. A significant number of interviewees said that they do not want to live with their children, either because relations were strained or because they do not want to burden their children. In the cities particularly, the interviewees said that they do not know their neighbours. They had a feeling that the neighbours do not care about them. In addition there is some evidence that violence towards old people within the family is quite common in present-day Estonia. Some older women feel unsafe with family members, especially with adult sons.

At the same time, the study (Tulva et al. 1999) found that every fifth retired person helps her/his grandchildren or children economically or practically. People also continually develop coping strategies. For example, in 1993, over half of the people in Tallinnn were growing food in their own gardens. The old women in the countryside deliver food from gardens to their relatives in cities, too.

The findings suggest that elderly people confront several difficulties concerning their everyday lives. Old people who belong to the ethnic minorities face special problems, including language problems, identity issues and the experience of exclusion or discrimination. Yet ageing as such is neither a disease nor a threat or problem; rather, the social reconstruction of age is one of the most profound social changes since the Second World War (Therborn 1995). In the entire industrialized world the proportion of older citizens is increasing, and that also means the proportion of frail older people. In Estonia, compared to western states, the change has been very rapid. At the same time, from the gender perspective, the status of ageing and also that of the frail elderly and their care will increasingly be more feminized (see Rauhala et al 1996).

In terms of social policy, Estonia's new Law of Social Care opens up a number of possibilities for helping people who cannot deal with their problems on their own. This was the first law for social care to be enacted in any of the former socialist republics. It regulates the services and determines conditions for applying for aid, relief and financing. Non-institutional care has been extensively developed in Estonia. In the cases of extreme need, retired persons are eligible for support from social services in the form of money or food and clothing. Social services are also provided by the church and volunteer organizations. Care and charity movements were not active before the 1990s. Their social services are in great demand by elderly people. Similarly since 1988 a vigorous citizens voluntary initiative has emerged in Estonia. In many, if not most of these new organizations, the role of women, especially retired women, is notable as both clients and volunteers. There are also signs that elderly women play an important role in informal social networks outside their families.

Conclusions

Wars, collectivization, industrialization, urbanization, repressed tensions among ethnic groups, as well as Stalin's terror moulded the lives of practically every family in the Soviet Union (Gerasimova 1996). The collapse of the Soviet Union in 1991 struck the societies unexpectedly in the sense that no socio-economic transition programme existed. Estonia has historically developed its political, economical and cultural relations with its neighbours: Russia, Latvia and the Scandinavian countries, and has had connections with Germany as well. At the moment, after 50 years of Soviet control, Estonia is searching for its own way to develop civil society and social policy.

A significant issue for social policy in the 1990s in all western countries is the care of the disabled elderly. There are, in principle, three ways to assign responsibility for the care of dependent people; to the state, to the market (private enterprises) and to the institutions of civil society (family, social networks, voluntary organizations). Different methods used by modern states have begun in very similar situations where the church, family and relatives had the responsibilities of these three spheres. Different politics and cultural traditions have led to various solutions for combining the responsibilities. Still, in every instance the care is gendered so that the women more often do the practical work.

Estonian social policy is oriented to support people who are most in need. The elderly need not only economic support (pensions, insurance) but also health-care services and a variety of non-institutional care services. In the future, physical and material as well as social support for the elderly can be organized through the networks of volunteers, neighbours, families and paid workers. They can be financed by the charity, by the municipalities, by the employers or employees, by old people themselves or by the state. In any circumstances the role of women is crucial.

An analysis of social policy and the elderly in Europe (Baldock and Evers 1991) concludes that it is a mistake to associate old age with need and dependency. The authors' review of European care systems shows that ageing as such does not mean illness or dependency, as retired people make a major contribution to caring, whether it be of grandchildren, less-able adult children or other older people. From the point of view of social policy, elderly women can be considered as a resource as well as a challenge to society. We note also that in practice elderly women can be seen as both care-givers and care receivers. In addition, they must be seen as active actors in every sphere of society - in the realm of policy, in social organizations, in education, in social networks, in the family and community.

The consequences of ageing for the elderly depend on the social context and social system where ageing takes place. In Scandinavian societies two basic changes can be seen which affect the way care is organized in the society and are connected with the individualism that characterizes modern society. First, disabled people are considered to have a right to their own homes. Second, the relationship between parents and children has become more equal as the economic dependence of children upon their parents has diminished as a result of the improving social security system. In addition, mothers do not like their daughters to have to work as their maids along with holding a regular job and taking care of their own home and family (Waerness 1990). In the Scandinavian context the support of the welfare state has been important for the quality of life of elderly people (Koskinen 1994).

We suggest that older women in Estonia are both developing new activities and suffering or calmly reconciling themselves to the changes. Research into the realities of ageing is urgently needed, since at the present too little is known about the everyday life and circumstances of older people. Gender must not remain invisible in future research.

An adequate and effective social policy should take into account how elderly women view their situation themselves depending on their health, social activity, life experiences, economic positions, family relationships and their participation in educational and cultural activities. Only then can we construct a more concrete perception of the actual role of elderly women in civil society, as well as of their activities and their needs.

References

Acker, J. 1992. "Gendering Organizational Theory", in A.J. Mills and P. Tancred, eds., *Gendering Organizational Analysis*. Newbury Park, CA: Sage Publications, pp. 248-60.

Baldock, J. and A. Evers. 1991. "Citizenship and Frail Old People: Changing Patterns of Provision in Europe", in N. Wanning, ed., *Social Policy Review*. London: Longman, pp.101-27.

The Baltic States. A Reference Book. Tallinn 1991.

Cavalcanti, C. 1996. *Estonia Living Standards During the Transition - A Poverty Assesment*. Tallinn: Eesti Raamat.

Gerasimova, T. 1996. "Elderly Women - a Challenge to Russia", in A. Rotkirch and E. Haavio-Mannila, eds., *Women's Voices in Russia Today*. Avebury: Aldershot Press, pp.175-88.

Harding S. 1986. *The Science Question in Feminism*. Ithaca, NY and London: Cornell University Press.

Koskinen, S. 1994. "Gerontologinen sosiaalityö vanhuspolitiikan mikrorakenteena" (Social Work among the Elderly as a Microstructure of Social Policy for the Elderly). *Acta Universitatis Lapponiensis* 3. Lapin yliopisto, Rovaniemi.

Liljeström, M. 1993. "The Soviet Gender System: The Ideological Construction of Femininity and Masculinity in the 1970s", in M. Liljeström, E. Mäntysaari and A. Rosenholm, eds., *Gender Restructuring in Russian Studies*. Helsinki: University of Tampere.

Pierson, R. 1989. "Beautiful Soul or Just Warrior: Gender and War", *Gender & History* 1 (1): 77-86.

Rantalaiho L. and T. Heiskanen, eds. 1997. *Gendered Practices in Working Life*. London: Macmillan.

Rauhala, P.L, M. Andersson, G. Eydal, O. Ketola, and N.Warming. 1996. "Why Are Social Care Services a Gender Issue?" in J. Sipilä, ed., *Social Care Services: The Key to the Scandinavian Welfare Model*. Avebury: Aldershot Press, pp. 131-52

Satka, M. 1994. "Sota-ajan naiskansalaisen ihanteet naisjärjetöjen arjessa" (The ideals of women's citizenship through the everyday lives of women's organizations), in A. Anttonen, L. Henriksson and R. Nätkin, eds., *Naisten hyvinvointivaltio* (The Women's Welfare State). Helsinki: Vastapaino.

Sipilä, J. 1996. *Social Care Services: The Key to the Scandinavian Welfare Model*. Avebury: Aldershot Press.

Tedre, S. forthcoming. "Finnish Gender Contracts in Care of the Elderly - The Case of Public Home Help Services", *Joensuun yliopisto, yhteiskuntapolitiikan laitos. Joensuu*.

Therborn, G. 1995. *European Modernity and Beyond: The Trajectory of European Societies 1945-2000.* London and New Delhi: Sage Publications.

Tulva, T. 1995. "Viron sosiaalityön muotoutuminen murroskaudella (Formation of Social Work in Estonia under Transition Period)", *Acta Universitatis Lappoensis* 8. Rovaniemi.

_____. 1997. "Vana ja uus Eesti hoolekandes (Old and New: Estonian Welfare in Transition)', *Tallinnna Pedagoogikaûlikool. Sotsiaalteaduskond. Sotsiaaltööosakond.* Tallinn: AS SPIN PRESS.

Tulva, T., ed. 1997. *Some Aspects of Estonian Social Work and Social Policy.* Tallinn University of Educational Sciences. Tallinn: AS SPIN PRESS.

Tulava, T. 1998. *Teaduselt praktikale: Uurimusi ja arutlusi sotsiaaltöö teemadel.* (From theory to practice: studies and ideas about social work). Tallinna pedagoogikaülikool. Sotsiaaltöö osakond. Tallinn: Talinna pedagoogikaülikool.

Tulva, T., S. Tedre and S. Koskinen. 1999, *Eläkeläisten selviytyminen ja avun tarve Virossa* (The living conditions and the need of help among retired people in Estonia). *Gerontolgia* 3 (vol 13).

Urponen, K. and M. Vabar. 1997. "Problems and Alternatives for Estonian Social Policy", in T. Tulva, ed., *Some Aspects of Estonian Social Work and Social Policy.* Tallinn University of Educational Sciences. Tallinn: AS SPIN PRESS.

Värnik, A 1997. Enesetapud Eestis 1965-1995 *(Suicides in Estonia, 1965-1995). Tallinn: AS SPIN PRESS.*

Waerness, K. 1990. "Informal and Formal Care in Old Age. What Is Wrong with the New Ideology in Scandinavia Today?" in C. Ungerson, ed., *Gender and Caring. Work and Welfare in Britain and Scandinavia.* Hertfordshire, UK: Harvester Wheatsheaf, pp. 110-31.

World Bank. 1996, Estonia. *Living Standards During the Transition. A Poverty Assessment.* Report No 15647 - EE, Document of the World Bank. June 17.

Old Age, Gender and Marginality in Peru: Development for the Elderly

Fiona C. Clark

Abstract

The elderly are a neglected minority in Peruvian public and social policy and marginalized subjects within development initiatives and popular organizations. This paper brings together discussions of gender bias and life course in an analysis of the situation of the elderly in Lima, Peru. It illustrates the way in which the accumulation of gender bias affects women in later life, resulting in their economic and social marginalization. Looking at recent state reforms in Peru, in particular at structural adjustment and pension reform, it illustrates the economic exclusion suffered especially by elderly women. It analyzes the role of the family and urban social movements in reinforcing old people's social exclusion and ultimately highlights the inherently gendered nature of old age. Finally, it looks at current initiatives to include elderly women in development programmes, and the need to acknowledge old age and ageing as legitimate and pressing development issues in order to avert an old-age crisis.

Introduction: An Ageing World

In Latin America, as in other parts of the world, increasing numbers of people are surviving into old age and their presence in the population is becoming more marked. In 1980 the total population of Latin America was 363.7 million, with the elderly (those over age 60) numbering 23.3

million (6.4 per cent). The elderly population is expected to reach 7.2 per cent (41 million) by the year 2000 and 10.8 per cent (93 million) by the year 2025 (Gutierrez Robledo 1989). Such demographic change poses a great challenge to governments and policymakers for the 21st century as the proportion of elderly people in Latin America increases without the accompanying rise in affluence required to cater for their needs. Peru's elderly currently run to roughly 1.5 million people (of which 30 per cent live in Lima), making up 7 per cent of the population. As such, "Peru is still a predominantly 'young' country and thus the elderly sector has, frankly, been largely left by the wayside" (interview with Dra. Blanca Deacon, *ProVida*, Lima, June 1998). Central to this issue is the gendered nature of old age and the accumulation of gender bias experienced by many elderly women that has so far gone unacknowledged.

A wealth of work exists on gender inequalities in Latin America illustrating how development processes have exacerbated gender gaps (Fisher 1993; Jaquette 1989; Jelin 1992; Lind 1992; Moser 1993; Nash and Safa 1986; Radcliffe and Westwood 1993). Research has, however, tended to concentrate on the inequalities that affect girls or women in the 'productive' part of their life-course, while ignoring the relative disadvantage women suffer later on in life (Gorman 1995, Tout 1989). The gender gap in life expectancy (with women generally outliving men) and the propensity of women to get married young, to older men, means that early widowhood, loneliness and dependency are almost inevitable for women in old age. Their opportunities are significantly limited due to the accumulated gender bias experienced earlier in life.

Women's relative disadvantage in life, through gender bias in health, education, and employment, means that they can face more severe difficulties in old age than men. "Elderly women are likely to suffer problems accruing not only from present abandonment, but also from earlier disadvantage" (Tout 1989: 289). In fact "It is precisely the accumulating disadvantage they suffer in later life, that makes women in poverty particularly vulnerable" (Gorman 1995:122). We cannot approach women as a homogeneous category as their situation will vary depending on marital status, residential status, family circumstances and private transfers, among others. Yet, women in general have to cope with irregular and unreliable income flows during their productive years and older women are therefore less likely than men to be able to secure economic stability for their later, 'unproductive' years which, along with poorer education and opportunity, considerably reduces their chance of independence. The gender bias in opportunity and access to resources continues into old age, when women suffer further exclusion from pension funds and social security support. The characteristics of gender relations in Peru mean that the experience of old age is similarly gendered, with significant consequences for the marginalization of elderly women.

The situation of Peru's *ancianos* (elderly), a minority long neglected, is currently being compounded by conditions of economic austerity and structural adjustment, as the state, the family and community organizations are undergoing a period of reform, leaving the elderly marginalized from all three. The ageing of the population and the feminization of old age, as more and more people survive into old age and women's longevity typically exceeds that of men, means that many people are living out their later years in poverty, isolation and abandonment. Yet old age is a time and a term that is still excluded from daily life, community development and development agendas in general. This paper explores the relationship between old age, gender and marginality in the context of reforms and shortfalls within formal and informal support networks for the elderly in Peru. After a brief discussion of Peru's ageing population and the feminization of old age, it concentrates on recent reforms within the state to highlight the gender, formal economy and urban bias in access to pension funds and economic stability in old age. The assumed passivity and burden of elderly women is challenged through an analysis of elderly women's role within the household, and a look at women's social movements.

The paper is based on personal research carried out in 1996 and 1998 in two low-income communities and one middle-income community in Lima. The research area was chosen with the aim of pointing out gaps within the Gender and Development literature that tend to obscure the presence of the elderly, challenging discussions around state reform and structural adjustment in Latin America, and also to challenge the popular beliefs around women's organization and the women's movement in Peru. Since the situations described are by no means exclusive to Peru, I hope to highlight some of the issues concerning gender, poverty and marginality in old age that can and do affect virtually any region.

A State in Transition: Economic Reform in Peru

The situation that faced President Fujimori on his election in 1990 was one of long-term economic crisis and a state of civil war. By 1990 58 per cent of Peru's population was estimated to be living below the poverty line, and the poverty gap, or percentage difference between the richest and poorest per capita income was calculated at 23 per cent (IADB 1997).[1] Since then, Peru has undergone significant changes - politically, economically and socially. The severe austerity measures introduced by President Fujimori in 1990 formed part of the reforms that kick-started Peru's economic recovery after the profound crisis of the 1980s. In a period that has come to be known as the Fuji-Shock, Fujimori embraced neo-liberal policies wholeheartedly and introduced his own stabilization policies in an attempt to regain the support of international financial institutions and encourage foreign investment.[2] Public expenditure was cut, a stringent taxation system was introduced, the currency was devalued and large-scale privatization of state-owned enterprises got underway. Since 1990 Fujimori has privatized, amongst others, the electricity company, the telephone service and parts of the education system, and introduced a private pension scheme (Barrientos 1995; 1996, PROMPERU 1997). These measures had considerable impact on various sectors of society, including the elderly population, in terms of their poverty and economic exclusion.

HelpAge International argues that the 'old age crisis' (World Bank 1994) is not so much a result of demographic change but rather the result of the negative social impacts of structural adjustment policies on the poor and vulnerable, and most notably on poor women and older people (HAI 1995). Therefore, they suggest that the situation of the elderly (and particularly elderly women) in Latin America has been exacerbated by the economic crisis of the 1980s and early 1990s and the adoption of neo-liberal economic policies. A variety of literature highlights the gender bias in structural adjustment policies, suggesting that in general it is women who suffer more in times of austerity and economic rationalization (Beneria and Feldman 1992; Cornia et al 1987; Elson 1995; Glewwe and Detray 1991; Moser 1990; Tanski 1994; Tinker 1990). These analyses however have failed to address the issue of elderly women, the effect of austerity on their lives and their role in survival strategies. Social security reform and public expenditure reduction, as important components of

---

[1] It is worth noting that the main indicators of 'poverty' tend to be infant mortality rate, levels of child nutrition and real income of people in the 'productive' labour force. Such analysis obscures the conditions for the elderly as they are excluded from, or rather 'invisible' in such data sets. Poverty in the elderly population may therefore be more severe than general poverty levels indicate (INEI/UNDP 1997).

[2] This process was finalized with the signing of Peru into the Brady Plan in May 1996.

structural adjustment programmes, have affected pension funds and health services particularly badly (Barrientos 1996).

Peru's Pension Reform

In the 1980s, pension systems throughout Latin America were beset by inefficiency and poor rates of returns and investment, ultimately leading to their financial collapse with a pronounced fall in the ratio of contributors to beneficiaries (Lloyd-Sherlock 1992; 1997). Peru was no exception. Thus, the neo-liberal economic package adopted by President Fujimori to eradicate government inefficiency and reduce state intervention included a privately funded pension scheme. The *Sistema Privado de Pensiones* (Private Pension System SPP), which now runs parallel to the old *Sistema Nacional de Pensiones* (National Pension System SNP), was introduced in June 1993 and follows the Chilean model almost to the letter (Barrientos 1996; Clark 1998; Clark and Laurie, forthcoming; Downs 1997, Ruiz 1998). While elements of the reforms have been beneficial, a number of shortfalls can be identified. For despite better, more profitable financial investment, the post-reform system perpetuates the same gender, formal sector and urban biases of the old system, hampering the participation of poorer workers and especially limiting women's ability to make contributions or receive financial benefits.

The coverage of the Peruvian pension system is still very low. Of the population aged 60 and over in 1993, 36.5 per cent were still economically active (of which 78.1 per cent were men). Of the 63.5 per cent who were no longer economically active only 21.3 per cent received a pension, 53 per cent of them living in Lima (*INEI* 1994). Since the reform, still only 38 per cent of Peru's economically active population (EAP) are covered by some sort of pension scheme, with 20 per cent in the public pension system and 18 per cent in the private one (Downs 1997). This means that many people are forced to work late into life in order to survive. This is especially true for women, who either rely on their husband's pension or have to go without altogether. *INEI* data indicate that in 1994, 90.6 per cent of people aged 60 or over in Peru who received a state pension were men. Of those reliant on the spouse's pension 99.6 per cent were women, reflecting the presence of women in the household and their limited access to formal economy employment and associated pension schemes. As one analyst concludes, "for many women in developing countries the descent into total dependency begins with the death of the husband" (Gorman 1995:121). A widow's pension in the private pension system is 42 per cent of her husband's full pension, with no dependent children and 35 per cent with them (Ruiz 1998). The widow, in addition to the loss of her husband, therefore also has to face widowhood with more than a 50 per cent reduction of her spouse's pension, reducing many elderly women to poverty.[3]

Similarly, the affiliation rate of women to either the public or the private pension schemes is very low. In May 1998 the percentage of female affiliates in the private pension scheme was roughly 30 per cent (of which the majority were not near pensionable age), significantly above the national pension system's 9.4 per cent, but limitations and biases against women's participation still exist (SAFP 1998). Both the state and the private pension scheme focus on formal wages and salaries, and consequently, coverage is concentrated in the high-income, urban and formal sectors of the economy (Cox and Jimenez 1992), thus limiting most women's access to them.

A woman's opportunity to participate in pension schemes is significantly limited by the accumulated gender bias suffered through disadvantages in education and the labour market. While there has been an increase in the participation of women in the Peruvian labour force in recent years (Burgos 1990; Tanski 1994), this has occurred mainly in the informal sector. Opportunities for women within the formal economy are limited due to women's lack of education and the need to combine waged work with reproductive tasks: "Because women also have to fulfil home production or domestic roles, they have greater time and mobility constraints, which can result in their 'preference' for choosing lower paying (informal) jobs that are nevertheless compatible with child care" (Tanski 1994:1633). Furthermore, gender segregation within the labour market is such that women are confined to certain gender-ascribed occupations which are usually less well paid and carried out in worse conditions than much of men's work (MacEwan Scott 1995; Beneria and Feldman 1992).

The minimum recommended contribution period in order to accrue the equivalent of a minimum pension is 20 years.[4] This contribution

---

[3] A woman's pension does not include a survivor's pension for her husband, were she to die before him (Ruiz 1998).

[4] In other Latin American countries, this requirement refers to eligibility for a minimum pension. In order to qualify for the minimum pension set by the government, the member needs to be able to show at least 20 years of contribution into the fund. Peru is the only

period can be problematic for many people, but women have particular difficulty due to frequent gaps in their employment and low, unreliable income flows. Furthermore, a significant part of women's earnings is more likely to be made up of non-monetary income by payment in kind or private transfers (Grown and Sebstad 1989; Moser 1981; Leacock and Safa 1986), which makes the calculation of pension contributions very difficult. Thus many women's productive work and type of income do not facilitate regular contributions to a pension fund.

This problem - and that of informal sector workers in general - is two sided. On the one hand, women working in the informal sector are unlikely to receive sufficient regular income to be able to contribute to a pension fund (whether public or private) and accrue a sufficient amount for their old age. Moreover, even those informal sector workers who do accrue sufficient income may not want to register in a pension fund due to the requirement to declare their income in order to calculate the contribution -- which may force them to pay taxes, something that informal sector

Table 1: Pension Contributions for Dependent and Independent Workers

| | Dependent worker | | Independent or informal worker | |
| | SPP | SNP | SPP | SNP |
	worker paid	*worker paid*	*worker paid*	*worker paid*
obligatory contribution	*8%	8%	8%	8%
commission for AFP[a]	2%	2.5%	2%	2.5%
insurance	1.5%	2.5%	1.5%	2.5%
total	11.5%	13%	11.5%	13%
	employer paid	*employer paid*	*worker paid*	*worker paid*
Health insurance	4.5%	4.5%	4.5%	4.5%
FONAVE ◊	4.5%	4.5%	4.5%	4.5%
tax	1.5%	1.5%	1%	N.A.
total	10.5%	10.5%	10%	9%
TOTAL	22%	24.5%	21.5%	24%
Worker's share	11.5%	13%	21.5%	24%

* Percentage of worker's income,
[a] Administradoras de Fondos de Pensiones (Pension Fund Administrators)
◊ *Fondo Nacional de Vivienda* (National Fund for Housing)
Source Constructed from interview with Hilman Farfán Ruiz, SAFP, June 1998

Latin American pension system not to have a guaranteed minimum pension (Downs 1997).

workers are generally able to avoid. In fact, many workers continue to see pension contributions as a tax which reduces their income, and not as an investment in the future (Downs 1997; Cox and Jimenez 1992). Furthermore, the cost of investing in a pension fund is far higher for an informal or independent worker than for a dependent one, whose employer covers half the costs. The incentives for low-income and informal sector workers to invest in a pension fund are therefore few, and a life punctuated by gender bias increases the risk of economic difficulty for women in old age.

On the other hand, the likelihood that contributions by informal sector workers will be inconsistent, thereby reducing revenue to the fund's administrators, means there is little incentive for the AFPs to encourage low, irregular income earners to invest in their pension fund (with high competition between the five funds for economic viability and higher profit margins, see Downs 1997). AFPs typically pursue customers with high incomes who make regular contributions into their accounts. Women therefore are not seen as an attractive investment as a result of the predicted gaps in their income, due not only to child bearing but also to their more insecure and unreliable employment and incomes.

Besides the economic difficulties in which this leaves elderly women, their lack of access to a pension is yet another denial of their life-time's work. Just as "employment gives a person the recognition of doing something worth his or her while" (Sen, quoted in Bhalla and Lapeyre 1997:420), I would argue that a decent pension acknowledges a lifetime of hard work, recognizing the contribution made by the worker and justifying his or her inclusion in the economic and social processes of the community. However, many elderly are marginalized from their communities, firstly through lack of income, but also through the conceptualization of what constitutes 'work' and the 'worker'. A woman's lack of a pension further undervalues the work that she has done throughout her life and confines her again to the notion of mother and wife inherent in her gender role. Furthermore, this work so often goes undervalued by the women themselves.

> Frequently an elderly woman, when asked if she 'works' will reply 'no', even though she spends most of her day selling vegetables or fruit in the market, or selling home prepared food in the street ... this is a problem in society that this kind of informal work is not given the value it deserves and is not seen

as 'work'. (Elia Luna, PROMUDEH-Ministry for the Promotion of Women and Human Development, Lima, July 1998)

The creation of a private pension scheme, while avoiding the corruption and inefficiency notorious in state institutions and improving the investment portfolio and profit returns for affiliates, fails to address underlying inequalities and reinforces the gender, urban and formal economy biases that lead to the exclusion of a growing (and the poorest) proportion of the population from receiving benefits. The reform of the pension system cannot happen in isolation, but needs to be seen in context with the other sectors of the economy and the way in which this affects enrolment for the lower-income groups. If Peru is really to avert its old age crisis, then a more concerted effort needs to be made to address inherent structural gender and formal sector biases within the labour market and the economy. There is an urgent need for a model designed specifically for independent workers, and it is essential that this takes into account the gendered nature of work and incomes if women are to enjoy at least some economic independence and stability in old age.

Gender and Social Marginalization

Besides economic differences, older men and women also experience different social and familial relationships which shape their adaptation to later life. Nan Stevens, in an article on elderly widows, states that "well-being in widowhood is a function of gender, background resources, primary relationships and relational needs" (Stevens 1995:45). The results of questionnaires carried out with an elderly people's club in the middle income area of *Pueblo Libre* showed that an elder person's experience of old age depended largely on their role within the family home and their gender role and the responsibilities it ascribes them.

The gender division of labour ascribes men and women certain jobs and roles throughout their life course (Katz and Monk 1993), until the point in old age where the loss of these roles poses a significant obstacle to adaptation to late adulthood and is one of the principal factors in the social exclusion of the older person. Dra. Blanca Deacon of *ProVida* emphasises the fact that both men and women suffer role losses, but that the severity of this loss depends on the individual's ability to accept it and adapt accordingly.

> For the man it is very difficult to accept his state of 'unemployment', it takes a lot for him to accept that he no longer has a title as a worker and it takes him time to adapt and make

the first step. Socio-cultural factors play a large role in the elderly person's adaptation to his or her later life. (Lima, June 1998)

Discussions with Dra. Deacon and responses to the questionnaires confirm Stevens' point that women are better able to adapt as they have had to face many role changes in their lives:

Throughout adulthood women are subjected to repeated role loss and the necessity for readjustment, a socialisation process that facilitates the adjustment of women in old age. Their lifelong socialisation which involves dealing with certain societal disadvantages and adapting to change within their multiple careers as workers, housewives, wives and mothers, helps many women develop a kind of flexibility. (Stevens 1995 :55)

Furthermore, women in old age, even if they lose their role as worker, rarely lose their role as wife, mother or grandmother. Two-thirds of respondents to questionnaires claimed that a man's life would in fact be more difficult in old age as he does not have the same domestic role as the woman to keep him occupied and give him a role in old age:

Women do not get depressed as much, as they have things at home to do, but men get depressed easily and feel they are of no more use to work...

A woman's life in old age is more bearable than a man's as she can accompany her daughter or daughter in law in raising the grandchildren...

When a man retires he easily gets depressed and gets in the way at home, the woman has house chores to do to keep her occupied. ...(Members of club de ancianos 'Autocuidado 19', ProVida, Lima, July 1998) [5]

While this continuation of a role into old age may be seen as advantageous by some women, it also means more work. Not only do women continue to serve their husbands (if these are still alive) but also their children and grandchildren, thus providing a potential source of relief to the household workload. Elia Luna of *PROMUDEH* turns this 'advantage' for women around:

---

[5] Interestingly it was the women respondents who were conscious of this difference. The male respondents claimed there to be no difference at all in the experience of old age for men and women, except perhaps health differences.

Elderly men live a very different reality to elderly women as the men have been attended and served all their life and this continues into old age, whereas women have, in our culture, always been the servers and the submissive and they continue to do so in older age ... They are the tired ones now. (July 1998)

Much literature emphasizes the fact that care for the elderly has 'traditionally' been the responsibility of the extended family (HAI 1995, Gutierrez Robledo 1989; Tout 1989), although the quality of care is seldom questioned. Yet evidence suggests that social and economic changes have created a situation where the needs and integration of the elderly are increasingly marginalized. Whereas previously, old people were rare within the Peruvian family due to low life expectancy, today's family is faced with the longer survival of its older members, increasing the potential burden on the family resource base - particularly as the opportunities for elderly people (and especially elderly women) to find paid work and contribute to household finances are few. Research by HelpAge International suggests that "where elderly people live with their adult children, the presence of an extra person strains the limited resources of the family (particularly if that person is not in the labour market), reinforcing the elderly people's view of themselves as a burden" (in Gorman 1995:120).

My own research, however, suggests that contrary to being a burden, the grandparent often takes over the mother's household domestic duties in order to release her for responsibilities of 'productive' work. "Child minding by grandparents for their working children is exchanged for care and protection of the older family members" (Gorman 1995:120). However, this invisible and unremunerated work by (mostly) elderly women very often goes unrecognized, thus reinforcing the view of the elderly as 'unproductive' and in need of care and financial support. The image of *'pobrecito anciano'* portrays the older person as a passive victim of their age rather than a potentially active, productive and beneficial citizen. I would suggest that the role of the grandparent (and especially the grandmother) may well be very important in supporting the reproductive tasks of the family (and thus indirectly the 'productive work'). This is especially the case in the rising number of female-headed households where problems are becoming increasingly diverse (Burgos 1990; Chant 1997; Moore 1994; Moser 1993; Tanski 1994).

Thus old age, like other periods in the life cycle, is complex and diverse, and is influenced by a multitude of factors that determine the older person's well-being and social marginalization. All elderly people suffer, through their explicit marginalization from most societies, but their suffering is influenced by their gender role and gender identity, which in turn affect their financial, material and social resources in old age. Although beyond the scope of this paper, race and ethnicity also have great bearing on the exclusion of the elderly, especially as many of the elderly in the urban peripheral areas of Lima are migrants from the mainly Quechua speaking highlands of Peru (see Clark 1998; Clark and Laurie forthcoming; De la Cadena 1998).

Marginalization of the Elderly: A Challenge for Urban Social Movements

Another factor influencing the *ancianos'* poverty and social exclusion is their involvement and role in the community. In Lima, a city renowned for its successful social movements, it is assumed that communities work together to provide safety nets for those elderly people unable to provide for themselves. The 1980s and 1990s have witnessed a deluge of academic writing on the social dynamics of collective action in Latin America (Escobar and Alvarez 1992; Fisher 1993; Jaquette 1989; Moser and Peake 1987; Nash and Safa 1986; Radcliffe and Westwood 1993). In Peru, women's grassroots activities have become emblematic of the 'new social movements' (see Escobar and Alvarez 1992, Jelin 1992). I would like to challenge the success of these organizations by reviewing the extent to which they have incorporated the elderly and especially elderly women as both benefactors and social actors. I will focus especially on the *Comedores Populares* (soup kitchens) and the *Vaso de Leche* (glass of milk) programme which reflect different types of Latin American urban social movements and are well known outside Peru.

Both the *Comedores Populares* and *Vaso de Leche* were set up at the start of the 1980s, as an attempt to cushion against the economic crisis. While the *Comedores Populares* were started as a strategy by grassroots women to ensure the survival of their households (Barrig 1996; Moser and Peake 1987), the *Vaso de Leche* programme was a state-implemented initiative designed to improve child nutrition specifically, but also to include pregnant women and the elderly in its target group. Both these organizations are now controlled by women's groups. Although both are heralded as successful grassroots women's organizations in the gender and development and poverty literature, my research suggests that the elderly remain invisible as actual benefactors or participants in these programmes. Neither the need of elderly women for these organisations nor their support for them is recognized. Despite the fact that the elderly constitute a major target group, they are generally excluded from these organizations.

Discussions with the *dirigentes* (leaders) of the Clubs de Tercer Edad in Lima showed that none of the groups had managed to receive any help for their members from the local *Comedores,* despite having asked and pressured them many times. Unless the elderly can afford to pay a contribution to the *Comedor* (1-2 *soles* a week), they do not receive any help. The director of the club *San Juan de Dios* had managed to arrange with the local municipality to have six of their members eat in the municipal *Comedor.* However, as this *Comedor* is situated down in the main part of *independencia* (a ten-minute bus ride or half an hour walk away), the chosen six could not go and eat as they could not pay the bus fare and it was too far for them to walk down and up the steep hill.

Similar accounts were given with regard to the V*aso de Leche* programme:

> Even the *Vaso de Leche* hasn't given me any help. I went and said to them, 'Please, I too need milk', but they said, 'for old women, no. This is for babies, for the little ones'. (Señora, member of Club de la Tercer Edad, San Juan de Dios, 1998)

The *Vaso de Leche* programme is one of the few in Peru which actually attempted to address the needs of the elderly and include them in the initial planning process. However, because of internal corruption and difficult economic circumstances, the elderly have once again been marginalized as a 'low priority'.[6]

> There they clearly told me that the V*aso de Leche* was only for children. I even stood in the doorway waiting for left-overs, and still they didn't give me any'. (Señora, member of Club de la Tercer Edad, San Juan de Dios, 1998)

The *Club de Tercer Edad San Juan de Dios*has managed to come to an arrangement with the local V*aso de Leche* that gives the group twelve

---

[6] There was much speculation in the interviews on the running of both programmes, with group members claiming that the people that worked in the programmes kept the food and milk for themselves and that money went astray.

bags of milk and seven bags of oats per week.[7] The leader of the group collects the milk and the oats together for six or seven weeks until there is enough for everyone (two bags of milk and one of oats each). This means that each individual receives a ration from the *Vaso de Leche* every six to seven weeks which they should be receiving every week. This was organized through the *Club de Tercer Edad* rather than the local committees in charge of administering the programme.

The stories abound, but the point to be made here is that many of the elderly in the urban peripheral areas of Lima, that are perhaps most in need of assistance with their food, are being excluded from the benefits of the above organizations.

Furthermore, both the *Vaso de Leche* programmes and the *Comedores Populares* are viewed as having led to the empowerment of grassroots women, enabling them to enter the public and political arena of everyday life within the urban peripheral settlements of Lima (Arana Ward 1996; Barrig 1991; 1996, Bonini 1989; Moser and Peake 1987). However, one observer argues that analyses of these organizations (especially through gender and development paradigms) "have led to the promotion of certain categories of women (young, single, metropolitan) at the expense of older, 'provincial' women" (Laurie, in press). Much of women's involvement in the community and community organizations is under the premise of their role as mothers; thus elderly women, having passed the reproductive stage, are assumed to have outlived this role. Consequently, elderly women are assumed to play no active part in the running of these organizations and furthermore to be neither empowered by nor involved in them.

Existing literature and public opinion both herald the involvement of young women and mothers in the success of the *Comedores Populares* and the *Vaso de Leche* programmes. While their involvement is of course crucial and visible, interview material showed that these women often in fact do not have or make the time to participate fully in the running of the programmes. Rather it is often the elderly women and grandmothers that organize and work in these groups. Thus despite the fact that the elderly are excluded as beneficiaries of these programmes (Clark and Laurie forthcoming), many elderly women in fact play a crucial role in supporting them, either directly or indirectly, as can be seen in the

---

[7] Each bag of milk makes a litre, enough to mix with half a bag of oats for one family breakfast.

remarks of a young mother in the *Vaso de Leche* Tablada de Lurin in Lima:

> In *comité* number six, there is nothing but arguments, 'I don't have time to go, you should go ... the only one who goes (to pick up the milk) is my mother, my mother and the neighbour, while the other women there sit idle with their husbands and children and don't help with even one glass of milk. All her life my mother has gone and fetched the milk, ever since the centre opened, while other *Señoras* sit and complain that 'no, I can't go because I have to look after my children, I can't go because I've too much to do'... and my mother? I suppose she doesn't have anything better to do? She, as it happens, has to look after her grandchildren because her daughters are out working. (1996)

This woman's comments challenge two important assumptions about the *Vaso de Leche* programme and organizations like it. First, it makes the point that, instead of 'empowering' women and relieving them of their drudgery, participation in such community organizations puts an extra burden on some women who already face a heavy workload and responsibility in looking after their family, the household and, especially in female-headed households, also performing remunerated work. Second, it shows that under such circumstances the running and continuing success of such programmes, very often in fact, relies on the work of elderly household members, and grandmothers in particular. Their perceived passivity and status as *'pobrecita'*, victims of their age and a burden to their families, obscures the value of the work and support elderly women give to their families and the local community. The help of the grandmother within the household (described above) may be what allows the younger women time to participate in the activities of the *Comedor Popular* or the *Vaso de Leche* - if the grandmother herself does not also take on this responsibility.

The social exclusion that many elderly suffer through being denied access to the benefits of programmes such as the two described above is unjustified, especially in the face of the crucial support that many of them lend to their households in the form of child care and domestic work. Also, the importance to these elderly women themselves of their participation in the *Vaso de Leche*, the *Comedores* and other such organizations often goes unacknowledged. All too often elderly women are faced with the reality that, having outlived the reproductive part of their life cycle, they are assumed to be useless and 'beyond their time', and present a burden to the family and the community, and often perceive themselves as such. The following remarks, however, indicate how important participation in such organizations can be for elderly women and what effect the exclusion from them can have on their lives.

> I have always been in the *Vaso de Leche* and the *Comedores*, but once I got older and started not feeling so well, I had to withdraw from my activities. I felt very poorly and so I had to stop. So now I sit here, stuck in my house, I am left very lonely. I had got used to always mixing with local people and having contact with local institutions. Now I've been left feeling very alone, uncomfortable. It really hit me hard and I was very depressed. I saw myself getting worse because I wasn't participating anymore. So that's when I decided to form my own group, of *Señoras* like me, a group for elderly people. So since 1993, my husband and I have been working on this - working, working - but still we receive no help and yet every day I see more elderly people, lonely ... (Señora, age 62, Club de Tercer Edad 'Los Tigres', El Ermitaño, Independencia 1998)

The majority of the members of the clubs are women, emphasizing that they are as important to them as they are assumed to be to younger women. I in fact would argue that for reasons of community integration and reducing their social marginality, the involvement of older women in community organizations such as these is very important. Furthermore, these women, while they are fit and healthy enough, may have more 'spare time' than their daughters, depending on whether they have responsibilities in the household or as child care providers or whether they continue to work. They provide a potentially large and relatively undemanding group of participants for the efficient execution of programmes such as the *Vaso de Leche* and the *Comedores Populares*.

Those lauding the successes of Lima's grassroots organizations have assumed them to be beneficial to the community as a whole. Focusing largely on the role of women as mothers and activists, they have emphasized the empowerment or upward mobility that involvement in community activities can bring for potential women leaders. Yet, few have looked at whether some groups may be excluded from the organizations' activities and no one has acknowledged the work that elderly members of the community may do to support them, because often their support occurs within the 'black-box' of the household and is seen merely as a 'household strategy' for the management of time and resources. In most analyses of

Lima's successful urban social movements, elderly people are assumed to be passive recipients of aid rather than social actors.

By outlining the multiplicity of factors that influence the social well-being of the elderly in Lima I have tried to highlight the social marginality that many of them experience. The gendered nature of old age has a strong influence on the adaptation of men and women to the later stage of their life. Urban social movements play a significant role in the magnitude of the exclusion of the elderly through, at times, denying them involvement as benefactors and recognition as social actors.

I would also like to stress that, while women face a structural disadvantage through gender bias within the education system, labour market, access to pension systems and society's structure in general, it is not always the case that elderly women suffer more than elderly men. As a result of the gendered nature of old age, men and women sometimes suffer quite different social losses, in which elderly men can even be disadvantaged over women, but both face the same difficulties of poverty, illness and social exclusion. Thus we will look briefly at some initiatives currently being undertaken to deal with this exclusion.

Too Old for 'Development'?

The Peruvian Government has no official policies or laws to protect the elderly and up until recently little attention was paid to their needs. However, recent initiatives by non-governmental organizations (NGOs) illustrate the ways in which development issues and programmes have been adapted to work with the elderly. Data gathered at *ProVida Peru,* which works to improve the situation of Peru's elderly, demonstrate the potential for inclusion of the elderly in development, focusing on poverty alleviation strategies, literacy programmes, preventative health programmes, and social integration.

Many stereotypical characteristics of old age are seen as the antithesis of development (Gorman 1995), thus marginalizing the elderly from the planning and implementation of development projects. *ProVida Peru* outlines three basic problems confronting elderly people: poverty, illness and loneliness. The issue that *ProVida* aims to address first is poverty, the basic needs of the elderly for food, clothing and medicine. Through the initial 'recruitment' of women who had been involved in the local *clubs de madres* (women's clubs) and therefore had the experience of organizing themselves, *ProVida* started to form *Clubs de Abuelos* (grandparent clubs) in the urban peripheral area of *El Callao.*[8]

In order to assess their needs and involve them in the planning of new facilities for the elderly, *ProVida*'s first initiative was to create *Comedores* specifically for the elderly. Elderly women who are fit and at least semi-independent physically and mentally, work in and run the *Comedor* to help older people in their community who are more dependent and fragile. In return for their work the women receive a certain number of rations for themselves and their families, as in other *Comedores Populares.* Out of these *Comedores* grew 'occupational workshops' which the elderly themselves started. Through the mere action of organizing themselves into groups, these elderly women have created their own space and opportunity to voice their needs and ideas as well as answering a practical need for food and support within the community. As a result, they are more visible in the collective. The rotating credit scheme, the literacy programme and the preventative health clubs also initiated by *ProVida* have been equally successful and are true paths to allowing the older person a more active, visible and respectfed role in the community.

Giving the Elderly Credit

Small-scale credit schemes are widely discussed in the gender and development literature with examples such as the Grameen Bank gaining worldwide recognition. The emphasis has generally been laid on enhancing women's empowerment and independence through access to credit, which is typically difficult for women to obtain due to structural gender bias in access to land, capital and material assets. The view of women in many societies as not being viable credit subjects extends to older people. According to Dra. Blanca Deacon of ProVida: "When an older person goes to a bank asking for a loan, apart from the fact that the person is already older, they may not have the papers which they are asked for, nor retain the minimum assets required for a viable loan application."

This is especially the case for elderly women, who suffer the double disadvantage of gender and age. ProVida's rotating credit scheme started with a group of elderly women from El Callao, and now works with

---

[8] *ProVida* has eight of these clubs in *El Callao* grouping together close to 400 elderly people and also has a number of old people's clubs in the middle-income area of *Pueblo Libre.*

some 70 elderly women, with the aim of turning them into viable credit subjects. Dra. Blanca Deacon explains how it works:

> One of the principal characteristics of our organization is that 95 per cent of the members are women, and so we have seen how these women have taken on many challenges in their two-fold condition of marginalization as women, and as elderly women. These women have therefore formed small trades of their own which allow them a form of subsistence and enable them to contribute to the family resources. The most important aspect is finding economic viability for these women, which in turn brings social viability in terms of a more respected space within the family for the fact that the elderly woman can participate and have a certain amount of independence.

She adds that repayment rates and viability of the loans have proved very favourable in comparison to the figures of other credit subjects: "The need and will of these elderly women to demonstrate to themselves, their families and whoever they owe, that they are an economically viable subject and can pay back the loans are very strong commitments for them. So we have not had to pressure them much for repayment."

As perhaps the only opportunity for elderly people to gain access to credit, the project has been used as an example to other NGOs at a HelpAge International conference in Ecuador in 1997. This example shows that credit schemes can successfully be extended to elderly members of the population and can be particularly beneficial to elderly women who have less access to financial assets (whether savings or pensions) and material assets. Preliminary results show that the income-generation activity of the elderly women has not only revitalized their sense of worth and usefulness, but also raised their respect within their families.

Although much of the debate about women's credit programmes has emphasized the lack of attention to inherent power (gender) relations within the household, more studies of this kind are required, looking at intergenerational power relations that are often present within families and households. Goetz and Sengupta (1996) argue that it is not enough merely to give women credit, but that we have to look at internal power relations within the household and determine to what extent women have control over the way the money they earn is used. Similarly, care needs to be taken in how the money the elderly make is used and who has control over it once it enters the household (Is it spent on the older person or does it go towards the food, schooling and health of the grandchildren?).

Never Too Late to Learn

Another issue currently hampering the serious involvement of elderly women in development programmes is their lack of literacy - a prerequisite for participation in many NGO activities. *ProVida* is the first institution in Peru to offer literacy programmes for the elderly, maintaining that through the process of learning to read and write, older people will also increase their concentration, their memory and their coordination. Yet *ProVida* met surprise and scepticism in implementing the programme. Dra. Blanca Deacon describes this reaction:

Many people thought teaching the elderly to read and write was foolish and a waste of time, even members of the Ministry for Education when we suggested the programme and were applying for funding, were amazed that we should try to expect people of that age to start learning to read and write. Well, there are many reasons why literacy is an important factor in elderly people's lives: firstly for their own dignity, so that the grandparent is not left aside in the last years of their life, secondly so that they can be informed on what is going on around them, read the newspaper, so that they can share things with other people ...

Illiteracy can be a key factor in the social exclusion of elderly members of the community. Interviews with *El Grupo Vida* in *Tablada* proved that illiteracy indeed posed daily problems to the elderly and that a literacy programme would be welcomed by many of the elderly. One woman, a member of *El Grupo Vida* in Tablada de Lurin, said:

I am worse off still as I do not even know my alphabet, I don't have any studies at all, I can't inform myself or anything. I always tell my grandchildren, 'do your homework, study hard so that you don't have to suffer like I did'. It would be useful to know how to read and write. Often my granddaughter is doing her homework and she comes and asks, 'Granny, what does this mean'? or, 'How do I do this sum or multiplication'? Or whatever. What do I do? I don't know. How can one help if one doesn't know oneself?

This statement shows that illiteracy can be a point of embarrassment and difficulty for elderly people in their daily life and that many would benefit greatly from being taught to read and write, even if only to be able to help the grandchildren with their homework. Considering the amount of time older people spend with their grandchildren this is a valid point. An older woman's illiteracy is once again a hangover of her gender assigned opportunities in younger life, as girls (especially in rural areas) are far less likely to receive a formal education than are boys.[9] "Illiteracy limits the individual in knowing and being able to articulate their rights and is also associated with other cultural factors that further the individual's social exclusion, such as gender and ethno-cultural origin" (Figueroa et al. 1996:115).

Illiteracy is often associated with helplessness and can hinder people from being able to look after themselves in later life, which exacerbates the image of the old person as a victim of their age and puts them into the role of passive recipient of aid, rather than a potential social actor in their own right. Thus *ProVida* works to change the attitudes not only of the communities in which it works and society in general but also of the older people themselves - helping to nurture a more positive and inclusive image of the older person. Further to the creation of this image is encouraging elderly people to take a more active role in their own well-being.

Helping People to Help Themselves

ProVida runs a preventative health programme called *auto-cuidado* (self-care), which encourages the older person to take responsibility for their own well-being (physical, mental and social) and not to rely on the family or medical services to care for them. The programme was started in the middle-income area of *Pueblo Libre* with, again, a majority of women. It addresses the processes of ageing (biological, psychological and social), different pathologies of illnesses to which the elderly are prone and extends this knowledge to the living surroundings and the community with the aim of creating a more healthy living environment for the older person, his or her family and the community. While the main goal is that the elderly themselves take an active role in improving both their quality of life and that of their living environment, the programme also tries to dissipate conventional stereotypes of the older person within society and by the older person themselves. Dra. Blanca Deacon explains:

> It has taken a long time and much hard work to change the public image of 'pobrecito anciano', 'they need help' or 'what

---

[9] In Peru in 1993, 70.2% of those without any level of education were women. Of those age 60 and over, 48.4% of women, compared to 21.6% of men, had no level of education (INEI 1995).

are *ProVida* going to give us, what do they have to offer us?' by the anciano themselves. Basically our work strives to encourage the anciano to create their own space and a greater presence in the community.

A major problem facing the elderly is society's perception of old age and the negative connotations that accompany this perception, often shared by the elderly themselves. The societal values placed on being old and the social barriers this creates for the older person are some of the most difficult obstacles to overcome, involving a lack of self-esteem, feelings of worthlessness and uselessness and a retreat into passivity. Gender again plays a large role in creating these identities and elderly women may suffer still more under images of submissiveness and inferiority, especially vis-à-vis their daughters or sons-in-law.[10]

More importantly, the misguided perception of 'old age' as something that only affects old people and is only of concern to them is equally badly informed. Ageing is a long process which, I argue, starts from the day we are born and, as such, affects all of us in every part of our life, not just beyond the age of 60 or 65. Close reading of questionnaires showed that many of the participants felt that a programme such as *auto-cuidado* should be extended to all areas and all ages. Thus it would help all of us, both to understand the ageing process better and to 'age' more healthily. More importantly, it will prepare younger generations for old age in economic, social and physical terms by extending discussion of the phenomenon into all realms of society and daily life, thus allowing a deeper understanding of elderly people and their problems and difficulties. This in turn would improve their status and position within society and unravel many of the stereotypes that currently surround them.

Returning to the debate on gender bias and life course, if all the rights and demands made by gender and development practitioners were realized, women would not suffer the way they do in old age. But so far, the connection between the demands of young women and the needs of elderly women has not been made. Therefore, while it is important to work on the 'strategic', political level and push for a wider recognition of the needs and

---

[10] I am referring here to the specific societal norms in Lima. In other areas of the world, such as India, the power and control of the older woman over her daughter-in-law is well documented.

capabilities of the elder person within the government, local institutions and the community itself, we must not lose sight of the immediate needs of these individuals in terms of daily survival.

Policy Implications : Averting Peru's Old-Age Crisis

This paper has argued that issues of age and gender combine to disadvantage elderly women in Lima, and deepen their economic and social exclusion. The reforms within the state have had little positive effect on the situation of elderly people as gender, formal sector and urban biases persist within the Peruvian pension system and within the education system and the labour market. Leaving pension funds to market forces has brought little benefit to the poorer sectors of the population. Policies of structural adjustment and economic austerity have further eroded the family's resource base, which, along with the gendered nature of old age has great impact on the marginalization and economic exclusion of the older person. Yet, research shows that in some instances the presence of an older family member (especially the grandmother) can in fact be a great resource to the family as they take over certain domestic and child-care responsibilities to release their daughters (and daughters-in-law) into the labour force. This work however, remains largely invisible and undervalued.

The discussion has been designed to illustrate that 'development' is relevant to the elderly and that development projects (and gender and development initiatives in particular) should and can work as successfully with this age groups as they do with others. The fact remains that these people are old, they are nearing the end of their life and suffer a number of physical and at times mental limitations that deter government agencies, development organizations and communities alike from believing there is anything to invest in. However, the analysis of NGO initiatives in Lima shows that development projects in fact lend themselves just as well to members of the older population as they do to younger generations. Credit schemes, literacy programmes and health promotion are important ways to combat the poverty and exclusion that many elderly people suffer. Elderly women can be just as viable as credit subjects, income generators and participants in urban social movements, and can be as receptive to training and learning as younger women. Furthermore, they can provide a significant support to the family and the community through their active participation.

I do not wish to homogenize 'older women' any more than younger ones, and their participation depends on similar factors of family responsibilities, economic resources and education, with the added limitation of declining good health. However, there are many older members of the community, both men and women, who are fit and well enough to help and support those who are not, as illustrated by *ProVida*'s *Comedores de Ancianos*.

In addition to their economic exclusion and linguistic and cultural barriers, an important problem facing Lima's *anciano*, is the attitude towards old people, ageing and old age held by the state, society and old people themselves. A concerted effort needs to be made to dispel stereotypes and convert the perception of the elderly from one of passive victims of their age in need of charity and constant help, to a more positive and constructive vision that acknowledges the older person's accrued wealth of knowledge, experience and work and gives them credit as potentially active social agents for the community. Not only should the elderly themselves receive wider acknowledgement and credit for their contribution to their community, but society in general needs to deal with old age. With adequate planning and awareness the economic and social exclusion discussed here can be at least reduced, if not entirely avoided. Not only is development relevant to the elderly, but the elderly, and issues concerning ageing, are relevant to development.

If the state is determined to reduce poverty and dependency, it needs to address the elderly as a growing and progressively poorer sector of the population. It needs to do more than open the pension system to market forces and rather look at ways to increase participation in the pension scheme, by giving the AFPs more incentives to recruit low income workers, and provide some kind of safety net to those who are not within reach of the pension system. The emphasis needs to be not only on giving people a good start in life, which is the focus of most development programmes (child nutrition, education and training), but also on ensuring that the population is able to advance and prepare for later life in financial, health and social terms.

Furthermore, policies for the elderly need to be informed by gender analysis and contextualized with issues of race and socio-economic status, so as to understand the multi-faceted experience faced by old people in Peru and elsewhere. A principal problem that I encountered is that the concept of ageing and old people is pushed to the end of the line, as it is in our lives, and is seen as something separate to the world of production, progress and development. Similarly, old age and the fate of elderly women has not featured highly on the gender and development agenda.

The remark, "We deal with women not with elderly people", which I received when trying to make contact with one leading Limeñan feminist organization, exemplifies the fact that the elderly are seen as a separate population group and are not integrated into discussions of gender and development, despite the gendered experience of old age. In an article on gender and culture in later life Katsuri Sen (1995:36) points out that:

> The lack of attention to the ways in which women's gender identity links with ageing deepens structural subordination and reinforces traditional patriarchal stereotypes, implying that women's life-cycles come to an end between the age of 44 and 50 years, with the loss of the natural capacity to reproduce... this renders older women invisible as a group.

Why is it that contemporary feminism and debates around gender and development in Peru have tended to ignore the issue of elderly women? Despite the strong presence of the feminist movement in Peru since the 1970s (see Vargas 1991), and a number of advances on gender and development issues both before and after the Fourth World Conference on Women in Beijing, gender issues continue to be marginalized within government policy and community development. As Mili Castro of Grupo Vida in Tablada put it:

> The majority of women have not thought about their gender roles or how this affects their life. They will tell you how much they suffered and how hard they have had to work but they will say 'I suffered because I am poor', rather than 'I suffered because I am poor and a woman'.

None of the women's centres or feminist organizations in Lima had any information on elderly women or elderly people in general. The issue, therefore, is plagued by a *doble encrucijada* (double intersection) of the lack of a gender analysis in addressing the situation of the elderly and failure to include the elderly in gender analysis and in the gender and development agenda in Peru. It is clear that elderly people suffer by the mere fact that the aged are an excluded 'last minority' in society. Furthermore, this suffering is heavily influenced by gender, and men and women have some different needs in old age as they have in previous stages of the life cycle. Social development organizations need to acknowledge the importance of investing in the elderly and the ageing as a means of addressing sustainability and continuity of their aims and objectives. Elderly women suffer precisely from the accumulation of the gender bias described for younger women in so much of the gender and development literature and they are therefore equally worthy of attention in gender and development debates. It is, therefore, with this paper that I hope to make a start on redressing these conceptual gaps in research and development practices.

References

Arana Ward, M. 1996. "Mother Knows Best in Lima Shanty Towns", *The Guardian Weekly* (October 3, 1996), Peru: *Washington Post.*

Barrientos, A. 1995. "Pension Reform in Latin America", *Ageing and Society* 15, pp. 407-14.

_____. 1996. "Pension Reform and Pension Coverage in Chile: Lessons for Other Countries", *Bulletin of Latin American Research* 15 (3): 309-22.

Barrig, M. 1991. "Women and Development in Peru: Old Models, New Actors" *Environment and Urbanisation* 3 (2): 66-70.

_____. 1996. "Women, Collective Kitchens and the Crisis of the State in Peru", in L. Autler, ed., *Emergencies, Women and Crisis in Latin America.* Los Angeles: University of California Press.

Beneria, L. and S. Feldman, eds. 1992. *Unequal Burden: Economic Crisis, Persistent Poverty, and Women's Work.* Boulder, CO: Westview Press.

Bhalla, A. and F. Lapeyre. 1997. "Social Exclusion: Towards an Analytical and Operational Framework", *Development and Change* 28, pp. 413-33.

Bonini, C. 1989. *Efectos de la Crisis sobre los Comedores Populares de Villa El Salvador,* (Effects of the Crisis on the Soup Kitchens of Villa El Salvador) Lima: SUMBI.

Burgos, H. 1990. "Mujer y trabajo: tambien con el sudor en su frente" (Women and Work: also with Sweaty Brows), *Quehacer* 66, pp. 86-95.

Chant, S. 1997. *Women-Headed Households: Diversity and Dynamics in the Developing World.* New York and London: Macmillan.

Clark, F.C. 1998. "Old Age, Gender and Exclusion: Development for the Elderly: A Case Study of Lima, Peru", Master's Dissertation, University of East Anglia, U.K.

Clark, F.C. and N. Laurie. forthcoming. "Old Age, Gender and Marginality in Peru: A State in Transition", *Bulletin of Latin American Research.*

Cornia, G. et al. 1987. *Adjustment with a Human Face: Protecting the Vulnerable and Promoting Growth.* New York and London: Oxford University Press.

Cox, D. and E. Jimenez. 1992. "Social Security and Private Transfers in Developing Countries: The Case of Peru", *The World Bank Economic Review* 6(1): 155-69.

De La Cadena, M. 1998. "Silent Racism and Intellectual Superiority in Peru", *Bulletin of Latin American Research* 17 (2): 143-64.

Downs, K. 1997. "The Private Pension Fund System of Peru: Policies to Improve Investment Returns and Diversification", in PROMPERU, *Peru: Beyond the Reforms.* PROMPERU Summer Research Internship Program: Field Reports, Lima.

Elson, D. ed. 1995. *Male Bias in the Development Process.* Manchester: Manchester University Press.

Escobar, A. and S.E. Alvarez. 1992. *The Making of Latin American Social Movements: Identity, Strategy and Democracy.* Boulder, CO: Westview Press.

Figueroa, A., T. Altamirano and D. Sulmont. 1996. *Exclusion Social y Desigualdad en el Perú* (Social Exclusion and Inequality in Peru). Lima: IILS/ UNDP.

Fisher, J. 1993. *Out of the Shadows: Women, Resistance and Politics in South America.* London: Latin America Bureau.

Gorman, M. 1995. "Older People in Development: The Last Minority?", *Development in Practice* 5 (2): 117-27.

Glewwe, P. and D. Detray. 1991. "The Poor in Latin America during Adjustment: A Case Study of Peru", *Economic Development and Cultural Change* 40 (1): 27-54.

Goetz, A.M. and R. Sengupta. 1996. "Who Takes the Credit? Gender, Power and Control over Loans in Rural Bangladesh", *World Development* 24 (1): 45-63.

Grown, C. and J. Sebstad. 1989. "Introduction: Towards a Wider Perspective of Women's Employment", *World Development* 17 (7): 937-52.

Guttierrez Robledo, L.M. 1989. "The Ageing Situation in Latin America", *Impact of Science on Society* 39 (1): 65-80.

HelpAge International (HAI). 1995. *Older Women in Development*, edited by Katrina Payne. New York: HelpAge International.

IADB (Inter American Development Bank). 1997. http://database.iadb.org/INT/ BRPTNET/ brptpubframe.htm

INEI (Instituto Nacional de Estadísticas e Información). 1994. *Censo Nacional 1993 (FUNAP) Resultados Definitivos: nivel provincial y distrital - Provincia de Lima, Departamento de Lima* (National Census 1993 - Final Results - Province and Department of Lima), No 2., Lima.

———. 1995. *Peru: Perfil sociodemográfico de la Tercer Edad.*(Peru: Socio-demographic Profile of the Elderly) Lima.

INEI/UNDP. 1997. *Informe sobre el Desarrollo Humano del Peru: indices e indicadores* (Report on the Human Development of Peru), Lima.

Jaquette, J.S., ed. 1989. *The Women's Movement in Latin America: Feminism and the Transition to Democracy.* London: Unwyn and Hyman.

Jelin, E., ed. 1992. *Women and Social Change in Latin America.* London: Zed Books.

Katz, C. and J. Monk., eds. 1993. *Full Circles: Geographies of Women over the Life-course.* New York and London: Routledge.

Laurie, N. in press. "State-backed Work Programmes and the Regendering of Work in Peru: Negotiating Femininity in 'The Provinces'", *Environment and Planning.*

Leacock, E. and H.I. Safa. 1986. *Women's Work.* Westport, CT: Bergin & Garvey Publishers.

Lind, A.C. 1992. "Power, Gender and Development: Popular Women's Organizations and the Politics of Needs in Ecuador", in Escobar and Alvarez, *The Making of Latin American Social Movements : Identity, Strategy and Democracy.* Boulder, CO: Westview Press.

Lloyd-Sherlock, P. 1992. *Social Insurance Reform in an Ageing World: the Case of Latin America.* The Development Economics Programme No. 39. London: LSE.

_____. 1997. "Models of Public Sector Intervention: Providing for the Elderly in Argentina", *Journal of Latin American Studies* 29, pp. 1-24

Macewan Scott, A. 1995. "Informal Sector or Female Sector? Gender Bias in Urban Labour Market Models", in D. Elson, *Male Bias in the Development Process,* pp. 105-32. Manchester: Manchester University Press.

Moore, H. 1994. *Is There a Crisis in the Family?,* Occasional Paper No. 3, World Summit for Social Development, UNRISD.

Moser, C.O.N. 1981. "Surviving the Suburbios', *Women and the Informal Sector,* IDS Bulletin 12 (3): 19-29.

_____. 1990. *Adjustment from Below: Low Income Women, Time and the Triple Role in Guayaquil, Ecuador.* London: LSE.

_____. 1993. *Gender Planning and Development: Theory, Practice and Training.* Routledge.

Moser, C.O.N. and L. Peake. 1987. *Women, Human Settlements and Housing.* London: Tavistock.

Nash J. and H. Safa, eds.1986. *Women and Change in Latin America.* Greenport, CT: Bergin & Garvey Publishers.

PROMPERU .1997. *Magical Peru.* Revista Internacional del Perú, Lima.

Radcliffe, S. and S. Westwood, eds. 1993. *Viva: Women and Popular Protest in Latin America.* New York and London: Routledge.

SAFP (Superintendencia de Administradoras Privadas de Fondos de Pensiones). 1998. "Afiliaciones, prestaciones, inversiones, rentabilidad, gestión" (Affiliation, Lending, Investment, Profits, Management), *Boletin Informativo Mensual* No. 04-98, Lima.

Sen, K. 1995. "Gender, Culture and Later Life: A Dilemma for Contemporary Feminism", *Gender and Development: Societies in Transformation,* 3(3) pp. 36-42.

Stevens, N. 1995. "Gender and Adaptation to Widowhood in Later Life", *Ageing and Society* 15, pp. 37-58.

Tanski, J.M. 1994. "The Impact of Crisis, Stabilisation and Structural Adjustment on Women in Lima", *World Development* 22 (11): 1627-642.

Tinker, I., ed. 1990. *Persistent Inequalities: Women and World Development.* New York and London: Oxford University Press.

Tout, K. 1989. *Ageing in Developing Countries.* HelpAge International. New York and London: Oxford University Press.

UN (United Nations). 1991. *The World Ageing Situation*, World Assembly on Ageing, Centre for Social Development and Humanitarian Aid. New York: United Nations.

Vargas, V. 1991. "The Women's Movement in Peru: Streams, Spaces and Knots", *European Review of Latin American and Caribbean Studies* 50, pp. 7-50.

World Bank. 1994) *Averting the Old Age Crisis: Policies to Protect the Old and Promote Growth.* World Bank Policy Research Report. New York: Oxford University Press.

Interviews

ADITEI *Asociación Distrital de la Tercer Edad de Independencia* [District Association of Elderly People in Independencia], Interview with leaders of elderly people's clubs, Independencia, Lima, 15 June 1998.

Altamirano, Teofilo, anthropologist, *Pontífica Universidad Católica del Perú*, 3 July 1998.

Barreto, Luz, Director, *Centro Proceso Social*, 8 June 1998.

Bravo Castillo, Oscar, Coordinator, M*esa redonda de trabajo de ONGs sobre ancianidad* [Round table of NGOs for old age], Lima, 15 June 1998.

Club de Tercer Edad : 'El Grupo Vida', Tablada de Lurin, Lima, July 1998.

Club de Tercer Edad : 'San Juan de Dios', Independencia, Lima, June 1998.

Club de la Tercer Edad : 'Los Tigres', Independencia , Lima, June 1998.

Castro, Mili, Director, *El Grupo Vida*, Tablada de Lurin, Lima, 13 July 1998.

Deacon Castillo, Dra. Blanca, Director, *ProVida*, Lima, 23 June 1998.

Luna, Elia, PROMUDEH *Ministerio de la Promoción para la Mujer y el Desarrollo Humano - Parte Adulto Mayor* (Ministry for the Promotion of the Woman and Human Development - Section for the Elderly Adult), Lima, July 23, 1998.

ProVida - Club de Auto-Cuidado 19, Pueblo Libre, Lima, June-July 1998.

Ruiz, H.F. *Superintendencia de Administradoras de Fondos de Pensiones (SAFP),* Research and Planning Section, Lima, 16 June 1998.

Caring for the Care-givers: Challenges for Italian Social Policy

Giovanni Lamura, Maria Gabriella Melchiorre, and Massimo Mengani

Abstract

Italy's population is ageing rapidly: people over 60 years old are estimated at 23 per cent of the population, one of the highest in the world. One consequence is the increasing number of frail elderly who need medical and nursing help as well as daily support. Traditionally, informal support to the disabled elderly has been given by the family, mostly by its females, especially wives, daughters and daughters-in-law. However, reduction of average family size, increased participation of women in the labour market and the declining value in Italian society of unpaid care-giving and household work are making it more and more difficult to meet the increased demand for elderly care by traditional means. This puts pressure on middle-aged women, many of whom are torn by the desire to not give up their jobs, on the one hand, and the growing requests for help from their ageing parents, on the other. Many female elderly care-givers suffer from stress, depression and/or other symptoms of distress deriving from the burden of being at the same time working women and still primarily responsible for the care of the elderly parents.

Among the suggestions which female care-givers themselves propose to remedy this situation is the development of home elderly care - which in Italy is still very rare - as well as of systematic support services which explicitly target care-givers. Also needed are longer paid or unpaid leave periods for working care-givers and better recognition of their work in terms not only of financial remuneration but also of pension benefits.

Introduction: Ageing and Elderly Care in Italy

In 1996 the number of 60-year-old residents in Italy, estimated at 22.6 per cent of the total population (Eurostat 1997: 28), was already among the highest in the world (U.S. Bureau of Census 1996) and might get as high as one in four by 2004 (ISTAT 1997: 218-22). The nation's ageing process has been extremely fast, since in 1951 the number of people over age 60 numbered only half of what they do today (ISTAT 1995a: 11). This trend is even more marked for the population over age 65[1], which more than doubled, from 8.2 per cent in 1960 to 16.8 per cent in 1996, so that today 38.2 per cent of Italian families have at least one elderly member (ISTAT 1997a: 22).

The Italian National Statistical Institute (ISTAT) calculated that in 1994, more than one in five elderly (20.9%, or 1,875,000 people) were disabled in at least one Activity of Daily Living (ADL); 4.5 per cent (409,000 people) were confined to their home and 2.0 per cent (176,000 people) were bedridden (ISTAT 1997a: 28). These data refer only to those living at home and are therefore underestimated, as they exclude people in nursing homes or hospitals, where the ratio of disabled persons is higher (Kane et al.1991: 62). Taking this institutionalized population into account using current prevalence coefficients it is estimated that the number of disabled elderly - currently over 2 million if we consider the mildest disability form, or below 200,000 if we regard the bedridden elderly - will increase by nearly 50 per cent in the next 25 years, when disability will affect nearly 3 million people in at least one ADL and leave about 270,000 people nearly totally non-self-sufficient (Mengani et al. 1996: 143-44). It should be underlined that one disabled elderly person out of three lives alone - in 1990 (the last year of available data) about 511,000 persons, or 31.1 per cent of disabled persons over 65 years who were residing at home.

In Italy, the law traditionally distinguishes two sectors of elderly care: health care and social care. Historically and until the early 1970s, the central government tried to respond to the needs of the elderly through the provincial branch offices of the Ministry of Interior as well as through numerous public 'assistance and charity' institutions, both local and national. During the 1970s, there was an attempt to rationalize and decentralize the social and health functions of the so-called

---

[1] Unless otherwise indicated, this is the age limit used to indicate that a person or a population is 'elderly'.

'territorial institutions' - that is, the 20 regions and over 8,000 communes - through the abolition of redundant public institutions. In addition, all commune-level social-care functions were concentrated under the control of regions, while health-sector functions were concentrated in the Local Health Units (ASLs) which constitute the Italian National Health System.

This operation was successful only for the health sector, since it combined functions previously fragmented among different ministries and institutions under the care of the Health Ministry. Social care, by contrast, despite parliamentary efforts, was never organized in a general reform bill (Disegno di Legge del Governo 1998; Paci 1996: 9). This failure has impeded the transfer of functions to the territorial institutions and has virtually blocked a great part of the regional legislative activity in this field, thus contributing to a high degree of uncertainty about the objectives and activities in the field of social care.

The main consequence is a lack of integration between the health and social-care services. Such integration, while clearly stated as an objective was never made part of national legislation, leaving it to the regions to adopt provisions on this matter. This has resulted in great territorial variability, since an integrated health and social services system exists only in a few regions in northern and central Italy - e.g., Emilia Romagna, Tuscany and Liguria - and much less frequently in the South, where finance is uncertain. In fact, while the National Health Service (SSN) is responsible for health costs, responsibility for social-care services rests with the commune, which often results in attempts by both institutions to shift responsibility for both aspects to the other. This has negative effects on the cared-for and their families, not only from a financial point of view, but also in terms of practitioners' attitude, timeliness and quality of care in general (Dogliotti 1994: 67-72).

While the social-care sector has been at a sort of standstill, the health-care sector has recently been more dynamic, at least on a planning level. Towards the end of the 1980s the idea began to take shape of creating so-called *Residenze Sanitarie Assistenziali* (Health Care Residences, or HCRs), 'mixed' structures providing medical and social care together, in order to support the growing number of non-self-sufficient elderly who could not be cared for at home for 'proven lack of suitable family support allowing necessary continuous medical treatment and care to be supplied at home'. This proposal, included in the financial law of 1988, stated that - at an overall cost of about 30,000 billion lire (about US$20 billion) over ten years - 140,000 beds would be supplied, serving only 2 per cent of the elderly (Ministero della Sanità 1995: 304). Today, at the end of the ten year plan - only 24,000 beds have been authorised, only 17 per cent of the original goal (Presidenza del Consiglio dei Ministri 1998:42).

This result is even more disappointing considering that HCRs were also included in the Health Protection Plan for the Elderly passed in 1992. This plan specified how HCRs should be organized, proposing some innovative methods of primary elderly care, such as Integrated Home Care (Hanau 1994:65) - which includes home-based social, psychological, nursing and rehabilitation support - and Home Hospitalization (Fabris 1997) - consisting of home-based nursing care, medical visits and specialized advice (Ministero della Sanità 1995: 300-4). In addition, a campaign has recently been launched to improve quality of care and promote a so-called service culture, designed to offer care that is both more efficient and more respectful of the users, through an increased emphasis on the regions and the ASLs and a general reorganization of their functions.

Yet, more than five years after the Plan was adopted, results are well below those expected. The hoped-for unification of care levels and health supply has been realised only partially, since not all regions have implemented the home services provided for by law, and only some have adopted a three-year plan specifically for the elderly (CENSIS 1996: 36-49). As a consequence, Integrated Home Care is carried out in only a few hundred of the over 8,000 communes (Lucchetti and Lamura 1998) - mainly highly urbanized ones, reaching less than 0.3 per cent of the elderly (CENSIS 1996:48), and Home Hospitalization is practiced in a very few small experimental units (Santanera et al. 1994: 96-97), thus totally insufficient to cover existing demand. All this, despite the fact that recent studies have pointed out the positive impact of home help for non-self-sufficient elderly patients on the health of their care-givers. These data show that care-givers' stress levels tend to substantially decrease when the cared-for person takes advantage of a home hospitalization service, especially if compared to those who have an institutionalized relative, among whom an increase in the stress level is on the contrary reported (Scarafiotti et al 1996: 297).

As noted, assistance to the elderly is carried out by the state, primarily through state allowances and general legislative schemes, and by the local authorities (regions and communes) and SSN branch offices, the ASLs. While the organization and planning of health and social services is done by the regions, the communes and ASLs ensure their implementation, by fixing modalities, times, costs, and management. In particular, services for the elderly can be divided into three categories:

- exclusively health-care services;
- socio-health services;
- exclusively social services.

Health-care services - usually guaranteed by the ASL or certified health centres - as well as socio-health services are funded by SSN and are therefore generally free for people whose complaints and income fall within the limits stated by the law. The ASL is, however, responsible for both kinds of service. The commune is responsible for social and financial, through its own municipal budget, possibly with a patient contribution. Municipal services do not usually undergo regular audits, so they vary widely depending on the practice of each municipal administration.

The problem of overlap between institutions was addressed through the creation of the so-called Geriatric Assessment Units (UVGs), interdisciplinary bodies made up of health and social personnel to ensure coordination among the different services, in order to provide for the multidimensional needs of the elderly. In fact, however, the elderly and their families still often find themselves alone in the search for proper care. One factor is that Italian public welfare institutions are better at providing monetary transfers than direct services - so recipients have not only the freedom but also the burden of deciding how to use their allowances.

The Health-Care Sector

In Italy health services are offered primarily through three 'poles', formally separate but in practice integrated: the general practitioner, the ASL district and the hospital. The general practitioner is the professional institutionally responsible for supplying free, continuous primary care (except on weekends, when the Emergency Care Units are on duty) - in the office, at home or by phone - to any Italian patient of any age. Specialist treatment and laboratory services are supplied by ASL - which operates through the ambulatory structures of ASL districts - and by the hospital.

The SSN is centered around the general practitioner, who is responsible for the patient, both for primary care and for specialist and lab service referrals. It is the practitioner's task to provide so-called

Scheduled Home Care (ADP), as well as care to residents in nursing homes, in cooperation with the district and hospital ambulatory services. However, while the hospital carries out the practitioner's instructions regarding treatment, it has autonomy regarding patient admittance. In addition, the location of hospitals and districts is quite varied, regarding not only number and size but also efficiency and quality of services. This creates overlapping roles and a lack of coordination between hospital and practitioners (Abate et al. 1995: 32-33).

The Social Care Sector

The social care sector includes both formal and informal care provision. Formal care concerns state subsidies to the cared-for as well as the provision of services in clinics or at the elderly person's home, by public or private paid personnel. Informal care concerns the elderly person's informal network of support, made up of family members, neighbours and volunteers.

Depending on the type and degree of disability, non-self-sufficient people can receive economic support through a special fund provided by the Ministry of the Interior (Adamo et al. 1997). People who are partially disabled (i.e., reduced to three-fourths of working capability) and have a yearly income lower than 6.2 million lire can apply for an allowance of about 5 million lire a year. The income requirement is much less rigid -- as it increases to almost 23 million lire a year - for people who are partially blind or deaf, who, regardless of income, can apply for a further allowance, amounting to 1.1 million lire for blind people and 3.7 million lire for deaf people. The latter amount can also be received by people affected by mild blindness (between 1/10 and 1/20) but only if they are unemployed and with a yearly income less than 9.5 million lire. In case of total blindness or total disability, the amount of the allowance remains the same, but it is granted only if income is lower than 22.8 million lire. These people can also apply for the so called 'companion payment', which is not income-tested and amounts to 9 million lire a year (12.3 million lire in case of total blindness), provided the disabled person does not enjoy free institutionalization.

In short, annual disability payments can vary from a minimum of 1 million lire in the case of a partially blind person with a yearly income over 22.8 million lire, to 17.7 million lire in the case of a totally blind person with income under 22.8 million lire, receiving both the disability pension and the 'companion payment'. To give an idea of the purchasing power involved, in 1995, the average yearly expense of one elderly person living alone was about 17.6 million lire, meaning that only the allowance for total blindness could assure the same level of consumption.

The number of disability allowances has greatly increased over the years, especially those to people over 65 years old, whose number more than tripled between 1984 and 1995 (Ministero degli Interni 1988, 1991 and 1998). In part due to local patronage (Paci 1990: 83) the distribution of such allowances is very irregular. In some central and southern regions (Umbria, Abruzzo and Sardinia), for example, the percentage of non-military disabled people (32-34%) was almost double that (16-17%) in the north (Piedmont, Lombardy and Veneto) in 1994 (Adamo et al. 1997:103). Recently, however, there has been an effort to limit this abuse; between 1997 and 1998 some 23 per cent of disability pensions were revoked on review (Carli 1998), and both disability pensions and companion payments to people over 65 have declined.

In the last few years, local subsidies have also been provided by several regional and municipal administrations in central Italy (Trentino-Alto-Adige, Emilia-Romegna and Tuscany), distributed to families who care for non-self-sufficient elderly in their own home (Credendino 1997:70; Sabbatini 1998). These contributions - which usually total less than 600,000 lire per month - are meant to be used mainly to cover expenses of home help and, unlike the state allowance, are means-tested. In some cases - as in Tuscany - it is possible to use this regional support to cover care provided by persons outside the family, such as friends or neighbours.

Municipal Social Services

The tasks of addressing elderly care needs fall to the commune-level social services - albeit coordinated by the provinces according to regional guidelines. However, owing to the failure to enact comprehensive national legislation, the regions vary widely both in the level of expenditure and in types of intervention (Adamo et al. 1997). Per capita expenditure by the local authorities for social care averages 138,000 lire in northern Italy, almost double that in the South (70,000 lire) - and the share of such expenditure of total commune expenses ranges from about 20 per cent (in Valle d'Aosta and Friuli Venezia-Giulia), to 7 per cent (Molise, Campania, Basilicata and Calabria).

In some regions, as noted, the integration of commune social services with those supplied by the ASLs has resulted in the creation of multidisciplinary Units of Geriatric Assessment (UVGs) made up of municipal and medical staff, which undertake a full assessment of the health and socio-economic needs of the elderly, so as to provide integrated care. In fact, the systematic diffusion of these UVGs all over the country is one of the priority actions stated in the National Health Scheme for the period 1998 to 2000 (ASI 1998: XVII).

In many local situations, however, the management of social care for the non-self-sufficient elderly remains separate from health care, and the work of the commune is focused primarily on providing socio-economic services, in some cases combined with health care. Among the most common are:

- *economic assistance allowances* (temporary or continuous) to help with household bills, medical care not provided for by SSN, etc.;
- *social and health home care services* that is, domestic services such as housework, bathing and toileting, feeding, laundry, and transportation, to allow non-self-sufficient people, whether elderly or not, to keep their own habits in the home environment;
- *hospitality in nursing homes*;
- *preventive socialization services* (for self-sufficient and partially non-self-sufficient persons): holiday breaks and recreational centres (Labos 1988).

Nursing Homes

Italian nursing homes historically have served indigent people who were unable to lead independent lives. Although they often took in, besides the poor, chronically weak, sick and old people, economic status was the critical factor in admission, a fact reflected in the partial self-sufficiency of most in-patients. Today - in part due to the introduction of principles of managed competition and the market economy (Vineis and Paci 1995), making it less convenient for hospitals to accept elderly patients who usually require relatively long hospital stays - nursing homes increasingly tend to admit the very old, seriously disabled elderly, whose care and treatment require more qualified personnel (Mengani 1993: 48).

Most nursing homes are not modernised, meaning that the increasing demand for care facilities for the severely disabled elderly is largely unmet, as reflected in the fact that nursing homes presently host about 2-3 per cent of those over 65 years old (Facchini 1997:288), far below that of most European countries (Glendinning and McLaughlin 1993: 8). In 1994, nursing homes for the elderly numbered 4,836, with an estimated 287,500 beds, the majority (83%) in medium-sized structures (11-100 beds) (Renzi et al. 1994).

This low utilization of nursing homes, especially in the South, seems to reflect a general attitude among elderly people, who declare that they would like 'to die at home' (Bavazzano and Taiti 1996: 16), stay in the place they live and absolutely refuse to be transferred to outside institutions (Cataldi and Pace 1997: 329). These data are corroborated by hospital mortality rates, which show that only one elderly person in three (34%) dies in hospital, compared to the much higher rates (50-80%) in the United States, Canada or France (Buratta and Crialesi 1996: 481). This should be viewed in the context of the traditionally strong -- though rapidly diminishing - support provided by family members, rather than as a consequence of the existence of alternative solutions, which remain relatively scarce.

Family Care of Older People

As noted, most elderly people in Italy have traditionally found help within their own immediate family, whether they continue to live in their own home or go to live with other family members. In fact, many elderly, while not cohabiting with other family members, have a so-called 'intimacy at a distance' relationship with them, as can be seen by the fact that 59 per cent of elderly who live alone see their offspring once a day, 20 per cent more than once a week and only 13 per cent less frequently (Ditch 1995: 120). This helps keep usage of formal care services by elderly people relatively low - as seen with respect to nursing homes - making informal family care a widespread phenomenon. Cautious estimates indicate that about 75-80 per cent of care for the elderly - including support for the disabled ranging from economic support to physical care, psychological and relational support - is provided within the informal network of the enlarged family (Ditch et al 1995; Pernigotti 1994). This confirms the role of the family as a 'productive organization' which - broadly speaking - produces goods and supplies services according to the needs of its members (Vicarelli 1994; Paci 1980): to improve or mitigate the economic condition of the poor elderly person (Florea 1994); to prevent dependency and progressive chronic illness requiring institutionalization (Sau 1994); and to integrate possible home-care services at a local level, thus improving their functioning.

Support from other sources, here only summarized, is much less substantial. The enlarged network of relatives, particularly active in rural communities, can sometimes represent a concomitant care support for the elderly and a physical-psychological help to the care-giver (Serini 1994). Collaboration from neighbours - which can range from carrying out errands to keeping the old person company or keeping an eye on him or her to provide a small break to the family care-giver - seems to concern the minority of the elderly population (Mengani 1995: 102-3). Volunteers also play a part, though often limited to urban areas and concentrated in institutes and hospitals; in 1996 1,280 volunteer organizations were working in the elderly-care sector, involving almost 70,000 volunteers (Manzi 1996: 72) and often providing support and counselling in place of more formal services (Spadin 1998: 49). Volunteer efforts sometimes included conscientious objectors (those opting for civil rather than military service), which have become a growing resource for municipal care services (Taccani et al. 1997). Such non-familial support sources tend to be sporadic and poorly coordinated, providing only little support to the role traditionally played by the Italian family (Facchini 1997).

In short, the family today often finds itself alone in managing the increased care needs of the elderly just at a time when its ability to provide such support is decreasing. From a demographic point of view, the drop in the fertility rate on the one hand, and the reduction in average family size on the other (see Table 1), combine to shrink the network of informal care which can be supplied within the family structure, thus increasing the dependency of single elderly people upon the community. Another factor here is the growing presence of women in the labour market, reducing the number of 'pure' housewives and figures traditionally 'delegated' to care-giving. Elderly care in Italy, as elsewhere (Estes et al 1993; Giumelli 1994), is mainly supplied by the female members of the family (Facchini 1994a). The INRCA study in central Italy shows that of a sample of 171 care-givers of disabled people over 75 years old, more than four out of five (80.7%) are women (Lamura et al. 1998). Data from Lombardy, one of the most industrialized areas of the country, show that care-giving occupies the majority of middle-aged women (45-65 years), since 56 per cent state that they have provided some kind of domestic work or nursing care to their parents in the last six months (Facchini 1994a: 110-11).

Table 1: Average Household Size, 1951-2024

	Historical series 1951-1994					Projections 2009-2039		
	1951 -52	1960 -61	1970 -71	1980 -81	1994	2009 -10	2024	2039
Fertility rate	2.3	2.4	2.4	1.6	1.2	1.5	...	...
Average number of members per household	4.0	3.6	3.3	3.0	2.7	2.3	2.1	2.0

Sources:Fertitlity rate - Eurostat 1997: 116, 208, Household size - Golini et al. 1995: 11-12; ISTAT 1990: 165-67.

The diffusion of female care-giving in the whole country is likely to be even broader, since it does not take into account at least two phenomena: women who as spouses care for their disabled husbands; and the persistence, in less industrialized areas, of traditions connected with higher rates of family - i.e., female - support. In fact, wives seem to be those who more than anyone else are 'morally and factually obliged' to care for a disabled elderly; in their absence the daughters must take over, followed by the daughters-in-law (Horl 1988; Baldassarre 1995). Talk of 'family care' thus becomes a euphemism, as most of the care-giving tasks are performed by women (Boccacin 1990; Aveni Casucci et al. 1995). Sons do not have such obligations; it is emblematic that the daughters, even if they live further away than the sons, visit their parents more often and have much greater contact with them (Negri 1994).

Women's care-giving tasks are also often combined with the helping role as a grandmother, a figure who is more and more involved in looking after the children of daughters and daughters-in law, who often are new mothers - due to higher age at the birth of the first child - and involved in work outside the home (Buratta and Crialesi 1996; Melchiorre and Vicarelli 1995). This plurality of roles - daughter, wife, mother, grandmother, working woman - is certainly not irrelevant to the fact that middle-aged women, especially if 'full-time' care-givers, experience a relatively high risk of depression and stress (Cigoli and Gilli 1992). Factors such as the loss of friends, of leisure time, as well as of the 'right to have holiday' (Mengani and Lamura 1997) should not be under-estimated, since they represent consequences which, in some cases, fall on the daughter-in-law who cares for her mother-in-law, rather than on the husband/son. Thus, it is mainly women who continue to bear the weight of the inadequacies of the Italian welfare state, characterized - in all care sectors -- by a lack of services which relies on, and in turn generates, exploitation and lack of recognition of unpaid family work carried out by mothers, wives and daughters (Sgritta 1996).

Table 2 shows an increase in female labour-market participation - along with a decline in male participation - over the past three decades.

Table 2: Activity Rate by Sex, 1960-1995		
Year	Males	Females
1960	62.5	26.4
1965	59.3	22.8
1970	56.6	21.8
1975	54.6	22.4
1980	54.4	26.0
1985	54.7	28.2
1990	54.8	30.6
1995	51.7	29.

Sources: ISTAT. 1997b: 241-42; 1986: 26; 1995: 25.

The importance of this phenomenon, which has been accompanied by claims of equal career and professional opportunity for women, shows how urgently the challenge of reconciling work outside the home, housework and care-giving demands reforms of the Italian welfare system. In fact, the growing burden of care-giving for elderly family members clashes with women's greater participation in the labour market, a situation which for many women means that they remain obliged to find work characterized by marginality, seasonality and discontinuity (Vinay 1991). In 1995 only 2.8 per cent of men worked part-time compared to 12.3 per cent of women, so that 70 per cent of part-time employees were female, employed primarily in the services sector, where there is more flexibility (Barile 1990).

Thus we can speak not only of women's 'double presence', in the family and in the labour market (Balbo 1978; Saraceno 1978), but of a 'triple presence', when the tasks, already numerous in the family, are incremented by caring for elderly parents or parents-in-law (Facchini

1994b; Bimbi 1993). It is therefore not surprising if sometimes women who are overburdened on more than one front make the decision - just how voluntarily should be more deeply investigated - to give up paid work: a choice with consequences which are not limited to a loss of immediate income, but are also long-term, as they determine a loss of pension benefits (Lamura 1997). For similar reasons, following a trend already experienced by other industrialized countries (Neysmith and Aronson 1997:482), more and more families, especially in urban areas, try to find help through the support provided by foreign immigrants, who often are asked to carry out elderly care-giving tasks on a live-in basis (Melchiorre 1994; 1997).

The crisis of traditional elderly care-giving patterns provided by the Italian family and its female members is confirmed, though indirectly, by recent research results. A 1993-94 survey among the 223 elderly recipients of Municipal Home Care provided by the city of Ancona on the Adriatic coast shows that, while 65 per cent stated that they receive visits from family members, only 47 per cent said they got concrete support from them, and 35 per cent of those interviewed admitted having to resort to private paid services (Mengani 1995:105). A 1994 study of an elderly population in a mountain area of central Italy (Lamura et al. 1997) found that 89 per cent of the 139 persons over 65 years interviewed stated that they received help from their family, consisting mainly of friendship and company, and much less of effective help in personal care and housework. Comparing data from a similar study in the same community in 1980, the study suggests that the elderly now show a greater acceptance (or less aversion) towards nursing homes than in the past.

These results, rather than questioning the primary role of the Italian family in care-giving, actually underline the 'growing difficulty of combining this task with other daily activities, such as work, looking after children and other members of the family' (Mengani et al 1996a). They provide evidence of how the family itself increasingly needs support, if it wants to be able to care for its weaker members without having to substitute, at its own expense, the responsibilities of the state and public care services. Otherwise the danger is that the family might end up in a dual status: on the one hand a protector of the disabled elderly and on the other an 'object of intervention' (Scortegagna 1996), requiring help, relief, and protection. As such the family is subject to 'care-giving pathologies', linked to conflict between the needs of the elderly cared-for and the needs of the care-giver (Pernigotti 1994), resulting in anxiety, depression, insomnia, frustration, nervous breakdown or even drug use (Baldassarre 1995).

In this respect, it must be noted that assessment of the health of elderly care-givers has traditionally made little use of existing measures. Only in the last few years have there been signs of society-wide change, shown by a reappraisal of the value of service quality - not limited to the health field - in the eyes of the public. The Relative's Stress Scale (Greene et al. 1982) is the most commonly used assessment instrument, not only in hospital or ambulatory settings (Bartorelli 1997; Fabrello et al. 1997), but also for field research (Mengani and Lamura 1997).

Apart from this, the care-giver's health is generally assessed by non-specific and non-standardised techniques. An exception is the already mentioned survey conducted by INRCA in cooperation with CNR about 'the role of women in the family care of the elderly' (Mengani and Lamura 1997). This research, which is ongoing, utilizes the Montgomery Caregiver Burden Measures (Montgomery et al. 1985), together with a series of non-specific standardised instruments, such as the Norbeck Social Support Questionnaire (adapted from Norbeck et al. 1981), the modified Zung Self-rating Anxiety Scale and Zung Self-rating Depression Scale (Conti 1995) as well as the Life Satisfaction Index - A (Liang 1984).

The need for suitable evaluation instruments in this field, instruments which should also be sensitive to differences of gender, is affirmed by several authors and supported by research. Among these studies is the work by Leonardi in psychology, who has written guidelines 'for the analysis of women's daily life' (Leonardi 1996: 256-57), as well as that by Paoletti in the field of sociology and discourse analysis (Paoletti 1998).

Support for Care-givers

There is little legislation covering those who carry out care-giving tasks. Recently the options for part-time work were improved for public employees, but private employers oppose such options "because of economic disincentives resulting from the structure of social security" (Ditch et al 1995: 46). To the employee who has to look after an elderly person on a full-time basis - and cannot therefore profit by working part-time - Social Security Reform of 1995 - offers the option of paid leave, but only if the dependent family member co-habits with the employee, and more importantly, only up to a maximum of 25 days per year and 24 months in a working career (De Santis 1996: 265). For those who must dedicate themselves to periods of full-time care-giving - typically required in caring for a totally disabled elderly person - the only alternative presently available is to quit work for a period of 'unpaid leave', limited to one year or less (although legislation currently being debated would extend it to two years) (Cinque and Fucile 1998). Moreover this option exists as such only for civil servants, as in the private sector it often represents an 'easy way to lose one's job'.

The difficulties faced by those who try to reconcile work in the labour market with informal family tasks can be deduced from the results of a survey carried out in some Milanese firms with a high percentage of female employees (Bergamaschi et al. 1995). Thanks to pressure from female employees working night shifts - deemed dangerous by industrial medicine and permitted by Italian law only if agreed through collective bargaining - trade unions in 1989 were able to obtain an exemption from night shifts for women with children under six years of age or caring for elderly or handicapped family members. When this exemption was demanded for all female workers, the companies answered by closing the factories, and only after long negotiations, in 1994, did they permit a limited number of exemptions, on an individual basis. This shows once again how the needs of men and women differ, as men regard night shifts primarily as an opportunity for greater income, while women complain about the lack of time they cause (Fontana and Schifano 1987).

This brief overview can be integrated with the preliminary results of a current INRCA study based on structured interviews with 69 care-givers of non-self-sufficient elderly over age 75, 78 per cent of whom were women, 23 per cent working (in four out of five cases full-time), 41 per cent retired and 35 per cent housewives (Lamura et al. 1998).[2] *Among those who are still working*, most (62%) do not appear to suffer from the concomitant condition of care-giver and worker. Over a third (38%), however, complained of excessive rigidity at work - in terms of time schedules, leave of absence and holidays - as well as of lost career opportunities, in terms of more gratifying and/or better paid work, which would have meant moving or working full-time. *Among the non-employed care-givers* - housewives and pensioners - those who mention

---

[2] The survey is funded by the Italian National Council of Research (CNR) and carried out by the Istituto Nazionale di Ricovero e Cura Anziani (INRCA).

problems in their professional work due to care-giving activities drops to about 20 per cent, primarily linked to early retirement (among those who left work) and to 'it did not allow me to work' (among housewives). An interesting finding, in terms of recommendations, is the high number (about 50%) who state *that the solution that would most help to reconcile work and care-giving* is 'economic support to make it possible to better organize care-giving', combined among those who work with a request for external personnel to integrate family care.

The research data and experiences have shown that formal care solutions for the frail elderly and their care-givers are still insufficient and only partially in line with the changing needs of the users. The polarization of the existing alternatives, which are still limited to the choice between 'home' and 'nursing home' - which often means institution for poor elderly, rather than centres offering integrated medical and social care - is a clear indicator of this situation. Even less visible and accessible are services specifically designed for care-givers, whether monetary support or counselling and health monitoring (Saraceno 1997: 332).

There are, however, some signs of change. First, the Italian government has approved the addition of a special section devoted to the elderly within the National Health Scheme for 1998-2000 - the main objective of which is "to adopt policies of support to the families with elderly people in need of home care (also with a view to safeguarding the health of women who are, in most cases, the main person responsible for the assistance)" (ASI 1998: XVII).

Another welfare reform initiative is the proposal to set up a Fund for Non-self-sufficient People (Redazione 1997c: 28-29) suggested by a special commission nominated to analyze the "macroeconomic compatibility of social expenditure" in Italy. This would create a national fund "to assure all citizens financial assistance and medical care whenever the situation of non-self-sufficiency should occur." The fund should be financed through contributions from both workers and employers, as done in Germany (Lamura and Mengani 1995), and it should reward care-givers by granting pension benefits to those (family members or others) who provide assistance to the non-self-sufficient elderly or, should home care not be possible, an adequate allowance to the elderly for institutionalization. The reactions to this project have been varied. Some are strongly in favour, while others insist on the need to keep expenditure for the assistance of non-self-sufficient people in a health-care ambit, rather than shift them to a new Social Safety Department as suggested. The proposal to subsidize institutionalization has also been criticised, pointing out it might become an indirect push towards institutionalization of non-self-sufficient elderly people (Redazione 1997c: 24).

A further proposal comes from a Bill introduced by the Minister of Social Solidarity for a set of "norms to make working time, family time and care time compatible" (Adamo et al 1997, 134-140). The aim of this proposal, currently being debated, is to enable better coordination between work and family life, including the integration and the rationalisation of the existing laws. The main measures which have been proposed are three:

- long unpaid leaves from work (but calculated for pension purposes and career seniority), to assist one's spouse or relative (up to the third degree of consanguinity) needing assistance;
- funds to cover expenses incurred in such circumstances in the form of advances on future pay;
- incentives to employers who offer part-time work to employees who assist relatives.

The costs of these provisions would be covered through the creation of a National Fund for Flexibility, amounting to 130 billion lire in the first year and to 170 billion lire in the next two years. The proposal, which, despite problems concerning the worker's non-payment during the periods devoted to assistance, appears sound, may be too ambitious for the present, which is characterized by myriad regulations concerning flexibility, but paradoxically envisages only periods of temporary leave rather than horizontal or vertical part-time work (i.e., a reduced working schedule every day, or a number of free days every once in a while).

On the whole, however, all of the proposals appear to be too cautious and modest for a health system still mainly based on hospitalisation, rather than on protection from disease. This is demonstrated by the extremely low public expenditure on prevention, rehabilitation and primary assistance, while almost two-thirds of financial resources are absorbed by hospital care (Banchero 1998: 319-320). It should be noted that the level of health expenditure in the Italian GDP (5.4% in 1995) is not higher than that of other OECD countries (Grossi 1998: 42), but these resources are not well allocated. In this period of generalised cuts in public expenditure, the risk is that people with chronic disease will be 'expelled' from the health-care system, with a subsequent increase in pressure not only on the much weaker social assistance sector - but also on care-giving families.

Conclusions

If current trends continue, the main challenges for the social and health policies for the elderly in Italy can be summarized as follows.

With respect to formal care, there are two political priorities. The first centres on strengthening community care, through more integrated social, medical, nursing and rehabilitative home care, in order to keep the elderly person's home as 'the central point' of an 'enlarged household' (Gennaro 1996). Practitioners and formal home care-givers should be better trained to deal with the needs of the dependent elderly person, for instance through the provision of ad hoc preparation courses for 'care-givers of disabled elderly'.

The second priority is the improvement of residential care for the frail elderly, through the adoption of more quality- and user-oriented management formulas. This means a radical change in care services provided by existing structures - whether the traditional 'Casa di Riposo' or new Health-Care Residences - in order to move in the direction of the 'Service Centre' model (Mengani et al. 1996a). The Service Centre, intended to maintain direct and on-going contact with users in its own area, should work closely with other social and medical support structures (general practitioners, day centres, hospitals, community services) to coordinate such services as laundry, hot meals, and rehabilitation to both in-patients (even temporary ones) and external users.

The recourse to residential care - which in Italy has almost always meant institutionalization - could become, through coordination by a Service Centre, a sort of respite service, making it possible for families to take a temporary break, and offer qualified services to periodically substitute for the work of family members. The philosophy behind this approach is like that which inspired Denmark's Integrated Home Care Services, where an explicit goal is to involve nursing-home staff in home-care services and home-care workers in nursing homes (Coleman 1995: 461). The main purpose remains the development of a range of alternatives, so that users can select different services according to their needs, to delay as long as possible permanent institutionalization, and to avoid overburdening their families.

More systematic collaboration between the family and external formal supports is urgently needed. One way is to realize this widespread provision of training and information courses for informal care-givers, along the lines of those already tried by some municipalities and by countries such as Germany. Parallel to this, it is necessary to mobilize qualified personnel to give counselling to elderly needing care and to their families (Paoletti 1998: 25), so as to improve user access to existing support services (Barbero Avanzini 1994: 34).

Also critical is changing the approach of the general practitioner, who can provide support and advice to family care-givers (Baldassarre 1995), but still too often works independent from others involved in elderly care, especially the municipal support services. First signs of a more decisive change of mentality in this field are taking place on a local level, where integrated health and social elderly care services are being implemented by some municipalities.

The heart of the matter is the recognition of the 'subjective right of the family caregiver to respite measures', through a reconsideration of care-giving activities as 'intra-domestic work', and as such deserving to be safeguarded (Florea and Credendino 1996). To this end, a big step would be the reorganization of the Health-Care Residences in short-term respite services, but could also be brought about through measures similar to Great Britain's 'family placement scheme' (Coleman 1995: 469), according to which the cared-for person is hosted temporarily by a so-called 'placement family', often middle-aged women with a residential home or nursing background, paid by the local government. Care-giving activities could also be recognized by the provision of economic incentives - besides the existing companion payment, including benefits to those who care for disabled elderly. A further desirable measure - included in the proposals of the Ministerial Commission on the 'macroeconomic compatibility of social expenditure' - would be to recognize, for pension purposes, those periods of time which family members - or other informal figures - dedicate to care-giving tasks.

Better coordination is needed with regard to the variety of family, social and professional roles in which Italian care-givers - i.e., Italian women - are today absorbed. As far as the *labour market* is concerned, there is an urgent need for support measures which recognize, for instance, the right to periods of 'children leave' to care for parents, as various political parties and trade unions have long been requesting.

Besides part-time work, measures which could ease the present rigidity of labour activity and reconcile it with elderly care-giving are an increase in paid leave - similar to what is happening for instance in Sweden (Coleman 1995: 458) - as well as flexible time schedules. In general, what is needed is a philosophy of 'organized flexibility' which views a person in multiple roles, including worker, parent, and care-giver, in order to take into account the requirements of working hours, service hours, times of family life, and of their possible reciprocal influence on social life. As shown by surveys in other countries, the satisfactions of playing a variety of different roles can often prevent stress resulting from care-giving activity (Jenkins 1997), making it possible to carry out the latter in a coordinated manner with other tasks. In these conditions, it is not surprising that paid work can take on, for the care-giver, the role of a mental-physical 'break' and attenuate resentment towards care-giving, in the same way as external 'respite services' (Secchi and Andreini 1994; Dennerstein 1995; Murphey et al. 1997).

Here, too, it can be observed that concrete proposals are already available, including the 'norms to make working time, family time and care time compatible' - although it is hard to tell if and when they might become a reality. In conclusion, it is desirable to adopt a global approach to the care of the frail elderly, through the promotion of services which - without saddling the care-giver with further tasks or ignoring the needs of the cared-for elderly - can ensure both sides proper and flexible support, also through qualified and personalised counselling and supervision (Saraceno 1997: 332-35). The worry of containing medical expenditure, the short lengths of governments, and the actual tendency, reflected by the mass media, of highlighting longer life-spans and 'successful ageing' rather than the problems of the non-self-sufficient elderly and of their care-givers, have so far prevented the reforms needed to maximize public and private resources in a 'welfare mix' perspective (Fadiga Zanatta and Mirabile 1993; Carbonin et al. 1994).

It is to be hoped that recent indications of greater and more sensitive attention to the problem will continue, since the present generation of Italian care-givers will soon become the first generation of elderly needing external care and support services on a large scale. If policy-makers do nothing, there is considerable doubt about whether and in what shape current care-givers will reach older age, if their over-burdened present does not quickly improve.

References

Abate, G., A. Bavazzano, Di Iorio. 1995. *Assistenza Domiciliare Integrata (A.D.I.). Indagine conoscitiva sulla situazione nazionale.* Rome: Consiglio Nazionale delle Ricerche (Progetto Finalizzato Invecchiamento).

Adamo, S., M. Brunetti and L. Dragosei. 1997. Il ridisegno della spesa sociale. Studi sul *welfare* italiano. 3° rapporto: L'assistenza. Rome, Editrice Liberetà.

ASI (Agenzia Sanitaria Italiana). 1998. "Il testo del Piano sanitario nazionale per il triennio 1998-2000", *Inserto Speciale* 6 (20): I-XXIII.

Aveni Casucci, M.A., A. Cristini and M. Cesa-Bianchi. 1995. "Lavoro femminile e invecchiamento", *Giornale di Gerontologia* 43 (12): 771-76.

Balbo, L. 1978. "La doppia presenza", *Inchiesta,* n. 32 (monograph).

Baldassarre, G. 1995. "Il ruolo della famiglia nell'assistenza all'anziano non autosufficiente: problemi, risorse, proposte", *Giornale di Gerontologia* 43 (6): 303-11.

Banchero, A. 1998. "L'offerta di servizi: dall'assistenza primaria alla long-term care", in M. Trabucchi and F. Vanara, eds., *Rapporto Sanità '98. Priorità e finanziamento del Servizio sanitario nazionale: le fragilità.* Bologna: Il Mulino, pp. 315-43.

Barbero Avanzini, B. 1994. *Famiglia e servizi sociali.* Milan: Franco Angeli.

Barile, G. 1990. "Lavoro femminile e condizione familiar", *IRER Notizie* 36, pp. 7-18.

Bartorelli, L. 1997. "L'assistenza all'anziano demente", *Giornale di Gerontologia* 45 (9): 599-604.

Bavazzano, A., and P.G. Taiti. 1996. "L'assistenza alla persona anziana non autosufficiente", *Anziani oggi* 8 (1): 11-24.

Bergamaschi, M., E. Omodei Zorini and K. Schweizer. 1995. *Un benessere insopportabile. Identità femminile tra lavoro produttivo e lavoro di cura.* Milan: Franco Angeli.

Bimbi, F. 1993. "Gender, 'Gift Relationship' and the Welfare State Cultures in Italy", in J. Lewis, ed., *Women and Social Policies in Europe. Work, Family and the State.* London: Edward Elgar.

Boccacin, L. 1990. "Gli anziani e la salute. Il sostegno delle reti familiari", *La ricerca sociale* 43/44: pp. 113-29.

Buratta, V. and R. Crialesi. 1996. "Le famiglie dei disabili: profilo socio-demografico e relazionale", *Rassegna Italiana di Sociologia* 37 (3): 477-99.

Carbonin, P.U., R.Bernabei, A. Manto, A. Cocchi, M. Pahor and G. Gambassi. 1994. "Gli insuccessi delle politiche sanitarie per l'anziano e la crisi della Sanità nei Paesi Sviluppati", *Difesa Sociale* 73 (2): 135-62.

Caretta, F., M. Petrini and R. Bernabei. 1996. "Il paziente anziano demente: problemi assistenziali e famiglia", *Anziani Oggi* 3, pp. 39-63.

Carli, S. 1998. "Falso 1 invalido su 4: il Nord eguaglia il sud", *La Repubblica*, 25 July, p.25.

Cataldi, L. and R. Pace. 1997. "Integrazione tra assistenza domiciliare e reti familiari per la cura degli anziani", *Giornale di Gerontologia* 45 (5): 323-32.

CENSIS. 1996. *Home care per anziani. La mappa dell'offerta*, Milan: Franco Angeli.

Cigoli, V. and G. Gilli. 1992. "L'incontro tra famiglia e servizi", in V. Cigoli, ed., *Il corpo famigliare. L'anziano, la malattia, l'intreccio generazionale* Milan: Franco Angeli, pp. 235-52.

Cinque, G. and S. Fucile. 1998. "Non solo madri", *Libertà*, 3, pp. 12-15.

Coleman, B.J. 1995. "European Models of Long-term Care in the Home and Community", *International Journal of Health Services* 25 (3): 474.

Conti, C. 1995. "Le scale di valutazione in psichiatria", *Caratteristiche generali*. Turin: UTET Libreria.

Credendino, E. 1997. "La società degli anziani e i diritti della persona - La relazione tra carer e anziano non autosufficiente L'anziano come risorsa per la comunità". *La Rivista di Servizio Sociale* 37 (1): 65-77.

De Santis, L. 1996. "Increasing the Rights of Carers: An Initiative of the Italian Pensioners' Unions", in *Proceedings of the European Conference 'What Kind of Legal and Social Protection for Frail Older Persons? The Ageing Society and Personal Rights'*, Rome, 19-22 June. Rome: Fondazione Finney - Commission of the European Union, pp. 263-69.

Dennerstein, L. 1995. "Mental Health, Work, and Gender", *International Journal of Health Service* 3, pp. 503-9.

Disegno di Legge del Governo. 1998. "Disposizioni per la realizzazione del sistema integrato di interventi e servizi sociali", *Prospettive Assistenziali* 30 (122): 33-40.

Ditch, J., H. Barnes, J. Bradshaw, J. Commaille and T. Eardley. 1995. "A Synthesis of National Family Policies 1994". European Observatory on National Family Policies, University of York.

Dogliotti, M. 1994. "La posizione dei parenti e dei pubblici poteri", in M. Dogliotti, E. Ferrario, F. Santanera, eds, *I malati di Alzheimer: esigenze e diritti*. Turin: UTET Libreria.

Estes, C., J. H. Swan and Associates. 1993. *The Long Term Crisis. Elders Trapped in the No-care Zone*. Newbury Park, CA: Sage Publications.

Eurostat. 1997. *Demographic Statistics 1997*. Luxembourg: Office for Official Publications of the European Communities.

Fabrello, R., R. Girardello, A. Pilotto, M. Franceschi, and G. Valerio. 1997. "Stress del caregiver nell'assistenza del soggetto anziano non autosufficiente di sesso femminile, a domicilio", Giornale di Gerontologia 45 (3/4): 296.

Fabris, F. 1997. "L'ospedalizzazione a domicilio (O.D.)", *Geriatria* 9 (1): 13-18.

Facchini, C. 1994a. "Le donne nelle solidarietà familiari", in G. Lazzarini, ed., *Anziani e generazioni*. Milan: Franco Angeli, pp. 329-41.

_____. 1994b. "Women and the Network of Family Solidarities: The Italian Case", in P. Pitaud and R. Vercauteren, eds, *Vieillir dans les villes de l'Europe du sud*. Ramonville: Edition Érès, pp. 105-16.

_____. 1997. "Gli anziani e la solidarietà tra generazioni", in M. Barbagli and C. Saraceno, eds., *Lo stato della famiglia in Italia*. Bologna: Il Mulino, pp. 281-90.

Fadiga Zanatta, A.L. and M.L. Mirabile. 1993. *Demografia, Famiglia e Società. Come cambiano le donne*. Rome: Ediesse Editrice.

Florea, A. 1994. "Vita familiare e relazionale", in ISTISSS, ed., *La famiglia anziana: terza e quarta età a confronto* Rome: Ministero dell'Interno, pp. 47-86.

Florea, A. and E. Credendino. 1996. "Old Aged Families and Carers. Support Services and Protection Programmes: Fondazione Finney", in *Proceedings of the European Conference 'What Kind of Legal and Social Protection for Frail Older Persons? The Ageing Society and Personal Rights'*, 19-22 June. Rome: Fondazione Finney - Commission of the European Union, pp. 231-35.

Fontana, R. and P. Schifano. 1987. "Soggetti sociali non identificati: le turniste", *Studi Organizzativi* 18 (2): 79-109.

Gennaro, I. 1996. "Definition for a Home without Walls", in *Proceedings of the European Conference 'What Kind of Legal and Social Protection For Frail Older Persons? The Ageing Society and Personal Rights'*, 19-22 June. Rome: Fondazione Finney - Commission of the European Union, pp. 258-62.

Giumelli, G. 1994. "Informal Caregivers e persone anziane: alcune riflessioni", *Senectus* 1 (3): 9-19.

Glendinning, C.and E. McLaughlin. 1993. *Paying for Care: Lessons from Europe.* London: Social Security Advisory Committee, HMSO.

Golini A., A. De Simoni and F. Citoni. 1995. *Tre scenari per il possibile sviluppo della popolazione delle regioni italiane al 2044*, Rome: CNR-IRP.

Greene, J.G. et al. 1982. "Measuring Behavioural Disturbance of Elderly Demented Patients in the Community and Its Effects on Relatives: A Factor Analytic Study", *Age and Ageing* 11, pp. 121-26.

Grossi, B. 1998. "Il cambiamenti in atto nel Servizio Sanitario Nazionale", in M. Trabucchi and F. Vanara, eds, Rapporto Sanità '98, Priorità e finanziamento del Servizio sanitario nazionale: le fragilità. Bologna: Il Mulino, pp. 25-81.

Hanau, C. 1994. "La razionalità nella scelta dell'assistenza domiciliare", *L'Assistenza Sociale* 48 (1): 55-116.

Hanau, C. and E. Pipitone. 998. "Analisi della domanda di cure domiciliari", in tre U.S.S.L. di Milan, Quaderni di Cure Palliative, 4.

Horl, J. 1988. "Il ruolo delle reti informali e delle organizzazioni formali nel sostegno sociale", *La ricerca sociale* 37, pp. 68-92.

ISTAT. 1986. *Statistiche del lavoro* 26, Rome.

_____.1990. Sommario storico di statistiche sulla popolazione *1951-1987*, Rome.

_____. 1995a. *Introducing Italy* (bilingual Italian-English edition), Rome.

_____. 1995b. "III Relazione sulle condizioni di vita degli anziani in Italia, in Presidenza del Consiglio dei Ministri-Dipartimento per gli Affari Sociali", ed, *Relazione Biennale sulla condizione dell'anziano.* Rome: pp. 75-115.

_____. 1997. *Population Projections by Sex, Age and Region - 1.1.1996* (bilingual Italian-English edition). Rome.

_____. 1997a. *Anziani in Italia.* Bologna: Il Mulino.

_____. 1997b. *Annuario Statistico Italiano.* Rome.

Jamieson, A. 1992. *Home-care for Older People in Europe: A Comparison of Policies and Practices.* New York: Oxford Publications.

Jenkins, C.L. 1997. "Women, Work, and Care-giving: How Do These Roles Affect Women's Well-Being?", *Journal of Women and Aging* 9 (3): 27-45.

Kane, R.L., M. Saslow and T. Brundage. 1991. "Using ADLs to Establish Eligibility for Long-term Care among the Cognitively Impaired", *Gerontologist* 31 (1): 60-66.

Labos. 1988. *Quartà età e non autosufficienza,* Rome: Edizioni T.E.R.

Lamura, G. 1997. "Rapporto sui risultati dello studio pilota INRCA-CNR Il ruolo della donna nell'assistenza famigliare all'anziano non autosufficiente". Ancona, INRCA, unpublished manuscript.

Lamura, G. and M. Mengani. 1995. "La nuova 'assicurazione sociale dell'assistenza' tedesca", *La Rivista di Servizio Sociale* 35 (3): 33-47.

Lamura, G., M.G. Melchiorre and M. Mengani. 1998. "Il ruolo della donna nell'assistenza famigliare all'anziano", *Rapporto di sintesi sullo studio condotto presso 69 famiglie residenti nel Comune di Senigallia (An) nel periodo novembre-dicembre 1997.* Ancona: INRCA (in press).

Lamura, G., M. Giammarchi, and M. Mengani. 1997. "Social Change and Care Needs in an Elderly Mountain Rural Population in Central Italy", in G.R. Andrews, L.J. Mikita, M.M. Andrews, S.A. Pearson, A.J. Gregory, J.C. Hagger, eds., *XVI World Congress of Gerontology - Book of Abstracts* . Adelaide: International Association of Gerontology, pp. 527-28.

Lamura, G., P. Fioravanti, C. Giammarchi, and M. Mengani. 1997a. "Disability, Family Support and Care Services: Two Case Studies In Central Italy", in G.R. Andrews, L.J. Mikita, M.M. Andrews, S.A. Pearson, A.J. Gregory, J.C. Hagger, eds, *XVI World Congress of Gerontology - Book of Abstracts* . Adelaide: International Association of Gerontology.

Lamura, G., P. Fioravanti, C. Giammarchi, M. Mengani, and I. Paoletti. 1997b. "The Role of Women in the Family Care of Disabled Elderly", in G.R. Andrews, L.J. Mikita, M.M. Andrews, S.A. Pearson, A.J. Gregory, J.C. Hagger, eds., *XVI World Congress of Gerontology - Book of Abstracts* . Adelaide: International Association of Gerontology.

Leonardi, P. 1996. "Depressione e differenze di genere: interventi al femminile", *Epidemilogia & Prevenzione* 20 (2-3): 255-57.

Liang, J. 1984. "Dimensions of the Life Satisfaction Index A: A Structural Formulation", *Journal of Gerontology* 39, pp.613-22.

Lucchetti, M. and G. Lamura. 1998. "Le politiche per la salute degli anziani in Italia", in R. Colantonio, M. Lucchetti, A. Venturelli, eds, *Environment and Aging: The State of Research in Germany and Italy*, proceedings of the 5th Meeting of the Italian Association of the 'Alexander-von-Humboldt' Foundation Fellows, Urbino, 23-24 May 1997. Milan: Guerini Editore.

Manzi, N. 1996. "Volunteering and Frail Older Persons", in *Proceedings of the European Conference 'What Kind of Legal and Social Protection for Frail Older Persons? The Ageing Society and Personal Rights'*, 19-22 June. Rome: Fondazione Finney-Commission of the European Union, pp. 41-51.

Melchiorre, M.G. 1994. "Lavorare dove e perché", in G. Vicarelli, ed., *Di qua e di là dal mondo. Donne straniere nelle' Marche* Ancona: Istituto Gramsci, pp.47-74.

_____. 1997. "Le donne immigrate', in E. Moretti, G. Vicarelli, eds., *Una regione al bivio. Immigrati e mercato del lavoro nella Regione Marche.* Ancona: Osservatorio Regionale del Mercato del Lavoro, pp. 85-151.

Melchiorre, M.G. and G. Vicarelli. 1995. *I tempi di un centro urbano. Famiglie e servizi a Chiaravalle.* Chiaravalle: Amministrazione Comunale.

Mengani, M. 1993. "Il grado di autosufficienza degli anziani nelle Case di Riposo della Regione Marche", *Prisma* 11 (32): 1-76.

_____. 1995. "Il servizio di assistenza domiciliare". Ancona: Il Lavoro Editoriale.

Mengani, M. and C. Gagliardi. 1994. "I luoghi e le politiche a favore della popolazione anziana: la casa di riposo", *Marginalità e Società* 25: pp.61-73.

Mengani, M. and G. Lamura. 1997. "Attività di supporto, stile di vita e salute degli assistenti informali di anziani non autosufficienti: un'analisi qualitativa", Poster presented at the 42nd National Congress of the Italian Society of Geriatrics and Gerontology. Rome.

Mengani, M., C. Giammarchi, and G. Lamura. 1996. "L'aiuto assistenziale della famiglia agli anziani non autosufficienti rsidenti a domicilio: situazione attuale e prospettive future", *Difesa Sociale* 75 (4): 139-48.

_____. 1996a. "Family Care for the Disabled Elderly Residing at Home Present and Future", in *Proceedings of the European Conference 'What Kind of Legal and Social Protection for Frail Older Persons? The Ageing Society and Personal Rights'*, 19-22 June. Rome: Fondazione Finney-Commission of the European Union.

Ministero degli Interni. 1988. *Provvidenze legislative a favore dei mutilati ed invalidi civili, ciechi e sordomuti.* Rome: Ministero dell'Interno, Direzione Generale dei Servizi Civili, 1988, 1991.

_____. 1991. Provvidenze legislative a favore dei mutilati ed invalidi civili, ciechi e sordomuti. Rome, Ministero dell'Interno, Direzione Generale dei Servizi Civili, 1988.

_____. 1998. Provvidenze legislative a favore dei mutilati ed invalidi civili, ciechi e sordomuti. Rome, Ministero dell'Interno, Direzione Generale dei Servizi Civili (unpublished data).

Ministero della Sanità-Centro Studi. 1995. *Tutela della salute degli anziani: materiali e indirizzi per l'attuazione del progetto-obiettivo,* Rome: Istituto Poligrafico e Zecca dello Stato.

Montgomery, R.J.V., J.G. Gonyea and N.R. Hooyman. 1985. "Care-giving and the Experience of Subjective and Objective Burden", *Family Relations* 34, pp. 19-26.

Murphey, B., H. Schofield, J. Nankervis, S. Bloch, H. Herrman, and B. Singh. 1997. "Women with Multiple Roles: The Emotional Impact of Caring for Ageing Parents", *Ageing and Society* 17 (3): 277-91.

Negri, N. 1994. "Genitori e figli: egoismo, altruismo e senso del dovere", in G. Lazzarini, ed., *Anziani e generazioni.* Milan: Franco Angeli, pp. 315-28.

Neysmith, S.M. and J. Aronson. 1997. "Working Conditions in Home Care: Negotiating Race and Class Boundaries in Gendered Work", *International Journal of Health Services* 27 (3):479-99.

Norbeck, J.S., A.M. Lindseq, and V.L. Carrieri. 1981. "The Development of an Instrument to Measure Social Support", *Nursing Research* 30, pp. 264-69 (rep. in D. Wilkin, et al., *Measures of Need and Outcome for Primary Health Care.* Oxford: Oxford University Press, 1994).

Paci, M., ed.1980. *Famiglia e mercato del lavoro in una economia periferica* Milan: Franco Angeli.

_____.1990. *La sfida della cittadinanza sociale* Rome: Edizioni Lavoro.

_____.1996. "Disuguaglianza, esclusione e nuova domanda di welfare state", Alcune riflessioni, in E. Bartocci , ed., Disuguaglianza e stato sociale. Rome: Donzelli Editore.

Palmisano, F. 1996. "'Interdiction' and 'Incapacitation' - The Public Guardian", In *Proceedings of The European Conference 'What Kind of Legal and Social Protection for Frail Older Persons? The Ageing Society and Personal Rights',* 19-22 June. Rome: Fondazione Finney-Commission of the European Union, pp. 104-9.

Paoletti, I. 1998. "Caring for Older People: A Gendered Practice", Paper presented at the International Sociological Association (ISA) Conference, Montreal, 27 July-3 August.

Pernigotti, L. 1994. "L'anziano ammalato e la sua famiglia", in G. Lazzarini, ed., *Anziani e generazioni.* Milan: Franco Angeli, pp. 379-95.

Presidenza del Consiglio dei Minstri. 1998. "Relazione biennale al Parlamento sulla condizione dell'anziano 1996-1997".Rome: Istituto Poligrafico e Zecca dello Stato.

Redazione. 1997a. "La drammatica esperienza del figlio di una anziana malata cronica non autosufficiente", *Prospettive Assistenziali* 119, pp. 20-23.

_____. 1997b. "La Corte di Cassazione conferma il diritto dei malati cronici alle cure sanitarie", *Prospettive Assistenziali* 117, pp. 32-34.

_____. 1997c. "La relazione conclusiva della Commissione Onofri su previdenza, sanità e assistenza", *Prospettive Assistenzial* 118, pp. 24-31.

Renzi, C., R. Pavan, and M. Ulisse. 1994. "Registro Nazionale delle Case di Riposo", *Quaderni di Volontariato* 6, pp. 31-135.

Rozzini, R. 1996. "L'assistenza alle persone affette da demenza", *Gerontologia* 44 (10/11): 705-10.

Sabbatini, M. 1998. "Per gli anziani affido...sicuro", *Il Comune* 4, pp. 32.

Santanera, F., M.G. Breda and F. Dalmazio. 1994 *Anziani malati cronici: i diritti negati*. Turin: Utet Libreria.

Santanera, F. 1997. "Sancito dalla legge 4 agosto 1955 n. 692 il diritto degli anziani cronici non autosufficienti alle cure sanitarie, comprese quelle ospedaliere", *Prospettive Assistenzia* 119: pp. 5-7.

Saraceno, C. ed. 1978. *Il lavoro mal diviso,*. Bari: De Donato Editore.

_____. 1997. "Gli anziani fragili e le loro famiglie: risorse, vincoli e preconcetti nella definizione delle politche". Atti del Convegno 'La salute degli anziani in Italia', Roma 21-22 marzo 1995, CNR-IRP, pp. 323-337.

Sau, D. 1994. "Contributo dell'operatore all'adattamento ambientale dell'anziano istituzionalizzato ed alla conservazione dei rapporti con la famiglia", in G. Lazzarini, ed., *Anziani e generazioni*, Milan: Franco Angeli, pp. 441-46.

Scarafiotti, C., N. Aimonino Ricauda, P. Visentin, L. Angeloro and F. Fabris. 1996. "Caring Activities for Non Self-Reliant Old Aged and Support to the Families Within the Framework of A Local Geriatric Assistance Pattern", in *Proceedings of The European Conference 'What Kind of Legal and Social Protection for Frail Older Persons? The Ageing Society and Personal Rights'*, 19-22 June. Rome: Fondazione Finney-Commission of the European Union, pp. 296-99.

Scortegagna, R. 1996. "What Kind of Social and Legal Protection?" in *Proceedings of the European Conference 'What Kind of Legal and Social Protection for Frail Older Persons? The Ageing Society and Personal Rights'*, 19-22 June. Rome: Fondazione Finney - Commission of the European Union, pp. 300-5.

Secchi, M.G. and G. Andreini. 1994. "Servizi presenti, servizi possibili", in P. Taccani, ed., *Dentro la cura. Famiglie e anziani non autosufficienti* Milan: Franco Angeli, pp. 217-46.

Serini, R. 1994. "Invecchiare in provincia: differenze di genere e rapporti fra generazioni', in G. Lazzarini, ed., *Anziani e generazioni*. Milan: Franco Angeli, pp. 447-54.

Sgritta, G.B. 1996. "Famiglie e solidarietà intergenerazionale: transizione demografica o crisi politica", *Difesa Sociale*, 175 (5): 15-34.

Spadin, P. 1998. "Problema della famiglia e del carico assistenziale", in F. Marcellini, O. Scarpino, R. Fabri, *Conoscere il malato di Alzheimer.* Ancona: INRCA, pp. 25-29.

Taccani, P., S. Tramma and A. Barbieri Dotti. 1997. *Gli anziani nelle strutture residenziali.* Rome: Nuova Italia Scientifica.

U.S. Bureau of Census. 1997. *Global Aging into the 21ˢᵗ Century.* Washington DC: U.S. Government Printing Office.

Venchiarutti, A. 1996. "The Legal Protection of Disabled Old People", in *Proceedings of the European Conference 'What Kind of Legal and Social Protection for Frail Older Persons? The Ageing Society and Personal Rights',* 19-22 June. Rome: Fondazione Finney - Commission of the European Union.

Vicarelli, G. 1994. "Introduzione" in G. Vicarelli, ed. *Familia mirabilis. Ruoli femminili et reti familiari nelle Marche degli anni Novanta.* Ancona: Transeuropa, pp. 7-16.

Vinay, P., M.G. Melchiorre, M. Solsona, L. Suarez, R. Trevino, M.J. Gonzales, I.M. André, C. Ferreira, and M.E. Arroz. 1991. *Women of the South in European Integration: Problems and Prospects.*Brussels: DIOTIMA, Centre for Research on Women's Issues, Commission of the European Communities, Equal Opportunities Unit.

Vineis, P. and E. Paci. 1995. "Epidemiology and the Italian National Health Service", *Journal of Epidemiology and Community Health* 49, pp. 559-62.

Changing Aspects of Caring for Older Persons in Europe: Policy Data Requirements

Tatjana Sikoska

Abstract

This paper explores the issue of caring for older persons in changing contemporary western society. It looks at trends of change in formal and informal care-giving systems and their effects on the welfare of older persons, especially women. It argues that due to structural conditions of gender inequality, gender gaps in welfare benefits and emotional security will not only persist but also create further inequalities among different categories of women. It hence questions the adequacy of available approaches to data collection and compilation, arguing for more detailed statistical data and new methodological, conceptual and analytical approaches in addressing the issue of care-giving from a gender perspective.

The paper takes up two major issues for the principle of intergenerational solidarity: the impact of the fragmentation of the nuclear family upon intergenerational patterns of care as well as the impact of increased welfare cuts on the available support systems for the growing number of elderly and the implications for the intergenerational transfer of resources.

---

[1] This is a revised version of a paper presented at the ECE-INSTRAW-UNSD Joint Work Session on Gender Statistics, Conference of European Statisticians, 20-22 April 1998, Geneva.

Introduction

Increased life expectancy and decline in fertility rates in most of the developed countries have resulted in an ever-expanding category of elderly, non-working population. Life expectancy figures show that, more often than not, women outlive men; therefore, it is not surprising that they comprise a larger segment of this category. Women's socio-economic status, however, is different than that of men; hence, it requires special consideration when viewing the impact of the changing nature of the developed western society on the status of older persons.

Like other developed regions, Europe faces a strong trend of population decline and increased longevity, making the ageing of its population inevitable. Available data suggests that the male population aged 60 and over in 1990 comprised one-sixth of the total male population, whereas the proportion for females was more than a fifth. By the year 2025, elderly males will have risen to almost a quarter of the male population in Europe while elderly females will amount to three-tenths of the female population. Males aged 80 and over, accounted for 2 per cent of the male population in 1990, while females accounted for 4 per cent of the total female population. It is projected that by the year 2025, 3 per cent of the male and 6 per cent of the female population will be aged 80 and over (INSTRAW and UNSTAD 1993). These figures demand serious policy considerations regarding the availability of support systems for future cohorts of older persons, especially women. This is especially true in view of the fact that the post-war system of care-giving is gradually eroding.

Modern European society achieved its prosperity and social cohesion on the basis of the principle of intergenerational solidarity, which has two important characteristics: the intergenerational transfer of material wealth (social welfare system) and the intergenerational transfer of care (family relationships of caring for and by the elderly). Within such a system, women, due to their double gender roles as workers and as mothers and housekeepers, experienced conditions of double dependency at old age: to men (spouse) and to the state (welfare system). Accordingly, their living arrangements, access to social and health security and pension benefits were largely dependent upon their marital status and occupation. Available data (see e.g., Wolf 1989) on the living arrangements of older women in Europe and North America, indicate that there is a striking similarity in the patterns of life of older women in most of the developed countries in the post-war period. Large proportions of women live alone or in institutions, yet the majority of them live with other persons (mostly another older person, usually a spouse or a family member). However, this study projected trends for the next quarter century based on diverse demographic and economic variables that indicate that there will be a continuing growth in the extent to which older women will live alone.

Indeed, trends of change of the post-war family structures and the living arrangements and gradual erosion of the formal state-based caring systems not only confirm such projections but also pose serious threats that undermine the sustenance of the relatively wealthy, healthy and secure base of the European society. Changing patterns of family relationships and family forms suggest that that the nuclear family, which was the building block of the age of modernity, is undergoing a process of 'de-nuclearization', induced by changing socio-economic and cultural conditions. If this is indeed an accurate depiction of the direction of change, then, the question is: What awaits women will be ageing without the support of family bonds? The withering away of the welfare state, which has shared much of the care-giving responsibility with the nuclear family, and the persistence of gender-based labour-market inequalities further exacerbate the situation. While public consciousness is well aware of the emerging threats, little is known of the actual impact of change on the older women of today and those of the future. Therefore, the challenge that confronts the European community is to come up with alternative modalities through which the balance of intergenerational solidarity in caring for an ageing society can be re-established.

But in order to confront this challenge, comprehensive statistical data and indicators on the changing status and role of older persons, especially on older women, are needed. In addition to statistics and indicators based on the traditional sources of data, such as national censuses and household surveys, other sources are needed that would inform policy-makers on diverse aspects of the changing status of older women due to changes in the available support systems.

This paper presents a brief review of the economic participation of women in Europe in order to place the issue of their economic and social security at old age within an overall life cycle perspective. It then examines the issue of ageing in the western European context, from the point of view of the available support systems, both public and private, by assessing trends of change in the institutional manifestations of intergenerational solidarity, followed by policy recommendations.

Economic Participation of Women and Implications for Older Age Security

Since an increasing number of the European population will become old and a larger proportion of them will be women, the socio-economic security of older people has to be approached from a gender perspective and within the context of the changing nature of the available support systems. Crucial to this is an understanding of the socio-economic status of women of working age and its repercussions on their status in older age.

Despite great social and economic advances in Europe, persisting structural gender inequality has placed women in a disadvantaged position as compared to that of men. Women continue to face inequalities in employment patterns, wages and educational attainments. Women are easily excluded from labour markets and are less employed than men (in most of the European countries the rates vary between 2% and 16% for women and 2% and 13% for men) (ECE, 1995). Indeed, women continue performing double work, combining both paid and unpaid household and care-giving work or opt for full dedication to the unpaid household and care-giving work. For example, in half of the European countries (both EU and non-EU), household work is a common reason for women not to be economically active. In Turkey, more than 80 per cent of women who are not economically active attribute this to household work (ECE 1995).

In most European countries, men's labour-force participation rates are higher than those of women, with differences in favour of men, ranging from 5 per cent in Sweden to 48 per cent in Turkey (ECE 1995). The discrepancy in labour-force participation rates is even more accentuated for women and men with pre-school children. Countries such as the Netherlands, for example, show labour-activity rates for women only at 36 per cent, as compared to that of 95 per cent for men (*ibid.*). This means that many mothers with small children spend a very small proportion of their time in gainful employment.

Furthermore, there is very strong evidence that the labour market is sex segregated. Women dominate occupations related to services in shops (sales) and offices (administrative assistants, professionals), in care-giving activities (nurses), domestic work (helpers and cleaners) and housekeeping and professional cooks and waitresses. All these occupations are less well paid than those occupied by men.

In addition, many women perform their jobs on part-time or contractual bases. Available data (ECE 1995) suggests that, for example, in the Netherlands, more than half of the women work part-time, while in Switzerland, Norway, U.K., Sweden and Iceland, the percentage is between 40 per cent and 50 per cent. In Spain, 39 per cent of the women employees work on temporary contracts, while in most of other European countries, the proportion between women and men working on temporary contracts is higher for women.

The important question to be thus asked is: What are the implications of the persistent labour-market inequalities on the socio-economic and emotional security of older women? Naturally, one result is that there is less welfare and economic security than men. Since under the prevailing social security and pension systems, old-age benefits depend upon past work record and enrolment in social security programmes, women automatically tend to be discriminated against, because they work less in the formal labour market and are largely engaged in part-time jobs. They also have less capacity to make substantial contributions to private pension and other welfare schemes, because they earn less, undergo frequent career breaks, and experience less job security than men. Overall, they are more likely to have smaller benefits from the formal support system than men. As such, older women are more dependent upon spouse and family support, which most of the time implies that these women continue to provide care-giving and household work until their very old age.

The Changing European Family and Care-giving

The development of modern industrial society in Europe brought about profound changes in family and household structures. The nuclear family became the predominant form of social organization, although the persistence of extended and complex families in some eastern and southern European countries is still notable. With the emergence of the nuclear model, a consequent pattern of formal and informal support for the elderly was developed, providing relatively stable socio-economic and emotional security. Available statistical data derived from national censuses and household and labour-force surveys as well as from administrative and population registers provide a wealth of information on the health, housing, economic and emotional conditions of life of the older population.

However, changes in household composition are becoming increasingly visible within developed western societies. There is an ongoing process of transformation of the nuclear family model, with important consequences for the status and the position of older women both within the family and within the wider society. A process of 'de-nuclearization' is taking place, involving diversification of family forms and living arrangements, like single-parent family, consensual unions and living alone. Because of the declining propensity to marry and to remarry, and the increasing impact of divorce, the nuclear family is losing its dominance (UN 1994). In addition, increased globalization and labour-related movements within the European Union are bringing about significant changes in the traditional cultural perceptions of family as well as in family living arrangements. Parallel to these, data suggests that there is a significant increase in the participation of women in gainful employment as compared to that of earlier decades and a process of changing life patterns regarding intergenerational sharing of households, care-giving and care-receiving activities, and so on.

If available statistics indeed depict reality with regard to these trends, it becomes pertinent to address the issue of the effects of it on the status of the future older women. Four immediate possible scenarios could be drawn:

1) Older women will live alone (because they will either have no spouse or no children);
2) They will be more independent and self-reliant in caring for themselves (if their health and socio-economic status allow);
3) They are likely to have had a steady employment pattern, and thus, enrolment in available social security and personal/occupational saving schemes;
4) The need and demand for formal support schemes are likely to increase, since there will be less family support available.

These scenarios indeed raise some very important questions for policy-makers, such as: What type of institutional arrangements will be needed to meet the increasing need for formal support? What options are available to the older women under decreased family support and increased welfare cuts? Answers to these questions require not only improved statistical data but also improved methodology, along with new conceptual approaches to care-giving itself.

Confirmation of the trend towards diversification of family forms by existing data is not enough to meet the needs of policy planners and designers. Further knowledge of the real impact of the transformation of the nuclear family on the prospects of informal caring capacity is needed in order to formulate policies to rebuild the eroded balance of the post-war formal and informal care-giving systems. For that, comprehensive data on household structure is needed, not only disaggregated by age and sex but data that enables comparison of different variables related to:

- types of household arrangements;
- the position of the elderly in the household;
- the relationship with their children and/or relatives;
- the type and the extent of geographical mobility of household members and its impact on the relationship between the elderly and their children/relatives; and
- changes in the family values and structure and the interrelationships between the age structures and family structures.

Also, new conceptual and methodological approaches to care-giving, which in itself is a complex concept, involving different aspects for different people and at different times, are needed. If care given among members of a nuclear family type is difficult to conceptualize and measure, it will be even more difficult to do so when multiple forms of family/household arrangements are present, and different personal relationships and needs among family members are involved.

Formal Support Systems for Older Women

Ageing, in a functional sense, begins when a person retires and discontinues her/his active economic life. At this point in life there is a transition from economic independence to total dependency upon welfare provisions and/or family support. Post-war western European societies were characterized by smooth transition where the state and the family offered a variety of support schemes. But this balance is clearly eroding.

Implicit in the economic integration of the European continent (the European Single Market) is a serious dilemma: integration (deregulation and free movement of capital, goods, services and people) increases the demand for social insurance while simultaneously constraining the ability of governments to respond effectively to that demand. The question, therefore, is: How can the tension between globalization and the pressure to mitigate risks be eased?

Employers are less willing to provide the benefits of job security and stability, partly because of increased competition but also because their enhanced global mobility makes them less dependent on the good will of their local workforce. Governments are less able to sustain social safety nets, because an important part of their tax base has been cut loose as a result of the increased mobility of capital. Moreover, the ideological onslaught against the welfare state has paralyzed many governments and made them unable to respond to the domestic needs of a more integrated economy (Rodrik 1997).

Hence, European insurance-based social security systems have been running into three sorts of difficulties. First, the ageing of populations (especially Germany's) is making it harder to afford such generous ratios of out-of-work to in-work incomes without unacceptably high contribution rates. Second, international competition makes it harder to sustain high employer contributions that feed directly into labour costs. Third, insurance based on employment provides far less comprehensive protection in societies where work is becoming more fragile, and increasing numbers therefore fall through the net (Hirsch 1997).

Answers are being increasingly sought in the market. There is a wave of privatization of social security systems, and the emergence of various 'welfare packages and case management' schemes (in Britain). Lowering monthly pension payments (France) and introduction of private retirement systems, life insurance and other forms of life-time savings and investment for older age are being developed. Health care too, is increasingly being 'privatized' (even in Sweden), with more and more situations in which patients will have to pay privately. Combinations of public and community-based care-giving systems for the elderly have also emerged (the Netherlands).

Government programmes are not the only mechanism for reducing income risk. Private insurance, community support, and household transfers are also important. As markets spread and mobility increases, however, some of the informal mechanisms for alleviating income insecurity - such as community-based social services - will become harder to sustain (Rodrik 1997).

These changes raise serious concerns that need to be addressed by policy-makers. In particular, three aspects of the correlation between the transformation of the welfare system and old age security must be addressed:

1) The positive correlation between welfare cuts and rising poverty in Europe. A study carried out by EUROSTAT found that poverty is increasing in Europe, with one person in six living in a poor household (57 million people, or 17% of the population, lived in poverty in 1993). Poverty rates were lowest in countries with the most extensive welfare systems, led by Denmark, where only 6 per cent of the population is considered impoverished, and highest in countries with less social protection. Portugal had the highest rate of poverty, at 26 per cent, followed by Britain and Greece at 22 per cent. Fully one-third of the poor lived in households where at least one person worked, another third of the poor were retired, while 13 per cent were unemployed and 19 per cent were classified as inactive. Poverty rates were highest for single-parent households (36%), the elderly (27%), and families with three or more children (23%). More than half of all single-parent households in Britain and Ireland qualified as poor, while only 10 per cent of large families lived in poverty in Denmark and France, countries that maintain generous family benefits (Buerkle 1997).

2) Threats to the spirit of modern European society: solidarity and security for all. Is it possible to talk about security at older age when the very system of security is increasingly being tied to employment, while employment, in the traditional sense (full-time, job for life) is undergoing profound changes? This obvious shift from intergenerational solidarity to market-based risk mitigation urgently requires policies to secure the 'right to entitlement', independent of personal employment record and based on the simple fact of citizenship.

3) Threats to older persons', especially women's eligibility for support. Private insurance schemes are based on eligibility rules related to the economic capacity of the insured person, as well as other risk components. Given the fact that women are discriminated against in various ways in the labour market, they are also more prone to experience eligibility discrimination. Moreover, since those schemes are market-driven businesses, run by 'professional care-givers', they leave little or no space for older people's influence on the

type and scope of care provided. Such developments endanger older people's basic human rights, and thus must be addressed seriously. Likewise, we urgently need to determine how widespread such practices are and how they affect the economic and social security of older women. This should be done through assessment of the ability of women of working age (who live longer, are less employed than men, earn less, and have longer periods outside the labour market) to fit within such schemes.

Given these considerations, we need to look at the impact of the privatization of public pension systems, as well as health and other social security schemes, on the economic and social well-being of older women, and design policies to safeguard their socio-economic security. Data and statistical indicators are needed on a national and cross-national basis, on the following:

- changes in welfare policies in Europe and their implications for formal support systems for older persons;
- types and quantity of public and private sector support available to older women;
- eligibility rules for private social security schemes and their correlation to the ability of women to enroll, especially with regard to motherhood-related employment breaks;
- types of pension and other social security schemes in which women are currently enrolled;
- number of pensions received, disaggregated by sex;
- extent to which older women benefit from the public versus private social security schemes.

Conclusions, Policy Considerations and Recommendations

It has been argued that, due to gender inequality in labour-force participation and caring for children and the elderly, women are more likely to have smaller social-security benefits than men. Persistent cuts in welfare provisions and the changing nature of the available public support system for the older persons, combined with the family's changing capacity for care-giving, could further threaten the already fragile socio-economic security of older women. Indications that increased welfare cuts and privatization of the welfare system are affecting women more negatively than men are not enough to compel the needed policy response.

However, because these developments could produce situations of gross violations of the basic human rights of the elderly, especially older women, an informed policy response becomes crucial. This is especially true given the irreversible increase in the ratio of the elderly population as compared to the working-age one. Creative policies are needed to balance the stress this will place on state welfare programmes, on one hand and on the ability of the family to care for its elderly, on the other.

Considering the real scope of the problem, policy-makers need to become more sensitive and address the problems and particular needs of older women. They need to look closely at the causes for their lower economic security at older age from the point of view of a life-time pattern of inequality between women and men. Then, they must put forward a new policy agenda that will address the implications of the current changes in available support systems (formal and informal) from such a gender perspective.

Sound policies on ageing should be based on comprehensive data and innovative methodologies to analyze them. Yet, current methods and concepts applied in most data collection systems do not provide for sufficient information needed to carry out complex analysis on the status of older persons. Even less do they provide for gender-specific policies within the context of the changes in available support systems. Hence, gender-disaggregated longitudinal data on the socio-economic status of women throughout their life cycle, on the one hand, and gender-disaggregated data on the effects of the changing support systems on their socio-economic security, on the other, are needed.

First, changes in social security provisions in most European countries raise serious concerns with regard to rising poverty in Europe and possible threats to the basic human rights of older persons. Data is needed not only on the extent to which poverty is affecting older women but also on how poverty is correlated to the newly developed social security schemes. In order to evaluate these threats, measurement of the capacity of working-age women (who live longer, are less often employed than men, earn less, and have longer periods outside the labour market) to fit within newly developing social security schemes is needed. Measurement should be based on national and cross-national indicators that reveal:

- current trends of reform of the welfare policies in Europe;
- types and quantity of public and private sector support available to older persons;
- eligibility rules for enrolment in private social security schemes in relation to the ability of women to enroll;
- types of pension and other social security schemes women are currently enrolled in;
- quantity of pensions received, disaggregated by sex;
- the extent to which older persons benefit from the public social security schemes and the extent to which they benefit from the private social security schemes.

Second, policy-makers need to take into consideration the availability of family-based care in planning for future support to the older population. Knowledge of the household, based on data that contains variables related to its composition and structural distributions is essential for this. But more importantly, policy-makers must consider the trends of change in the nuclear family model. In addition to confirming the 'de-nuclearization' of the family by existing and new data, policy planners and designers need to go beyond this to focus on the real impact of the transformation of the nuclear family on future older women, especially in relation to the quantity and the quality of formal care-giving support systems. Thus, we need:

1) Comprehensive data on the household structure, disaggregated not only by age and sex but data that enables comparison of different variables related to:
   - types of household arrangements;
   - the position of the elderly in these household;
   - the relationship of older persons with their children and/or relatives;
   - type and extent of mobility of the household members and its impact on intergenerational relationships.
2) Cross-national and cross-class/ethnic group studies related to differentials, trends, determinant factors and consequences of changing household and family forms.
3) New conceptual and methodological approaches to care-giving that reflect the emergence of multiple forms of family/household arrangements and different personal relationships and needs among family members.

4) Research on care-giving activities performed by the elderly within the family and measurement and conceptualization of the 'in-kind' payment they receive for it, in order to adjust policies related to provision of formal support both to the elderly and support to the families that provide care.

Third, appropriate policy considerations should respond to the issue of greater mobility within the European Union, and the resulting geographical shifts in the demand for social security support. To this end, the following measures are suggested to improve data and methodological tools for the analysis of the migratory movements within the EU:

- Expand the range of factors that are examined in empirical studies of the determinants of migration, to include those related to socio-economic and cultural factors of the place of origin and place of destination.
- Distinguish the consequences of migration for the individual, the family, and the supply of formal caring facilities. The former two should reveal aspects such as quality of caring in relation to geographical proximity between family members, while the latter should indicate the quantity and quality of the available legal and institutional care.

Fourth, because the category elderly is not a homogeneous one, policy should be designed to address the differences within it. Drawing distinctions between frail and destitute older women and those capable of continuing with employment, requires data disaggregated by age, capacity to work and nature of care needed. Consequently, income-generation strategies for elderly women who are able to continue with employment could be pursued either in the informal or the formal sectors, as well as in the community and at the household level. The most optimal policy measures would require permanent training and acquisition of know-how in order to catch up with the changing nature of modern western European economies.[2] Yet, in the short run, it would be

---

[2] But the reality in Europe tends to be opposite. Unemployment is a problem throughout the EU. Its remedy has been seen, in part, in job-creation strategies that do not favour elderly people, including early retirement, seen throughout the continent. Such practices raise concerns not only about violations of human rights of the elderly, but also about their real economic impact. Since earlier retirement job-creation strategies produce more people who will become dependent upon the already overburdened social security systems, their economic effectiveness has yet to be seen. Comparative analysis, based on

appropriate to think about utilizing these elderly women's know-how as caretakers of both children and of older persons, provided that they are physically able to do so. First, because many women continue with care-taking jobs after their retirement. Second, because of the increasing proportions of older people as compared to people of working age and the consequent cuts in benefits, there will be less supply of care-givers and greater demand for them. And finally, because care-taking (at the household and community level) could be transformed into income-earning opportunity for the already vulnerable, elderly female population.[3]

Last but not least, we need to start thinking about old age and care-giving in different terms, so that cost-efficient, humanitarian and socially integrating care-giving arrangements can be designed.

---

accurate statistical data on the social costs of earlier retirement and the social benefits of the newly created jobs is needed.

[3] This does not mean that men should be excluded from care-giving jobs. On the contrary, they should be encouraged to take them, by giving caring a market value and by eliminating practices that set-up discriminatory rules about men's engagement in care-giving work.

References

Buerkle, Tom. 1997. "Testing the Welfare System", *International Herald Tribune,* 15 May.

Dueñas Loza, M. 1996. "Ageing: A Chronological Process in Life, Social and Economic Questions Arising from It", paper presented at the panel Living Longer, Living Better. Istanbul.

Gardener, K. 1997. "Labouring Under Delusions About Cost of Old Age", *Independent,* 17 February.

Hirsch, D. 1997. "Solidarity: the Missing Link in the UK's Welfare Chain", *New Statesman* 126 (2): 28.

Hohn, C.1994. "Ageing and the Family in the Context of Western-Type Developed Countries", in: *Ageing and the Family.* Proceedings of the United Nations International Conference. Kitaskyushu. 15-19 October, pp. 29-32.

INSTRAW. 1994. *The Migration of Women, Methodological Issues in the Measurement and Analysis of Internal and International Migration.* Santo Domingo, pp. 37-68.

_____. 1991. *Improving Concepts and Methods for Statistics and Indicators on the Situation of Elderly Women,* Santo Domingo.

_____ and UNSTAD. 1993. *The Situation of Elderly Women, Available Statistics and Indicators,* Santo Domingo.

Rodrik, D. 1997. "Sense and Nonsense in the Globalisation Debate", *Foreign Policy* 107(2): 22.

United Nations Secretariat. 1991. "Overview of Recent Research Findings on Population Ageing and the Family", paper presented at the Expert Group Meeting on *Integration of Ageing and Elderly Women into Development.* 7-11 October, Vienna.

United Nations. 1994. "Summary of the Discussion and the Papers", in *Ageing and the Family,* Proceedings of the United Nations International Conference, Kitaskyushu, 15-19 October.

United Nations. Centre for Social Development and Humanitarian Affairs, Division for the Advancement of Women. 1991. *Report from the Expert Meeting on Integration of Ageing and Elderly Women into Development.* 7-11 October, Vienna.

United Nations. Centre for Social Development and Humanitarian Affairs, Division for the Advancement of Women. 1991. "Integration of Ageing Women in Development: Choice or Necessity?", paper presented at the Expert Meeting on Integration of Ageing and Elderly Women into Development, 7-11 October, Vienna.

United Nations Economic Commission for Europe (ECE). 1995. *Women and Men in Europe and North America*. Geneva: ECE.

Wolf, D.A. 1989. "Changes in the households of older women: a cross-national study". Paper presented at the annual meeting of the Population Association of America, Baltimore, Maryland.

SECTION III

BYOND CARE-GIVING:IDENTITY AND EMPOWERMENT

Identity, Culture and Older Women

Noeleen O'Beirne

Abstract

This paper examines the manner in which the cultural production of gender intervenes in the constitution of older women's identity. Gender dictates historical representations of Woman and the disciplinary practices which regulate women's bodies. These practices are internalized and naturalized by repetition and validated by hegemonic discourses and mainstream representations of Woman. One consequence is the particular type of embodiment and subjectivity adopted by older women.

The cultural ideal of the feminine body is one that is young, white, slim and desirable, compared to which older women's bodies are presented as culturally incoherent. The incompatibility of these bodies with the feminine ideal elicits cultural reinterpretations of older women's bodies as grotesque and defective. This process militates against older women's adjustment to their ageing bodies and causes alienation from their bodies, exhibited in such interventions as cosmetic surgery, dieting, exercise and the use of anti-ageing creams. In the process of reconciliation to the feminine ideal, older women are reconstituted as economically viable 'units'.

I argue that if it is recognised that bodies are the end-product not only of biological and psychological attributes but also of culture, the possibility then exists to challenge and change the negative readings of older women's bodies. The un-thought of older women's bodies is the positive view that they are healthy, active, sexual, acceptable but different bodies. It is this alternate view which needs to be propagated in society.

Introduction

> One is not born, but rather, becomes a woman [...] it is civilisation as a whole that produces this creature, intermediate between male and eunuch, which is described as feminine. (Simone de Beauvoir 1960)

Ageism is a prevalent phenomenon in western society. While ageism is directed at both sexes there is a gendered difference in the degree to which it affects each sex with a markedly greater degree of marginalization displayed towards older women. Currently there is a shift in discourses of ageing where a more positive presentation defines it as a stage in the life cycle rather than an illness. This shift acknowledges the better health, education and spending power of an ageing population. in western society. However, when reference is made to the 'aged', it refers to a non-gender-specific and supposedly homogeneous group which, in effect, can be interpreted as male. When gender specificity is applied to the aged body, older women are 'abjectified' and pathologized through the definition of their bodies as defective and prone to diseases such as breast cancer, osteoporosis and hormonal deficiencies. As a consequence, older women's bodies are deemed to be in need of constant surveillance.

A cultural dread of ageing does not explain the attitudinal difference in society between male and female ageing bodies. Gendered differences which privilege the masculine remain operative in ageing, allowing older men to retain a greater degree of social status in the community and still to be considered sexual subjects. This paper argues that this discrimination is due to cultural interventions which in turn, impact on identity. Identity is formulated through culture by means of gender and representation, a normative process which reduces identity to a culturally intelligible and universalised mode of being.

Identity and Representation

Representation encompasses the production of a normative model, in this case of 'woman'. Socialization of subjects occurs through the internalization of the model by the subject and the correspondence between this internalization and the external model. The subjective identification with the model thereby constitutes a culturally intelligible identity or category of being a woman. It is through the prior acquisition of the identity of woman that a basis exists for older women's ascribed identity.

Anthropologist Sharon Kaufman maintains that chronological age is not central to the ageing person. She states, "Identity in old age - the ageless self - is founded on the present significance of past experience, the current rendering of meaningful symbols and events of a life" (1986: 26). Gendered meanings of particular aspects of a woman's life cycle, particularly that of her reproductive years, are formative of her feminine identity. The taking-in-charge of older women's bodies parallels earlier controls of women's bodies specifically as they relate to reproductive functions and their sexuality.

Cultural representations of ageing women in western society carry largely negative connotations. In western society the norm, 'woman' is represented as young, white, thin, physically and sexually attractive, and fertile. The older woman's body contests some but not necessarily all of these designations of what it is to be a 'woman'. The disparity that exists between older women's corporeality and normative representations of 'woman' may thus, for older women, engender an alienation from their bodies and a desire to defer ageing through a masquerade of youth which employs the use of pharmaceutical drugs, exercise, dieting, cosmetic surgery and denial.

Luce Irigaray, in describing the consequences for women of the culturally imaginary 'woman', unintentionally describes how an older woman is doubly absent, even less able to articulate her difference from the imaginary, let alone her deviation from the Ideal of the (masculine) Same. The impact that this location 'elsewhere' has, is that the older woman suffers disqualification as a woman because of her departure from the imaginary and is consequently unable "to articulate her difference. Thus she allows herself to be consumed again for new speculations, or thrown away as unfit for consumption" (Irigaray 1992: 228). While it is acknowledged that individual differences occur in the internalization of cultural representation, the influence of these differences in identity-formation is mediated by these images.

So it is that identity is moulded by normative processes constructed within specific cultural and historical contexts (Butler 1990, Johnson 1993, Foucault 1988). These normative processes "are produced through a range of institutional practices and associated forms of expertise. Participating in these institutional practices accustoms and trains individuals to act, think and desire according to particular sets of rules or norms" (Johnson 1993: 17).

How do cultural norms mould and produce a certain type of identity? The inscription, formation and regulation of the individual by externally imposed standards inform cultural stereotypes, normative discourses and institutional controls which are then adopted with individual variations. In psychoanalytic accounts the ideal model is the phallic or masculine, an accommodation to which entails in-built failure for the female sex. The adoption of culturally constructed characteristics of womanhood are accepted as natural by social consensus and become, as a consequence constitutive of female identity. It is logical then to expect that after a lifetime in which older women have conformed to cultural and institutional expectations of feminine identity, that they will acknowledge their difference from representations of 'woman' and attempt to identify with contemporary representations of what it is to be an older woman.

Bodies encompass the physiological, social, and symbolic body. The fit between corporeality, representation and subjectivity defines older women's bodies as 'failed' or defective bodies when compared to the hegemonic model of woman. The history of older women's bodies is necessarily bound up in that of woman, and, like her, has been affected by what Elizabeth Grosz refers to as the 'mire of biologism' (1994: 188). Susan Bordo's (1990:94) observation that in western culture the body is interpreted as a marker for internal order/disorder seems particularly apposite when applied to the older woman's body. For while the woman's body itself has been perceived as disordered, older women's bodies are evidence of an even more markedly chaotic corporeality in that they lack reproductive capacity, menstrual flow, have a non-functional uterus, breasts that no longer produce milk, bodies that have lost shape and are no longer marked as an objects of desire.

The very fact that older women have departed unwittingly but radically from the normative model of woman, threatens the gender order, strongly signifying the duplicity and in-built failure of the ideal, the 'truth' about being a woman. Older women's discontinuity as an object of libidinal desire, coupled with their infertile ageing bodies demonstrates the incoherence and instability of mainstream feminine discourses so that these discourses become contested sites.

If body shape can represent disorder, older women's bodies whose shape departs with ageing from the 'slim, trim' and sometimes anorexic models of normative femininity, represent disorder or, in Judith Butler's terms, a lack of 'cultural intelligibility'. This normative model ignores the fact that, throughout life, the body constantly engages in shape-shifting. But it is the non-reproductive bodies of older women which depart most radically from the concept of woman and its conflation with the maternal. This radical departure is heightened by the effects of reproductive ideology in the control, commercialization and 'subjectivation' of women's bodies.

Belonging is dependent on others' recognition. In women, this identification is based on sex, leading to "a conflation of the category of women with the ostensibly sexualized features of their bodies" (Butler 1990:19). But apart from the use of this conflation to trivialise and dominate women, does it not also serve to exclude women, particularly older women who are deemed asexual? Is this loss of a supposed identity one of the reasons why women have dreaded age? Why many, even today, remain secretive about their age and why they submit their bodies to rigourous diet, beauty and exercise routines and have facelifts in an attempt to deny their age?

Older women's loss of femininity and youth accounts for their social construction as lacking desire and therefore as being incapable of desire or belonging. Describing belonging as a "tenacious and fragile desire" (1996:8), Elspeth Probyn notes that it places one on the outside of belonging. I extend this to older women's desire to belong which places them as women on the outside of gender and facing "the knowledge of ever really and truly belonging" (*ibid.*). Butler, too, has described how the rigid application of gender identity has rendered deviant identities apparently incapable of being incorporated in the cultural matrix. While it was not Butler's intention to apply this proposition to older women, nevertheless it serves to explain the sense in which older women have been considered asexual, unbecoming, as not belonging. Their gender identity is unintelligible due to their failure to conform to gender norms and so older women appear as "logical impossibilities from within that domain" (1990: 17).

From this perspective, it is legitimate to argue that older women signal the failure of representations of femininity. While coherence and continuity of identity are due to socially instituted and maintained norms of intelligibility, judged by these norms, the older woman becomes an incoherent and discontinuous model of the feminine, potentially able to destabilize the very notion of woman. This leads to the consideration of the older women as a failed model of femininity in her departure from the ideal but in her difference from this ideal, she is representative of the instability of woman as a signifier. The destabilizing effect which older women have on the feminine ideal explains in part, the marginalization of older women in this culture and their exclusion from the public arena as well as their continued representation as physically weak, giving rise to the 'truth' of an older woman's body as diseased, particularly those parts of the anatomy which are associated with reproduction.

Normative models are propagated through a variety of methods which are reflected in and accessed through print media as well as fiction and non-fiction, television, radio, and the Internet. They are further spread by institutions such as schools, universities and other educational establishments; through knowledge regimes as in the research and teachings of medical and social sciences; in religion, in legislation and the administration of justice, government departments and welfare agencies. All these agencies reflect mainstream values in differing degrees.

Social Reproduction

Michel Foucault (1979) has described society's use of discursive practices to produce the bodies which it needs, that is, bodies that are governable and economically useful. It is through society's need to reproduce itself that it perceives as necessary the control of women's reproductive processes and sexuality. That this control reflects a masculine rather than feminine sexuality is a factor in the marginalization of older women whose departure from the image of the ideal 'woman' negates them as sexual beings. Their disqualification as sexual beings is reinforced by their representation as grotesque bodies, a body image to be avoided at all costs. This is compounded by the added consequence of woman being conflated with the maternal. The cessation of an older woman's reproductive years further disqualifies her as an ideal body. That the model woman, does not portray the embodiment of older women or reflect their lived experience of their bodies serves to alienate older women from their bodies.

If it is accepted that there is a need for particular types of bodies in the social field, older women's corporeal deviance necessitates their re-conversion into culturally intelligible and productive individuals. But how is this to be accomplished when, because of their deviation from the norm, older women become non-persons and objects of disciplinary practices which marginalize them?

The disorder of older women's bodies is countered by knowledge systems which reintegrate them as 'fit' subjects that are controllable and economically useful with a need to be under constant surveillance by the knowledge/power systems of the biological sciences and the welfare industry. Their bodies' gender code is re-inscribed as asexual and anomalous as women on the margins. Their destabilization of the signifier, woman, is neutralized and defused by their designation as defective bodies to be known, supervised, treated and normalized. In other words, older women are expected to internalize external standards.

Older women have had a lifetime of being subjected to the 'dominant reality' of being a woman. Culturally instituted factors such as gender and normative representation affect older women's subjectivity, as does their corporeality which becomes a cause of confusion when the feminine is used as a referent. Their bodies are irreducible to the feminine imaginary - young, thin and desirable. Among the discursive practices which aim to regulate women's embodiment is the pathologizing of their bodies. This establishes a need to control and monitor women's health, sexuality and the means of reproduction thereby allowing a conflation of woman with the maternal and a construction of desire.

Factors specific to the individual's personal history impinge on subjectivity. Memory or personal history is an important factor which can mediate in such a way as to block new becomings. Thus older women's recollection of what it is to be a woman impedes their incorporation as older women and incites denial of ageing and the use of strategies which mimic youthfulness. Gilles Deleuze explains how thought obstructs self-definition and reinforces old stereotypes: "we think according to a given method, but also [...] there is a more or less implicit, tacit or presupposed image of thought which determines our goals when we try to think" (1994:xvi).

Cultural Recognition and Belonging

What motivates older women to cooperate with their reinvention by yet another normative process? Is it the sense of belonging when they meet with social approval? Probyn speaks of desire producing modes of subjectification at the "level of the body" (1996:30). Older women cooperate because they have memorized and internalized the discursive knowledges which know the 'truth' of their being, a 'truth' already accepted and approved in the community. Their acceptance of these truths, while subjecting them, simultaneously provides a space within which they can exercise power. There are two aspects here: first, the reward and approval which older women receive for conforming to the stereotype which infantilizes and depicts them as dependent (it is often much easier not to 'rock the boat'); and second, the fact that by adopting this position the older woman can actually exercise a modicum of control over her own life. It can be a strategic use of mimesis.

It has already been noted that older women, along with women generally, are regulated through gender identifications which are contingent upon cultural intelligibility. It appears feasible then, that the element of usefulness and docility that discourses of femininity have produced in the younger woman's body could and would also be extended to older women. Jill Matthews states that women are self-aware and cognizant of the social prescriptions of gender normativity. She adds that the unstable nature of 'woman' is characterized in the slippage "between self-perception and others' recognition, between actuality and expectation, between behaviour and prescription" (1992:16).

Butler maintains that the deregulation of body margins is disruptive of what even constitutes a body (1990:133). If the surface of the body is accepted as one of the body's boundaries, older women's ageing bodies with their breakdown of bodily shape and elasticity of the skin are disruptive of feminine bodies as envisaged by western cultural norms. What is disruptive is liable to marginalization or expulsion. In this way older women's bodies become 'uncanny' bodies, others, even, of the feminine. The cultural response is that older women's ageing bodies are seen as grotesque and repulsive which leads to their representation as asexual and pathological. The dissonance which exists between an earlier internalization of society's representation of the feminine and their now ageing bodies, creates a tension for older women. The retention of this idealized memory of their bodies manifests itself as a rejection of their ageing bodies and in depression.

Along with the changes in body image and function, other tensions may arise and are experienced as a feeling of uselessness and futility. Many older women have been employed and face a further erosion of identity, the loss of a public persona, so that the identity crisis is not only of gender and self-identification, but also (familiar to many men) the loss of that aspect of identity which is synonymous with paid work.

Many older women experience a further loss, that of an intimate relationship, through death, divorce or separation. The loss of children has to be accommodated and the older woman may experience a sense of isolation. The destabilization of the biological, psychological and social factors which constitute identity as a woman serves to make identity problematic rather than reinforce and legitimate it. Women, moreover, have the ability to critically appraise and often determine the degree to which socially acceptable roles are adopted. However, these factors may facilitate, in turn, the assumption of a ready-made identity at a time of vulnerability when many adjustments both biological and psychological impinge on the process of becoming an older woman. It is not surprising then, that older women may be overwhelmed by these changes so that it becomes impossible for them to again 'reinvent the self'.

How is the older woman re-modelled so that she once again conforms to a norm which renders her a culturally intelligible subject in the socio-political field? The normative conflation of woman with the maternal (Irigaray 1992) is an important aspect in the formation of older women's subjectivity. It has already been noted that biologically, symbolically and socially, older women are unrepresentative of 'woman' and that, while the in-built corporeal failure implicit in normative models of the feminine affects all women, this failure is excessively exemplified in the older woman's body.

The first step in the 'rehabilitation' of older women's bodies as culturally intelligible is the re-coding of their bodies as asexual. Bodies such as older women's can be culturally intelligible only by being declared sexless. The coding of older women's bodies as asexual resonates with the oxymoronic attribution of asexuality to the maternal body displayed in such attitudes as the negative response to breast-feeding in public while public exposure of breasts as sexual icons (e.g., topless waitressing) is condoned. Having been declared asexual, older woman are next pathologized, treated and managed, to render their bodies economically viable.

Anatomy fails as a stable signifier of woman in more than one instance and menopause, where older female bodies cease menstruation and lose their reproductive capacity, constitutes their bodies as abnormal through the social significance of menstruation as a privileged site of "(normal) female bodies" (Gatens 1996a:9). The cultural correlation of menstruation with the biological normality of women's bodies has the effect of confirming the alienation older women, as women, may feel from their bodies. Menopause inscribes older women's bodies as doubly deficient because of their loss of desirability and fertility. It also contributes to a belief held by the medical profession that wombs and breasts are excessive bodily parts not integral to older women's bodies, a belief which has contributed to high rates of unnecessary hysterectomies and mastectomies when alternative traditional and non-traditional therapies may be more appropriate.

In a continuation of the control which bio-technology has already established over the maternal body, older women's bodies are seen as requiring intervention in the form of Hormone Replacement Therapy, screening programmes for breast and cervical cancer, pap smears and bone scans for osteoporosis. This constant monitoring of their medicalized bodies render older women the subject of the clinical gaze. While these interventions can be useful and life-saving measures, there is a high level of pressure applied to older women to participate in these procedures which fosters in them a nagging anxiety in relation to their bodies. The tendency for non-discrimination in the exercise of health-monitoring programmes, and the unwanted and harmful side effects that can eventuate, see the continuation of medicine's gate-keeping function in relation to women's bodies. Thus the portrayal of the older woman's body as pathological remains consistent with the medicalization of the reproductive functions of women's bodies.

Foucault identified the emergence, in the eighteenth century, of a discourse about the growth and control of population as an economic and political problem which gave rise to a technique of power. This technique of power targeted the regulation of sex as a means to provide wealth, manpower, growth and the utilization of resources for society (1990:25). One result of a politics of sex was that four strategic processes were established which provided "specific mechanisms of knowledge and power centering on sex" (1990:103). Despite noting the absence of an all-encompassing strategy, that sex as a strategy has heterogeneous forms and that it is impossible to reduce sex to its reproductive and adult function, Foucault identified two strategies specific to women and the maternal function, which ensured women's compliance and usefulness in the supply and control of populations; namely, the "hysterisation of women's bodies" and "a socialisation of procreative behaviour" (1990:104-05). At the same time as women occupied an essential position of supply and production in the economy of population, a politics of population in which men dominated the public arena of government, administration and industry, science and medicine undermined any power which might accrue to women from their vital role as child bearers.

The political strategies specific to the maternal function which saw the definition of women as inadequate and hysterical and therefore in need of control and monitoring, have no doubt impacted on older women, whose bodies are now marked as asexual. This is due to discourses which conflate the maternal with 'woman' and the cultural obsession which depicts desirable bodies as young and thin. There is a difference between being and becoming and while older women may 'be' mothers, they can no longer become mothers. As women they fail the representation of what is desirable and are consequently deemed undesirable. This radical departure from the recognized standards of gender intelligibility puts them beyond the borders of an Oedipalized sexuality (Grosz 1990:71). Because of this, older woman are the un-thought of a phallic sexual economy. Quite inadvertently, older women become an example of the Foucauldian notion of the body building its own resistances. Again, the reproductive organs of older women, when they exist, are reproductively functionless. This casts doubt on their status as women, if one accepts the paradigm which conflates women with the maternal.

Although the period in which a woman is fertile may span a period of some 30 years, she may only bear children for a short period of that time, and sometimes not at all, but, having given birth, her primary definition is as a mother and grandmother - not nurse, professor, office worker, engineer, even though she may be qualified in any of these or other occupations.

Some older women have never been mothers but this actuality is not reflected in society's diminutive term 'grannies', which has become an almost universal appellation in the press and television, particularly when coupled with anti-social incidents involving older women such as granny bashing, granny dumping, granny killers.

Irigaray speaks of the maternal as a function to which women are reduced in a phallocentric society. The extent to which this has been internalised is evident in a recurring theme of older women who perceive themselves to be lacking a function or purpose: 'I don't feel of use any more' or 'I feel I should do something useful'. In order to compensate for this lack, older women recoup their lost role of mother by reasserting a broader maternal role: a mothering or caring for the whole community.

The Struggle for Identity

While identity formation occurs in the interface between discursive practices and mediation of images and representations projected in mainstream society, an image of older women does not represent or correspond to older women's lived experience. Subjective experience then, gives rise to a problem of identity for older women through the dissonance which exists between older women's experience of their bodies and their representation in society.

A series of struggles takes place for the individual and for communities around identity; a struggle against "the abstractions, of economic and ideological state violence which ignore who we are individually, and also a refusal of a scientific or administrative inquisition which determines who one is" (Foucault 1983: 212). Foucault prioritizes the struggle against "the forms of subjection", seeing them as more important in the present context than "struggles against forms of domination and exploitation [which] have not disappeared" (1983: 213). While I do not subscribe to this view, seeing it as having a narrow context which relates primarily to western society, I nevertheless agree that it is important in relation to the individual. Indeed, Foucault himself has qualified his statement, adding: "It is certain that the mechanisms of subjection cannot be studied outside their relation to the mechanisms of exploitation and domination" (*ibid.*).

What are these 'forms of subjection' and how do they affect the individual? To understand this it is necessary to examine their theoretical base. The state is one mechanism which has made the struggle for new forms of subjectivity important since its rise in the sixteenth century, as a new form of power. However, state power, while political and concerned predominantly with society as a whole, nevertheless is both an 'individualizing and totalizing power' (Focault 1983: 213). Foucault considers the individualizing power wielded by the modern state, to be "a very sophisticated structure, in which individuals can be integrated, under one condition: that this individuality would be shaped in a new form, and submitted to a set of very specific patterns" (1983: 214). What Foucault defines as a form of secularized pastoral power has eventuated. It has two roles: "one, globalizing and quantitative, concerning the population; the other, analytical concerning the individual" (1983:215). With the refinement of these practices by the state, Foucault saw resistance as involving a refusal of what we are rather than a discovery of what we are (1983: 216).

In the modern state, power increasingly informs the daily lives of individuals and has, in tandem with knowledge, codified the manner in which the individual becomes a desiring subject. The assumption is that there is a stable subject who is the object of these regulatory practices but the very totalizing nature of these strategies of power/knowledge invites resistance.

Again, there is the gendered nature of a morality of behaviours which relate specifically to men in their conduct of matters relating to the "exercise of their rights, their power, their authority, and their liberty" (Foucault 1987: 23). This morality of behaviours presents an exclusively masculinist viewpoint that excludes women and as such is a male ethic which objectifies, trains, educates and monitors women who are under one's control, or avoids them if under the control of another man (*ibid.*: 22). Foucault has observed that the extent to which an individual adopts or modifies the ideal is a matter of degree. In other words, the morality of behaviours legitimates and institutionalizes the power and authority of men while ensuring the subjection of women to authority and denies women a role as autonomous, desiring subjects. This relationship to the self involves an external standard by which to judge oneself and adjust one's behaviour (*ibid.*: 28).

In other words, the individual institutes a regime of voluntary conformity or resistance to society's normative rules of behaviour as has already been noted in the case of older women. As a result, subjectivation becomes a 'relationship with oneself' that "is subject to a constant monitoring of thoughts, actions, and feelings in the endeavour to form oneself as an ethical subject" (Foucault 1987:30). But it also implies that one's use of the external standard as a measure, even when there is nonconformity, remains within the dominant paradigm. It is thus that older women by comparing themselves to the normative model of femininity find themselves lacking.

This demonstrates the strategies by which cultural norms exert influence on identity and are embedded in power-knowledge regimes. There are resistances to the imposition of normative control because there is always a resistance to power as it is inscribed on the body. The origin of one of these points of resistance is in the relation the individual woman has to herself, how she reacts to her experiences and how she mediates them. An instance of this is the by-no-means universal reaction in women to the ageing process: while some dread and deny their ageing, others are accepting and conform to cultural expectations, and still others find ageing a liberating process. The refusal of an identity that is imposed by external standards is a project which has significant repercussions for older women.

An interest in a history of thought rather than that of behaviours or representations aims to "define the conditions in which human beings 'problematise' what they are, what they do, and the world in which they live" (Foucault 1987: 10). It is a case of analyzing the investments that inform the stereotypical determinations of categories of identity. Because the individual is the interpreter of the standards of conduct or morality, individual differences will arise where 'the relation to oneself' assumes an 'independent status' (Deleuze 1992:100).

The individual "is coded or recoded within a 'moral' knowledge" (*ibid.*:103). Thus in daily life, the individual assumes an identity which is exterior to the person and through a folding of that external representation internalises that identity. The individual's subjectivation becomes subjection with power-knowledge as an active agent in the control and dependence of the individual who at the same time conforms to the measures and controls elicited by "all the techniques of moral and human sciences that go to make up a knowledge of the subject" (ibid.).

An application of this is older women's assumption of identities that are foreign to them and in conflict with their lived experience. Women's bodies have been heavily over-coded from the onset of womanhood by the twin vectors of sexuality and reproduction. The 'being-called' asexual marks older women's shift from the objectification of women's bodies to the 'abjectification' of older women's embodiment. A history of the gendered identity of woman provides the rationale for older women's assumption of an identity which results in their continued subjection as women. The displacement of an objectified mode of being for an abjectified mode occasions the tensions, contradictions and melancholia which impact, through memory, on the older woman's subjectivity.

In the cultural production of identity there is a presumption that an identity is fixed. This excludes difference and the capacity for change. Stasis is antithetical to "[t]he struggle for subjectivity", which "presents itself, therefore, as the right to difference, variation and metamorphosis" (Deleuze 1992:106). Modern subjectivity's rediscovery of bodies and pleasures is the result of the intensity of regulatory practices which target the body. This results in the production of a desiring subject, itself an interesting proposition from a feminist viewpoint, because 'woman' has traditionally been identified as an object rather than as a desiring subject and presumed to lack a desire of her own.

Memory, Melancholy and Mourning

While power-knowledge contributes to subjectivation and subjection, memory plays a vital role in the formation of subjectivity and as such is of particular relevance to older women, who have a lifetime of incorporated memories. How does the memory of being a woman affect older women? An effect of memory is that there is a retention of old beliefs and past learning which may no longer be relevant. In the case of older women, past events which are now irrelevant may be the performative acts which constituted her as a gendered being, a woman. In accessing bodies and desires, corporeality affects reactions and responses. These memories inhibit change and so block new becomings. In other words, the technologies of self instrumental in the constitution of the older woman may inhibit changes in her subjectivity which would constitute her an older woman.

Psychoanalytic accounts of melancholia see it as a psychological state brought about by the loss of a love-object which involves both an identification with and an incorporation of the other (Grosz 1990:128). Butler, in her discussion of Lacan's work on melancholy provides a framework for analyzing how memory and melancholy are intertwined and so affect women's subjectivity (Butler 1990). If this is applied to older women, their being the love-object, is revoked and their memory of being this desired object may cause older women to mourn the loss of love-relations.

The affect of melancholy on older women's subjectivity is explained by the internalization of gender norms allocated by culture to their sex and their adoption of the feminine but, as older women, the status of love-object is refused them. Consequently, older women are expected to divest themselves of their former identity as women. They are re-diagrammed, meaning that their former gender incorporation, while internalized as memory, must be renounced and forgotten. However, older women's identity still remains as women and is still part of their life stories, as the term 'older women' indicates. If older women are subsequently unable or find it hard to incorporate their subsequent asexual identity, melancholia may result as an affect of memory, a mourning for their past identities as feminine and youthful. It is only if older women refuse their new identity, as Foucault suggests, that they resist a melancholic identification.

The refusal of their new identity is not the same as its denial, a denial in which some older women engage in an attempt to maintain the masquerade as the desired object, which is more a submissive than a subversive engagement. When older women masquerade as younger women, it can be an almost literal transformation, aided by facelifts, collagen implants and cosmetics. Butler describes masquerade as having a double function which is identical to melancholy. It is a mode of inscription of melancholy, both in and on the body, and incorporates the other who has been refused, in this case, the older woman. A fusion of identity then occurs between the refuser and the refused, locating gender incorporation within the field of melancholy (Butler 1990: 50).

Although Butler is referring here to Lacan's proposition that the way the feminine masquerades as the phallus is consequently always aligned with melancholy, I wish to reinterpret this passage in the light of the double refusal which older women undergo. For older women, gender incorporation is a double masquerade in that they have already adopted the feminine masquerade as the desired object and, now that they are rejected as such, they must masquerade as woman trying to incorporate two contradictory identities. This signals what Butler terms 'identificatory failures' (1990: 56), which furthermore demonstrate that the symbolic "guarantees the failure of the tasks it commands" and in doing so exposes "the permanent impossibility of the realization of identity" (*ibid.*:57). If older women internalize the taboo imposed on them as the object of desire or appropriated feminine, then they will be able to assume a culturally intelligible identity as older women but will fail, on the other hand, to realize an identity in keeping with their relationship to themselves.

Butler comments that "the interior psychic space in which identifications are said to be preserved makes sense only if we can understand that interior space as a phantasised locale that serves yet another psychic function" (*ibid.*: 67). This psychic space appears to have much in common with memory. Butler suggests that psychoanalytic accounts of identification should be replaced by 'multiple and coexisting identifications'. These identifications produce oppositions, assemblages and discords which destabilise the position of masculine and feminine as defined by paternal law (*ibid.*). It is my argument that older women's identity produces both an internal conflict for the woman who has internalized the feminine and an external conflict within culture because her very corporeality does not conform to the gender configuration of the feminine, demonstrating that 'woman' has multiple meanings.

The infantilizing of the older woman is seen as a continuation of a lifetime of disciplinary practices which produce a subjected, female body. This commences with the body of the girl. Deleuze and Guattari see the girl's body as the first to be appropriated by society in order to fabricate opposable organisms (1994: 276). This allows dualism and domination of one organism over the other. It fosters societal conceptions that a woman remains not fully responsible, a 'girl', who never achieves adulthood or maturity in society's eyes. As such, a woman is no more entitled to autonomy and an assumption of a place in society than a child. The older woman's representation as dependent and in need of care reflects underlying attitudes to women. Women and older women do not imitate, identify or resemble a child but become girls through the societal appropriation of their bodies.

Older women are either non-existent, rarely portrayed or cast as inadequate socially, physically and mentally, in literature, television commercials, documentaries, films and character portrayals in dramas. Patricia Mellencamp comments on how a woman's body is viewed in popular culture and of the young/old divide between women: "TV etches an inadequate female body, an image of the classical body of Freud - irreparably divided by age and sex" (1992: 277). This image permeates our lives. She emphasizes the unitary interpretation of woman's body as "a sanctified image of the classical body [which] haunts television and our bathroom mirrors". She remarks that "in one regard [it] never changes - it is a youthful, thin body, air-brushed of blemishes, lines, and wrinkles" (*ibid.*: 279). Older women's bodies are seen as grotesque by comparison. However, Mellencamp suggests that there is a current shift in analysis from pleasure to anxiety, moving away from sexuality to economics "with money and appearances as the key to identity, away from inner recesses and towards surfaces, an overt rather than a covert operation" (*ibid.*).

There appears to be a belief that age is something to be avoided; that one must keep up appearances; not show one's age, in other words, masquerade as a younger woman. This is what is involved in Mellencamp's observation that there is a societal shift from pleasures of the body to an obsession with the appearance of the body. It is implied that if enough time and money are invested, age can be cured. There is disapproval of those older women who 'let themselves go'. This benefits the beauty industry, she notes, "when the cost of masquerade is calculated, keeping up appearances is an exhausting and unimaginably profitable business" (*ibid.*: 288).

In a viewpoint which differs from Butler's alignment of masquerade with melancholy, Kathleen Woodward uses Joan Riviere's analysis of femininity as masquerade and draws attention to competing views of masquerade: "as submission to dominant social codes and as *resistance* to them" (1991:153). If older women masquerade as both feminine and youthful, despite their corporeal departure from both models, the desire involved to occupy both positions indicates a wish to belong. The older woman is located on the outside of both femininity and youthfulness but, through her desire incited by her yearning for feminine belonging, she experiments with and experiences the becoming-woman and the becoming-young of her age.

Fear of ageing manifests in many women as a dread and a coyness about age - a reluctance in telling age and assertions of being younger than their chronological age in order to avoid an admission which alienates them from society. Mellencamp notes: "Women's 'loss' of youth as if it were a tangible object (not a time), measured by our faces and bodies, rather than a gain of wisdom and influence over time, is a manufactured fear that verges on a national obsessive-compulsion" (1992: 273). While in a society that privileges youthfulness, ageing is generally disparaged, older men do not suffer the same disapproval rating as older women. What is so ingrained, so endemic to white, western society that women, even comparatively young women, are reluctant to admit their age? What are the strictures which encourage this denial, and how do they come about? What effect does an age-repressing gerontophobia exert on the identity formation of older women? What possesses a society to engage in practices which induce large-scale masquerades of youth in a phantasmagorical body which ignores the changing nature of ageing?

Biopower and Fear of Death

Older women experience other bodily changes which differ on a gender and attitudinal basis but nevertheless affect the subjectivity of older women. A cultural preoccupation with 'biopower', the science of living, has resulted in a fear of death and a prolongation of life through bio-technology. The cultural discomfort experienced with ageing is associated with death and manifests itself through the association of death with the feminine. Celtic mythology's *banshee* and *cailleach dhu* are two such feminine figures who foretell death. This fear of death is generalized to a fear of older women, who are seen as harbingers of death. In an analysis of Cecelia Condit's videotape, *Not a Jealous Bone,* which deals with an ageing daughter's relationship with her mother whom the daughter has internalised negatively, Mellencamp interprets the fear of death as the catalyst in the relationship between the mother and the ageing daughter as a "failure to come to terms with that position of subjectivity and identity and meaning" (1992: 258). .

This linking of older women with death and the loss of their feminine identity can result in a denial of ageing. The denial of ageing is expressed in individual women in attempts to erase aged appearance through facelifts, use of cosmetic procedures (facial peels and collagen implants), dieting, body sculpting, exercise regimes and hair dyeing. Kathleen Woodward refers to these practices as 'the aging body-in-masquerade', the masquerade, of course, being one of femininity and youth (1991: 151).

Resistances

Older women have come to identify with representations which give rise to an alienation from their bodies. The cultural-social imaginaries of womanhood are varying and contradictory and manifest a component of in-built failure in that these normative models are disrupted by individual differences and ageing itself. What are the resistances that older women can employ to reconcile their psychological and physical being? Rather than being reactive, older women might ask themselves a series of questions in relation to their mode of life so that they might evaluate their life experiences. They could reflect on what has actually been achieved throughout their lives; what experiences have affected their value systems and acknowledge the positive contribution they have made to the community through the wisdom and skills which they have accumulated over a lifetime of experience. They could assess their experiences in the light of these values. In other words, older women are in a position to contemplate their relationship to self, a relationship which puts them in touch with who they are, what they can do and what they can be.

Then, too, the body is not a passive entity which is the subject of cultural constructions but is actively engaged in the assumption of, resistance to, or rejection of them. The focus, then, is on the individual's role in assuming 'pre-existing' models of identity such as that of 'woman'. Foucault's study of the manner in which a human being turns itself into a subject indicates that the individual becomes interested in what influences are brought to bear on the self and where they originate. Are they internal or external? Foucault refers to the broad basis of morality, one of which, a 'morality of behaviors', encompasses the individual's compliance with or transgression of normative rules and values (1987: 25).

The first step in resistance is to consider the possibility of new forms of subjectivity which are viable and non-hegemonic. By discovering new forms of subjectivity which result from a relationship to the self and its way of being in the world, the individual is repeatedly created anew. Again, while Foucault uses language which entirely overlooks specific references to the feminine, but which is nevertheless equally applicable to women, he judges these struggles for new forms of subjectivity to be a resistance to a technique of power which in everyday life categorizes and inscribes the individual with an identity which is imposed by normative values that are both recognized by the individual and evident to others (1983: 212). Foucault contends that a person is both recognized as, and becomes a subject in the socio-political field by adherence to these normative values.

With ageing, women experience changes in body image, sometimes with almost imperceptible thickenings and differences in mass and shape. Older women may feel that they inhabit an alien body which fails the criteria of femininity and its concomitant sexual attractiveness and reproductive ability. It is this discontinuity of the body, with its resultant deconstruction of the internalized discourses of normative femininity, that is often a contributing factor to a pervasive depression which sometimes characterizes post-menopausal women. But it is also this excess of discontinuity that exists between the body and dominant discourses of femininity which give rise to resistance. While it is probable that older women have internalized the role of woman, there is a realization of the instability of that category, an awareness that gives rise to questioning and, in some older women, a sense of freedom. As a result of this resistance, discourses of ageing become a contested site.

Implications

Older women are well-placed to exemplify thinking otherwise from normative prescriptions of identity, or, in Foucauldian terms, to be free of themselves. Their ties to cultural hegemony are more tenuous than at various ages throughout their life cycle and, because older women are already considered deviant and in need of re-identification, they have less to divest. Older women are in a prime position, with nothing to lose because they are already marginalized, and therefore have everything to gain by experimentation with relationships to the self. It is a period of their life cycle when older women need no longer continue the feminine masquerade because they have already been abjectified and marginalized by societal rejection of them as objects of desire.

Successful ageing has been identified as an ability to extract "from one's age the particles, the speeds and slownesses, the flows that constitute the youth of that age" (Deleuze and Guattari 1994: 277). The importance of freeing oneself from the identifications which have conditioned each individual, particularly as they relate to gender and sexuality, is that it is an important constituent in accessing the youth of that age and in liberating oneself. Older women's bodies have the ability to disrupt the normative processes which stratify bodies by their departure from the gender stereotypes of femininity.

While older women's bodies can elicit a mainstream reading as disjunctive, this is not the only possible reading. In fact, the hegemonic view is often presented as the 'only possible actual' (Gatens 1996b:183), and in relation to older women's bodies, the 'only possible actual' is their representation as grotesque, asexual, defective bodies. Gatens asserts that 'a Deleuzo-Spinozist approach' allows the possibility of thinking in terms other than the popularly-held representation (ibid.). The un-thought or other possible actual of older women's bodies is as sexy, unappropriated, healthy and complete. The older woman's body has shown that "the attempt to capture bodies in stable forms" is a fallacy; that there is always another possibility of being through the 'becomings of bodies' (*ibid.*: 182).

Just as the girl's body is the first body to be appropriated in the fabrication of 'opposable organisms' (Deleuze and Guattari 1994: 276) the older woman's body provides the final appropriation for the fabrication of oppositional bodies: young/old bodies, feminine/unfeminine bodies, desirable/undesirable bodies. A point of resistance, then, is to challenge the normalizing stereotypes of gender which circulate in society. In this process, discourses of gendered bodies should defer to, and be replaced by, accounts which acknowledge sexual difference and the dynamic nature of bodies.

Conclusion

Older women's bodies are the un-thought of contemporary culture - a result of their departure from the unitary model of woman except when they attempt to negate this departure in a masquerade of womanliness and youth. Judith Butler (1990) recognises the diversity of those represented by the normative category of 'woman' and proposes that the impossibility of describing and defining all who pass as women is a positive aspect for resisting this categorisation. As a category of 'woman', this is equally applicable to older women. Nobody can with surety define what constitutes an older woman, although a normative model is proffered by the 'experts' in the field of medicine, gerontology and the social sciences. Older women have had a variety of differing experiences as women that have impacted on whom they have become as older women. Within limits, older women, depending on social class and ethnicity, can choose to adopt the normative model or not. The 'contested meanings' attributed to older women's bodies demonstrate that normative models reflect society's creation of bodies which fit its economic needs, with the use of biopower as its rationale.

Moreover, the 'defective' body serves another social purpose in inciting desire for the ideal body. Butler proposes that "[t]he definitional incompleteness of the category [woman] might serve as a normative ideal relieved of coercive force" (1990:15). I have difficulty with the idea of normative ideals as divorced from coercive force and see this idea as a paradox. Even with the most idealistic intentions, I would see these ideals as instituting new 'regimes of truth'. However, I agree that the category, 'woman', is subject to definitional incompleteness as a means of incorporating the diversity of those who come under its umbrella (*ibid.*). If it is acknowledged that any category of women due to their diversity is incomplete, it can be recognized that older women have been marginalized and excluded because they have demonstrated in their persons that, as women, they differ from the normative model and so signify that 'woman' is not a stable signifier.

References

Bordo, S. 1990. "Reading the Slender Body", in M. Jacobus, E.F. Keller, S. Shuttleworth, eds., *Body/Politics: Women and the Discourses of Science.* New York: Routledge.

Butler, J. 1990. *Gender Trouble: Feminism and the Subversion of Identity.* New York: Routledge.

Deleuze, G. 1992. *Foucault.* Minneapolis, MN: University of Minnesota Press.

_____. 1994. *Difference and Repetition* (trans. Paul Patton). New York: Columbia University Press.

Deleuze, G. and F. Guattari. 1994. *A Thousand Plateaus: Capitalism and Schizophrenia* (trans. Brian Massumi). Minneapolis, MN: University of Minnesota Press.

Foucault, M. 1979. *Discipline and Punish: The Birth of the Prison* (trans. Alan Sheridan) New York: Vintage Books.

_____.1983. "The Subject and Power", in H. Dreyfus and P. Rabinow, eds., *Michel Foucault: Beyond Structuralism and Hermeneutics.* Chicago: University of Chicago Press.

_____. 1987. *The Use of Pleasure: The History of Sexuality Vol. 2* (trans. R. Hurley). London: Penguin Books.

_____. 1988. "Technologies of Self", L.H. Martin, H. Gutman, P. H. Hutton eds., *Technologies of the Self: A Seminar with Michel Foucault.* London: Tavistock.

_____.1990. *The History Of Sexuality: Vol. 1.* (trans. Robert Hurley), London: Penguin Books.

Gatens, M.1996a. *Imaginary Bodies: Ethics, Power and Corporeality,* London: Routledge.

Gatens, M. 1996b. "Through a Spinozist Lens: Ethology, Difference, Power", in P. Patton, ed., *Deleuze: A Critical Reader.* London: Blackwell.

Grosz, E. 1990. *Jacques Lacan: A Feminist Introduction.* Sydney: Allen & Unwin.

_____. 1994. *Volatile Bodies: Towards a Corporeal Feminism.* Sydney: Allen & Unwin.

Irigaray, L. 1992. *Speculum of the Other Woman* (trans. G. C. Bell). Ithaca, NY: Cornell University Press.

Johnson, L. 1993. *The Modern Girl: Girlhood and Growing Up.* Sydney: Allen & Unwin.

Kaufman, S.R. 1986. *The Ageless Self.* Madison, WI: University of Wisconsin Press.

Matthews, J. 1992. *Good and Mad Women: The Historical Construction of Femininity in Twentieth-Century Australia.* North Sydney: Allen & Unwin.

Mellencamp, P. 1992. *High Anxiety: Catastrophe, Age, and Comedy.* Bloomington, IN: Indiana University Press.

Probyn, E. 1996. *Outside Belongings.* New York: Routledge.

Woodward, K. 1991. *Aging and its Discontents: Freud and Other Fictions.* Bloomington, IN: Indiana University Press.

Silencing the Voices of Older Women
Rachel Josefowitz Siegel[1]

Abstract

While there are great variations in attitudes among ethnic and cultural groups, the woman over age 60, whom we shall call old, is an easy target for combined ageist and sexist myths and misconceptions about late life, including false assumptions about knowing and learning. Old mothers are also exposed to mother-blaming and false attributions of power. These undermine her ability to make herself heard and to be taken seriously within her own family as well as in the world at large. Having absorbed these negative stereotypes about herself, she has to overcome both internal and external obstacles before she can speak her own voice. The hiding of old women's wisdom and experience prevents women from forming alliances across generations and from taking political action on their own behalf. This article will focus primarily on mothers over age 60, who constitute a large proportion of the population of old women. Keeping in mind the enormous differences among old women, this is an attempt at identifying some of the factors that contribute to the silencing and discounting of old women to various degrees.

These observations are based on interviews with 56 women over the age of 60 (Siegel 1993), all living in the United States, as well as the author's extensive reading and personal experiences. Most of the women in the sample were white and heterosexual. They were reasonably healthy, living at home, and mostly, but not all, above the poverty line.

---

[1] With many thanks to the women over age 60, who have confided their experiences to me as friends and as interviewees, and especially to Gertrude Wolfner for critical reading, and to Mira J. Spektor and Marcia Cohn Spiegel for additional comments.

Nice Quiet Girls Become Silent Old Women

Women who are over age 60 as we approach the year 2000 still carry traces of early childhood messages. We were taught to be quiet in the presence of our elders, and to defer to male authority outside the home as well as to the men in the family. We were also taught to avoid conflict. These messages were frequently reinforced with physical or cruel punishments and threats, but even in gentler households, the lessons had the powerful backing of a predominantly unquestioned patriarchal social and educational system. The young girl growing up in the first 40 years of our century, learned at a young age, that women are not allowed to raise their voices like men or to make demands like men.

No matter how emancipated some of us are in our old age, or how well we have fought for women's equality in our adult years, we may still carry traces of early messages that interfere with asserting ourselves or speaking up in certain situations. On the whole, as old women we are more comfortable facilitating the speech of others, be they children, male partners, parents, or sisters, instead of speaking up for ourselves. Pauline Wengeroff, a Russian Jewish grandmother in her 70s, writing 100 years ago in 1898, had this to say:

> While to us, obedience to our parents' commands were sacred and inviolable, now, we must submit to our children, subordinating ourselves utterly to their wishes. As was once the case with regard to our parents, so now a word from our children enjoins us to be silent, to hold our tongues, and if this was difficult once, long ago, perhaps it is even more difficult now. If we, as children, listened while our parents told us of all they had experienced, we now keep silent and take careful note, full of pleasure and pride, as our children speak about their lives and ideals. The obsequiousness we show to our children, turns them into egotists and tyrants over us. (cited in Magnus forthcoming)

This passage could have been written today. Ms Wengeroff's words illustrate the internalized or learned self-silencing of her generation as well as ours, and the late life silencing of mothers in the presence of adult children.

By the time a woman has reached her sixtieth year, she has accumulated a lifetime of experiences that have reinforced the early messages. We have learned that our words are often minimized, distorted, not taken seriously, or not heard at all. In the workplace our ideas have often been ignored or co-opted by men without giving us credit, in academia our publications have not been cited as often as those of our male colleagues, in the lower paid occupations, our pay has not been equal to that of men for comparable work. In the home, if our partner is a man, his opinions and his preferences have been taken more seriously than ours. Those of us who are lesbians will have led a closeted life, never speaking of our sexual identity or life style, unless we have lived in or near a sizeable and visible lesbian community such as the San Francisco or New York City areas. We have been exposed to a lifetime of heterosexual assumptions about us, making us feel invisible as well as unheard. We have learned to be doubly silent as old women and as lesbians. Those of us who have experienced violence, and those who are handicapped, also refrain from speaking about that aspect of our lives.

All of us have learned that some topics are not welcomed by others. Our activities in the private domain, within the family, are not considered interesting conversation. Thus we keep silent about the familial aspects of our lives, except when we talk with other women. As we get older, even when we are passionately involved in other pursuits, more and more of our time and energy are focused on self and family, on health care and nutritional care. We find that a larger proportion of our daily concerns are not of interest to others.

These blockages of self-expression may make us feel that it simply does not pay to speak our own mind, unless the situation is extremely important to us. We may, however, have developed some less direct patterns of communicating. The polite and somewhat old-fashioned speech patterns of our generation can be very effective in some situations, although they are ridiculed by some younger people. We may be good at such strategies as cajoling, flattering, compromising, negotiating, palliating, and waiting for the right moment. These useful behaviours can add to our silencing, when they are misconstrued or criticized as female manipulations.

Feminist therapists have described these strategies as healthy survival tactics in a society that discourages the direct expression of women's voices. Other critics are not as kind. Some of us who have lived or still live in a long-term heterosexual relationship, have had enough time to find ways of communicating with our partners; sometimes even teaching our male partners some listening skills. Yet, we are often caught between the fear of being perceived as timid if we do not speak up, too aggressive when we speak forcefully and directly, and manipulative if we use indirect methods of communicating. As we get older, we have the additional problem of being deprived of sympathetic listeners when the age- and death-related topics that concern us are shunned by younger people, and sometimes by our own age-mates as well.

The long-term accumulation of relatively minor incidents that involve having our communications censored, ridiculed, discounted, and ignored can cause severe loss of self-esteem, depression, and stress-related physical symptoms.

Silence and Relationships

In thinking about the silencing of old women in our society, I have found it useful to use the concepts developed by Carol Gilligan and her colleagues in their studies of adolescent girls (Gilligan, Rogers and Tolman 1991). Briefly stated, these authors observed that adolescent girls were likely to censor their own feelings and preferences, essentially losing voice, in the service of maintaining or establishing connections or relationships with others. It is important to remember that ethnic and cultural variations exist among older women as well as among adolescents. It is likely, for instance, that African American women and Jewish women who have highly expressive speech patterns, may speak with more self-assurance than others; on the other hand, their sense of otherness may get in the way, depending on the environment in which they speak.

My interviews and conversations with old women seem to indicate a process similar to that of adolescents, when we maintain silences in order to remain connected or in relationship with the people in our lives whom we love and who are important to us. In the natural progression of ageing, we survive the loss of many friends and loved ones every year; even our doctors and other professionals retire or die, reducing our circle of supportive people. Our need to remain on good terms with those we love, and those who care for us, becomes more pressing when we are alone, and constantly reminded of our own mortality.

In social gatherings, we are often ignored or not invited at all, and if we are single we tend to lose the companionship of friends who are still coupled. Some of us are able to express our anger, others feel unwanted and depressed, thinking that it is all our fault. Older mothers, especially if our children live at a distance, often feel that our children's visits depend on how well we behave ourselves. We feel that we must not raise controversial issues, ask personal questions, suggest possible solutions or alternate ways of seeing a situation, criticize, or insist on doing things our own way. We feel that we must have done something wrong that keeps them away, or that they would come more often or stay longer if we did it right. Some older mothers have indeed been cut off from contact with adult children who have not spoken to their mothers for periods ranging from months to years; the rest of us are haunted by the fear of the same thing happening to us.

One mother in her 70s, upon returning from a brief visit with her previously estranged daughter, said: "If I speak funny, it's because I feel as if my tongue is shorter - I had to bite my tongue so many times." It is no accident that the emerging literature on midlife and old age is hardly ever written from the perspective of the older mother or older woman, except in praise of children and of families. The fear of being misunderstood, estranged, or cut off from our children keeps us from speaking of the pain.

The silencing that we absorbed in childhood, and experienced as adults, is now compounded by the silencing of old age. Our words are easily dismissed or ridiculed as Old Wives Tales, or in Yiddish as 'Bobbe Meises', grandmother stories. We now learn that we are not likely to find a listening audience, which causes us to discount our own wisdom. The silencing of old women seriously disrupts the flow of information and accumulated wisdom from one generation of women to the next, making it difficult to form long lasting alliances among women or to build effective power structures that could change society. Our silence thus helps to maintain the male-dominated status quo.

Silence Caused by Gendered Misconceptions About Old Age

'Old' is such an undesirable word in our society, that both men and women will do almost anything to avoid using it. When we can no longer call ourselves middle-aged, we are usually not willing to call ourselves old, but we begin to feel a significant shift into the later years of life (Siegel 1993). Age oppression is the only group discrimination that will eventually affect all of us if we live long enough (Sonderegger and Siegel 1990), but it is perhaps the least recognized and least understood oppression of our culture, and it includes obvious gender differences. By the time a woman reaches midlife, whatever the definition of that stage, or even earlier, she feels the impact of combined age and gender discrimination.

Old people are assumed to be incapable of new learning, in spite of a growing body of evidence showing that many old people continue to enjoy emotional and intellectual growth, as well as physical challenges in their last years of life. Bob G. Knight (1992), in a review of the literature on intelligence and memory in late life, reports that old people retain information when it is relevant and immediately applicable. Their poor performance on intelligence tests that require speed and yes or no answers does not indicate their true abilities, because they are slower in retrieving information from a very full memory bank, and they tend to see the world in its complexity, rather than in either/or categories. All this indicates an ongoing ability to learn, especially if it continues to be exercised.

Old men continue to be treated with a measure of dignity and respect for their accomplishments, even after retiring from positions of accomplishment. Old women are only rarely given such recognition. In the first place, fewer old women have had the opportunity to exercise our fullest potential and to rise to high levels of accomplishment; we are more likely to have been the unrecognized, behind-the-scenes facilitators of male accomplishments. Furthermore, old women, like women of all ages, are more likely to be judged by physical attractiveness than by personal accomplishments, and old is by definition considered unattractive in women, much more than it is in men.

Old women in general are still silenced within our own families as well as outside the home. Our words and concerns are not taken as seriously as the words of old men by the professionals who should be there to serve us, such as doctors, lawyers, therapists, and publishers. The lack of medical and psychological research on old women, compared to men, has been well-documented. In the media, images of old women are either absent, depicted as sentimentalized nurturers, or unattractive objects of ridicule. Old men tend to be portrayed as wise, attractive, distinguished and powerful. There has been some growth in the number of books and articles about old women that are written in the old woman's own voice, and many more are needed (see suggested readings). The women over 60 who were interviewed by the author, expressed astonishment and great satisfaction at the opportunity to be included in a publication about them. In one of the group interviews, a participant said: "We're never in the picture". The other women nodded in agreement.

The pathologizing of old women is another source of painful silencing. We are often labelled self-centered, depressed or paranoid, when we give voice to the anger, hopelessness, powerlessness and fear that can accompany the natural diminution of faculties in old age. Our families or care-givers, unwilling to face their own feelings about old age, may prefer to see our reactions as personal flaws or weaknesses, and so do we, instead of recognizing that these feelings are appropriate responses to our life situation. We have good reasons to feel depressed at times, and would like to be able to talk about it. Our feelings may well develop into worrisome symptoms if we are in an environment in which our complaints are dismissed or denied.

Silence Caused by Mother-Blaming

Many old women, whether they are heterosexual, bisexual or gay, are or have been mothers. The interactions between us and our adult daughters and sons have hardly ever been discussed from the ageing mother's perspective. While there is a great deal of professional as well as popular literature about ageing and about old mothers, most of it is written by and for middle-aged men and women. At best, such literature is a loving acknowledgement of the mother's contributions and sacrifices; often it is about taking care of her, and at worst it is mother-blaming. When mothers are blamed, we tend to internalize the blame, turning it into self-doubts and self-blame. We may choose to remain silent in order to avoid such blame. We may also remain silent when we are not invited to participate in conversations or when we sense a lack of interest in what we have to say.

Many daughters and sons maintain loving and respectful relationships with ageing mothers, providing care and emotional, physical and financial support as needed. Many families enjoy spending inter-generational time together without undue friction. Some adult sons and daughters may even seek advice from us, may value our opinions and our memories. These positive interactions, however, do not negate the fact that, on occasion for some and routinely for others, we are stifled, silenced and blamed, and that such negative interactions most often go unnoticed.

Paula Caplan (1989) has written extensively about how and how often therapists blame mothers and how our society teaches and encourages mother-blaming. Attributing blame to mothers is part of the more generalized woman-blaming that maintains the patriarchy. The easy scape-goating of mothers and of all women serves to deflect responsibility from the male-dominated institutions that fail to adequately serve children and families. Old mothers have been blamed when we no longer have the energy to be as helpful and available as used to be, when we could not protect our loved ones from violence or poverty, when our best efforts and our love were not sufficient to make up for the evils of an unfair society. We have been blamed when we are less than perfect and silent listeners, or when our words are not what the adult child wants to hear.

Those of us who are immigrant mothers or feminist mothers are subjected to additional blame, anger and disappointment from our children because we do not live by mainstream socially accepted norms; we do not fit in and we make it difficult for them to fit in. In some ways, we represent the extremes on a continuum of mothers who do not fit in, and who get blamed for holding on to or conveying the 'wrong' culture, the 'wrong' values, that is, the culture and values of origin, or the culture and values of resistance to the mainstream.

It is not unusual for mothers to end up feeling silenced within the family, by the fear of being blamed, misunderstood, or even punished for speaking our mind. The punishment takes the form of avoidance and distancing.

Gender Issues

Those of us who are mothers over 60 have lived through and have learned to adapt to enormous technological, social and economic changes. So have our children. Not least among these changes are the revolution in gender expectations and the partially aborted revolution in gender roles. These changes have created tensions between us and our daughters that differ somewhat from the tensions between us and our sons. While we are still perceived and resented as the conveyors of societal norms and gender expectations, we are also resented when we have become the conveyors of resistance to those norms and expectations. As mothers, we are often blamed for the unresolved tensions of a society in constant change.

The gender-related messages that we gave our children in the 1940s, 1950s and early 1960s have changed over the years. We have changed and grown, as have society's gender expectations and gender roles. Many of us had conveyed ambivalence and confusion as we tried so hard to be true to ourselves and to also adapt to a society that valued us less than men and did not want us to be treated as equals.

Mother-blaming by Daughters

It hurts, when we hear that a daughter does not want to become like her mother. Mother-blaming among women - by daughters, for instance - is an example of how oppressed people blame each other, seeing ourselves and each other through the negative lens of our oppressors. This kind of blaming within the oppressed group often takes the form of denying the oppression and assigning individual blame or pathology instead. Mother and daughter both mirror the attitudes of society towards women. We blame each other for making less than perfect life choices. We hardly ever realize that we will still be oppressed no matter what choices we make, as long as society favours men over women in so many spheres. There are times when the price is high, no matter what we choose.

The tensions between us and our adult daughters reflect the hurdles and disappointments that we both feel in a society that devalues us. Our attention focuses on each other instead of looking at our patriarchal society in which individual men and their male-dominated institutions are engaged in a sophisticated backlash against the gains that women have made.

Another source of blame lies in the expectation of greater intimacy with adult daughters than with sons, which can turn into a greater disappointment when it falls short of expectations. As feminist mothers we have tried to empower our daughters, and have urged them to expect equal treatment and equal rights. In some ways, you might say that we have tried to masculinize our daughters, teaching them the skills and attitudes that are admired in men. We may get blamed for having instilled impossible goals, since society has not changed enough to accept and reward women on an equal basis.

Fortunately, some of us have been able to resolve some of these issues with our daughters, we have broken the silence, we confide and empower each other, and we take pleasure in each other's company.

Mother-blaming by Sons

Mother-blaming by sons may well be an echoing of the demeaning and devaluing messages about mothers that our sons have heard from their fathers and other men, combined with the personal resentment or fear of losing male privileges. There may also be elements of envy at the closer relationships enjoyed and expected between mothers and daughters, combined with the anger of the little boy being taught to 'act like a man' when his attachment to his mother is still very strong. The tensions and silences between us and our adult sons also reflect the distancing from mothers that our society considers a healthy part of adult male development.

As feminist mothers, we have tried to empower our sons. We have urged them to give up some of the male attitudes and privileges that interfere with empathic and equal relationships. In some ways, you might say that we have tried to feminize our sons, teaching them skills and attitudes that are not valued by other men. As a result, our feminism can be perceived by sons as a threat to their masculinity; in Freudian terms, it can trigger a fear of castration. Some of us have noticed that any mention of feminist issues or ideas can provoke angry outbursts in our sons with all the rhetoric of the current male backlash. These outbursts are frequently followed by prolonged periods during which our sons put emotional and physical distance between themselves and us.

Fortunately, some of us have been able to resolve some of these issues with our sons; we have developed some measure of intimacy and meaningful communication across gender lines and across generations.

Silence Caused by Being Misunderstood

We are not only silenced; we are frequently misunderstood and mislabelled. In general, the people who write about us have no personal knowledge of late life. Feminists have shown how wrong men can be when making pronouncements about women. Therapists have paid attention to how wrong a parent can be in assessing a child's personality or the child's issues. That same wisdom has not been applied to understanding how wrong a younger person can be when making pronouncements about old women. Even the most loving sons or daughters, who think that they really understand us, may have no idea of what we are really thinking or feeling. We often become the repositories of other people's fantasies about old women; we may be idealized or demonized, but we are seldom understood.

A common myth about us is that we are apolitical. The women I interviewed and the women in my own support group are intensely engaged in the issues of our times, but we may chose not discuss these in mixed groups where we find it more difficult to be taken seriously. We relish the opportunity to talk politics and world issues among ourselves.

Silence Caused by the Myth of the All-powerful Mother

One of the factors that contributes to the misperceptions and silencing of old women, is the patriarchal assumption that exaggerates the power of women, in order to keep women in their proper place. When applied to old mothers, this confers power to our self-expression that we do not claim or want. We are often misperceived as overly powerful when in fact we may have even less power or control over our bodies, our families and our circumstances than we had when we were younger. The false attribution of power seems to give our children, and the experts who advise them, permission to resist our message, to discount our words, to criticize us or pathologize us by perceiving us as over-controlling.

We may well feel intimidated, as well as hurt and angry when an adult child says: 'You don't realize how powerful you are - or how powerful your words are. When you ask a question it feels like an interrogation, and when you make suggestions it feels like a criticism of how we do things.' We do not feel at all powerful during this interaction, and in most cases wanted only to understand the child's world or to share a piece of our own wisdom and experience. True enough, mothers, like other family members, may at times feel the right to be more intrusive than others, and may offer unsolicited advice, but when that happens, the 'child's' response is often more abusive than the mother's infringement.

Another element that contributes to the exaggerated attribution of power to mothers, is that many adults still assume that the mother's life never stops revolving around the child and that all of the mother's actions and decisions are child-centered and child-directed. We do indeed never stop feeling a deep attachment to our children and delight in their presence. But we also have needs and preferences of our own, and a life of our own. If we did not, we would be totally dependent on our spouse or children for the meaning of our lives, and would be considered a burden to them. The fact that we have our own life-direction may arouse complicated feelings in our partner, our adult children, and our critics. It may also be difficult for our children to take in the fact that we have changed over the years since they left home, especially when they live far away and only see us once or twice a year. We are no longer the mother they knew when they were growing up,

If we have achieved success outside the home and have become independent, we may be envied by our children, but if our whole life is centred on our children, we may be resented. Either way we lose. In order to diminish the critical voices surrounding us, we may learn to go about our business without talking about it.

The Silence of Minding Our Own Business

Popular wisdom conspires with psychological theorizing and self-help literature in advising mothers of adult sons and daughters to mind their own business. Under the label of respect, we are asked to bend over backwards in accepting our adult offspring's life choices, to stifle our own values and preferences, and to change our ways when we are with them. This may or may not be a good thing when the respect is mutual. The same attitude of respect however is not applied to mothers. We are often subject to overt or subtle criticism and disapproval of our own values, politics, lifestyles, ethnic and religious traditions, and of our lifetime habits of speech, dress, food and housekeeping. If we were to express similar disapproval, snickering, or criticism of our daughters and sons, we would suffer severe consequences.

When we accept our children's radical or innovative life choices, we are admired and idealized by some, and seen as deviant by others. But when we expect that kind of acceptance from our children, we are more likely to be perceived as rigid, demanding, domineering, and over-controlling. This double standard is in direct contradiction to how we were brought up, and how we expected to be treated in our old age. Even our simplest expression of individuality or opinions is often misperceived as an attack on our children. We are expected to be attentive listeners, continuing to provide unconditional love and acceptance, but we are not expected to receive the same in return.

These are but some of the ways in which our attempts to be heard and to be taken seriously are undermined within our own family. We may have to stifle our personality and our voice within the family, even when we have developed a strong and independent persona and voice in other areas of our lives.

The Silence of Loneliness and Grief

Since women's life expectancy is longer than that of men, a large percentage of old women are widows or sole survivors of an intimate relationship. The transition to living alone brings on the silence of loneliness. We now have no one to share our intimate moments, our joys, our worries, our hopes, our challenges or even the everyday details of our lives. We have no one to talk to without making a special effort to connect with someone outside the home. It is a major period of personal growth, as we learn to cope with the many deaths of loved ones and the additional losses of late life, the shift to retirement, the slowing down or diminishment of our faculties, the downsizing of our home and finances, the adjustment to illness, and so on. We may well feel more vulnerable and insecure than we have ever felt before, and yet we also discover strengths we never knew we had. On some level, whether actively or subconsciously, we are preoccupied with thoughts and preparations for the end of life, while we are living life as fully as we still can. We have few, if any, willing listeners as we grapple with these issues. We have periods of grieving for our partner, parents, siblings, friends, and are most likely doing it alone. Our need to talk about our grief most often exceeds the patience of potential listeners, and again, we turn to silence.

Those of us who are immigrants, and especially those who are survivors of the Holocaust or other forms of genocide, carry the additional burden of grieving in silence in a social environment that wants us to put all that behind and enjoy life. It is painful for us to talk about the trauma that we have experienced, and it is painful not to. It is difficult for us to convey our cultural heritage to our families and to our new hosts, and it is difficult to face death without being able to transmit that heritage.

Those who have been lesbians throughout our adult lives are likely to have lived in closeted, heterosexual pretence, unable to talk of the affectional and sexual dimensions of our lives. Our younger counterparts, and those who discovered a lesbian identity in late life, are more likely to have established supportive relationships with other lesbians, and been able to talk more openly of their sexual identities. When the lesbian partner is ill or dying, we do not have access to the medical or legal advantages that are taken for granted by heterosexual couples. We often face a major dilemma in trying to establish a health care proxy or in making financial provisions for the surviving partner. The silence of our sexual identities may catch up with lesbians in late life, when we face the possibility of having our true identities exposed through illness or death.

Legacies

In late life, old women are concerned with the emotional, cultural and financial legacy we leave behind. In the group interviews we talked of putting our house in order. Who will get our most cherished belongings, how to divide our assets, and perhaps most important, how to convey our values and our personal and family history. After a lifetime of taking care of others, women, much more than men, are concerned about not leaving too much work for our survivors after we die.

Many mothers feel an urge to reconnect with our children and grandchildren. We yearn to see more of them, to let them know who we really are and have been, and what has been important in our lives. Unfortunately, the fullness of our children's lives and the demands on their time do not always make this type of visiting possible. Our children, pressured by the demands of the corporate world, find it difficult to be as available to us as they would like to be, even when they live in the same community, which is less and less common.

"My daughter loves me, I know she does, but there is no room for me in her life", said a mother in her 80s, having recently moved to her daughter's community. Our children who are single parents or in dual career couples have special demands on their time and energy that cause them to even less available to us. They may however have more contact with us when they need us for various kinds of support.

Adult children may not be emotionally ready to receive the memories and family history that we wish to pass on, even when time is not the determining factor. They may not appreciate the gift, they may change the topic, drift off, or get edgy because the telling is perceived as an imposition of our values and our way of life. Or they may not want to focus on our mortality. Sometimes we are made to feel that there is something wrong with our efforts to transmit family or ethnic values. Grandchildren are often more eager to hear Grandma's stories, by-passing the complicated baggage that may exist between us and our children (Schlesinger 1997).

Beyond Silencing

Not all old women feel silenced. Not all old mothers feel silenced. The factors inhibiting speech usually affect one area of life more than another. The old woman who speaks well and freely at work may not do so at the doctor's office or at home; the old woman who speaks clearly at home may not do so in other places.

Many of us have found our voice through the women's movement. We found the support and skills to break out of the silence in small consciousness raising groups, among like-minded women friends, in larger feminist gatherings and conferences, and through woman-affirming literature. We have also been helped by the presence of ageing women leaders as role models in politics, in grassroots organizations, in labour unions and professions. We have found a tremendous amount of support among our age mates and in groups of women who share our concerns.

We hope that women who will reach their 60s in future decades will have benefited from the changes in gender expectations and in patterns of communication between generations. Younger men are better listeners and do more parenting. Younger families speak much more openly with each other than they did 50 or more years ago. We dare to hope that mother-blaming will also diminish as fathers take a more active role in parenting.

There is a great deal more to be said about the silencing of old women that goes beyond the scope of this presentation. My hope is that this is a beginning in the direction of making it possible for more old women to speak up and be heard.

Recommendations for Policy and Action

- Research about old women needs to be initiated, designed, and administered by women over 60 from the old woman's perspective, and must include the voices of old women.
- Educational policies at every age need to be sensitive and pro-active in facilitating and encouraging girls and women to speak up effectively, even in male-dominated environments.
- Educational curricula must include conflict-resolution skills.
- The training of lawyers, ministers, health-care providers and mental health workers must include better listening skills applied to old women.
- Old women need to be presented as role models and repositories of cultural wisdom in textbooks, media, and the arts.
- Information needs to be widely disseminated about the ability of old people to learn and to grow.
- The myths about the power of old women need to be exposed and replaced with accurate information.
- The myths about the unending availability and power of old mothers need to be exposed and replaced with accurate information.
- Friendships among old women need to be encouraged and facilitated.
- Publications about old women, written from their own perspectives, need to be widely distributed.
- Alliances between old women and younger women need to be fostered through workshops, conferences, and in small groups.
- Our society's high valuation of youth, strength, and independence needs to be re-examined in light of the realities of normal ageing, human vulnerability, and interdependence.

References

Caplan, P.J. 1989. *Don't Blame Mother: Mending the Mother-daughter Relationship*. New York: Harper and Row.

Gilligan, C., A. Rogers and D. Tannen, eds. 1991. *Women, Girls and Psychotherapy: Reframing Resistance*. Binghamton, NY: Haworth Press.

Knight, B.G. 1992. "Introduction", *Older Adults in Psychotherapy: Case Histories*. Newbury Park, CA: Sage Publications, pp. ix- xxiv.

Magnus, S. forthcoming. *Memoirs of the Grandmother: Scenes from the Cultural Life of Russian Jewry in the Nineteenth Century*, Vol.1. Translated from Wengeroff, Pauline. *Memoiren einer Grossmutter*. Berlin: Verlag von Poppelauer. 1913. By permission from University of California Press.

Schlesinger, R.A. 1997. "Personal Reflections on Being a Jewish Grandmother: L'Chol Dor Va Dor", in R. Siegel and E. Cole, eds., *Celebrating the Lives of Jewish Women: Patterns in a Feminist Sampler*. Binghamton, NY: Haworth Press.

Siegel, R.J. 1993. "Between Midlife and Old Age: Never Too Old to Learn", in E. Cole and N. Davis, eds., special issue on Women and Aging, *Journal of Women and Therapy*, Binghamton, NY: Haworth Press.

Sonderegger, T. and R.J. Siegel. 1990. "Ethical Considerations in Therapy with Older Women", in H. Lerman and N. Porter, eds., *Feminist Ethics in Psychotherapy*. New York: Springer.

Gendered Living Environments for the Elderly in Turkey and Sweden

E. Olcay İmamoglu and Vacit İmamoglu

Abstract

This paper reports on the physical, social and psychological conditions of Turkish elderly, both women and men, selected from small towns, cities and metropolitan areas, and compares them with a similar group of elderly women and men in Sweden.[1] Gender and cultural differences are found with regard to the nature of elderly people's social networks, physical environment and life satisfaction, and attitudes towards institutional living. The findings suggest ways to improve elderly living environments in Turkey.

Introduction

At the 1971 White House Conference on ageing, in Washington, DC, it was reported that the most important element in the lives of the elderly, aside from their spouses (cited in Carp 1976), was housing. In spite of its importance, however, housing should be considered not as an independent unit, but as one element in an interactive system; that is, housing conditions interact with other social and physical aspects of the older persons' living environments. Therefore, housing for the elderly should be understood as referring to their total living environments,

---

[1] Portions of this report have been published in İmamoglu and İmamoglu (1992 a, b), İmamoglu et al. (1993), and in the Habitat Preconference publication entitled, "Housing Question of the Others" (1996).

including their social and physical aspects. Hence, the goals of housing programmes have been extended beyond mere provision of physical shelter to improving the quality of life (Carp 1976). This understanding has given rise to an examination of what kind of living environments may be best for older people, which in turn requires a careful examination of the current living environments of the elderly.

In Turkey, consideration of the current living environments and special housing needs of the elderly has generally been neglected by social scientists as well as designers, planners and decision-makers. Not only the housing needs of the elderly, but virtually all dimensions of ageing have received no systematic research interest in Turkey. In contrast to developed countries, old age is not regarded as a problem in Turkey; however, due to the rapid social and economic changes taking place, already it is becoming more difficult to continue with conventional lifestyles and existing patterns of caring for the elderly, particularly in the cities, where both spouses often tend to work and live in three-bedroom flats designed for the prototypical nuclear family with two to three children. Furthermore, Turkish people in general are reluctant to accept old age as a problem because the Turkish culture is based on close-knit interpersonal relationships where support and sacrifice of parents towards their children, and the obedience to and responsibility of children to care for their parents in old age are widely accepted strong values (İmamoglu 1981; 1987; Kagitçíbasi 1982). However, unless the problems resulting from changing lifestyles are acknowledged and examined, alternative forms of accommodation, that would be more suitable to the needs of the elderly, cannot be provided.

This paper reports findings from a study of physical, social and psychological characteristics of people between the ages of 55 and 71, living in small towns, cities, and metropolitan areas. In the related literature, 'older persons' have been defined in terms of different variables, such as age, health, retirement, life events and the judgements of planners and investigators. Because of the importance of finances in problems of housing, it has been suggested that retirement may be a more useful index than age in defining the criterion group (Carp 1976). Accordingly, respondents in this study were either retired or if employed, over the age of 60. The Turkish study was part of a cross-cultural project, allowing a comparison with the Swedish case (İmamoglu et al 1993), and thus providing some suggestion as to the cross-cultural generalizability of the findings.

Method and Subjects

The Turkish sample consisted of 448 respondents (166 females, 282 males) between the ages of 55 and 71, with a mean age of 62.4. The sample was selected by partly stratified random sampling according to area, age, sex and retirement scheme. The objective was not to represent the whole population, but rather to represent different lifestyles in different geographical areas with varying levels of urbanization. Therefore, respondents were selected from ten different areas, namely, the western, northern, central, central-southern and south-eastern parts of Anatolia. These ten areas were considered in three groups representing the urbanisational level of the areas: a) Metropolitan - 57 females and l03 males, from İzmir and Ankara, cities of 1.5 - 2.3 million; b) City - 58 females and 86 males from Kayseri, Burdur, Zonguldak and Gaziantep, smaller cities of l00,000 - 400,000; c) Small Town - 51 females and 93 males from Bulancak, Safranbolu, Nazilli and Milas, small towns of l0,000 - 40,000, and the surrounding villages. Of the respondents only l4 had not yet retired; about three-fourths were not working, whereas the remaining were working after retirement. All respondents were living on some kind of social security.

The Swedish sample consisted of 502 respondents (245 females, 257 males) between the ages of 60 and 71, with a mean age of 65.2. As described more fully in Küller (l988), they were selected from five different localities, an inner-city area and a suburb of Malmö (a city of 225,000); a district in Karlskrona (a town of 30,000), and one island and one coastal area in the Karlskrona region. As noted above, the Turkish sample was somewhat younger than the Swedish; however, this is thought to be justifiable in view of the differences between the two countries in terms of life expectancy and retirement age. In l986, life expectancy in Turkey was 65 for females and 61 for males, while the corresponding values in Sweden were 80 and 74. Moreover, the retirement age in Turkey is 50 for females and 55 for males rather than 60 and 65, as is the case in Sweden. Thus, despite difference in chronological age, the two samples are considered to be fairly comparable in terms of psychological age.

The interview forms consisted of booklets of 376 questions for which respondents selected an answer and 84 open-ended questions. The questions were adapted to the Turkish situation from the English version of the original used by Küller (l988), making some appropriate changes and additions. The questions were arranged to progress from relatively objective ones about housing, neighbourhood and mobility patterns to the more personal ones about the social living environments, retirement experiences, recreation, health and psychological status of the respondents. Then there were some questions to be filled in by the interviewers about the physical environment and the interview situation. On average, interviews took 76 minutes in Turkey and 96 minutes in Sweden. The respondents generally were positive towards the interviews and most were willing to help again in the future.

Relations with Social Networks

The majority of the Turkish respondents were married and living with their spouses, only about 10 percent lived alone (İmamoglu and İmamoglu 1992a). Compared to the Swedes, the Turkish respondents seem to live not only in larger households, but also have larger external networks, with whom they interact more frequently (İmamoglu et al 1993). The differences between the two countries are especially large in terms of households, neighbours and workmates, with Turks reporting two to four times the number of individuals in these categories as Swedes.

The Turkish elderly appear to have larger social networks with whom they interact more frequently, particularly in smaller towns; mean frequency of social contacts decline with urbanization, except for interactions with children and siblings (İmamoglu and İmamoglu 1992b). However, even the Turks living in metropolitan areas have more social contacts compared to Swedes.

Evaluation of Living Environments

Although the Turkish elderly have larger social networks with whom they interact more frequently, they on the whole report feeling lonelier and feeling more negatively about ageing and their lives compared to Swedes (İmamoglu and İmamoglu 1992b; İmamoglu et al. 1993). These findings support the arguments that the higher expectations arising from close-knit social networks (Wellman 1979), may give rise to feelings of loneliness and dissatisfaction even if the quantity of interaction is adequate (Hirsch 1979; 1980; Rook 1987; Williams and Solano 1983). Having lived in a culture of close-knit interpersonal relationships, the Turkish respondents might have developed high interpersonal expectations, which at times may be unrealistic and lag behind the rapid social change taking place in Turkey. Feeling that what they get from their social network falls below their comparison level which they feel they deserve, they may end up being unsatisfied with their existing circumstances (Thibaut and Kelley 1959).

Apart from such cross-cultural differences, in both Sweden and Turkey, having more social contacts is related to feeling less lonely and more positively about ageing. Also in both countries, the lonelier respondents seem to feel more negatively about ageing, themselves and their lives (İmamoglu and İmamoglu 1992b). Thus, in both cultures, social contacts seem to help release feelings of loneliness and worries about ageing; however, in Turkey, frequency of social contacts also seems directly related to feeling satisfied with one's self and life; whereas they appear to be unrelated in Sweden. In other words, Turkey being more of a culture-of-relatedness where interdependence rather than independence is predominant (İmamoglu 1987), frequency of interactions with social networks seems to have far-reaching effects for the individuals' satisfaction with their selves and life situations.

In addition to the already close relationships with members of the social network, Turkish people seem to retain expectations and preferences for even closer relationships. For example, a strong cultural difference is noted in terms of preference for living next-door to one's children and their families, which, in contrast to Swedes and the English, is strongly favoured by Turks (İmamoglu et al. 1993; Mikellides and Willcocks 1987). Other investigators have also noted that the spatial proximity of the separate Turkish family and kin households, even in urban areas, symbolizes and enhances the close family and kin bonds which tend to generalize to neighbourhoods (Olson 1982; Senyapílí 1978). In general, although the majority of Turkish families are nuclear (Timur 1972; İmamoglu and İmamoglu 1992a), the functions of an extended family are served, whereby close family ties extending into kinship relations provide material and psychological support when needed. Such interpersonal bonds seem to be very important for the general psychological well-being of Turkish individuals, such that reduced frequency of interactions tends to relate not only to feelings of loneliness but also to negative feelings about self, life and ageing. The Turkish elderly give more importance to the 'people' in their neighbourhoods than do the Swedish and the British elderly (İmamoglu and İmamoglu 1990; Küller et al 1990). In other words, personal (home-related) and interpersonal variables seem to be the most important aspects of living environments for the Turkish elderly, which does not seem to change as a result of urbanization (İmamoglu and İmamoglu 1992a).

Cross-Cultural Similarities and Differences Concerning Gender

In both countries, females interact relatively more frequently with their children and males with their workmates, thus confirming the stereotypical gender-role differences of the family-oriented women and the work-oriented men even during retirement. Furthermore, females in both countries report feeling more loneliness, insecurity and fears of not being able to care for themselves. Thus, women in both cultures seem to experience more negative feelings than men in and around retirement. One possible explanation for this may be that males are more reluctant to admit their negative feelings about ageing and loneliness. Although congruent with the traditional less-expressive male role, there was also some contrary evidence; for example, both Turkish and the Swedish males reported more feelings of not being needed than did Swedish females (İmamoglu et al. 1993).

Another explanation for these observed gender differences might be women's higher expectations for close meaningful interpersonal relationships (Sarason, Shearin, Pierce and Sarason 1987). Dyadic relationships between men have been reported to lack intimacy, often resembling parallel play or meeting work-oriented goals rather than truly interpersonal needs (cited in Lowenthal and Robinson 1976). Women, on the other hand, having lived their lives with more other-oriented social-emotional investments and concerns, may experience feelings of loneliness relative to their prior life stages, as well as insecurities and fears about ageing and not being able to care for themselves. After all, they were the ones to care for others, but who will care for them if they find themselves unable to do so?

In general, gender differences seem to be more pronounced in Turkey than in Sweden. This may reflect a sharper differentiation of lifestyles in Turkey by gender. Although formal gender equality was secured in Turkey by means of laws and regulations following the establishment of the Republic, beliefs and traditions concerning gender issues have tended to lag behind these legal changes, especially in the rural areas.

Turkish males on the whole tend to be in a more advantageous position compared to their female counterparts, a situation reflected in attitudes towards ageing. Turkish men have larger social networks and interact more frequently with them; have more positive self-images, and more positive attitudes towards getting older (İmamoglu et al. 1993). These findings are consistent with reports of Turkish men being sheltered from new gender role demands paralleling urban change (Kandiyoti 1982). Thus, male Turks seem to continue their well-sheltered position during the time of retirement as well. They are not only well cared for at home but also seem to continue their interpersonal ties with their workmates and other friends. In fact, mean frequency of interaction with friends appears to be highest for Turkish males and lowest for Swedish males (İmamoglu et al. 1993). This difference probably is due to the availability of neighbourhood coffee-houses in Turkey where most retired males meet. It supports anthropological reports that Turkish young men spend a lot of time together and develop intense friendships with each other (Olson 1982). Although the sex of friends interacted with was not specified in our study, Turkish males' frequent interactions with their friends may be interpreted as a continuation into old age of a pattern observed in their youth.

Turkish females, lacking access to coffee-houses, interact more with their neighbours as well as their children. It is a widespread practice for Turkish women to even have structured reception days for social visits; interactions with neighbours tend to be very frequent, sometimes continuing on a daily basis, in the form of visits for morning coffee or afternoon tea. Thus Turkish women have more frequent interactions than Turkish men in their close social network of children and neighbours. They have both larger networks and more frequent interactions compared to both Swedish men and women (İmamoglu et al. 1993).

Still, Turkish female respondents' assessment of their psychological well-being seems more negative than that of the other comparison groups. In addition to their negative feelings about ageing and of loneliness, which appear to be shared by the Swedish women, Turkish women's judgement of their own self-image is very low, whereas Swedish females have equally positive self-images as Swedish males. Compared to others, Turkish females report feeling older and judge their health to be inferior. They also have highest feelings of not being needed (İmamoglu et al. 1993). Thus Turkish elderly women's psychological self-assessment points to their more disadvantageous position relative both to men of their own country and to Swedish women.

This pattern of gender differences does not seem to change as a function of the urbanization level of the area of residence (İmamoglu and İmamoglu 1990, 1992b). Elderly women need to develop alternative ways of viewing their life situations as harmonious consequences of lives spent in worthwhile personal and impersonal endeavours. Such an outcome is not a natural concomitant of retirement but requires dramatic changes in the mental outlooks of both men and women towards valuing human qualities in every person regardless of sex.

Physical Environmental Conditions and Life Satisfaction

Comparisons of the physical environments of the Turkish elderly, at different levels of urbanization, indicate that conditions are quite similar in terms of dwelling standards, prosperity, evaluations of dwellings and neighbourhoods, as well as size of households (İmamoglu and İmamoglu 1992a). In fact, there appear to be more differences between the living conditions of the central and squatter areas of the metropolitan areas on the physical environmental indices rather than between small towns, cities and metropolises. However, although the physical living conditions of the elderly generally do not differ as a function of urbanization, and those observed differences with regards to the indices of dwelling facilities and location standards tend to favour the metropolitan areas, still, life satisfaction of Turkish elderly decreases from small towns to metropolises. In other words, the elderly report feeling less satisfied with their lives as a function of urbanization. Possibly the causes of this decline in life satisfaction might be related to the social changes accompanying urbanisation.

Several findings support this argument. First, among the seven qualities valued in living environments, the elderly in general consider the personal (home-related) and interpersonal aspects of their neighbourhoods most important; followed by the functional and natural characteristics; while the architectural and recreational aspects are least important (İmamoglu and İmamoglu 1992a). This is in contrast to some other cultures; for example, the elderly in Britain, who rank dwelling most important, rank people in the neighbourhood fifth in importance (Mikellides and Willcocks 1987); similarly, in Sweden dwelling is ranked second while people are ranked fourth (Küller et al. 1990). Thus, dwellings and people seem to constitute the most important aspects of the living environment for elderly people in Turkey.

In spite of this importance attributed to the social environment, the Turkish elderly seem to be less satisfied with the social aspects of their living environments as a function of urbanization. For example, the means for the size of social networks and the frequency of interactions with their social networks decline with urbanization, except for interactions with children and siblings (İmamoglu and İmamoglu 1990; 1992b). Furthermore, with increasing age the elderly report feeling more loneliness (İmamoglu and İmamoglu 1992b).

Attitudes Towards Institutional Living

Significant cross-cultural differences were observed concerning both attitudes towards institutional living and the relationships between these attitudes and those involving current life situations (İmamoglu and İmamoglu 1992b). The Turkish elderly generally are more negative towards institutional living than the Swedish. For the Turkish elderly, having fewer social contacts, feeling lonelier and feeling more negatively about ageing and current life situation are related to more favourable attitudes towards institutional living. In contrast, for the Swedish respondents, the only related variable of frequency of social contacts is positively correlated with the attitude towards institutional living. In other words, while the Turkish elderly seem to view institutional living as a last resort, this is not so for the Swedish elderly who seem to feel relatively more favourable towards institutional living.

One reason for the generally negative attitudes of the Turkish elderly towards institutional living may be found in the strongly held cultural values of interpersonal relatedness and embeddedness, upon which one's sense of being seems to depend. Another reason may derive from the Turkish elderly respondents' notions of institutions. In Turkey, the institutional services for the elderly are generally limited to old folks homes which are inhabited by only a very small proportion of the elderly, most of whom lack alternative means of support and accommodation (Özer 1990). By contrast, in countries such as Sweden, where there are numerous institutions offering high-quality services to a great number of the elderly population, such institutions may seem as available alternatives without negative personal implications for their inhabitants.

In spite of the generally negative attitudes towards institutional living in Turkey, related attitudes become less negative with urbanization and age. This change is important, since large cities can be considered the barometers of social change and hence indicative of future trends. The age effect implies that after age 60, people might start thinking more realistically about the problems of ageing, and hence, might look relatively more favourably on alternative living styles beyond normative values. Thus, the social changes accompanying urbanization, as well as reduced social contacts and increased feelings of loneliness accompanying ageing, might lead the Turkish elderly to be more positive towards alternative living styles (İmamoglu and İmamoglu 1992b). In fact, a comparison of the Turkish elderly residing in high- or low-quality institutions indicated that although their attitudes towards institutional living in general appeared to be relatively resistant to change, high-quality institutions were perceived as good options by the elderly residing there; and that apart from the option of a high-quality institution, being better educated and being a female seemed to play a role in deciding to move to an institution (Imamo_lu and Kílíç in press).

Recommendations for Planners and Designers

Our findings suggest the need to plan special living environments in Turkey, particularly for the metropolitan elderly, which would provide more opportunities for meaningful social interactions. According to Turkish laws, each healthy citizen of 60 years and over is eligible to live in the state-owned institutions for the elderly. However, in a country of 60 million there are only about 90 such institutions, mostly of low quality (Özer 1990); by contrast, in England, with a similar population, the number of institutions for the elderly is 1990 (Weal and Weal 1988). The fact that the attitudes of the elderly in Turkey tend to be relatively more positive towards institutional living with increasing age and urbanization, indicates that the demand for alternative living patterns, including institutional living, might be expected to increase in the near future, particularly in metropolitan areas.

In particular, women who were found to have worries about getting old and not being able to care for themselves might be expected to be relatively more receptive to alternative means of living. Accordingly, they appear to favour sheltered housing relatively more than men who generally have the opportunity to rely on women to be taken care of (İmamoglu and İmamoglu 1990; 1992b). In fact, a follow-up study indicated that of the Turkish elderly residing in institutions, women appear to have moved to the institutions more voluntarily than have men and seem to be more satisfied with both institutional living and life in general (İmamoglu and Kílíç in press).

Our findings concerning size and composition of households, indicate that the elderly in Turkey generally do not live in extended families. However, they tend to have more frequent contacts with larger social networks even in metropolitan areas, and furthermore, desire even closer relationships compared to the older people from other countries, such as Sweden and England (İmamoglu and İmamoglu 1990, 1992b; İmamoglu et al. 1993; Mikellides and Willcocks 1987). The living environments in Turkey tend to be characterized by functional and psychological extendedness rather than physical space. Thus, the independent living units for the elderly should be organized in such a way as to satisfy the needs for such social interdependencies.

Apart from the needs for interdependence between family units, the desires of the elderly for same-age companionship also need to be considered by designers and planners. The respondents in our study indicated a preference for being with people of their own age groups (İmamoglu and İmamoglu 1992a). However, while providing opportunities for same-age companionship, it should also be noted that old age is a natural stage of life which cannot be segregated from the natural flow of life, but instead needs to be integrated into the social and physical aspects of living environments in a meaningful manner. Another related consideration should be that the elderly do not constitute a homogeneous group; for example, with respect to preferences for living in an area mostly with older people, they seem to be divided into two extremes, with about half favouring and the other half rejecting such arrangements. Furthermore, preference for being with older people appear to be relatively higher in smaller towns and to decrease as a function of urbanization (İmamoglu and İmamoglu 1992a).

Perhaps another important consideration at this point might be that the older people should have control over their lifestyles. Therefore, it would be advisable to provide various housing alternatives so that the older people can have the opportunity to choose the type of living environment that best suits their needs. These can range from independent housing units, with varying size and plans, where minimal supportive services are provided within interdependent social communities, to institutional living where more services are provided without degrading human needs and rights for privacy, companionship and growth.

Finding optimum solutions that are compatible with the related values of the Turkish culture and that meet the changing needs of the country's elderly requires the concerned ingenuity of our planners and designers. The challenge for the designer is to manipulate the physical environment in such a way as not only to make up for the reductions in life satisfaction experienced by the elderly, but also to endow this final developmental stage of individuals with the meaning, growth and fulfilment it deserves (İmamoglu and İmamoglu 1992a). A first step towards achieving this aim might be to regard the elderly (as well as all 'others'), not as 'others', but as 'human beings'.

References

Carp, F. M. 1976. "Environment and Ageing", in D. Stokols and I. Altman, eds., *Handbook of Environmental Psychology* 1, pp. 329-60.

Cutrona, C.E. 1986. "Objective Determinants of Perceived Social Support", *Journal of Personality and Social Psychology* 50, pp. 349-55.

Hirsch, B.J. 1979. "Psychological dimensions of social networks: A multimethod analysis". *American Journal of Community Psychology*, 7, 263-277.

_____. 1980. "Natural support systems and coping with major life changes". *American Journal of Community Psychology*, 8, 159-173.

İmamoglu, E.O. 1981. "Yarının büyükleri nasıl yetisiyor?' (How are future adults being raised?), paper presented at the 'Cumhuriyet Türkiye'sinde İnsan, Toplum ve Bilim Semineri', Middle East Technical University, Ankara.

_____. 1987. "An Interdependence Model of Human Development", in Ç. Kagıtçıbası, ed., Growth and Progress in *Cross-Cultural Psychology*. Lisse: Swets and Zeitlinger.

_____ and V. İmamoglu. 1990. "Currrent Life Situations and Attitudes of the Turkish Elderly towards Institutional Living", in H. Pamir, V. İmamoglu, and N. Teymur, eds., *Culture, Space and History* 3, Ankara: METU Faculty of Architecture Press.

_____. 1992a. "Housing and Living Environments of the Turkish Elderly", *Journal of Environmental Psychology* 12, pp. 1-9.

_____. 1992b. "Life Situations and Attitudes of the Turkish Elderly towards Institutional Living Within a Cross-Cultural Perspective", *Journal of Gerontology: Psychological Sciences* 47 (2): 102-8.

_____ and N. Kılíç. In press. "A Social Psychological comparison of the Elderly Residing at High or Low Quality Institutions", *Journal of Environmental Psychology*.

İmamoglu, E.O., R. Küller, V. İmamoglu and M. Küller. 1993. "The Social Psychological Worlds of Swedes and Turks in and around Retirement", *Journal of Cross-Cultural Psychology* 24 (1): 26-41.

Kagıtçıbası, Ç. 1982. The Changing Value of Children in Turkey (Publication No. 60-E), Honolulu, Hl: East-West Publication Institute.

Kandiyoti, D. 1982. "Urban Change and Women's Roles in Turkey: An Overview and Evaluation", in Ç. Kagıtçıbası, ed., *Sex Roles, Family and Community in Turkey*. Bloomington: Indiana University: Turkish Studies 3.

Küller, R. 1988. "Housing for the Elderly in Sweden", in D. Canter, M. Krampen and D. Stea, eds., *Environmental Policy, Assessment and*

Communication: Ethnoscapes 2. Avebury: Aldershot Press, pp. 199-224.

Küller, M., R. Küller, E.O. İmamoglu and V. İmamoglu. 1990. "Health and Outdoor Environment for the Elderly", in H. Pamir, V. İmamoglu, and N. Teymur, eds., *Culture, Space and History* - Proceedings of the Eleventh Biennial Conference of IAPS 3, Ankara: Faculty of Architecture Press, pp. 236-45.

Lowenthal, M.S. and B. Robinson. 1976. "Social Networks and Isolation", in R.H. Binstock and E. Shanas, eds., *Handbook of Ageing and the Social Sciences*. New York: Van Nostrand.

Mikellides, B. and J. Willcocks. 1987. "Environment and retirement", Unpublished Report, Oxford Polytechnic.

Olson, E.A. 1982. "Duofocal Family Structure and an Alternative Model of Husband-Wife Relationships", in Ç. Kagitçíbasí, ed., *Sex Roles, Family and Community in Turkey*. Bloomington: Indiana University Turkish Studies 3.

Özer, Ö. 1990. "Housing for the Elderly", Unpublished Masters of Architecture thesis, Middle East Technical University, Ankara.

Rook, K.S. 1987. "Reciprocity of Social Exchange and Social Satisfaction Among Older Women", *Journal of Personality and Social Psychology* 52, pp. 145-54.

Sarason, B.R., E.N. Shearin, G.E. Pierce and I.G. Sarason. 1987. "Interrelations of Social Support Measures: Theoretical and Practical Implications", *Journal of Personality and Social Psychology* 52, pp. 813-32.

Senyapíli,T. 1978. Bütünlesmemis Kentli Nüfus Sorunu (The Problem of Unintegrated Urban Population). Ankara: Middle East Technical University Press.

Thibaut, J.W. and H.H. Kelley. 1959. *The Social Psychology of Groups*. New York: John Wiley.

Timur, S. 1972. *Türkiye'de Aile Yapísí* (Family Structure in Turkey). Ankara: Hacettepe University Publications, D-15.

Weal, U. and F. Weal. 1988. *Housing the Elderly, Option and Design*. London: Mitchell.

Wellman, B. 1979. "The Community Question", *American Journal of Sociology* 84, pp. 1201-31.

Williams, J.G. and C.H. Solano. 1983. "The Social Reality of Feeling Lonely: Friendship and Reciprocation", *Personality and Social Psychology Bulletin* 9, pp. 237-42.

Navigating in Unknown Waters: Canadian Widows Negotiating Relationships

Deborah Kestin van den Hoonaard

Abstract

This paper explores the social meaning of widowhood for older Canadian women. One of the most challenging aspects of life for widows is in the area of relationships, as indicated in their characterization of the social world as a 'couples' world'. In the absence of norms about behaviour to expect from friends, widows find that they are 'dropped' by many of their friends. Similarly, relationships with adult children are also affected by unclear expectations. Finally, widows need to find new ways to interact with men, whether or not they want to remarry. The paper therefore looks at the strategies women use to move from a couple identity that once seemed natural to being single, which requires conscious effort. The data consist of in-depth interviews, workshop observation, and a focus group comprised of widows.

Introduction

Becoming a widow is one of the most profound changes a woman faces in her adult life. She must learn to live alone after many years of sharing day-to-day life with the same person and most likely learn to live on a fraction of the income she and her husband had shared. But perhaps the most significant change is that she now becomes a single woman living in a couples' world. This transition affects all her relationships, notably relationships with her (and her husbands') friends, relationships with her children, and relationships with other men.

The data on which the paper is based come from a study that examined the social meaning of widowhood from the perspective of women who actually experienced it.[1] It consists of in-depth interviews with 29 women in New Brunswick, Canada, ranging in age from 53 to 87 years old, who had been widowed within the previous five years, plus observation of a six-week workshop, Striving on Your Own, conducted by the Third Age Centre at St. Thomas University, and a focus group comprised of widows who commented on the findings.

Relationships with Friends

When their husbands die, the way women interact with their friends changes. The women interviewed describe the obligations they have towards their friends, the foremost being 'keeping up appearances'[2] and not seeming too depressed, both of which seem fairly clear-cut. What they felt they could reasonably expect from their friends was more problematic. For most of those interviewed, these expectations are surrounded by uncertainty and ambiguity.

Keeping Up Appearances

Most women averred that it was important to keep up appearances around other people. They felt they should not cry, be very depressed, or talk about their husbands too much in front of others. Several commented that if you need to cry, you should cry alone. It was not their friends' responsibility to cope with the loss of their husband, but theirs (often alone). If you cried in front of your friends or appeared too depressed, they said, you would 'depress your friends; bore everybody; drive people crazy; or burden people'.

Women explained that the felt others would not understand and would get fed up with a widow who was always sad. One woman (Lynn) said that "if I'd have wept and wailed and howled in [my friends'] soup for the last six months ... [my husband] would be very upset with at me ... very disapproving ... ashamed of me."

---

[1] The study was funded by a Community Researcher Award from Health Canada's National Health Research and Development Program. The Third Age Centre at St. Thomas University, Fredericton, New Brunswick, was a partner in the research.
[2] Quotations unless otherwise specified, are taken verbatim from interview transcripts and all names are pseudonyms.

A few women did not have much patience for widows who could not control their emotions in public. They were as unsympathetic towards those who broke the 'feeling rules' as those who had not experienced widowhood themselves. Feeling rules are the guidelines that direct "how we want to try to feel" (Hochschild 1979: 563). We know if we are conforming to or breaking feeling rules by others' reactions to the emotions we project. Some women had widowed friends who they said were too depressing to be with. One woman avoided her own sister because she was crying all the time. This inclination to keep away from depressing widows was reinforced by others.

Nonetheless, a few widows did identify settings in which they were able to share their grief with a group or an individual who understood what they were going through. Some attended a support group for widows where talking about their feelings was both expected and helpful (van den Hoonaard 1997). Others identified a particular widowed friend with whom they could, as one of them (Audrey) put it, "talk and share ... similar experiences".

Reciprocity is the necessary ingredient for a woman being able to let go and talk about what it really felt like to lose her husband.[3] For the women who lost patience with other widows who talked about their loss all the time, it was they who felt burdened by unwanted confidences. For all the women, they knew that their married friends would not understand how they felt. Confining their emotions to the proper context required great control. As Doris commented: "Well, you're going to go away from here thinking that I'm fine and I feel fine. Maybe you won't be at the end of the road 'til I'll be weeping, but that's all right."

Although there are rules regarding the display and even the feeling of emotions in response to the loss of one's spouse, it is less clear what widows have the right to expect from their friends as well as what their own obligations are in order for friendships to be maintained.

Expectations

Because there do not seem to be any generally accepted norms for interaction, women's interpretation of what has occurred in any relationship is very much affected by what they had assumed was their right to expect from their friends. These expectations had a great

---

[3] See Hochschild (1973) for a discussion of the 'sibling bond' based on reciprocity and similarity of situations that developed among a group of widows living in a subsidized apartment building.

influence over their explanation of how their relationships changed. For example, when a woman becomes widowed, she is 'dropped' by at least some of her friends (see, e.g. Lopata 1996; van den Hoonaard 1994). This was common knowledge among many women before they experienced it, but some were surprised that it happened to them.

Lopata (1996:160-61) has suggested that this surprise may be a result of a confusion between 'friendly relations', which carry minimal obligations and 'friendship', which implies more extensive obligations. While this may be true in some cases, the picture may be more complex. Some women recount the loss of long-term friendships, which had included much reciprocal assistance and sharing of confidences (MacRae 1996:386).

Eileen, for example, recounted the demise of her friendship with a woman she had considered a very good friend. Eileen explained that, not only had she known this friend for years, but, when the friend had been seriously ill, Eileen had been there when she came back from the hospital: "[I] spent months going to her house, helping her out". Eileen had thought they were very close friends. After her husband died, Eileen said, "I called her and I went to her house ... she was very pleased and wanted to see me ... and I said to her, 'I was here three weeks ago' ... this is the last time I'm coming ... Now the ball's in your park. Now, if you don't call me, that means our friendship is finished." And it was.

Eileen felt that she had given her friend every chance to continue the relationship. In contrast, Eileen explained that she had people she considered acquaintances who have become good friends since her husband's death: "they called me and invited me to the house for supper or lunch". She noted that there were those who she "expected to be here all the time, to be friends with, to call you, who haven't and others ... that you didn't expect are the ones that really come forward".

Older widows' interpretations of the nature of these lost relationships may not be accurate. Rather, it may be that their expectations of how their friends should provide support have affected their understanding of the friendships. Many expected their friends to call, invite, include, or drive them to events. Thus, although Emily's friends from a social organization invited her to a social evening being held by the organisation, she felt that they should have offered to drive her there. Because they did not offer to drive her, she did not go and felt excluded.

Peg, on the other hand, felt that it was her responsibility to keep in touch with her friends. She described a number of occasions when she invited people to her home and made conscious efforts to stay in touch with others. It did not trouble her that she had to make the effort. In fact, this was simply the way she expected things to be. Lynn also saw keeping friendships going as primarily her responsibility. She expected to get fewer invitations, but commented that she was "determined to have luncheon parties and dinner parties ... that's the only way I'm going to keep in contact with these people ... I can't expect to get invited out if I don't receive." Contrast this approach to that of Eileen, who noted: "I've given [my friend] the chance."

Others, who felt neglected, conceded that they had not called their friends who had disappeared. Perhaps, as single women, they, like some widows interviewed in a previous study in Florida (van den Hoonaard 1994), did not feel that they were in the position to proffer an invitation. Being widowed confers a lowered status (Lopata 1976), and may, therefore, upset the equality that is a hallmark of friendship (Allan 1979; Lopata 1975; Suttles 1970) as well as shift obligations onto one member of the relationship to take the initiative to keep it going. Because the role of 'friend' is not institutionalized, norms are often unclear as well as idiosyncratic (Matthews 1986:158). In some cases, it appears that both the widow and her friends each assumed the other now had that obligation, which led to the termination of the friendship.

Concentrating on disappointments, however, presents only part of the picture. Women also received unexpected support and help. Many found that there were people who came through for them in ways they did not expect. For example, it was not uncommon for neighbours, particularly younger neighbours, to provide instrumental support. Emily found that a few younger business acquaintances rolled up the garden hose and did other such tasks around the house. As well, there were people who provided unexpected emotional support. As Eileen said: "People that were acquaintances have become good friends."

Marie, a nurse, found unexpected support from people she worked with, offering her a cup of tea or asking how she was doing. "I did not think they cared that much", she explained. Even a small gesture from an unexpected source sometimes made a real difference: Marilyn explained that the "girl at the checkout" at the grocery store "brought a little bunch of flowers".

Single women were most likely to become close friends, sometimes unexpectedly. Lydia was surprised "that there were so many people around to do things with ... looking for friendship". Others picked up friendships with other widows. Edith said that losing her husband "made me more aware of other people". She was disappointed with her married friends who had not called but knew this had been her own reaction before her husband died.

'They Have Their Own Life': Relationships with Children

Widows' relationships with their adult children reflect an upset of a lifelong equilibrium and a need to find a new balance. Women's descriptions of these relationships since their husbands' deaths brings into focus the need for older mothers and adult children to find a balance between the children's concern for their mothers and their ability to recognize that their mothers are capable of making decisions and living alone. In their day-to-day interactions, a balance between privacy and support typifies a comfortable situation.

'I must look after Mama'

Widows' children often see them as more vulnerable after the loss of their husbands and react by becoming protective. 'I must look after Mama' is what Eleanor reported one of her sons had said when he learned she had become a widow. Widows want their children to acknowledge their loss and to be available to support them both emotionally and instrumentally. However, when the equilibrium becomes skewed towards over-protectiveness, many feel besieged in their struggle to build a new life for themselves.

Muriel felt that her daughter's inclination to take over grew out of a misunderstanding of how her marriage had worked. She said that her daughter had thought that her husband had been in charge but that this perception was incorrect. This led to an immediate confrontation. The initial problem was Muriel's daughter's questioning her capacity to make decisions. She feels that if she had not displayed some strength right away, a pattern might have been set up resulting in her daughter's making all the decisions for her and her becoming dependent on her daughter. Now, she feels that her daughter knows her better than she had before and grew up quite a bit [and] learned something.

Eileen found that her daughters' attempts to be protective grew out of their concern for her safety. She reported that they "made me go through a whole bunch of medical tests ... get a new car ... In fact, they wanted me to get a phone in the car." Her daughters also questioned her ability to make decisions and worried that she would run out of money. Eileen took a middle road. She complied with some of her children's wishes but made it quite clear to them that "I haven't lost my mind yet; I know what I want and I know what I'm going to do." Like Muriel, Eileen succeeded in training her children to give her the space she needed.

Relationships with sons may be more problematic. They, too, are eager to protect their mothers from perceived vulnerability, but are not as willing to back off when their mothers try to tell them that they are being too protective. This is exemplified by sons' reactions to their mothers' buying a new car. Polly's sons insisted on coming with her when she was negotiating the price of a used car she was buying. She felt that she knew the asking price was fair because she had been looking for a few weeks, but her sons said: "No, one of us will go with you."

While Judy did not find that her son insisted on being involved in the buying of a new car, his comments suggest a certain level of condescension in referring to her as the little old lady from Pasadena when she bought a sports car.[4] This son has also begun to admonish his mother to be careful driving. Judy refers to this as a role reversal, which highlights the potential for her son to make all her important decisions for her. This role reversal is not total because Judy and other women in this situation may or may not acquiesce and become like obedient children.

Edith has experienced the most extreme example of role reversal. Not only do her sons want to take over car maintenance, they also react strongly if Edith says anything that is upsetting: "He came one lunch time and I was crying and he said, 'Mom, you shouldn't be crying ... you should be glad Dad's out of his agony' ... if I say anything to my son that's upsetting to him, he says, 'Oh, Mom, you shouldn't be thinking that way'."[5]

---

[4] Cars are one of the last areas that are still almost totally in the province of men. See Berger (1986) for a discussion of the growth of folklore surrounding women's supposed inability to deal with cars and driving.

[5] Sometimes Edith does seem to be using emotional blackmail. She reports commenting: "I say sometimes I feel nobody cares whether I'm here or not. I know they're busy..." So

But, it does not stop there. Edith's sons insist that she let them know where she is when not at home at night: "I call them and I say ... 'I'm here tonight' or something ...Goodness, I'm not a child!" Her sons are pressuring her to sell her home and move into a mobile home. Her reaction: "I've lived here thirty-eight years. I fell down the stairs once, now I'm going to move . . . 'No', I said, 'I don't tell you how to live your life ... so you're not gong to tell me'."

Nonetheless, Edith reports that her eldest son "went around to all my sons and said, 'And you keep on at Mom'." She finds that her sons frequently put pressure on her to allow them to make important decisions for her. They do not treat her like the competent adult she feels she is.

It is clear that Edith finds her relationship with her sons almost smothering. Polly, on the other hand, appreciates the concern associated with her son's concern for her welfare. This is illustrated by the difference in they way she relates her experiences. Polly now lives in an apartment that her son put in over the garage on his property:

> Now, my other son ... when we first started talking about building this place, he said, 'Mom, I won't rest until you're in town ... Every time I call you and you don't answer, I have you laying at the bottom of those stairs ...' I find that they worry more about me.

But, for Polly this has worked out well. She feels that she and her son and daughter-in-law have a good balance between their desire to know that she's safe and their privacy and independence. Polly makes an effort to ensure that neither she nor her son's family intrude on one another.

Other women report that their children did not take over their lives or try to protect them. Several think that their children saw them as quite competent even before their husbands died. For example, Emily and her husband had been in business together. Interestingly, the example she chose to explain that her children felt she would be able to make important decisions involved buying a car: "As far as knowing what to do, like buying my car, my kids feel that I should know ... simply because I worked, I think."

---

although some of her sons' reactions are clearly protective, this is not always the reason for their being upset at what she says.

Because she does not feel she has to struggle with her children to retain her independence Emily feels free to ask them for advice: "not necessarily that I'm gong to do what they tell me ... And if I made a decision to sell the house, I'd talk to them all." Lydia credits having had a responsible position in a large, voluntary organization with letting her children know that she is able to look after herself while Peg sees her strong personality throughout life as important. For others, it is simply that their children see them as competent adults.

Trust is an integral part of this type of relationship. Because their children have not overreacted to their mothers losing their husbands by treating them like children, several women commented that they know that if they do become incompetent in some way as they get older, they can trust their children to tell them when they can no longer function independently: Sarah, for example, says: "But I told [my children] if ... I'm starting to leave the stove on or I'm falling down ... Then you talk me into selling [the house]."

But whether or not an individual woman is satisfied with the level of concern on the part of her children, she does find that the centre of the family has changed. As Blanche said: "It used to be Mom and the kids. Now, it's reversed, the kids and there's Mom."[6]

Close Feelings

For the most part widows report that their relationships with their children are close. This became apparent when I asked if their relationships with their children had changed since the deaths of their husbands. Martha reported that her relationships with her children had changed very little: "We've always been a close family ... sort of concerned for each other." Those women who do report a changed relationship, most often couch it in the direction of a stronger rather than a more distant relationship. For example, Eileen said, "I think it's gotten stronger, really." Doris remarked, "I see more of them, it's a closer relationship." Audrey's daughter and son-in-law have become more considerate, she says, "more concerned about ... letting me know where they are."

---

[6] Dr. Joyce Brothers (1990), in an account of her experience with becoming a widow, notes that her children became the centre of the family after her husband's death.

But characterizing relationships simply as changed or unchanged conceals the complex and subjective nature of women's feelings about their relationships with their children, which are partially grounded in objectively measurable actions, but are significantly affected by their expectations about what their children should do for and/or with them.

Several studies have shown that North American women generally prefer to live alone rather than with their children once they have become widows (Doyle et al. 1994; Fengler et al. 1983). In the present study, although participants also stated that they preferred living alone, several were quite pleased to report that their children had offered to have them move in with them. Their reasons for declining such an invitation reflect a desire not to threaten a good relationship. As Peg explained: "I definitely think it would be a disastrous to live with your children ... It's been offered to me by my daughter, but I said, 'No, I don't think so'." [7]

Both of Eleanor's daughters-in-law offered to have her come live with them, but she would have had to move quite some distance to live with either one:

> I'd never be happy in Ontario ... I would have [my son and his family] there ... granted you make new friends, but I don't want to go up there ... I have a good relationship [with my sons] ... I don't ever want to feel that I'm smothering them.

Cathy's experience of moving into the same apartment building as one of her daughters demonstrates that women's concern that living too close to their children might damage their relationship has merit. She has moved away from friends, thus isolating herself, and, although it is more convenient she observed that perhaps she's living a little too close. Cathy's emotional needs require more than her daughter can give. The hoped-for emotional support has not developed. Cathy spoke again and again about her disappointment and feeling that she had expected too much.

Eileen's decisions regarding living arrangements reflect a more conscious exploration of the balance between privacy and independence than did Cathy's. Her initial concerns about leaving her house empty when she travels led to an idea to build a new wing onto her daughter's house, creating a small apartment. She waited a year after coming to this

---

[7] It is interesting to note that Peg's father had lived with her for about the last 10 years of his life and she said that this had been a good arrangement. Nonetheless, she felt strongly that living with either of her children might jeopardize their relationship.

conclusion before listing her own house for sale. Eileen explained her decision: "I could be close and at the same time I could have my independence." This move was instigated by Eileen, and her focus on her own privacy and independence reflects an approach that adds the needed balance to her relationship with her daughter.

Simply acknowledging a particularly difficult time is also very meaningful. One of Eleanor's sons remembered to call her on the anniversary of her husband's death as well as on Father's Day because he knew that those days would be very hard days for her. Audrey has one daughter, who lives in Australia who sent flowers on the anniversary of her husband's death. The geographic distance allows these adult children to show their concern without the risk of feeling overwhelmed.

Neglecting to notice an important date can be very hurtful. Cathy was not only disappointed but hurt by her daughters' not understanding how meaningful her fiftieth wedding anniversary was to her:

> This was our fiftieth anniversary ... I was talking to [one of my daughters] and I said, 'This is our anniversary.' She said, 'Yes, I know, Mom ... I know,' she said, 'but Dad's dead,' she said, 'Dad's gone.' So I said, 'Dad's gone, but I'm still here.' It really hurt me, really hurt me.'

Cathy and her daughters have not yet found a balance between what she needs to assuage her loneliness and what they feel is reasonable. This may be the reason they tried to underplay the importance of Cathy's fiftieth wedding anniversary.

Weekends are particularly difficult times for widows. Three reported that they often spend their weekends with their children. Doris said:

> Weekends were bad and weekends are still bad if I'm alone, but I'm most fortunate because the one son isn't married, and there's been very few weekends since his father died that he hasn't come ... and spent the better part of a day ... My daughter [also] comes most weekends.

Audrey's daughter knows that her mother finds hearing particular hymns difficult and puts her arm around her mother when they are sung at church, while Sarah's daughter knows that one of the things Sarah misses most is having tea with her husband when returning from an evening out:

Now the kids always come in with me and say, why even if it's eleven o'clock and [my daughter] has so far to go, she says, 'Oh, I think I'll have a cup of tea before I go,' or something like that. I know why they're doing it ... they always do that.

For women who live quite close to their children, it is the day-to-day thoughtfulness that defines their relationship. Martha has one daughter who "hardly misses a day she doesn't call me." Her other two daughters are not as conscientious, but they do say they want her to call them:

The second one is terrible ... she is very busy ... she just doesn't have the time, so I'll call her and I'll say, 'Oh, you're alive. I just called to make sure you're still there.' She says, 'Well, Mom, I'm so glad you called ... I do neglect.' But I don't let it bother me ... she's busy.

Martha's third daughter lives right up the road from her and also depends on her mother to keep in touch. Martha's explanation is that the two inattentive daughters have very busy lives. Therefore, it is only reasonable that she takes responsibility for initiating their contacts. This is compensated for by their not feeling that Martha is intruding by calling or visiting them when she feels like it. The balance between this feeling of appropriate caring and over-protection makes the difference between a mother's being satisfied or dissatisfied with her relationship with her adult children.

Several women maintain balance by adding reciprocity to the relationship. For example, Eileen takes care of her grandchildren when her daughter travels, and her daughter includes her in many family outings. Judy and her sons joke that she will make her special goulash and that they will come visit her with their friends. Florence's son invites her for dinner regularly, and she, in turn, will often cook food in quantity and invite him and his family to join her.

Sarah's discussion of her relationship with her children reflects a very refined system of maintaining balance in their relationship. The foundation is a broad understanding of their not intruding on one another: "And my family, well, they're just wonderful; they're friends as well as family. If I need anything, I only have to make a phone call. And if I don't want them around, they don't crowd me."

In exchange, Sarah handles her difficult times by herself: "I don't feel sorry for myself ... just sit down and say, 'now look, this is the way things are'." Sarah recounted a number of arrangements that rest on the firm foundation of reciprocity she has established with her children. They asked her not to learn to drive because they felt they would worry about her. In return, they said, "We'll take you any place you want to go." Sarah feels very comfortable calling on her children if there is something she cannot fix but usually tries to fix things herself before calling on them. She enjoyed explaining that after she had spent over an hour putting up one of a set of new venetian blinds, her son came to help. She went into another room for just a few minutes, and when she returned, he said: "Your blind's up ... I could have done that the first time, but I knew you wanted to do it."

Sarah spends her winters in Florida, which means that she needs someone to pay her local bills for her and to keep an eye on her house. Sarah's daughter pays the bills for her, and her son checks on her house for her. The reciprocity involved is very ingenious: "My son is very fond of ice cream, and he can't get cable [TV] ... So I fill the freezer downstairs with ice cream, and I know he'll be down to watch TV. And he watches the house." In addition, Sarah's granddaughter, who attends university, if she wants to entertain, she brings the kids down, cooks them supper. For Sarah, there is the tremendous benefit of having family members check her house in an unpredictable but reliable fashion.

Not everyone is successful at maintaining or implementing a reciprocal relationship. For example, Sylvia has tried to persuade her children to visit her by offering them whatever they want to take of the nice things her husband left her. This has not been effective, and she fears she will soon have to call an antique dealer. Edith, whose sons have become domineering, has tried to achieve reciprocity by inviting them to have holiday meals at her home, but they insist she come to theirs, thus reinforcing the unequal dimension that has become a part of their relationship. Cathy, who is so aware that she is overwhelming her daughters, who live in the same town, talks of moving to another town where she has a daughter who does not have a job. She hopes they will be company for one another.

For women who do not live near their children, the telephone can be a life-line that results in a long-distance relationship becoming close. Lydia, for example, has a closer relationship with her daughter who lives out of the province than she does with the one who lives a 15-minute drive away. Unfortunately, long-distance phone-calling can be very expensive, and this affects Sylvia, whose children all live in the United States: "I'm a demon on the phone. I call home too many times ... I talked to my daughter last night ... I just had something to tell her ... that's so expensive, on a smaller budget, you see." For Sylvia, finding the balance between finances and loneliness is not an easy task.

Relationships with Men

As challenging as relationships with friends and adult children can be, those with men were even more complicated and ambiguous. As wives, these women had known how to act with their husbands and with men who were either single or married. Once they found themselves single, they had to decide whether or not they were interested in getting married again. Even if they did not want to remarry, they had to figure out new ways to interact with men, both to avoid being misunderstood and because norms regarding relationships between unmarried men and women have changed in the 20, 30 or 50 years since they had had to negotiate these relationships.

Negotiating Relationships with Men

Although they showed very little inclination to become romantically involved or to remarry, these widows did want male company, whether simply for the companionship or for physical, albeit not intimate, contact.

Sylvia and June expressed a desire to have someone to go out with: "Just to go out for dinner ... and dancing for a few hours." Others missed the type of conversation they have with men. Audrey commented that she actually preferred conversations with men to those with women but that a man would misunderstand her intent. He might think: "You're looking for a husband, and that's not necessarily it - it's nice just to have a friend." Both women and men often think that a cross-gender friendship implies romance, courtship, and an intimate sexual relationship (Adams 1985).

Several women would like male companionship for the physical contact. Only a few brought up issues of sexual intimacy. For most, this simply referred to hugging. But three women in their fifties spoke specifically about missing sexual intimacy. Audrey said: "Even the sex thing, I mean, I found that hard, really lonely ... sexual desire ... and no way of fulfilling that."

June, whose husband had Alzheimer's disease, had been faithful to her husband, but they had not had a sexual relationship for some time because of his illness. She said that she did not miss that aspect of the relationship, "because I didn't have it for so long".

For the few who did comment on issues of intimacy, the changing mores regarding sex provided a challenge. Going out with a man for the first time could be traumatizing. Some women remarked that they had felt like adolescents again at the first beginnings of some sort of physical relationship. When these women were growing up, intimate relationships were, for the most part, confined to marriage, and although a few of them were almost apologetic about their 'outdated' moral standards, they were not about to "crawl into bed with somebody", as Emily put it, because "there has to be a relationship". As Eleanor commented: "And I don't believe in jumping in bed with every man that comes along." Several women felt that men do not share this reluctance to engage in a casual sexual relationship. This was a cause for concern among most of the women.

Edith, for example, had gone out to dinner with someone thinking that they were just going to go out and just talk. The man she was with wanted her to "go around with him ... away with him ... you wouldn't imagine that at our age, but he did". She went on to state that men are different from women in this regard. Living together without marrying was also not a viable option for these widows.

A safer avenue is hugging. Martha and Sharon relied on specific men at their church for hugs. The safety of the setting was underlined for both of them because the hugs took place in the presence of the men's wives and were so obviously harmless that nobody found them a threat. Sharon explained: "Like B. and I, we'd never think anything of it, we'd start hugging each other up [at church], but [his wife] is such a sweetheart." June had found a safe environment in the formal ballroom-dancing setting. Studios provide a partner, and it is understood that you do not date anybody or anything. Her dancing provided her a place where she could "dance with someone and I think I'm dancing with my husband." For this reason she only frequented the better studios and avoided public dances.

Some noted that they were careful to arrange their relationships in such a way as to avoid gossip. Peg has very strict rules about when male visitors leave her house at night because she lives in a small town where she feels others would notice and comment on late-night visitors. Audrey commented that in her small town if you showed up at market on Saturday morning, it means you slept together Friday night. Even though they went to great lengths to avoid misunderstandings, the women felt that many married women considered them a threat. This has been a constant finding in research on widowhood and is not surprising. Some men, particularly single men, also assumed that widows were interested in them and reacted as if they were threatened. For example, Marion said, "If you bake bread or give them something, they get ... all nervous ... I have to be very careful not to overwhelm them, I guess." Some of the widows interviewed simply felt they have to disabuse men of the assumption that they were interested in more than conversation or companionship.

The motives of men were also problematic. Two contrasting stories highlight this difficulty. First, Audrey told me the story of a phone call she received from a man who had seen her at the cemetery when she was visiting her husband's grave. He had been visiting his wife's grave. This man was interested in getting together. Audrey's reaction was to avoid him. Marilyn, on the other hand, also received attention from a man who noticed her at the cemetery. When he approached her and started up a conversation, she made the same assumption Audrey had made, and her reaction was almost identical: "I felt sorry for him." But it turned out that the man had seen some young men with beer bottles in the area the night before and was simply warning her to be careful: "I immediately jumped to the conclusion he was going to come there and meet me the next night", she said.

Both women felt vulnerable and uncertain because of the new basis on which they were meeting and interacting with men. They jumped to conclusions about the men's intentions, one seemingly inferring his intentions correctly, the other incorrectly.

Significant Relationships

Although most widows did not want to remarry and few reported having a more than superficial relationship with any men, there were three women who each had a relationship that was important enough that it came up continually during our interviews in response to various questions.[8] Audrey needed to make a decision about whether to move towards remarriage. The situation was difficult both because her male friend has emotional baggage that he has to get rid of and because of others' reactions to the relationship. Her story did not resemble the story of a young woman looking towards a first marriage with innocent excitement. Rather she was dealing with divorce, AIDS, as well as the cautionary tales she had heard about second marriages.

Eleanor, who also thought that she might someday remarry, was involved with a slightly younger man who had never been married. The relationship dominated her thoughts so that almost any question I might ask ended up with conversing about some aspect of their relationship. She said that she and this man were the victims of matchmakers - "Our best friends think it would be wonderful if we could get together" - and of gossip - "There's one lady who has decided to make it her business to see if she can get us anywhere together" - and her children also had reactions to her seeing this man so steadily: "And it wouldn't have mattered if it had been Jesus, himself come back, [my son] would not have liked him because nobody's ever going to take his father's place."[9]

Sharon also had a male friend with whom she spent a great deal of time, but unlike both Eleanor and Audrey she had no intention of ever remarrying, and made that quite clear to me. She was one of the few widows who had developed a more-than-superficial relationship with a man in a way that was comfortable to them both. She had made it quite clear that she had no intention of remarrying or living together from the outset of their relationship.

Sharon's relationship allowed her and her friend to talk to each other about their late spouses.[10] They went for walks, out to supper, and took short trips together. Sharon believed that they were meant for each other at this point in their lives to fulfil a need. In fact, she had asked her

---

[8] As Becker (1970) noted long ago, the evidential value of statements, which are volunteered rather than directed by a question from the researcher, is very strong. Two of these three women brought up issues about their relationships with men in response to a variety of questions, many seemingly not connected to these associations. It is clear that the issues were of great concern to the women.

[9] The inhibiting affect of adult children may be significant in women's ideas about remarriage. Zheng Wu (1995:729) notes that the incidence of remarriage among widows with adult children is 93% lower than it is among women with no children.

[10] Usually, both women and men talk to women about their emotional suffering at this time.

husband to look after her from the next world and thought that her male friend might be her husband's way of making sure that she was all right. Nonetheless, Sharon felt guilty after their first supper together.

Discussion

When women lose their spouses, their relationships change in ways they could not predict and that make negotiating those relationships challenging. At the most obvious level, widows experience the loss of their friends. The violation of expectations is one of the primary contributors to this loss. Their friendships may be based on "highly valued, if rarely discussed, norms that have evolved over the course of their relationship" (Rook 1989:171). Unmet expectations are based on what women think their friends should do now that they are widows. Both in dealings with friends and with children, women need to 'keep up appearances' and not appear too needy. With friends, this means that women see the need to keep the depth of emotional suffering to themselves; with children, they attempt to maintain a balance between the support they receive from their children and what they contribute to the relationship.

When women do manage to find this symmetry in their relationships with children and friends, they talk about it with a sense of pride and accomplishment. Both independence and self-reliance are characteristics that women are pleased to be able to assign to themselves. One way they accomplish this is by making sure they do not impose burdens on their adult children. They conform to cultural norms of being self-sufficient and allowing their children to 'live their own lives' as well as providing care for their children (Aronson 1990: 71). We can see the strength of these prescriptions by looking at the comments of the women who have not succeeded in limiting their own need for emotional support. In Cathy's story, for example, there are numerous references to her expecting too much from her daughters in combination with her feeling hurt that her daughters act insensitive to her loneliness. This guilt and shame (Aronson 1990:76) reflect how deeply the norm of being undemanding is internalized.

Feeling comfortable with children who live far away is less complicated. Adult children, who live far away, feel less susceptible to their mothers' wanting too much and becoming a burden. They, therefore feel free to send flowers and phone on difficult anniversaries. There are few problems with children who have moved far from home. The 'intimacy at a distance' (Rosenmayr 1977) that these women are able to maintain with their children is satisfying and adequate to meet their expectations.[11]

Women report closer relationships with daughters than with sons. Although both react to their fathers' deaths by trying to protect their mothers and control their lives, daughters are more amenable to their mothers' wishes to be treated like adults.[12] Perhaps, the expectation of closeness results in the extent of disappointment women express when their daughters do not seem to be sympathetic enough.

Relationships with men present different challenges. Some women choose to live in a world of women because they believe that friendship between a man and a woman is at best difficult and conceivably not even possible (Wright 1991). In either case, the norms of comfortable interaction simply are not there. The problem is trying to decode approaches from men - is he after a romantic relationship or simply wanting to be a friend?

Changing mores are another obstacle to continuing relationships with men. Many women assume that men will want to have sexually intimate relationships with them sooner than they would be comfortable. Uncertainty about men's attitudes may prevent some from trying out a romantic relationship. Women, who want 'safe' avenues for non-romantic relationships with men, show creativity in finding viable settings. Perhaps this is because, particularly in this generation, many women have reached this point in their lives "without being exposed to real models for non-courting, cross-sex friendships" (Adams 1985: 608). When safe environments do not exist, women seem to shy away from interacting with men at all.

Women do learn new ways of interacting by using strategies that allow them to negotiate relationships and use the term 'couples' world' to communicate their feeling of not fitting into society in a comfortable way. The couple identity with which they and others identified them had been an effortless one; it just seemed natural and easy. Learning to interact and be a woman alone required a more conscious effort for the

---

[11] It should be remembered, however, that most of these women also have at least one adult child who does live within driving distance.

[12] See Hansson and Remondet (1988) for a discussion of the challenges older widows sometimes have in trying to maintain personal control and independence in their relationships with their children, particularly sons.

widow, herself, and for others who interacted with her. Participants in this study navigated the unknown waters of their widowhood with varying degrees of success, but most developed effective strategies for finding rewarding relationships.

References

Adams, R.G. 1985. "People Would Talk: Normative Barriers to Cross-Sex Friendship for Elderly Women", *The Gerontologist* 25(6): 605-11.

Allan, G.A. 1979. *A Sociology of Friendship and Kinship*, London: George Allen & Unwin.

Aronson, J. 1990. "Women's Perspectives on Informal Care of the Elderly: Public Ideology and Personal Experience of Giving and Receiving Care", *Ageing and Society* 10, pp. 61-84.

Becker, H.S. 1970. *Sociological Work: Method and Substance*. Chicago: Aldine Publishing.

Berger, M.L. 1986. "Women Drivers: The Emergence of Folklore and Stereotypic Opinions Concerning Feminine Automotive Behavior", *Women's Studies International Forum* 9 (3): 257-63.

Brothers, J. 1990. *Widowed*. New York: Simon & Schuster.

Doyle,V. 1994. "It's My Turn Now: The Choice of Older Women to Live Alone", Gerontology Research Centre, Simon Fraser University at Harbour Centre.

Doyle, V. with B. Backman, E. Cassiday, B. Cumby, B. Ferneyhouch, J. Florczyk, W. Gladman, P. Hall, P. Joyce, A. MacLean, M. Miller, P. Rafferty, R. Rile, D. Ritchie, J. Smith, D. Trohan and V. Ward. 1994. *It's My Turn Now: the choice of older women to live alone*. Vancouver: Gerontology Research Centre at Simon Fraser University.

Fengler, A.P., N. Danigelis and V.C. Little. 1983. "Late Life Satisfaction and Household Structure: Living with Others and Living Alone", *Ageing and Society* 3, pp. 357-77.

Hansson, R.O. and J.H. Remondet. 1988. "Old Age and Widowhood: Issues of Personal Control and Independence", *Journal of Social Issues* 44 (3): 159-74.

Hochschild, A.R. 1973. *The Unexpected Community: Portrait of an Old-Age Subculture*. Englewood Cliffs, NJ: Prentice Hall.

_____. 1979. "Emotion Work, Feeling Rules, and Social Structure", *American Journal of Sociology* 85(3):551-75.

Lopata, H.Z. 1975. "Couple-Companionate Relationships in Marriage and Widowhood", in N. Glazer-Malbin, ed., *Old Family/New Family: Interpersonal Relationships*. New York: D. Van Nostrand, pp. 119-49.

_____. 1976. "Widows as a Minority Group", in B.D. Bell, ed., *Contemporary Social Gerontology*. Springfield, IL: Charles C. Thomas, pp. 348-55.

_____. 1996. *Current Widowhood: Myths and Realities*. Thousand Oaks, CA: Sage Publications.

MacRae, H. 1996. "Strong and Enduring Ties: Older Women and Their Friends", *Canadian Journal on Aging* 15 (3): 374-92.

Matthews, S.H. 1986. *Friendships Through the Life Course: Oral Biographies in Old Age*. Beverly Hills, CA: Sage Publications.

Rook. K.S. 1989. "Strains in Older Adult Friendship", in R.G. Adams and R. Blieszner, eds., *Older Adult Friendship: Structure and Process*. Newbury Park, CA: Sage Publications, pp. 166-94.

Rosenmayr, L. 1977. "The Family - A Source of Hope for the Elderly?", in E. Shanas and M.B. Sussman, eds., *Family, Bureaucracy, and the Elderly.* Durham, NC: Duke University Press, pp. 132-57.

Suttles, G.D. 1970. "Friendship as a Social Institution", in G.C. McCall, ed., *Social Relationships*, Chicago: Aldine Publishing, pp. 95-135.

van den Hoonaard, D.K. 1994. "Paradise Lost: Widowhood in a Florida Retirement Community", *Journal of Aging Studies* 8 (2): 121-32.

_____. 1997. "Learning to Be a Widow: The Contributions of Support Groups and other Organizations to Older Women's Transition to Widowhood", paper presented to the symposium 'Beyond Pills and Pamphlets: Positive Approaches to the Stresses that Women Face in Later Life', at Aging: Dreams and Realities, Canadian Association on Gerontology, October 23-26, Calgary.

Wright, P.H. 1991. "Gender Differences in Adults' Same- and Cross-Gender Friendships", in R.G. Adams and R. Blieszner, eds., *Older Adult Friendship: Structure and Process* Newbury Park, CA: Sage Publications, pp. 197-221..

Wu, Z. 1995. "Remarriage after Widowhood: a Marital History Study of Older Canadians", *Canadian Journal on Aging* 14 (4): 719-73.

Age, Migration, Gender and Empowerment: Older Migrant Women in Europe

Gail Wilson, Helen Cylwik, Angela Grotheer and Lydia Potts[1]

Abstract

Despite the invisibility of migrant women in migration theory, available statistics and interview studies suggests that women have always migrated, but that their numbers are increasing as the world demand for women's paid labour increases. This paper argues that recent migration has not necessarily been a negative experience for women, and many have been able to build on their experience in later life to achieve their own objectives rather than those of the male-oriented migration project offered in the literature. The authors' research with older Cypriot and Turkish migrant women suggests that economic opportunities and changing relations of patriarchal power in the migrant community, and in the countries of origin and countries of destination, allow, but do not guarantee, empowerment for older women. Much depends on working conditions and access to welfare benefits in the country of destination. Women who have accumulated some pension and health entitlements may prefer itinerant retirement, moving between their countries of origin and the country of migration for long or short visits. They enhance their well-being by keeping in touch with grandchildren and with their roots, and can very often make their own decisions independent of their male relatives.

---

[1] We would like thank the British Council for the grant 'Ageing, Migration, Gender and Ethnicity: cross-cultural theory building using comparative empirical data' and Dagmar Lorenz-Meyer for her help and support. Translations are our own throughout.

Introduction

Older women are often assumed to be disempowered and migrant older women still more disempowered than others. The aim of this paper is to show that such an oversimplified approach denies the ways that older women successfully resist patriarchal and racist constraints. Although not all older women are able to benefit from migration, a growing number are finding ways of acting within the constraints imposed on them and are making their own life-enhancing choices once they reach retirement age. We focus on migrant communities, mainly in western Europe, drawing on French, German and British writing and on our own qualitative research with older Cypriot and Turkish migrant women.

We start from the assumption that the relationship between women and empowerment is never a simple one-way process of more or less power. Women interact over the life course with different structures and in different ways that can be both empowering and disempowering. We define empowerment as the ability to choose or to exercise agency. However, agency should not be seen as a purely individualistic project as it has tended to be for male migrants. Any concept of women's agency has to recognize that women are more socially constrained than men and operate more within non-individualistic family- or community-oriented contexts. In other words, women may make choices that can be experienced as positively empowering without necessarily seeing themselves as individuals in the sense of 'the rational economic individual'. Women's choices may fall within male definitions of agency but they also have a wider range of ways of expressing and empowering themselves.

In the context of migration, the interactions of changing social, economic and political structures produce situations that can be experienced by older women as empowering in some ways, while still being disempowering in others. We do not argue that migration automatically empowers women; rather, that some outcomes of migration in old age indicate that women develop a range of possibilities and can exercise choice and agency over wide areas of their lives as opposed to being disempowered or even completely ignored. Before looking at the actual experience of women migrants, we consider the invisibility of women in migration theory and indicate gender-related areas of difference between men and women migrants.

The Male Migration Project and the Invisibility of (Older) Women Migrants

Theorists of labour migration have presented a process which is gender-free and hence implicitly masculine (see e.g., Cohen 1995 who mentions women once in a world survey of migration -- in the context of 'Emerging Trends'). According to European migration theorists, young or midlife men move to better themselves economically and their migration project is only successful if they return to their countries of origin (see Dietzel-Papakyriakou 1993a). Many who intended to return do not do so, which leads to two related discourses: the failure of the migration project and the 'myth of return'. Both are rooted in male experiences of migration and male interpretations of those experiences.

The emphasis on failure can be related to the intersection of a number of discourses. The first is the link between migration and economic individualism. The migrant, or since refugees and asylum seekers have become such a big component of migration figures, the *economic* migrant, is assumed to move because work is available or because wages are higher. Migrants are thus automatically absorbed into an ideology of market capitalism and are assumed to act as rational economic individuals. From this it follows quite naturally that migration or the migration project, should be evaluated in terms of economic success. The migrant must become materially better off and preferably acquire new skills, or he will have failed. Since the mass of labour migrants start low down in the socio-economic hierarchy in their countries of destination and have to compete with racism and various forms of social and political discrimination, it is not surprising that many economic migrants are rapidly labelled as 'failures'.

However, when labour migrants are reasonably successful in terms of acquiring training, skills and money, they are liable to find themselves the subject of nationalist condemnation. Successful migrants who do not return may be condemned in the same way as migrant intellectuals and professionals, for taking part in a brain drain and depriving their countries of much-needed expertise. They become moral rather than economic failures. French Islamic intellectuals (Samaoli 1991; Sayad 1991; Kiwan 1992) have expressed a related discourse in terms of a religious rather than an economic imperative to return to an Islamic state. According to this theological interpretation, economic migration may be allowed for younger men, but old men are expected to attend to spiritual affairs. They cannot do so satisfactorily while they remain on infidel territory and so continued residence in Europe automatically becomes a sign of religious dereliction. Sayad (1991), for example, says that migrants who stay in France are lost in spiritual darkness and are like "rags of rotting flesh on a gangrenous corpse".

The growth in the number of asylum seekers and refugees has blurred the accepted distinction between immigrants who aimed to move countries permanently and labour migrants who expected to stay for a short time. It seems likely that this distinction was never as clear-cut to the migrants themselves as it was to theorists in countries of destination. Many, if not most, express a wish to return to their countries of origin. However, the emotional wish to return to the place of birth, or childhood home, is a widespread phenomenon and not confined to migrants. Older men and women look back on their childhood and on the cultures that they grew up with. Often they contrast these past cultures unfavourably with the present. Such thoughts and feelings appear to be common to a large majority of older people in all cultures and can be described as nostalgia.

However, as most older men and women know, there is no returning to the past. Return to a physical place is more possible than return to times past, but countries can be so changed, both physically and socially, that they are no longer the same place that they were some 50 years previously. Migrants who have been identified as endorsing the myth of return are also recorded as knowing that it is only a myth, a wish that cannot be fulfilled. As they age, they may increasingly recognize that they will never return, as Noiriel has documented for older migrants in France: "The majority of our interviews show that older immigrants, whatever their nationality are imbued with a longing to return to the homeland which they know in their hearts is impossible" (1992:14). Like other writers (Zehraoui 1994; Dietzel-Papakyiakou 1993b), Noiriel interprets the recognition that return is impossible as evidence for the failure of the migration project, without recognizing the component of nostalgia in the discourse.

In contrast to the labour-importing countries in continental Europe, most migrants to the U.K. were Commonwealth citizens who had the right to settle and they were reluctantly perceived as intending to stay. Older migrants were and are recorded as saying that when they first came they intended to return (see below), but this is not a dominant discourse and the myth of return has not been developed as a component of the migrant experience. Thus for example Blakemore and Boneham (1994), while focusing strongly on male migrants, make no mention of return as a feature of U.K. migration. The theoretical problem in countries of immigration such as Britain and the United States is that migrants are frequently defined as 'disadvantaged' (Markides 1983) in the same way as native inhabitants of deprived areas, African Americans or Native Americans. The weakness of this approach is that by focusing on the characteristics of current disadvantage and looking at individuals and groups cross-sectionally rather than taking a life-course approach, the fact of migration is ignored. The forms of social organization, resources and other attributes that may distinguish migrants and their communities from others become invisible and are not investigated or validated.

Failure of the migration project and the myth of return rest on an out-dated view of global relations. The one-off journey out and the definitive return in triumph or as failure, are no longer parts of the migration experience (assuming they ever were). The globalization of world economies has greatly changed the spatial relations that underpin migration. Even for long distance migrants, for example from southern Europe, India or Africa to the United States or Australia, there is now the possibility of return for long or short stays. There may still be some economic migrants who are genuinely unable to return because they cannot save up for an air fare and have no family network to provide the money, but most now have a choice. The revolution in costs of long-distance travel means that most migrants can afford to return 'home' from time to time if they wish. Even if they do not return, migrants may be able to maintain much stronger links with their own culture than in the past, thanks to global telecommunications, satellite and cable television and local ethnic radio stations.

Even so, when and if they return, migrants are likely to find a 'home' that is greatly changed. Many find it difficult to settle back into a society which frequently regards them as 'foreign'. It is normal for returning migrants to be spoken of as the 'Americans' or the 'Hawaiians' in the Philippines (Pertierra 1992), the 'English' in Cyprus (Anthias 1992) or 'Alamanyali' in Turkey, meaning 'people from Germany', irrespective of the host country in which they actually lived. (Abadan-Unat 1995:283). They no longer belong to the home culture in the same way as those who never moved and who have changed as the culture changed.

Migration theory, as an implicitly male construct, has not seen women as economic agents and rarely viewed them as taking the decision to migrate in their own right. Many authors write as if women migrated solely as dependants. For example Samaoli writing of North African women migrants in France, says that "the great majority remain completely ignored, eternally dependent on their husbands, without training or professional qualifications, without an occupation or work and without access to their own resources, which cuts them off from any desire for independence or autonomy" (Samaoli 1991: 168). In Germany Abadan-Unat (1985) saw Turkish women migrants as pushed into migration by male family members, a view echoed by Bennholdt-Thomsen et al. (1987). The fact is that women have always migrated as individuals. As early as 1907, 200,000 migrant women were employed in Germany, constituting more than a quarter of the total foreign labour force (Potts 1990).

Campani (1995) argues that global changes in labour markets have shown a falling demand for men's labour and a rising demand for women's labour. In Europe women were post-war labour migrants long before 1974 when restrictions were placed on new labour migration and, in theory, family reunification became the dominant form of migration to Europe (INSTRAW 1994). Germany for example, promoted the recruitment of foreign workers from the 1950s onwards on the basis of a general consensus that the limits of mobilizing married [German] women had been reached. This import of so-called *man*power was supported by the Turkish government (Martin 1991) in order to reduce unemployment as Turkish agriculture mechanized and in the hope of increasing income from remittances (Abadan-Unat 1986). Although the public perception was that men were recruited, the number of contracts officially given to women was considerable. In 1968, women made up 29.6 per cent of migrant workers from Turkey (Mehrländer 1969, cited in Treibel 1988). This contradicts the common assumption that migrant women in general were latecomers. Although it was officially men who were recruited, the contribution of women was large. In 1968 ,the percentage of women among migrant workers from Turkey was 29.6 per cent (Mehrländer 1969, cited in Treibel 1988). Assumptions about return also ignore women, who are once again assumed (wrongly) to follow a male relative (Potts and Grotheer 1997). Castles and Miller (1998) note that the expectation that migrant workers will be temporary residents appears always to be wrong, and the European labour-importing countries are no exception.

As pointed out in *The Migration of Women* (INSTRAW 1994), when women are asked why they migrated their reasons are less likely to be seen as economic than in the case of men. A woman who says she migrated to better her family, for example, is likely to be recorded as migrating for family reasons, not for economic reasons. Her aim is, however, economic. Just as the economic aims of women migrants appear to be more family-oriented than individually-oriented, so the outcomes of women's migration projects need to be theorized from the point of view of women. Individual women have traditionally migrated to support their families or as family members following male relatives. Women who migrated to improve the economic standing of their families are likely to measure their success in terms of the health and welfare of their families. It follows that women's migration projects must be seen as different from men's on a material level. Older women migrants may, and do express nostalgia but, as shown below, they are less likely to wish to make a permanent return to their countries of origin.

Migration as Empowering Women in Later Life

The rest of the paper looks at the relationships between migration and the empowerment of older women. We first discuss the structures within which migrant women live their lives and the ways in which the intersections of these structures combine to create situations in which older migrant women can resist patriarchal power and make their own choices. The separation between structures of ageing, gender relations, culture and economic power is artificial since all interact, along with others which are not discussed here. We separate them in order to show some of the different ways in which older women can order their lives and make their own choices. As indicated above, empowerment is not a simple concept, especially for women migrants who often come from cultures where individualism is not a widely held value. The situation of married women noted by Sharma in north India is not uncommon still:

> It was only in the rather unusual situation in which a woman's relationship with her husband and his kin had deteriorated to the point where she no longer identified herself with the interests of his household, that she would realise subjectively the true extent of her economic dependence (Sharma 1978: 266).

Even unmarried women who may indeed migrate for adventure and for economic advancement (see below), may also see themselves as part of a family unit. However, this ability to identify with the interests of others does not prevent women from resisting patriarchy or from exercising agency (see Patel, forthcoming) and becoming more or less empowered over the life course.

Boundaries of Old Age

In the European countries of destination, old age is defined as age 60 or 65 but poor working conditions, low pay, bad housing and racism can affect migrants so that they age sooner than the average for the dominant population. They may find themselves unable to work or denied work in ageist societies. In any case, the bureaucratic definitions of old age which mark western welfare states may have little meaning in cultures of origin. Adult children, or grandparenthood, or menopause may mark the boundaries of old age for women. In most cultures of origin the stage of being defined as old brings greater freedom to women. As Lechien reports, once her children leave home a woman can "consider herself old" and she reaches the age when she "can do anything" (Lechien 1992a: 91). Divorce, like widowhood, may also be more acceptable in old age. The other advantage for older women is that it is normal in most migrant cultures for older people to be respected in ways that are quite alien to western European culture and there is not the same stigma in being old. This does not mean that migrant elders are content with the degree of respect that they receive from younger members of their communities (complaints about the young by the old are a common feature of all cultures past and present), but migrant older women have, in general, less reason to fear old age than native western Europeans and they have more culturally accepted alternatives open to them (see below).

Gender Relations

Gender relations cannot be considered as static, and older migrant women find themselves at the intersection of (at least) three sets of changing gender relations. In the first place, there are the gender relations in the country of origin. Globalization, economic change and modernization have reduced the power of tradition and with it some aspects of the disempowerment of women. However, in many countries the ability of women to resist patriarchal domination depends on a life-long process of building networks and alliances among other women and female relatives. Women who have been away for long periods are disadvantaged because they are unlikely to have been able to maintain and develop a full set of networks. They may also feel different from women who have not moved and find it harder to fit in to the communities of their birth if they return.

In contrast, gender relations in the migrant community sometimes remain conservative, at least in terms of rhetoric, even though the reality may have been greatly changed by migration. It is not clear how far migration changes gender relations in migrant communities. While many French commentators assume that migration cuts women off from their networks and disempowers them, even in France this view is not uniform. Our own interviews suggest that migration can greatly weaken the power of husbands and other male relatives. Husbands alone, without the added sanctions of a community, were frequently reported as unable to stop their wives from taking paid work. A younger Greek Cypriot woman in Britain reported: "I think things have changed a bit. It wasn't just the opposition from parents, it was also the extended family. My dad was encouraged to throw my brother out because he wanted to grow his hair, in fact he did grow it". Her mother then explained that she had insisted that her son stay because hair could be cut when the fashion passed and relatives should not be allowed to control the family's behaviour.

Finally, older migrant women experience to greater or lesser degree, the changing gender relations in the country of destination. Gender relations outside the migrant community can be disempowering when they reflect patriarchal views on whether women should work. German legislation, for example, made it difficult for women who migrated as dependants to take formal employment and many chose to set up their own businesses. However, changes in the dominant culture which have led to more women entering the paid labour force also benefit migrant women, even though they often got low-paid jobs. The ability to earn is recorded as empowering migrant women. For many, however, it was the long-term differences in gender relations which encouraged them to stay. Equal-opportunity legislation, the right to justice (however restricted in practice) and easier divorce were valued by some migrant women:

> *Mrs. T*: I'll tell you the truth, it was my intention to come and return to Cyprus. But later I liked it. I found the environment pleasing, the restrictions in Cyprus and you know I found that women were more modern (had more freedom). She didn't have the stranglehold of her parents and relations not allowing her to go out ... I found that women had many more rights in England than in Cyprus. As a moral woman I did not want to abuse my freedom. I got a job in Lyons the cake shop selling cakes and enrolled at the Pitman college. I attended for a year. That was the reason why my parents agreed to me staying in England. They were very strict. (older Greek Cypriot migrant to England)

The other aspect of gender relations in countries of destination that has greatly empowered some, though not all migrant women, is the assumption that women will organize gendered community activities. Women's groups, social activities, care for frail elders and, sometimes, early years education, were all seen as stereotypically women's activities by national and local funders. In France (Lechien 1992b) and in the U.K. (Cylwik and Wilson 1996) women achieved positions of responsibility in state-subsidized voluntary groups. Sometimes their activities could be linked to a cultural career (see below). In Germany where volunteer organizations were largely controlled by native Germans, migrant organisations developed relatively late (Cylwik and Spohn n.d.)

Culture

Migrant intellectuals have often described women as extremely disadvantaged: Zehraoui (1994: 64-5) says women's migration reinforces male power and cuts women off, leaving them without female resources or language or access to society, but he assumes that women's migration is always determined by men. Our interviews indicated that women's roles were very different in later life whatever they might have been immediately after migration. Older women have a wide range of positive roles that they can perform in their communities. In the first place, they usually belong to cultures where old age is respected. As Simics (1986) found, older women (and men) have the opportunity to develop a late-life cultural career. They are the repositories of cultural memory and they have the time to organize and run cultural societies. Among Greek Cypriots there was also the opportunity to do church work. Women taught in language schools and were in demand to help their grandchildren maintain competence in the language of 'home'. One women explained how she had mobilized her community which was small and some miles from the main concentration of Greek Cypriots: "I lived in Hackney and I had to get 15 children for them [a Greek school] to provide transport to take them to Camden Town. Slowly, slowly I managed to get this number and the bus used to come. My eldest son managed to get O-level [primary level] Greek; the youngest left Greek school once the eldest one had finished". As mentioned, welfare organizations for migrants have been increasingly supported by state funds and offer a range of possible roles for active women.

Women who organized cultural activities had to learn to negotiate with the dominant culture. For many, this began when they had children and were exposed to local health and education services. As Zehraoui (1994) notes in a more positive mood, women were the leaders in absorbing and understanding aspects of the dominant culture. In other words, women were often at the forefront of change in migrant communities.

Economic Power

Over the life course migrant women may accumulate direct and indirect economic power. Their ability to do so depends to some degree on the citizenship and trade union policies of the countries of destination. If migrants have access to citizenship welfare benefits or if trade unions have successfully negotiated for migrant workers to have the same rights to welfare as native workers (so that migrant labour does not undercut native workers), some of the worst effects of old age can be avoided. The main problem in many countries is that whatever their legal rights, migrants may fear to claim certain benefits because they may be deported - a common problem in Germany where most migrants have no citizenship rights (see Cylwik and Spohn n.d.).

Women who were only allowed to enter the country as dependants with a guarantee that they would be supported by a relative are in a much weaker position. They are most likely to be older widows who have joined their children under family reunification policies, but they cannot claim any form of public support and, if anything happens to their children, they are liable to deportation and extreme poverty. Similarly, migrants who have no legal status, or migrants to countries where welfare benefits are minimal, as in the Pacific rim countries, are likely to be unable to draw any benefit from remaining beyond their retirement age unless they are providing indirect economic support to their families. If they have no savings, their labour will have been wholly expropriated by the country of destination.

Women who were able to find jobs in unionized sectors such as the health service in Britain or municipal or public services in France had access to pensions and other workplace benefits. Contract workers in Germany also gained pensions that assure a relatively good standard of living in countries of origin. There is evidence that even a low pension is helpful for elders who have to negotiate for care or support with other members of their families. In other cases the pension may go to support younger family members who cannot find work and so is less immediately beneficial. As long as inflation or unfavourable exchange rates do not reduce the value of pensions, older men and women have a choice of where to live in later life. Many now choose to move between countries and to benefit from warmer climates and lower living costs for part of the year, while retaining a base near their families in the country of destination.

Although women have not been theorized as being economic migrants, once in the country of destination, many revealed great ingenuity and determination in finding paid work:

> Then I started to work at this department store as a packer [...]. From a girl I learned that child minders were wanted in two nursery schools. They accepted me. In the afternoons I helped at a tailor's shop. [Later] I opened my own. In the morning I worked at the nursery school and in the afternoon in my tailor's shop. I think I can't be without this work. (Turkish woman migrant to Germany, owner of a tailoring shop, age 52)

Women who already had families when they migrated may have been forced into part-time work or may not have been able to take any paid work while their children were young. They are likely to have fewer pension contributions than others and to end up with lower pensions. However, in countries such as France or Britain where there are national minima which can be paid to older people on low incomes, women who migrated during their working lives may still benefit, either directly or through their husbands.

Indirect Economic Power

Although unpaid work is still ignored by economists and not recorded in national productivity statistics, it can confer indirect economic power on women. Inability to take paid work, contrary to the theory propounded for (male) migrants by Sayad: "it is work that gives birth to the immigrant, that brings him into being; it is work also which kills him, denies him and relegates him to non-being when it ends" (1991:61), is not a disaster for all woman migrants. Often they belong to cultures where women are not expected to take paid work but are extremely important in maintaining family and community links. Their ability to network may be crucial even after migration, and they may be supported by other women relatives in a network of transnational family links (Wilson 1987). In later life their children and grandchildren may still rely on them for child care and a wide range of practical and emotional support. It is often the unpaid work of grandmothers which allows daughters or daughters-in-law to take paid work and this essential input can determine the prosperity of the wider family. Of course, caring for children, like most aspects of empowerment for women in later life, is not unproblematic. For example:

> Yes caring - I don't know, do I care? I look after my grandson from N. Sometimes he stays here for two weeks. And this granddaughter, I raised her, because her mother always worked. Well, I cook and look after my family, my husband, my daughter, my niece and my grandchild. But if anybody gets ill and is in need of care, I will care at any time for this person. That can be my mother-in-law, my husband or my two aunties in Turkey. (Turkish migrant to Germany, age 56)

The speaker is used to moving between countries and she may well decide once she retires, to spend the year partly in Turkey and partly in Germany. Older women who can negotiate itinerant retirement are relieved of the burden of caring for parts of the year.

Individual Choices

We have indicated that women make a range of choices over the life course and that these choices have been largely ignored by migration theorists. The decision to migrate is itself made independently by married and unmarried women. For example, one Turkish woman who came to Germany with her girlfriend, recounted how she had kept the project from her family until she got a work contract in Germany so that her husband could not object to her leaving. Later on, her paid work actually provided the economic basis for her to file for a divorce, as it did for the two other divorced women in the Turkish sample. Another explained:

> Our first daughter had died of diphtheria, we didn't have the money to take her to the doctor. Then I said to my husband, 'It can't go on like that. I want a good future for my second daughter.' Then for this daughter, I went to Germany, because my husband's family was too big, my husband's money wasn't enough. I wanted to earn for my daughter and that wasn't possible in Turkey. (Turkish migrant to Germany, age 51)

Once the women had migrated, a range of possibilities, including divorce, opened up which would have been impossible, for cultural or economic reasons, if they had not migrated:

I already did not want the last one, three children were enough. And then I went to the doctor (for a removal of the uterus) and he gave me the pill. (Turkish migrant to Germany, age 51)

Work is good for my legs. And then I wanted to have my own money. I have grandchildren now who have birthdays or there are holidays, and then I want to buy presents with my own money. My husband is a pensioner now and I don't want to take his money. ... My husband didn't agree at all. I did it anyway. He didn't want to have my money in his account. So I put it in the account of my daughter. (Turkish migrant to Germany, age 59)

The idea that migration is a failure unless crowned by return is essentially part of a male-dominated discourse. It has always had dubious validity even for men, but for women it is largely irrelevant. When children and grandchildren are settled in the country of migration, to return 'home' and leave them, does not represent success. The solution for many women is to spend part of the year in the country of origin where the climate is typically milder, and part with family in the country of destination, where health care is more easily available. In later life many migrant women are no longer so closely tied to or dependent on their husbands or other male relatives. As Zehraoui says, with typical male focus, a man "may desert the family and go and live permanently or for part of the year in the house he has built at home. His family is likely to remain in France" (Zehraoui 102-03). In other words, his wife can make her own decision on whether or not to accompany him.

Conclusion

The more we consider women's migration, the less relevance the standard male migration project appears to have for women. While nostalgia is always present, there is no reason to assume that women automatically wish to return to their countries of origin, and much to suggest that many do not. Increasing numbers of older women migrants can and do exercise powers of choice. The clearest demonstration of this is their choice of residence. We do not know how important the new trends in the migration of older men and women are. We have no theoretical framework for recording return migration or itinerant migration of older people or poorer people. The idea that older migrant women might be making choices about where to spend their retirement has been slow to catch on. However, it is increasingly noted that older men and women spend different parts of the year in different countries.

They may go on extended visits to the homeland or they may commute around to the families of their children in different countries.

Such choices were not possible in the past, when travel was expensive and time-consuming. As noted above, globalization in the form of inexpensive, fast travel, less expensive telephone communication and the dissemination of cable and satellite television, now brings transnational families and communities closer together. Neither migration nor return need any longer be definitive. Even those who remain in the country of destination can choose if they wish, to live almost wholly within their own cultures once they retire. They can watch their own television programmes, read the ethnic press and socialize with their families or with culturally defined secular or religious organizations. In addition, the extent of international visiting, for holidays or for family events and festivals seems to be greatly under-recorded by researchers who may regard migrant communities as too deprived to take part in international tourism.

In our view, it is not so much the fact that older migrants are developing patterns of itinerant retirement that is important but that there are gender differences in how itinerant retirement has developed. While men are known to be more likely to favour a definitive return to the country of origin (though even with men, large numbers do not) women have been recorded as very much more ambivalent. They may realize that they will have greater difficulties adjusting to the more restrictive society in the country of origin, as noted, although the main factor appears to be the presence of children and grandchildren in the country of destination.

It follows that some older migrant women are able to combine resources gained from their positions as elders in their own communities, as grandmothers with a defined and valuable economic and educational role to play, as paid workers with some savings or pension rights, and as agents of change in gender relations, to enhance their control over their own lives. They may be able to negotiate a position in their families, cultural groups and the wider society that balances the respect due to age in their own cultures and their position as migrants.

This is not to say that all migrant women are empowered, or that the power they achieve is adequate. In the first place, many women are disempowered by migration since the customs and networks within which they traditionally resisted patriarchy are weakened. For migrant women there are structures which enable them to increase their autonomy but their ability to make the most of resources leading to empowerment must depend on chance as well as on individual agency. They operate against a background of economic deprivation, discrimination and racism in the country of migration and may not always be able to overcome their structural disadvantages.

In the future much will depend on the ability of migrant women to acquire economic resources over the life course, and it is here that national and international agencies have most to offer. Regulations which establish minimum rights, employment conditions and pension entitlements for women migrants are essential and can be furthered by national and international trade union organizations as well as by state and UN agencies. There will still be women migrants who fall outside the scope of national and international laws and agreements but that is no reason for not trying to improve working conditions for those who qualify.

We can conclude that women's migration projects (if they exist as a valid concept) are very different from men's. They are less likely to result in 'failure' in later life and more likely to enhance women's life choices. Older migrant women may choose to return permanently to their countries of origin, but often they do not, and their choice is respected. Their husbands may wish to return and some will do so, but older women may either stay near their children and grandchildren or insist on itinerant return (life in two places). In Europe or increasingly in North America, women may choose to spend the warmer months near their immediate families, but in winter they can return to their extended families in Africa, Asia or southern Europe. This choice of lifestyle enhances health, enhances roots and cultural identity, and enables the maintenance of contact with grandchildren. It is a gendered choice that is not confined to older women but is very much more commonly made by them than by older men.

References

Abadan-Unat, N. 1985. *Die Frau in der türkischen Gesellschaft*. Frankfurt/Main: Dagyeli.

_____. 1986. *Women in the Developing World: Evidence from Turkey* . Denver, CO: University of Denver Press.

_____. 1995. "Turkish Migration to Europe", in R. Cohen, ed., *The Cambridge Survey of World Migration*. Cambridge: Cambridge University Press, pp. 279-84.

Anthias, F. 1992. *Ethnicity, Class, Gender and Migration*. Greek-Cypriots in Britain. Avebury: Aldershot Press.

Bennholdt-Thomsen, V. et al. 1987. *Frauen aus der Türkei kommen in die Bundesrepublik*. Münster.

Blakemore, K. and M. Boneham. 1994. *Age, Race and Ethnicity*. Buckingham: Open University Press.

Campani, G.1995. "Women Migrants: From Marginal Subjects to Social Actors", in R. Cohen, ed., *The Cambridge Survey of World Migration*. Cambridge: Cambridge University Press, pp. 546-50.

Cohen, R. ed. 1995. "Prologue", in *The Cambridge Survey of World Migration*. Cambridge, Cambridge University Press.

Castles, S. and M.J. Miller. 1998. *The Age of Migration*. Basingstoke: Macmillan.

Cylwik, H. and M. Spohn. n.d. "The Impact of Structure on Choices Made by Male Migrants in the Later Stages of the Life Course: Cypriots in Britain and Turks in Germany", unpublished paper.

Cylwik, H and G. Wilson. 1996. *Capacity Building in the Cypriot Communities*. London: London School of Economics.

Dietzel-Papakyriakou, M. 1993a. "Ältere Ausländer in der Bundesrepublik Deutschland. Zwischen Ausländersozialarbeit und Altenhilfe", in *Informationsdienst zur Ausländerarbeit* (iza), Heft 3, S.43-53.

_____. 1993b. "Altern in der Migration. Die Arbeitsmigranten vor dem Dilemma: zurückkehren oder bleiben", *Soziologische Gegenwartsfragen*, Band 54. Stuttgart.

Kiwan, C. 1992. "L'identite Sociale d'une 'Grand Personne': M.K., un 'gars Francais-Algerien-Musulman' retraite a Nemours". Paris: Fonds d'Action Sociales, pp. 213-312.

Krueger, D. and L. Potts. 1997. "Zwischen Isolation und transnationaler Familie. Soziale netzweke von Migrantinnen der esten Generation aus der Tuerkei", *IZA - Zeitschrift fuer Migration und soziale Arbeit* 2, pp. 36-41.

Lechien, M.H. 1992a. "Rappel de la problematique de l'enquete qualitative", in G. Noiriel, *Le Vieillissement des Immigres en Region Parisienne*. Paris: Fonds d'Action Sociale.

_____. 1992b. "Logiques de l'enracinement et vieillissement d'un reseau de solidarite entre francais et immigres; La fin d'une ASTI (Association de Solidarite avec les Travailleurs Immigres)" in G. Noiriel, *Le Vieillissement des Immigres en Region Parisienne*. Paris: Fonds d'Action Sociale, pp. 99-212.

Lorenz-Meyer, D. and A. Grotheer. forthcoming. "The Impact of Social Institutions and Family Tradition on the Provision of Care in German and Turkish Migrant Families" in S.Arber and C.Attias-Donfut, eds., *Changing Generational Contracts. The State and the Family across Cultures*. London: Routledge.

Martin, P.L. 1991. *The Unfinished Story: Turkish Labour Migration to Western Europe with Special Reference to the Federal Republic of Germany*. Geneva: ILO.

Markides, K.S. 1983. "Minority Aging", in M.W. Riley, B.B. Hess, and K. Bond, *Aging in Society* . Hillsdale NJ: Erlbaum Inc.

Naegele, G., E. Olbermann, and M. Dietzel-Papakyriakou. 1997. "Aelter werden in der Migration. Eine neue Herausforderung fuer die kommunale Sozialpolitik", *Sozialer Fortschritt 46* (4): 81-86.

Noiriel, G. 1992. *Le Vieillissement des Immigres en Region Parisienne*, Paris: Fonds d'Action Sociale.

Patel, T. forthcoming. "The Precious Few: Women's Agency, Household Development and Fertility in Rural Rajasthan", *Journal of Comparative Family Studies.*

Pertierra, R. ed. 1992. *Remittances and Returnees.* Quezon City: New Day Publishers.

Potts, L. 1990. *The World Labour Market. A History of Migration.* London: Zed Books.

Potts, L. and A. Grotheer. 1997. "Arbeitsmigration als Frauenprojekt? Migrantinnen aus der Türkei zur retrospektiven Evaluation der Migration", in U. Loeber-Pautsch et al., eds., *Quer zu den Disziplinen. Beiträge aus der Sozial-, Umwelt- und Wissenschaftsforschung.* Hannover: Offizin, S., pp. 77-101.

Sàmaoli, O. 1991. "Les immigres dans la vieillesse", *gerontologie et societe* 56, pp.167-73.

Sayad, A. 1991. *L'immigration ou les paradoxes de l'alterite.* Brussels: Editions universitaires de De Boeck Universite.

_____. 1993. *Vieillir ... dans l'immigration' in Vieillir et Mourir en Exil Immigration Maghrebine et Vieillissement.* Lyon: Presse Universitaire de Lyon.

Sharma, U. 1978. "Women Migrants in North India", In P. Caplan and J. Bujra, eds., *Women United Women Divided.* London: Tavistock Publications.

Simics, A., (1986), "Ethnicity as a Career for the Elderly: The Serbian-American Case", *Journal of Applied Gerontology* 6 (1): 113-26.

Treibel, A. 1988. *Engagement und Distanzierung in der westdeutschen.* Auslanderforschung: eine Untersuchung ihrer soziologischen Beitrage Stuttgart: Enke.

INSTRAW (United Nations International Research and Training Institute for the Advancement of Women). 1994. *The Migration of Women* . Santo Domingo: INSTRAW.

Wilson, G., (1987), "Women's Work: The Role of Grandparents in Intergenerational Transfers", *The Sociological Review* 35 (4): 703-20.

Zehraoui, A. 1994. *L'Immigration de l'homme seul a la famille.* Paris: Ciemi L'Harmattan.

Notes on Contributors

Sara Arber is Professor and Head of the Department of Sociology at the University. Her research is focused on gender and ageing, as well as inequalities in health. She is co-author/co-editor of *Women and Working Lives* (Macmillan, 1992, with Nigel Gilbert), *Ageing, Independence and the Life Course* (Jessica Kingsley, 1993, with Maria Evandrou), *Gender and Later Life* (1991) and Connecting Gender and Ageing (1995).

Maribel Blasco is Research Officer on the Economic and Social Research Council project: 'Gendered Housing: Identity and Independence in Urban Mexico', led by Ann Varley at the Department of Geography, University College London. She is currently completing her Ph.D. dissertation for the Department of International Development Studies at Roskilde University, Denmark, on low-income students' experiences of secondary education in urban Guadalajara, Mexico. She has contributed an article on this subject to a UNESCO publication on Educational Reform in the South (1998).

Antony de Bono M.D., is Director of the International Institute on Ageing United Nations-Malta. As Chairman of the Advisory Committee and Main Committee of the UN World Assembly on Ageing 1980-82, he played a major role in reaching consensus on the Vienna International Plan of Action on Ageing, for which he composed the Preamble. Under his direction the Institute has already more than doubled its commitment to implementing the Plan of Action in the Developing Countries, by greatly expanding its 'in situ' courses and introducing an Interactive Distance Learning Programme on Ageing. He regards the role of Women as the key factor in the whole phenomenon of ageing in the next century.

Helen Cylwik is a former research officer and current research student at the London School of Economics. She is a second generation Cypriot and has worked in the Cypriot community in London.

Fiona Catherine Clark completed a BA in Human Geography at the University of Newcastle upon Tyne. Since 1995, her work has been based in Peru, focusing on the well-being of elderly people and especially gender bias and its consequences for women (and men) in old age. She received an MA in Gender Analysis of Development from the School of Development Studies at the University of East Anglia, U.K. and is currently working in the Urban Peace Program, Latin American Division of the World Bank.

Hugh Davies is Lecturer in Economics, Birkbeck College, University of London. He is the author of numerous publications, many with Heather Joshi, including "Gender and Income Inequality in the U.K. 1968-1990: The Feminization of Earning or of Poverty?" *Journal of the Royal Statistical Society*, Series A (January 1998). His research interests include family economics, income distribution and pensions.

Jay Ginn is a Research Fellow in the Sociology Department at the University of Surrey, researching the changing pensions mix in Britain. She has published widely on gender and pensions and has co-authored/co-edited two books with Sara Arber; *Gender and Later Life* (Sage, 1991) and *Connecting Gender and Ageing* (Open University Press, 1995).

Angela Grotheer is a research officer at Carl von Ossietizky Univerisitaet, Oldenburg who has worked with older and younger Turkish women migrants in Germany.

Deborah K. van den Hoonaard is Associate Professor in the Gerontology Programme at St. Thomas University, Fredericton, New Brunswick, Canada. A sociologist, she received a Ph.D. from Loyola University of Chicago. The paper in this volume is taken from her forthcoming book, *The Widowed Self: Older Women's Journey through Widowhood*. She is currently working on a textbook entitled A Critical Sociology of Aging.

E.Olcay İmamoglu is a professor of social psychology at the Middle East Technical University, Turkey. She has received her B.S. degree in psychology from METU; her M.A. degree in social psychology from the University of Iowa, U.S.A., her Ph.D. in developmental social psychology from the University of Strathclyde in Scotland. Among her research interests are social cognition, close relationships with particular reference to gender and marriage; and assessment of home environments with special reference to children, women and the elderly.

Vacit İmamoglu is a professor of architecture at the Middle East Technical University, Turkey. He received his B.Arch. and M.Arch. from METU, M.Sc. from Pratt Institute in U.S.A. and Ph.D. from the University of Strathclyde, Scotland. He carried research on traditional Turkish houses, particularly in Kayseri and Southeastern Anatolia, spaciousness and assessment of interiors, and various housing projects including children and elderly.

Misa Izuhara completed her Ph.D. at the University of Bristol, UK and is currently Research Associate of Urban Studies at School for Policy Studies, the University of Bristol. Her research interests are in the areas of urban planning, housing studies, aging and gender issues. She is currently undertaking post-doctoral research, funded by Tokyo Metropolitan Institute of Gerontology, on housing, old age and welfare systems through the experiences of older Japanese immigrants in transitional welfare states.

Heather Joshi is Professor of Economic Demography and Deputy Director of the Centre for Longitudinal Studies, Institute of Education, University of London. Her research interests are in the areas of gender, the family and the labour market. She is the author of numerous articles on gender and economic justice and co-author (with P. Paci) of *Unequal Pay between Women and Men* (MIT Press, 1998).

Giovanni Lamura is a social researcher at the Italian National Research Centre on Aging (INRCA), Ancona, a public institute financed by the Italian Ministry of Health which carries out health care and scientific research in the field of the elderly. He received his Ph.D. from the University of Bremen (Germany) in 1995, and is currently working at two main research projects in the field of caregiving: "The role of women in the family care of the elderly", financed by the Italian National Research Council, and "Carers of Older People in Europe" (COPE), a research network involving seven European countries and supported by the European Commission within the Biomedical and Health Research Programme.

Maria Gabriella Melchiorre is a researcher connected with the Institutes of Economic History and Sociology and of Demography and Statistics of the Ancona University of Economics, where she is engaged in research on migration and gender studies. She also works with the Italian National Research Centre on Aging (INRCA) on research focused on issues related to aging and elderly care. Currently she is involved in research on "The role of women in the family care of the elderly" financed by the Italian National Research Council.

Massimo Mengani is Senior Researcher at the Italian National Research Centre on Aging (INRCA), where he supervises the Centre of Social-Territorial Planning. He also works as a consultant for both public agencies and private companies, and has been project leader in Italian and European research networks. Author of numerous books, reports and articles on social and health problems of the elderly - especially the disabled elderly living at home or in nursing homes - he is currently directing the research project "The role of women in the family care of the elderly" financed by the Italian National Research Council.

Noeleen O'Beirne completed a Ph.D. in Women and Ageing at the University of Western Sydney, Nepean. A member of WARN (Women and Ageing Research Network), she has given papers at national and international conferences on women and ageing and has published numerous articles in working papers and conference proceedings. She has two articles in an edited collection, *Revisioning Ageing*, which is to be released early next year. O'Beirne is herself an older woman in her late sixties.

Laura Katz Olson Professor of Government at Lehigh University in Bethlehem, PA, specializes in ageing and public policy. She is the author of *The Greying of the World: Who Will Take Care of the Frail Elderly*, *The Political Economy of Aging: The State, Private Power*, and *Social Welfare*, and co-editor of *Aging and Public Policy: The Politics of Growing Old in America*. She has published widely in the field of ageing on topics such as private pension funds, the Social Security system, problems of older women, and long-term care. Dr. Olson has worked as a policy analyst for the Social Security administration and has been a Gerontological Fellow and Fulbright Scholar. She also has been active in community organizations on behalf of the elderly.

Isabella Paoletti Ph.D., is presently conducting research for the Social and Economic Research Department of INRCA, Ancona, Italy. She has worked extensively on older women's issues and published numerous books and articles, including, most recently, *Being an Older Woman: A Study in the Social Production of Identity* (Hillsdale, NJ: 1998) and "Handling 'Incoherence' According to the Speaker's On-sight

Categorisation" (with Erlbaum), in C. Antaki and S. Widdicombe, eds., *Identities in Talk* (London: Sage Publications, 1998).

Romana Peronacicontributed to this work while she was in the Department of Economics, Birkbeck College, University of London. Her research interests are in family economics and the labour market. She has published numerous articles on gender and economics, including "How Do Couples Spend their Time? Hours of Market and Domestic Work Time in British Partnerships" (with Hugh Davies, Heather Joshi and Mark Killingsworth).

Lydia Potts is Lecturer at Carl von Ossietzky Universitaet, Oldenburg and author of *The World Labour Market. A History of Migration* (London: Zed Books, 1990).

Russell Rimmer Reader in Mathematics at Deakin University in Melbourne, carries out research on the issue of equity at the workplace. He has made quantitative studies of questions concerning young people, women and aborigines in Australia and has researched age as a factor in growing income inequality. His books include *More Brilliant Careers and Income Distribution in a Corporate Economy*. His latest research is about measuring the outcomes of welfare policies.

Rachel Josefowitz Siegel, MSW, is a writer and lecturer who recently retired from her feminist psychotherapy private practice. She has written extensively on Jewish women and on women's ageing. A 74-year-old Jewish widow, living in Ithaca NY, she loves the company of her daughter, two sons, and her grandchildren, and enjoys her garden and her feminist friends and colleagues.

Tatjana Sikoskais Social Affairs Officer in the Research and Training Unit of INSTRAW. She holds a "Graduate Lawyer" degree from the Faculty of Law of the University of Ciriulus and Methodus, Skkopje, the former Yugoslav Republic of Macedonia and a M.A. in Politics and Alternative Development Strategies from the Institute of Social Studies (ISS) The Hague, The Netherlands. Immediately after finalizing her M.A. studies, she worked at ISS as a research assistant in the areas of women and communications and the politics of social movements, during which time she became closely involved in gender and development issues.

Silva Tedreis Assistant Professor in the Department of Social Policy at Joensuu University in Finland. Her research area is comparative social policy for the elderly and its impacts on the provision of welfare and women's position in both public and private life, a subject on which she has published several studies.

Taimi Tulvais Professor and Head of the Department of Social Work at Tallinn University of Educational Sciences in Estonia. She is the founder of post-Soviet social work education in 1991 and has published books and articles on social welfare in several languages.

Ann Varley, lecturer in Geography at University College London, has written widely about housing, gender relations and the urban household. She is co-author, with A. Gilbert, of *Landlord and Tenant: Housing the Poor in Urban Mexico* (Routledge, 1991) and co-editor, with E. Fernandes of *Illegal Cities: Law and Urban Change in Developing Countries* (Zed Books, 1998), and has authored a chapter in the forthcoming *The Hidden Histories of Gender and the State in Latin America*, edited by Elizabeth Dore and Maxine Molyneux (Duke University Press). She has advised on gender issues at UNIFEM, the National Women's Programme in Mexico, and the Gender Research on Urban Planning, Housing and Everyday Life (GRUPHEL) group in southern Africa.

Caroline L. Weber holds a B.Sc. in economics (M.I.T.) and an M.Sc. and Ph.D. in human resource management from Cornell University. Her main research interests are in the area of compensation, strategic human resource management and planning, health and safety, and the overall effectiveness of human resource management systems. In addition to having written monographs and book chapters, her written work has appeared in referred journals such as *Relations Industrielles*, the *Academy of Management Journal*, the *Journal of Applied Psychology* and *Compensation and Benefits Review*. As an Associate Professor she teaches courses on various topics in human resource management and organizational theory at the graduate level in the School of Industrial Relations and the School of Business at Queen's University in Kingston, Ontario. As of 19 July she is on leave from Queen's to serve as Director of the Women's Bureau in Human Resources Development Canada.

Gail Wilson is Senior Lecturer in Ageing and Social Policy, London School of Economics, London, and author of numerous articles on issues concerning the elderly.

Irene Zeilinger a self-defense teacher and NGO consultant in Brussels, studied sociology and development politics at the University of Vienna. Her dissertation is entitled "Elderly Women in sub-Saharan Africa: an Analysis of the Gender Statistics in the UN System."

Isik Urla Zeytinoglu is a Professor at the MGD School of Business and is the Principal Investigator at McMaster Research Centre for the Promotion of Women's Health, McMaster University, Hamilton, Ontario, Canada. Her B.A. and M.B.A. degrees are from Faculty of Business Administration, Bogazici University, Istanbul, Turkey and her M.A. and Ph.D. degrees are from the Wharton Business School, University of Pennsylvania, Philadelphia, U.S.A. Dr. Zeytinogluy conducts research on part-time and nonstandard work, employer flexibility stratgies, gender and work, women's occupational health and global human resource management and itnernational industrial relations topics.